DISSOLUTION

OF THE

VIRGINIA COMPANY

The Failure of a Colonial Experiment

BY

WESLEY FRANK CRAVEN, Ph.D.

GLOUCESTER, MASS.
PETER SMITH
1964

Printed in the United States of America

To

MY MOTHER AND FATHER

PREFACE

THE place which this volume is intended to fill has been outlined in the introductory chapter. It is necessary to add only that the sketch there given of the historiography of the subject was not designed as a complete study of the conclusions found by all the historians who have passed judgment on the dissolution of the company. It is offered as no more than an attempt to indicate those works and influences which have been of chief importance in evolving the popular political interpretation of the causes for the company's fall.

I wish also to recognize certain obligations incurred in the preparation of the volume. All students of early Virginia are deeply indebted to Miss Susan M. Kingsbury for her valuable services in editing the official records of the company's courts. Her work also in securing for the Library of Congress transcripts of important documents and of official and private correspondence relating to the colony's affairs is of inestimable aid to the American student. It is to be hoped that the two further volumes of the company's records designed to include this material will appear at an early date. Through the courtesy of Dr. J. Franklin Jameson, I was permitted to examine these two volumes, the one in galley proof and the other in manuscript. Most of the documents had been studied in the original, but this opportunity to go through the complete collections of Miss Kingsbury was of great help in verifying the author's notes and in avoiding errors of omission. In the bibliography and in footnotes I have attempted to recognize more fully my obligation to Dr. Jameson and Miss Kingsbury. The editors of *The American Historical Review* and of *The Hispanic American Historical Review* have kindly consented to the use of certain material relating to the company's affairs which I had previously presented in articles appearing in these journals. I am indebted also to the officials of the New York Public Library and of the Public Record Office in London for many courtesies.

To Professor Charles H. Hull of Cornell University and to Professor Wallace Notestein of Yale University I would express my appreciation for helpful criticism and encouragement given in the earliest stage of the study, and to Professor W. T. Laprade of Duke University for his kindness in reading the completed manuscript and for certain revisions suggested by him. It has also been read by my colleagues, Professor John Musser and James O. Wettereau, to whom I am deeply obligated for their useful suggestions. They are in no way, however, to be held responsible for the contents and conclusions of the book. For aid in reading the proof I wish to thank another colleague, Professor W. K. Ferguson.

The old style dates have been followed throughout.

W. F. Craven

May, 1932.

CONTENTS

CHAPTER I
INTRODUCTORY

ALTHOUGH the British people have founded colonies in the four corners of the globe and in the course of three centuries have come to hold sway over the fortunes of a quarter of the world's population, Virginia has held a place unique in the history of English expansion since first she stirred the imagination as " Earth's only paradise." Neither India with her unvarying lure for the occident, nor Australasia with her Southern Cross, nor the West Indies with their lingering tradition of the " Spanish main," can summon the same dramatic attraction that clings to the first permanent English settlement in the new world. This effort

> . . . to plant a nation
> Where none before hath stood

involved many new and unprecedented ventures: the first important transfer of British stock to a distant shore, the first hard lessons in the art of colonization, the first vague indications of a colonial policy, the first attempts to adjust English customs and institutions to the conditions of the American continent, the first representative assembly in the western hemisphere, the first justices of peace, and the first introduction of the common law into America — all of them calculated to stir the interest both of contemporaries and of succeeding generations of students.

Nor has Virginia's later history detracted in any way from the interest in her earlier days. Rather, the development in the colonial period of a planter society of gentlemen and country estates, her greatness in the American Revolution, her contributions to the founding of the republic, and her preëminent leadership in the nation through the services of a long line of distinguished sons have served to give Virginia's history a growing importance.

And yet the very features of her history which have given it especial interest have at times proved a weakness in its writing. The natural tendency in historiography is to read backward from some dramatic event, to search out the causes and influences moving forward to some important milepost in the progresses and processions of mankind. But while it is perhaps unavoidable, and even at times necessary for purposes of convenience and organization, the practise involves a danger of losing the proper perspective and of reading alien ideas and motives into the annals of an earlier period. Until comparatively recent years, American colonial history was written from the starting point of the Revolution with many consequent errors of fact and interpretation. English scholars, busy with a wealth of material for study of their own national origins and slow to awaken to the interest and significance of their imperial history, were content to leave the seventeenth century colonial movement largely to the labors of American students, who sought not so much to understand English colonization in all its aspects, as to find the *Genesis of the United States,* to trace the *First Republic in America,* or to study the *Cradle of the Nation.* Virginia by her later membership in the American union was of more interest than Bermuda or Barbados, and her historians have been more concerned with tracing back the roots from which grew her later fame than with the problem of understanding this early commercial adventure by English enterprise. Thus the contemporary point of view has been frequently wanting in the writing of Virginia's history, and serious misinterpretations of men and events have entered into the story.

The outstanding instance is the interpretation of the five year period in which Sir Edwin Sandys directed the fortunes of the London Company from his election as treasurer in 1619 to the dissolution of the company in 1624. A story justly famous, and rendered highly colorful by the most bitter factional strife among the adventurers, it presents one of the most complicated problems of colonial history. Yet by the attachment of undue significance to certain political features of the story, notably the establishment of the Virginia Assembly in 1619, it has been reduced to simple terms, and the final dissolution of the company by royal power has been explained as the result of a long-standing political quarrel in which the adventurers divided according to their opinions on government in England and democracy in Virginia.

Sandys, supported by the earl of Southampton, Lord Cavendish, Sir Edward Sackville, and Nicholas and John Ferrar, stands in the popular tradition as leader of the so-called " patriot party," opposed and frustrated in his far-sighted plans by a " court party " of Sir Thomas Smith, Alderman Johnson, the earl of Warwick, and Nathaniel Rich, who after many futile efforts to overthrow the " patriots " finally conspired with James I to bring about that which they could not accomplish by their own votes. In the works of the most extreme exponents of this interpretation King James assumes a position not altogether unlike that of King George, Smith and Warwick in their short-sightedness are comparable to Grenville and North, and Sandys stands forth as one of the earliest patriots of American history. Certain economic difficulties, the exceptionally high mortality of Sandys' colonists and the financial ruin of the company, are not altogether ignored, but they are considered of secondary importance, rather in the nature of an excuse for the proceedings against Sandys than as the true cause. Such an interpretation receives some degree of plausibility from Sandys' prominence in the parliamentary struggle with James, but even so his lack of royal favor was no more than a contributing factor in his troubles with the company, and a political interpretation has been

the result of misplaced emphasis. By it Sandys' true purposes as a colonizer and the significance of an important
movement in the history of English colonization have been
in large part lost.

The introduction of this interpretation into the accepted
history of Virginia affords an interesting study of the various influences and pitfalls to which historical writings are
ever a prey. Robert Beverly, the first native historian of
Virginia, strangely enough presented in his *History and
Present State of Virginia,* published at London in 1705,
the most accurate explanation of the company's dissolution
to appear for two centuries. Not yet aware of the full significance of the provision made for the government of the
colony in the last years of the company, he summed up
the events leading to the dissolution as arising from the
fact that the adventurers by " frequent Acts of Mismanagement " had " met with vast Losses and Misfortunes." His
account is sketchy and inadequate; he is mistaken in the
date by two years, but he comes nearer the essential truth
than his more thorough going successors when he explains
that " The fatal Consequences of the Company's Male-
Administration cried so loud, that King *Charles* the First,
coming to the Crown of *England,* had a tender Concern
for the poor People that had been betray'd thither and
lost. Upon which Consideration he dissolved the Company
in the Year 1626, reducing the Country and Government
into his own immediate Direction, . . ." [1]

The evidences upon which he based his story were, according to modern standards of scholarship, few and inadequate. For the formative period of the colony, to which
he devoted a third of his space, he seems to have relied
chiefly upon Purchas and Captain John Smith. And it was
from the latter that he drew his conclusions as to the causes
of the company's dissolution. The reliability of Smith's
Generall Historie of Virginia has, needless to say, been the

---

[1] Robert Beverly, *History and Present State of Virginia,* London, 1705, p. 45.

subject of much controversy. The extolment of his own part in the early trials of the colony, his harsh judgment of many other prominent leaders in the movement, and his tendency to heroics have laid him open to severe criticism. But allowing for the exaggeration of his own importance, it must be recognized that his works contain much reliable information and that he himself was a man of real courage and strength. And with no intention or desire to reopen the famous John Smith controversy of a generation ago, it should be recorded in his behalf that his judgment of the conditions in the colony and their causes in the mal-administration of the company through the years immediately preceding its fall are supported in the main by a careful study of sources now at hand.[2]

In 1747 Rev. William Stith published at Williamsburg the first important secondary account of Virginia's early stages, a *History of the First Discovery and Settlement of Virginia*, a book which left a lasting impression upon the accepted interpretation of the colony's origins. Although drawing heavily upon John Smith and Robert Beverly, he depended chiefly upon the official records of the company for the period of Sandys' control, and rejecting the conclusions of his predecessors attributed Sir Edwin's fall to the trickery of the king and the treachery of Warwick and Smith. There is reflected in Stith's history the rapidly growing spirit of independence and colonial self-confidence of his day, which rested upon the colonists' sense of achievement, and expressed itself in an increasing pride in their strength, in an awakening to the value of their traditions, to which Stith himself was an important contributor, and in resentment at any failure on the part of England to recognize their importance and to provide for their interests. Any appraisal of his work must take into consideration this spirit as expressed by him in the preface, where he speaks of James' relations with the company as

[2] *Infra*, pp. 295-298.

full of "such mean Arts and Fraud, and such little trick-
ing, as highly misbecome Majesty." "And I am much
mistaken," he continued, "if his arbitrary Proceedings
and unjust Designs will appear from any Part of his History more fully, than from these Transactions with the
Company and Colony; which have been thus far unknown
to the English Historians, and will perhaps be still thought
too insignificant for their Notice." [3] Stith wrote as an American, conscious of the importance of Virginia's early history
and traditions. He seems to have been the first to use copies
of the company's charters, the instructions to Governor
Yeardley in 1618 and to Governor Wyatt in 1621, the ordinance for the Virginia Assembly, and the papers regarding
the state of the colony under Smith and Sandys sent home
by the assembly in 1624. His book first presents Sandys and
his supporters as the defenders of these chartered rights
against the unworthy designs of James I.

But perhaps the point may be overemphasized, for despite his admiration of Sandys and praise of the company,
he arrives at the not surprising conclusion for his day that
the dissolution of the company was "an event certainly of
Benefit and Advantage to the Country, as we in America
find by Experience, that it is better to be under Royal government, than in the hands of Proprietors, in what shape
or Manner soever." [4] And his chief errors of interpretation may be traced directly to a reliance upon the official
minutes of the Virginia courts from 1619 to 1624, which
again he was the first historian to use.

To accept the court minutes at face value, as Stith and
most of his successors have done, is to arrive inevitably at
the most favorable interpretation of Sandys' administration. Like most other sources from which the company's
later history must be written, the court records are de-

[3] William Stith, *History of the First Discovery and Settlement of Virginia*, New
York, 1865, p. vii.
[4] *Ibid.*, p. 329.

cidedly partisan and prejudiced documents. Sandys was ever anxious to present to the courts and the country the most favorable impression of conditions in the colony. He accordingly held back much unfavorable information, and the picture of Virginia's state as it was read into the court minutes was such as was calculated to encourage the adventurers to further contributions and a continued support of Sandys' policies. Nor can a just estimate be made of the grounds of opposition to him, for while the speeches and arguments of his supporters are reported in full, those of his opponents are either omitted or blurred over in such a fashion as to leave a distinctly unfavorable impression of their motives. The accuracy of the minutes was more than once challenged in the courts,[5] especially at the time of the royal investigation of 1623 when Nathaniel Rich's insistent demand for the delivery to the privy council of the "blurred" minute books suggests the charge that official records had been subjected to no little editing.[6] It is, of course, impossible to determine to what extent this charge was justified,[7] but at any rate, the reliability of the court records must be seriously questioned, and their partisan character is indisputable.

Stith's explanation of the company's fall is not surprising to one acquainted with the official minutes. Sandys' administration, we find, was one of consistent improvement coming to an unhappy end largely because of the reprehen-

[5] *Records of the Virginia Company*, ed. Susan M. Kingsbury, Washington, 1906, I, 366, 372; II, 180-187, 188-189, 197, 199-213, 498-500. (Hereafter cited as *Records*.)

[6] Manchester Papers, 330, 347.

[7] Considerable support is given to Rich's charge by Professor Scott's discovery in the Ferrar Papers at Magdalene College, Cambridge, of a "blurred" copy of the minutes for an extraordinary court of the Bermuda Company held on March 17, 1623, in which there are to be found certain alterations in the hand of Deputy John Ferrar tending to improve the arguments of his own partisans, and certain mutilations in the copy of his opponent's arguments. The speech of Richard Edwards is so heavily inked (or blurred) out that only the opening sentences are legible.—W. R. Scott, *Constitution and Finance of English, Scottish and Irish Joint-Stock Companies to 1720*, Cambridge, 1910, II, 274.

sible opposition of his opponents. Warwick assumes the rôle of the villain who encouraged men like Captain Martin to complain against the company in order to stir up trouble under cover of which he might avoid being called to account for his own misdealings and selfish exploitations. This, as so much else in Stith's volume, is taken almost verbatim from papers prepared by the company in its own defense at the time of the royal investigation and written into the court minutes. Nor was Stith the last to accept at full value these papers written in the height of passion when intense partisan hatred rendered impossible an impartial relation of facts. Many errors have entered into the written history of the company because of the disposition to accept Sandys' statements of his own case as true and unbiased, while rejecting the mass of evidence presented against him because of its obvious bias. The truth is that Sandys' supporters were governed as much by factional prejudice as were their opponents, and the only hope of an accurate explanation of events is to weigh the statements of one against the other. Stith, not having access to the papers of Sandys' opponents, drew his conclusions almost entirely from the evidence compiled in defense of the dominant faction. James I, by no means indisposed to assume direct control over Virginia now that it had been brought to a state of great promise, is pictured as preparing the way for his treacherous dealings with the company by oppressive and illegal impositions on tobacco which reduced the adventurers to his mercy. And even though Stith considered the dissolution of the company an event of great benefit to Virginia, he concludes that its chartered rights had never been legally annulled.

Although Stith appreciated the possible influence of Sandys' unpopularity at court and of the prominent rôle taken by several adventurers in opposition to the royal prerogative through the sessions of the Parliament of 1621, his interpretation is not essentially political. It is rather the explanation advanced at the time by Sandys' supporters. In it, however, there are to be found several important ideas upon which the political thesis later came to rest. The extolling of Sandys, Southampton, and the Ferrars, the discrediting of Smith and Warwick, and the charge of their unholy alliance with the court for purposes of obstructing the company's leadership are all essential to the thesis which rose to favor in the nineteenth century. It remained merely for historians of the national period, searching out the origins of the American republic, to elevate the political features of the story into the position of paramount importance.

A work of great influence in the formation of our national history was Peter Peckard's *Memoirs of the Life of Mr. Nicholas Ferrar* published at Cambridge in 1790. It is based largely upon a manuscript written about 1654 by John Ferrar in commemoration of his brother, Nicholas, who had died in 1637. The Ferrars have enjoyed an unusually favored position in the company's history, especially Nicholas, who by his staunch support of Sandys and his saintly character has proven particularly attractive to American historians. It so happens that John was a man of much greater importance in the company, but due to the unselfish praise of his brother and the fact that Nicholas was deputy at the trying time of the royal investigation, John has been given a place of secondary importance. The significance of Ferrar's memoirs lies in his emphasis on the sinister influence of the famous Count Gondomar, ambassador for Spain at the court of James I. Sandys' struggles in Virginia coincided with those years in which the ascendency of the Spanish ambassador over the king and court was the cause of the deepest and most bitter resentment to the English people. The possibility of a successful attack by the Spaniard had long been considered one of the most potent threats to Virginia's success, and although the apprehension at the time of Sandys' control was probably greater than the actual danger, it is not surprising that in explaining the king's interference with the company the suspicion grew that he was urged on by Gondomar. The extent to which this was true cannot be determined, but in any attempt to settle the question it should be remembered that matters of far more consequence on the continent probably relegated Virginia to a position of comparative unimportance in the efforts of the Spanish embassy, and that some of the most active and bitter enemies of Spain, notably the Rich group, were to be found in the so-called court party of opposition to Sandys. Certainly the reliability of Ferrar's account, written largely from memory several decades after the event, is subject to serious question.

The story is that Gondomar " by his extraordinary craft and various intrigues " so wrought upon a weak prince that in the end he was able to suppress one of the most flourishing commercial companies in England. But the point that caught the eye of Americans was the argument supposedly used by Gondomar to persuade the king, which was an appeal to James' prejudice against the political opinions of the company's leaders. He was reported to have said to James: " That though they might have a fair pretence for their meetings, yet he would find in the end that court would prove a seminary for a seditious Parliament." [8] This oft repeated quotation, which by its frequent repetition alone has contributed greatly to fixing the political interpretation in the popular tradition, came to John Ferrar in a very roundabout fashion. He had it from Southampton, who had been told by the marquis of Hamilton and the earl of Pembroke that they had heard Gondomar make this statement to the king. A story at third hand quoted from memory thirty years later is clearly of doubt-

[8] Peter Peckard, *Memoirs of the Life of Mr. Nicholas Ferrar*, Cambridge, 1790, 115-116.

ful historical value.[9] Of only one thing can we be sure, that Sandys' partisans were convinced that they suffered in part by the pernicious influence of Gondomar and that this conviction may have rested to some extent on fact. But there is not sufficient justification for the unusual importance that has been attached to this story of obviously doubtful authenticity.

Nevertheless, it enjoys a prominent position in the histories which followed after Peckard, and was of great aid to those who were disposed to emphasize the political features of the company's history. The keynote is political in the frequently inaccurate *History of Virginia* by John Daly Burk, an expatriated Irishman who dedicated his three volumes to Thomas Jefferson.[10] George Bancroft, though recognizing the company's failure in Virginia, considered the dissolution to have come mainly from James' dislike of Sandys and his fear of " a seditious parliament." [11] It is found later in the volume of Charles Campbell, who explains that James, " already jealous of the growing power and republican spirit of the Virginia Company, was rendered still more inimical by the malign influence of Count Gondomar." The massacre afforded occasion to frame a plausible pretext for annulling the company's charter on grounds of mismanagement.[12] And Edward D. Neill, in a work composed largely of excerpts from court minutes and correspondence of the Virginia council, places great reliance in Ferrar's explanation of the motives governing

[9] Ferrar's memory may have been prompted by an account of the company's history written from memory about 1644 by Arthur Wodenoth and published in 1651. Wodenoth was a cousin to Ferrar, and it is likely that he saw and read the tract while writing the memoirs in 1654. Wodenoth also relates this reference to the company as "a seditious parliament." *Infra*, pp. 16-18.

[10] John Daly Burk, *History of Virginia from Its First Settlement to the Present Day*, 3 vols., Petersburg, 1804-1805.

[11] George Bancroft, *History of the United States of America*, New York, 1884, I, 129-130.

[12] Charles Campbell, *History of the Colony and Ancient Dominion of Virginia*, Philadelphia, 1860, p. 169.

12   DISSOLUTION OF THE VIRGINIA COMPANY

the action of James and of Sandys' opponents in the company.[13] But there was little in any of these works that added materially to Stith and Peckard. It was left to Alexander Brown, by far the most interesting character of all Virginia's historians, to fill out and complete the political interpretation of the company's history.

A native of Virginia living at Norwood Post Office in Nelson County, Brown early professed an interest in American history, but undertook no independent researches or writings of his own until late in life. In 1876 his interest was especially stirred by the famous " John Smith controversy " in which the Pocahontas incident was made a sort of test issue for determining the reliability of Smith's works on the early history of Virginia. The controversy dates from 1859 when Charles Deane of Cambridge, Massachusetts, edited and printed a copy of Wingfield's " Discourse of Virginia," which was the next year included in the *Collections of the American Antiquarian Society*. The editor in his notes raised the question of Smith's veracity in the account of the celebrated incident in which Pocahontas was reported to have saved the captain's life.[14] Within a few months the Honorable Wyndham Robertson, a former governor of Virginia claiming descent from Pocahontas, challenged Deane's conclusions in a paper read before the Virginia Historical Society entitled " The Marriage of Pocahontas," [15] and with these opening guns there was begun one of the most prolonged scholarly disputes of American history. The civil war brought an enforced truce, but the controversy was reopened almost immediately after the cessation of hostilities. In 1866 Deane reprinted Smith's " True Relation of Virginia," again questioning the truthfulness of Smith in this one

[13] Edward Duffield Neill, *History of the Virginia Company of London*, Albany, 1869, pp. 385-387.
[14] *Transactions and Collections of the American Antiquarian Society*, IV (1860), 92 n.
[15] Later published in *The Historical Magazine*, IV (1860), 289-296.

point although he considered much else of his work of real value, and he was shortly sustained in these views by Henry Adams writing in the *North American Review*.[16] The present writer does not propose to trace the history of this extended dispute which attracted widespread interest both in America and in England and in time called forth the opinions, on one side or the other, of George Bancroft, Henry Cabot Lodge, Henry Stevens, Moses Coit Tyler, J. H. Lefroy, Charles Dudley Warner, J. A. Doyle, Edward Arber, and John Fiske.

Its importance for our purpose is that it was the occasion for Brown's embarkation into the field of history. W. W. Henry, a Virginian, had recently defended Smith in *Potter's American Monthly* when Mr. Brown in 1876 decided to make a study for his own satisfaction of all available materials. The controversy by this date had broadened out into the larger question of the general reliability of Smith as Virginia's first historian, and the result of two years' study was a complete rejection of Smith and the conviction that by following him the true *motif* of Virginia's history had been wholly lost. Convinced that " a great historic wrong had been done the real founders of our country," Brown determined " to go regularly to work and try to find out exactly in what the historic wrong consisted, and the causes of it; to correct the wrong and to remove the causes of it, if I could," considering it a " very proper " task for a Virginian. He began independent research in 1878, but his real efforts date from 1880 when he retired from business on account of deafness and henceforth devoted his time and funds to the correction of Virginia's history.[17]

He correctly saw that a proper understanding of Virginia's origins depended upon a more complete knowl-

---

[16] *North American Review*, CIV (1867), 1-30.
[17] Alexander Brown, *English Politics in Early Virginia History*, Boston and New York, 1901, pp. 179-180.

edge of the sources, that many important documents and facts pertaining to the company and its leaders were as yet unknown. By prodigious labor he collected in the following decade a mass of documentary material relating to the formative period of the colony's history, a part of which he published in 1890 in *The Genesis of the United States*, covering the period from 1606 to 1616.[18] This, his most valuable work, contained copies, excerpts, and references to many documents which served to fill out the original material available for the study of the company's fortunes.

Curiously enough, however, as he continued to study the period after 1616 he became quite dissatisfied with the *Genesis*, for through a more thorough knowledge of the subsequent years he was convinced that the history of the company was primarily that of a political movement, which caused him to revise some of the opinions on men and events advanced in his first book. There he had quarrelled with Smith, holding him and his friends " solely and personally responsible for the wrong done by his history," but now he felt that he had been mistaken in overlooking the important fact that Smith's book had been licensed by the crown and that it therefore conformed to the political purposes of the court party. He saw as he had not seen before that the erroneous interpretation of Virginia's history was the result of a deliberate plot by James I to conceal the manner in which he had conspired to defeat the patriotic ends of Sir Edwin Sandys. The disappearance of the original records of the company and the loss of many other valuable evidences of its history, which ordinarily would be attributed to carelessness and the usual circumstances by which so many important sources for historical writings have been lost, were to Brown proof of a deliberate attempt to destroy the records, merely the

[18] Alexander Brown, *Genesis of the United States*, 2 vols., Boston and New York, 1890.

first stage of a studied effort by James and his successors down to George III, through their control over the sources, to rob America of its rightful heritage.[19]

Since his purpose in writing the *Genesis* had been " to defend our founders of that period from the unjust charges of the contemporary historian," Sir Thomas Smith and his supporters were portrayed in heroic proportions and James I was presented as a true friend of the colony. But now that he saw that " politics was the mother's milk of Virginia " and that he had failed to give proper consideration to political conditions in England and to the fact that Sir Thomas eventually united with the national court party, he reversed his judgment of both men. As he explains:

> So far from having implicated James I and the Court party in any way in the matter, I had looked upon them as the great friends of the whole movement, and had regarded the royal manuscript evidences — written by the king, by his Privy Councillors and other royal officials, and by others to the king and to the royal officials — as being official and entirely reliable evidences, when as a matter of fact these evidences are *ex parte,* and almost entirely in accord with the political purposes of the Court party to conceal or obscure — rather than to give — any facts favorable to the political purposes of the opponent Patriot party.[20]

And so with one stroke of the pen he discarded as unreliable the whole mass of official papers relating to the later

[19] *English Politics in Early Virginia History*, pp. 180-181. Part II of this work (pp. 59-86) is described as "An outline of the effort of the Court party in England to obliterate the true history of the origin of this nation; showing how a great historic wrong was done our patriotic founders by James I, his commissioned officials, and licensed historians." Part III (pp. 87-150) is entitled, "The influence of politics on the historic record while the evidences continued under the control of the crown,—an outline of the contest over our political and historic rights between the Court and Patriot parties, from 1625 until the Patriots determined to secure their political rights by force of arms in 1776,— showing the ways by which the original historic wrong was supported and perpetuated under the crown."

[20] *Ibid.*, p. 182.

years of the company, and proceeded to build his case partly upon partisan evidences left by the Sandys faction and partly upon a pure flight of patriotic fancy. The result was *The First Republic in America*,[21] a work of far less worth than his earlier *Genesis,* but regarded with pride by its author as " the first effort to restore to our foundation as a nation the inspiring political features of which it was robbed by those who controlled the evidences and the histories under the crown." [22]

In building up his thesis for the *First Republic,* he placed great reliance on an account of the company's history written by Arthur Wodenoth about 1644, which is of interest not merely because of the significance attached to it by Brown but because it is the source of several catch phrases that by their frequent quotation have helped to perpetuate the political interpretation of the company's fall. Wodenoth, a former adventurer of the Virginia Company and a first cousin to the Ferrars, was deputy governor of the Bermuda Company at the time of writing " An Account and Observation taken by A. W. a true friend and Servant to Sir *John Danvers* and the Parliament-interest, containing a great part of his [i.e., Danvers'] more Publick Transactions concerning the Plantation of Virginia." Written in praise of Danvers, his patron and one of Sandys' staunchest supporters, and entirely from memory, at a time when the issues between parliament and the Stuart monarchy had finally been submitted to the arbitrament of arms, and composed with something of a hope that the rights of the old London Company might in time be revived, the historical value of the tract is obviously open to serious question. He left the manuscript, containing no dates at all, to his cousin William Wodenoth with instructions to publish it at some seasonable time, and suggested that if it were possible to consult the company rec-

---

[21] Alexander Brown, *First Republic in America*, Boston and New York, 1898.
[22] Brown, *English Politics in Early Virginia History*, p. 184.

ords and the official orders of the council he might add
" the yeer of our Lord in the Margent at every main Trans-
action." It was not published until 1651, after William
Wodenoth's death, when it appeared with several papers
relating to Bermuda and was presented to the Somers Islands adventurers shortly after their election of Danvers as
governor of the company.[23]

Wodenoth's account is one of confused sequences in
which his memory seems frequently to have been prompted
by the stirring events of the time at which he wrote. In
his mind the first difficulties with the king arose from
the pernicious influence of the Spanish ambassador, and
many honorable men, he wrote, finding the " pulse of the
Court beating wholly in observance of the *Spanish* Coun-
sells and ends, by interrupting at home, and barring our
trade to the *W. Indies*," saw in Virginia a place of honorable employment and in Bermuda an island which by its
natural strength and its situation promised security for
warlike shipping and navigation throughout the English
plantations. Frequent consideration of these affairs in the
courts of adventurers had been the occasion of King James'
passionate speech that " The Virginia Company was a
seminary for a seditious Parliament." They were protected by their patent, however, from the " Prerogative-
destructive intrusion" until certain ill-affected adventurers undertook to disturb and interrupt the regular
proceedings of the courts, thereby giving James opportunity to express his dislike of Sandys and other patriotic
leaders. Having found great neglect in Sir Thomas Smith's
care for Virginia and many shortcomings in his accounts,
he was finally displaced by Sir Edwin Sandys, who proceeded with many improvements in the conduct of the
business until at the end of his first year as governor the

[23] *A Short Collection of the Most Remarkable Passages from the originall to the
dissolution of the Virginia Company*, printed by Richard Cotes for Edward Husband, London, 1651.

king, influenced by Smith who hoped to cover up his own errors, refused to allow his reëlection. When the adventurers protested, James in great passion declared Sandys to be his greatest enemy and returned no other answer but " Choose the Devill, if you will, but not Sir Edwin Sandys." But after the selection of the earl of Southampton the business proceeded peacefully except for the interruptions of Smith's supporters, who when the company continued in its efforts to call them to account for their former corrupt practises appealed to the court, and were warmly supported by the " Spaniolized faction of the Council Board and the King's Bed-chamber." The remainder of the tract is a distorted and confused story of the events leading to the final dissolution of the company, in which Lord Treasurer Middlesex is represented as making a " specious overture " in the offer of the tobacco monopoly, which by the efforts of " many ingenuous persons " brought the adventurers into " eminent distraction " and thereby prepared the way for an " inquisition " by the crown into the company's affairs.

There is a kernel of truth in Wodenoth's relation of these disputes, but it is colored by his partisanship and lost in much second-hand information quoted from memory. He was correct in attributing the first division in the company to differences over economic problems, it is undoubtedly true that Sandys was far from enjoying royal favor and that Smith, a man of great means and influence, used whatever weight he could command in high places to combat Sandys, but what he failed to see is that no serious procedure against the company itself was undertaken until Sandys' maladministration had reduced the company to bankruptcy and the planters to a miserable state of famine, disease, and death. Brown, who in the *First Republic* seems to have been the first historian to use this tract, makes the same mistake in underestimating the importance of more mundane considerations of economic conditions.

He too saw that the original dispute related purely to business, but after Smith sought aid at court the issue becomes to him almost entirely political, and upon the patriotic interpretation of an Englishman — Wodenoth makes no reference to the government of the colony, nor does he once mention the Virginia Assembly — he superimposes the patriotic interpretation of an American.

Nor was the *First Republic* the last product of one of the most prolific pens of the day. Brown was to write yet another book defending his thesis and pushing the political interpretation of Virginia's history to even more extreme limits. The *First Republic* was not altogether favorably received. Several reviewers in leading historical magazines objected to its distinctly patriotic and nationalistic flavor. Others, notably W. W. Henry, not yet ready to surrender their faith in John Smith, took issue with him in his complete repudiation of the gallant captain as an historian. And still others dared to suggest that " We will have to look further north for the first republic in America." In answer to these various " misrepresentations " of his work, he published and circulated at his own expense in the fall of 1898 " The History of our Earliest History; an appeal for the truth of history in vindication of our legitimate origin as a nation, as an act of justice to our founders, and as an incentive to patriotism." [24] The following January he answered the criticisms of the John Smith advocates in a reply to Mr. Henry appearing in the *Virginia Magazine of History and Biography*.[25] And in 1901 he published another volume of some 275 pages in defense of his thesis. *English Politics in Early Virginia History* was an apology for Brown.

An interesting influence affecting this last statement of his patriotic interpretation was that of sectional feeling in America. For although Brown in answer to his critics

[24] Brown, *English Politics in Early Virginia History*, p. 187.
[25] *Virginia Magazine of History and Biography*, VI, 324-334.

roundly and soundly condemned the interference of sectionalism with the true relation of a common history, there can be little doubt that the rival claims of the Virginia Assembly and the New England town meeting as the roots from which grew America's matchless political institutions had a decided effect in producing his overstatement of Virginia's claims. The New England school comes dangerously near an alliance with John Smith and James Stuart in the suppression of truth. And with something of the resentment of a prophet without honor in his own country, he proceeds to develop a personal grievance against a curious company of King James and his successors, Captain Smith and his supporters, American publishers and Yankee reviewers — all of whom had joined hands in frustrating his patriotic purpose of vindicating the founders of our nation. " I have had to contend with the almost insurmountable obstacles placed in the way of finding the facts by James I., his commissioned officials, and licensed historians," he wrote, it being a work of great difficulty to compile a book " correcting the wrong impressions which have resulted from an almost absolute control over the history and all evidences for nearly one hundred and fifty years by the crown officials." Then after the work was done it was difficult to find a publisher " liberal enough and patriotic enough to undertake the publication of an article or a book opposing opinions which have grown gray with age and become popular." And even when published, the author must yet suffer the persecution of those slow to surrender ideas venerated by age, and of those who fall back upon sectional politics to perpetuate an " historic wrong." " The court which licensed the publication of Smith's history," he concluded, " would have burnt my books and imprisoned me; but thanks to the immortal principles which inspired our founders, the advocates of John Smith could only ' roast ' my books and abuse me." [26]

[26] Brown, *English Politics in Early Virginia History*, pp. 185-187.

The purpose, therefore, in a volume dedicated " to those citizens of the Republic who wish to render historic justice to the Patriots who instituted the popular course of government in this country," was to " show more clearly than I have yet done the correct political and historical point of view; the real importance of the movement; the political character of the historic wrong done those who, under the charters of 1609 and 1612, inaugurated a popular course of government in this country; the political influences which swayed opinions, evidences, and histories under James I., and the political influences which have been instrumental in upholding the evidences and purposes of the crown ever since." [27]

Thus it may be seen that Brown's patriotic reading of Virginia's history has never been universally accepted. Yet it has found its way into the textbooks and into the general histories of the colonial period, some of them written by reputable scholars, until it has become well established in the popular tradition. Of considerable influence in its acceptance were the writings of John Fiske whose *Old Virginia and Her Neighbours*,[28] appearing almost simultaneously with the *First Republic,* through its pungent style and moving story did much to popularize the interpretation presented in Brown's more heavily documented volume.

The work of revision, though early begun, has proceeded but slowly. The late Professor Channing within a few years effected a partial revision by calling attention to certain economic conditions of colony and company which he considered to have had an important bearing on the government's attitude, but he did not seem quite certain as to whether he should regard these economic factors of primary or of secondary importance and in a general

---

[27] *Ibid.*, p. 189.
[28] John Fiske, *Old Virginia and Her Neighbours*, 2 vols., Boston and New York, 1899.

history of the United States he did not have space to give the subject adequate analysis.[29] Professor Beer, while studying the origins of the British colonial system, revised the hitherto accepted and unfavorable interpretation of the course followed by the Rich group in the famous tobacco disputes which immediately preceded the royal investigation that led to the company's fall.[30] And Professor W. R. Scott in 1910 took sharp issue with the American interpretation in a short survey of the histories of the Virginia and Bermuda companies that continues to be the most satisfactory treatment of the subject. He lacked space and time, however, to make it a definitive study. The topic is introduced in a general survey of joint-stock companies, and the author's treatment suffers somewhat from the fact that his natural interest in the machinery and functioning of the company leads to the neglect of certain other factors of equal importance. Nor can one avoid the feeling at times that he is a bit severe in his judgment of Sandys.[31]

Other scholars have found it difficult to accept the political interpretation because of the impossibility of fitting the leading characters into the rôles so prepared for them.[32] A fuller understanding of men and events in Jacobean England has shown that the division in the company could not have been according to political opinions, that men like Nathaniel Rich and the earl of Warwick are entitled to a position hardly second even to Sandys in the opposition to the crown, and that they were the most consistent opponents of the pro-Spanish party to be found in England. And withal, the increasing disposition among stu-

[29] Edward Channing, *History of the United States,* New York, 1905, I, 193, 205-206, 223-225.

[30] G. L. Beer, *Origins of the British Colonial System,* New York, 1922 (first published in 1908), p. 133.

[31] Scott, *Joint-Stock Companies to 1720,* II, 266-289.

[32] A. P. Newton, *Colonizing Activities of English Puritans,* New Haven, 1915, pp. 20-21; see also by same author brief summary of question in *Cambridge History of the British Empire,* New York, 1929, I, 149-151.

dents to regard seventeenth century colonization as above all else an economic movement has tended to discredit a thesis resting on the assumption that the movement was primarily political in character and in motives.

But although the political explanation of the company's later years has been rejected in scholarly circles, the story has not been rewritten on the basis of adequate research. It is to fill this long recognized need that the present work is undertaken. It is offered as something more than an attempt to disprove a false thesis. Rather it is hoped to fill in certain gaps in the story that have resulted from too great a dependence upon incomplete and partisan sources and to correct certain misinterpretations which have necessarily found their way into studies giving undue emphasis to the political features of the company's affairs.

CHAPTER II
EARLY HOPES AND DISAPPOINTMENTS

THE most common error in writing the history of the Virginia Company has been a failure to understand the fundamental character of that corporation. Whatever else may have entered into the activities of the company, it was primarily a business organization with large sums of capital invested by adventurers whose chief interest lay in the returns expected from their investment. Their motives were not entirely selfish; their desire to render a public service is unquestionable. They intended to aid England in the solution of her economic and social problems by increasing her trade, by relieving her of a dependence upon other countries for certain necessary commodities, and by relieving her congested state of population. Yet even these considerations of public welfare were not wholly divorced from the idea that in fulfilling its higher purposes there was to be found the best guarantee of financial reward for the company, and hence the best assurance of profit for each individual adventurer. The true *motif* of the company's history is economic rather than political. To make the business pay was the first aim of all — as Sandys himself expressed it, " that whereon all men's eyes were fixed " [1] — and other matters were of but secondary interest. Even the question of the colony's government was decided largely upon the question of what form would best promote the peace and content necessary to the prosperity of the plantation.

The story of the five year period through which Sandys guided the destinies of Virginia is no exception. He came into office immediately after a complete and thorough reorganization of the company's affairs, and his administration marks the last attempt of the company to build up a paying business in accordance with prevailing ideas on

[1] *Records*, I, 482.

colonization. The reforms of 1618, to which he contributed much, and his own election were due to the failures and disappointments experienced under the leadership of Sir Thomas Smith. The bitter factionalism with which he had to contend for five years was the product of these same earlier disappointments and of the conflicting interests of various groups of adventurers. And his fall, accompanied by the dissolution of the company, is attributable to a failure to realize the hopes and aims of a profitable business at home and a prosperous colony in America.

The key to the company's history, both before and after Sandys' election, is to be found in the fact that the business of colonization was yet in its earliest experimental stage when many errors of judgment were inevitable and reality often proved contrary to theory. In any attempt to judge the record of the Virginia adventurers, it should not be forgotten that they were truly adventurers in a new and uncharted field of commercial speculation with little in the way of previous experience to guide them.

The most experienced, and at the same time the most substantial, of their number were London merchants. Foremost among these was Sir Thomas Smith, who for thirteen years served as governor of the company and for almost half as long directed the fortunes of its sister corporation, the Bermuda Company. At the founding of the Virginia colony he was one of the most seasoned veterans of the commercial expansion that had glorified the Elizabethan era. Born of a merchant's family in the year of the good queen's accession, he rose to rapid wealth and distinction and became active in practically every trading venture of his day. He was a prominent member of the Haberdasher's and Skinner's companies, he frequently invested in adventures for the Northwest Passage, was deeply interested in the Levant Company, was for a time governor of the Muscovy Company, and for many years was the governor and leading spirit of the East India Company. The merchants who followed Smith's leadership regarded Virginia as merely one other of their numerous commercial ventures, though in common with imperialists of all ages they were convinced of a service rendered to the country in the promotion of their own interests. They were not unnaturally disposed to draw heavily upon their experience in the older corporations trading to the east of England. There can be little doubt that they approached the West with something of the same hopes and methods with which they plied their trade in India, the Levant, and the Baltic. But conditions for eastern trade were quite different from those of the primitive and sparsely settled West, and the attempt to adapt the old machinery and methods to problems of western trade must explain in part the early failures of commercial companies in America.

Second only to the merchants in importance was an influential and powerful group led by the Rich family, Lord Robert Rich and his more famous namesake and son, who as the second earl of Warwick was destined to become the most consistent supporter of colonization in seventeenth century England. While they frequently held important commercial interests in the city, they are better known for their more colorful participation in Elizabethan piracy. Their interest in Virginia was not unlike that of Smith, but there was with them perhaps more consideration of the advantage to be gained by a base for piracy in America and of the strategic value of the colonial port in time of war. They played an important role in the founding of colonies, but their roving adventures, though adding much to the knowledge of and interest in the new world, can be said to have done little to acquaint them with the actual problems of western colonization.

A third body of adventurers were endowed even less by experience to undertake the serious business at hand. They present an interesting cross-section of the English people

— merchants of small means infected by the microbe of speculation, country gentry stirred by the appeal of an adventurous enterprise, and great lords who now added Virginia to the patronage of men of letters, to the support of charities, and to their social activities as one more object for the devotion of their wealth and leisure. The idea of rendering some public service, of building up England's wealth, of making her economically independent, of asserting her rightful position in the world, of relieving her congestion of population, of converting the savage natives of America, and, generally speaking, of promoting those " religious and public ends " for which the business was undertaken carried a special force with these men. In common with other adventurers they anticipated some profit upon their investment, but there was an additional compensation for them in the honor and credit of their connection with an enterprise serving such worthy and lofty purposes. Individually they were of less importance in the company, and at first, having no special cause to realize their voting strength as a group and no recognized leadership of their own, they followed the merchants with patriotic enthusiasm and optimistic expectation of early rewards in wealth and honor. In time, however, with the bitter disappointments of repeated failure there emerged from their own number an effective leader in the person of Sir Edwin Sandys who organized them to bring about the ultimate overthrow of the merchants in one last attempt to realize the original purposes of the company.

Sandys, a man of varied activities and accomplishments, was born the second son of an archbishop of York in 1561. Educated at Oxford and Middle Temple, he is best known for his leadership of the opposition to the crown in the house of commons, which he first entered in 1586. There he exhibited those qualities of mind and leadership which mark him as one of the greatest parliamentarians of history. But though one of the most gifted and able men of the time, with an unusual capacity to inspire his followers and a rare devotion to duty, there was little in his background or in his experience to qualify him for the direction of a great commercial company. Moreover, his steadfast opposition to King James won him the thorough dislike of his sovereign, and as Professor Channing has suggested, he ought never to have been selected to head a business that was dependent in so many ways upon royal favor.

His strongest allies in the Virginia Company were Henry Wriothesley, third earl of Southampton, and John Ferrar. Southampton, a handsome, scholarly, accomplished, and impetuous nobleman, is chiefly known for his patronage of Shakespeare, his frequent court brawls, and his support of voyages for discovery and colonization in America. He had been imprisoned for his connection with the Essex affair, but was restored to favor upon the accession of King James. On account of Salisbury's distrust of him, however, he was denied anything more than ornamental offices and honors, and in time he drew away from the court. Sandys claimed to have converted him from Catholicism, and at the time of his governorship of the Virginia Company he was prominent in the opposition to the royal favorite, the duke of Buckingham. John Ferrar sprang from a merchant family of some prominence in London. He was a loyal and devoted follower of Sandys, and for three years was primarily responsible for attending to the ordinary business details of buying and shipping supplies, equipping and transporting colonists, and keeping the company's books. His work, as we shall see, offers a clear demonstration of the inability of seventeenth century Englishmen, even when business men of experience, to appreciate the fundamental problems of American colonization.

The purposes which inspired these various groups of adventurers to undertake the colonization of Virginia were a confused heritage of the sixteenth century. There were hopes of gold and other precious metals. There were plans

for voyages of discovery in search of a passage to the East
Indies. There were expectations of a valuable trade with
the natives. There were anticipations of advantage in
plundering the Spanish West Indies. And there were also
ill-defined plans for colonization, but with no clear idea
of the staples to be promoted or the manner of their promotion, except that somehow the labor of the colonists
should produce certain commodities needed in England,
of which naval stores seemed to be of greatest importance.

Being thus in the position of expecting almost anything
and everything of America, it was inevitable that their
first experience should be one of many disappointments
necessitating some revision in their hopes and methods.
There were two such periods when the adventurers
paused to reform their lines, to restate their purposes, to
apply the lessons apparent in previous mistakes by a reorganization of the company's machinery, and then to advance with renewed enthusiasm to a more determined
effort at successful colonization. The first of these was in
1609 and the second came nine years later.

The background of the reorganization of 1618, with
which the present study begins, is to be found in the
failure of the changes effected immediately after 1609 to
achieve the ends for which they had been designed. An
attempt had been made to remedy the demonstrated defects in the government of the colony and in the organization and powers of the adventurers through the charters
of 1609 and 1612, by which the London Company was
incorporated as a joint-stock company with the organization common to commercial companies of the time. The
most significant feature of this change was that full control, both economic and political, was for the first time
placed in the hands of the adventurers. The royal council
established in 1606 relinquished its powers to another
which formed a vital and integral part of the company's
machinery, the members of which were drawn from the

adventurers and were held directly responsible to them rather than to the king or the privy council. Acting as a sort of standing committee of the company, this new council for Virginia served thereafter as the permanent administrative body of the corporation. The main burden of work fell upon its members, who decided upon questions of policy, interceded with the government in behalf of the company, handled correspondence and instructions for colonial officials, drew up and issued numerous public statements which became an important work in maintaining the "reputation" of the business, and attended to numerous administrative details.[2] In the period of this study, due to the withdrawal over long periods of the Smith-Warwick faction, it became practically a steering committee for the majority party.

The acts of the council, however, were subject to approval by the adventurers, who exercised their voice in the business through two types of general meetings or courts. Authority was given to hold once a week, or more often if necessary, "a Court and Assembly," at which a quorum was to consist of five councillors including the treasurer or his deputy, the two principal officers of the company, and fifteen at least of the "Generality," with power to attend to "all such casual and particular Occurrences, and accidental Matters, of less Consequence and Weight, as shall from time to time happen, touching and concerning" the plantation. But for the settlement of more important matters, such as concerned "the Manner of Government from time to time to be used, the Ordering and disposing of the Lands and Possessions, and the Settling and Establishing of a Trade there, or such like," there were to be held "four Great and General Courts of the Council and Company of Adventurers for Virginia," commonly known as quarter courts. Among the duties of

[2] See *Orders and Constitutions* in Force, *Tracts*, Washington, 1844, III, No. 6, pp. 6, 9.

the quarter courts were the selection of councillors and officials for both company and colony, the settlement of policy, the control of trade, the distribution and disposal of lands, and the enactment of such laws as were necessary for the government of the company and the colony, in which last function they were restricted only by the requirement that their enactments be not contrary to the laws of England.[3]

The authority of the treasurer and company in London was exercised in Virginia through a governor and council appointed by and responsible to the adventurers at home. The chief weakness in the government of the first three years was remedied by giving the governor a superior authority and position which he held by commission from England and not at the will of his fellow councillors. But while the governor enjoyed considerable freedom in the performance of his office, both he and the council were always bound by instructions from the company.

Thus with the exception of the addition of the Virginia Assembly in 1619 there was completed by 1612 the general outline of the governmental machinery by which the affairs of the plantation were governed until the dissolution of the company in 1624. Of chief significance is the fact that the government was centered in the company at London, which selected all officials, passed laws for the colony, and issued instructions controlling both the economic and political life of the colony without much distinction between that which was economic and that which was political. In this work the company was relieved of any direct control by the crown, and thereby exercised practically an independent jurisdiction. It has been often overlooked that it was this whole machinery, and not any one part of it, by which the adventurers directed the economic and political affairs of the business that contemporaries referred to as the " government of Virginia." The ultimate

[3] *Ibid.*, III, No. 6, p. 1.

authority resided with the adventurers who exercised their right of control through an equal franchise which paid no heed either to the sum adventured or to the quality of persons. And when the "government of Virginia" was attacked as democratic the reference was to its most democratic feature, the equal voice of several hundred stockholders in the government of the company's business.[4]

This reorganization of the company was accompanied by renewed efforts for the development of the colony. A wave of enthusiasm swept over England, and men from all walks of life rallied to the support of Virginia in response to numerous appeals that went throughout the country. Their expectations of wealth and honorable achievement were only slightly less extravagant than before, but there was now less disposition to expect sudden and extraordinary profit by the discovery of precious metals or through some other short cut to wealth. Instead, their energies were directed more fully to ordinary colonization as the surest hope of drawing from Virginia those benefits expected for themselves and for England. This belief in colonization as the best method for the development of Virginia was not entirely new. It had been held by many before the company was organized, but its acceptance by the generality of adventurers required more time than was necessary in the case of closer students of colonization. After 1609 the chief attention of all concerned was concentrated on the task of sending a sufficient labor supply to produce in Virginia the commodities that would find a ready and profitable market at home, and the colony assumed the features of a large plantation which became the common type of early settlements in North America.

There were many points of comparison between the Virginia plantation and a feudal manor. It was practically a private estate farmed for the profit of its absentee landlord, the London Company, which expected to realize on

[4] *Infra*, pp. 282-285.

its investment by the sale of commodities produced on the plantation. The labor was supplied by indentured servants, and there was for a time an absence of private property. From the common land of the company and from the neighboring forests and waters they were to draw their food supply and timber, tar, pitch, turpentine, flax, hemp, and other such staple commodities that could be shipped back for sale in England. The landlord's interests were represented by the governor, into whose hands were given both economic and political control over the settlement. The first organization had to be partly in the nature of government, but it was primarily an administrative organization for economic purposes. The maintenance of order was essential to the peace and content of the settlers and thus to the economic development of the colony. Government was primarily for economic motives, and so it remained throughout the history of the company.[5]

For a few years the adventurers followed this new venture with energy and enthusiasm. But as year after year brought only a few samples of the colony's productions and little more than disappointing reports of lack of progress, the enthusiasm of the adventurers disappeared. In the four years that followed after 1614 life in the company reached a low ebb, many adventurers dropped out, and attendance at courts dwindled to a very small number.[6] The treasury was exhausted, and by the spring of 1618 the company's debts were estimated at between eight and nine thousand pounds. Few new adventurers entered to replenish the common stock, and subscriptions went uncollected until by 1620 a total of some £16,000 of uncollected subscriptions stood on the company's books.[7] In 1616 it became necessary, in view of the lack of public funds, to resort to the practise of a subsidiary joint-stock

[5] An excellent outline of this type of colony is found in L. D. Scisco's "Plantation Type of Colony," *American Historical Review*, VIII (1903), 260-270.
[6] *Records*, II, 350, 394.
[7] *Ibid.*, I, 350, 390, 397.

company to supply the colonists, and from then on the Magazine, a " Society of Particular Adventurers for Traffic with the People of Virginia in Joint Stock," became the customary means of supply. It was practically a separate company having the right of furnishing supplies, the profits of which were divided among the adventurers according to the amount they invested in the ventures. The Magazine was administered by a director and a committee of five councillors. Its business was transacted in its own separate courts, but its accounts were subject to the supervision of auditors appointed by the company.[8] The well known Alderman Johnson, son-in-law and business associate of Sir Thomas Smith, was at the head of the Magazine, and he and Smith were the chief adventurers therein.

While a small group of merchants thus endeavored to realize a profit through the use of the company's monopoly of supply and trade, the efforts of the company itself were few and feeble. Some of its leaders were interested in other commercial enterprises of more promise, and were accused, perhaps with some justice, of neglecting Virginia on this account. Many adventurers lost faith in the prospects of the colony, and disturbing rumors derogatory to the climate and soil of Virginia were bruited about the city and country. Any really progressive policy for the further development of the colony was abandoned, and a state of faction and strife not uncommon to a failing business became the prevailing order in the Virginia courts.

The colony was left largely to its own course. Only a few new colonists were sent to replenish its population. In 1616 the inhabitants numbered 351 men, women, and children, which as John Rolfe declared was " a small number to advance so great a worke." [9] This small band was composed of those who had become accustomed to the

---

[8] P. A. Bruce, *Economic History of Virginia in the Seventeenth Century*, New York, 1896, II, 259-261.

[9] John Rolfe, "Relation of the State of Virginia" [1617], pub. in *Virginia Historical Register*, I (1848), 107.

hardships of a frontier community, and as the " old planters " they formed the nucleus around which the population of Virginia was to grow. Yet in April, 1618, the settlers were only 400, among whom, according to Sandys,
only 200 were able to " set hand to husbandry and but one
Plough was going in all the Country, which was the fruit
of full 12 years labour and above one hundred thousand
marks expences . . . over and above the sum of between
8 and 9000 pounds Debt into which the Company was
brought, and besides the great expences of particular Adventurers." [10]

Left in this fashion with no constructive guidance from
the company, it is not surprising that the colony's development followed certain lines which in the end produced
as much dissatisfaction among the adventurers as did the
unhappy state of affairs in the company. In 1618 it was
discovered to the consternation of many stockholders that
almost the entire investment of the common stock in the
public estate and property of the company had been allowed to waste away until almost nothing of value remained to show for an investment estimated at £75,000.
The first step toward the decline of the company's plantation, or " publique " as it was known, had come in 1614.
The seven year term of service of the oldest inhabitants
expired in that year, and there were present for the first
time in the colony free laborers. Some of these returned
to England, but others elected to remain in Virginia where
it became the practise to allot them small individual tracts
of land on a formal tenure. By the end of 1614 there were
eighty-one such tenant farms in the colony.[11]

It is not known whether Governor Dale or the company was responsible for the initiation of this policy, but
it seems to have won approval both in Virginia and at
home. There was probably some disposition to believe
that the encouragement thus given to private enterprise

[10] *Records*, I, 350.   [11] Scisco, *loc. cit.*, VIII, 264-265, 267.

offered better promise of putting the colony on its feet than further attempts to farm the land directly. Regardless of the opinions held by the leading adventurers, however, the condition of the company forbad any energetic attempts at keeping up or improving the old plantation. And since few new settlers were sent to replenish the labor supply, the private plantations increased in number as each year brought to an end the indentured term of additional groups of older settlers, while the laborers left to work directly for the company's profit became fewer in number. At Governor Argall's arrival in 1617 the larger part of the settlers were tenant farmers, and his administration of two years witnessed the practical disappearance of the company's plantation.

Captain Samuel Argall's record as the governor of Virginia will probably always remain a controversial subject. The records are so few and contradictory that it is impossible to pass a satisfactory judgment on the man. He was censured by the company while Smith was still in power, and George Yeardley, who succeeded him in 1619, sailed with instructions to try him on several counts of neglect and malfeasance. Indeed, the feeling against him was so great in the winter of 1618–1619 that his patron and friend, Sir Robert Rich, privately dispatched a boat to Virginia to fetch him away before Yeardley's arrival.[12] Sandys condemned the man and his administration as governed wholly by personal greed, and there has been some tendency to accept this as the judgment of history.

But while it is quite probable that Argall had several private projects which were of more interest to him than the company's estate, there are undoubtedly some things to be said in his behalf. It was a difficult task to govern Virginia from 1617–1619 — to satisfy a group of disappointed adventurers at home and a band of colonists in Virginia whose state was none too happy. He received from

12 *Records*, II, 404.

the company only fitful and inadequate help, and on the whole he was left to make the best possible use of that at hand. And that was little enough. The old plantation of the company was in a poor state and it may have seemed to him of little use to attempt its further development without adequate supply and support from England. Nor were the planters doing any too well on their own estates. Already they were showing a disposition to apply their labor chiefly to tobacco, which was one of the factors producing a food shortage to embarrass further his administration. Moreover, their tobacco was usually of a poor sort, and the price they demanded for it had forced the Magazine merchants to raise their prices with the consequent complaints of exorbitant prices. The problem of maintaining peace, complicated by the break-up of the colony's unity, the usual tendency to lawlessness among a frontier people, and the old problem of idleness led him to an especially strict enforcement of martial law, which brought of course the cry of oppression. Complaints from Virginia found their way to England where groups of adventurers took them up and added them as fuel to the fires of faction growing out of their own discontent. Colonists looking for someone upon whom they might fasten the blame for their unhappy state quite naturally picked the company's agent in the colony, and so did many adventurers. There can be no doubt that many both in England and Virginia were looking for a scapegoat, and the governor was a natural choice.

It would have been hard for anyone to have filled Argall's position satisfactorily. It is only necessary to remember the numerous failures, fights, and factions that mark the history of so many governors in the early years of the American colonies to understand the difficulties of his position during the brewing of the most violent storm that marks early colonial history. And in whatever judgment is made of the man it will be well to weigh the words of John Rolfe who in a letter of 1620 to Sandys could not

" but reveal " the sorrow he felt at hearing the " many accusations heaped upon Captain Argall," who he was persuaded would " answer well for himself." When these matters came to trial, he continued: " I assure you that you shall find many dishonest and faithless men to Captain Argall, who have received much kindness at his hands and to his face will contradict, and be ashamed of much, which in his absence they have intimated against him. Lastly, I speak on my own experience for these 11 years, I never amongst so few have seen so many false-hearted, envious and malitious people (yea amongst some who march in the better rank) nor shall you ever hear of any the justest Governor here, who shall live free from their scandals and shameless exclamations, if way be given to their reports." [13]

Whether Argall should be held chiefly responsible for the conditions which prevailed during his governorship or not, they were nevertheless among the foremost causes of dissatisfaction which prompted ever increasing attacks upon the manner in which the business was being conducted. Especially objectionable was the decay of the public land. In 1619 Sandys summed up the colony's history in the preceding years, declaring that " as the Private Plantation began thus to increase so contrary wise the estate of the Publique . . . grew into utter consumption." The chief blame for this he put upon Argall, who upon his arrival in May, 1617 had found a portion of land called the Company's Garden which yielded an annual profit of £300. Fifty-four servants were employed on this land and the salt-works. Eighty-one tenants yielded a rent in corn and services which with the tribute corn of the natives amounted to 1200 English bushels per year. In addition there had been eighty kine and eighty-eight goats. But two years later " this whole State of the publique was gone and Consumed, there being not left at that time to the Company

[13] Rolfe to Sandys, January, 1620, Ferrar Papers.

either the land aforesaid or Any Tenant, Servant, Rent, or Tribute Corn, Cow, or Saltwork and but six Goats only, without one penny yielded to the Company for their so great loss in way of Accompt or restitution to this very day." [14]

This break-up of the company's plantation into individual holdings had been accompanied by another development of paramount importance in the economic life of Virginia, which became also a cause of great dissatisfaction among the adventurers. By 1613 it had been found that Virginia tobacco was of such quality that it could be marketed in England. It was a crop on which a quick return could be secured, and the colonists within the next few years turned to it as their staple commodity. Although some few pounds of tobacco were brought into England by Sir Thomas Smith in 1614,[15] the really rapid increase in its production came after 1616. In this year there were only 2,500 pounds of tobacco imported from Virginia and Bermuda, but the next year the total was 18,839 pounds, and in 1618 the figures rise to 49,518.[16]

Thus it may be seen that this signal development in the economic life of the colony coincided with Argall's administration and the events within the company which prepared the way for Sandys' rise to leadership in the courts. It was in many ways a fortunate discovery for Virginia, for the continuance of supplies in after years, when the company itself was frequently unable to provide them out of its own funds, depended upon the production of some staple in the sale of which there was hope for profit. It was the prospect of a load of tobacco on the return voyage that carried many a ship across the Atlantic with

[14] *Records*, I, 350-351.   [16] *Ibid.*, p. 526.
[15] "Lord Sackville's Papers respecting Virginia, 1613-1631," pub. in *American Historical Review*, XXVII (1922), 496. The papers included here of Lionel Cranfield, surveyor-general of the customs from 1613 and lord treasurer after 1621, furnish the most accurate index to importations of tobacco into England.

supplies upon which at times depended the very existence of the colony. A reawakened interest too among some of the London merchants may have been due to the possibilities offered by tobacco.

But at the same time there were disadvantages which were to have tremendous effects on Virginia's history. The rapid development of tobacco accompanied the break-up of the colony's economic unity. The governor no longer held the same effective control over tillage with the result that planters neglected those commodities which had not proved profitable, and the economic life of the colony tended to become one-sided through an unwholesome dependence upon one commodity. The danger of this condition became obvious at an early date because of the neglect of food crops along with others. Governor Dale found it necessary as early as 1616 to require each man to "set two acres of ground with corn" to prevent a food shortage.[17] Such laws, however, were difficult to enforce, and the colony became increasingly dependent upon supplies from home for the necessities of life.[18]

This development was not only opposed to the best opinion in England on tobacco,[19] but the resulting unhealthy economic condition produced a concern which was another important factor prompting discontent among a group of adventurers forming under the leadership of Sandys. Shortly after his election he complained that while three years before twelve several commodities had been returned from Virginia to the honor of the company, since then little had been sent home except tobacco and sassafras, "which the people there wholly applying had by this misgovernment reduced themselves into an extremity of being ready to starve, unless the Magazine this last year had supplied them with Corn and Cattle from hence." [20]

---

[17] Rolfe, *loc. cit.*, I, 108.

[18] *Records*, I, 266-267.

[19] An excellent treatment of the deeply rooted aversion to tobacco in England is found in Beer, *Origins of the British Colonial System*, pp. 78-100.

[20] *Records*, I, 266-267.

These conditions in company and colony were calculated to breed discontent, faction, and rivalry. The development of the private plantation undoubtedly added much to the immediate content of the colonists, which was increased by the discovery of a profitable staple and the conclusion of a peace with the natives. But while John Rolfe, writing in 1617 to deny the " many imputations " which " disgraced " Virginia, could speak of " everie man sitting under his fig tree in safety, gathering and reaping the fruits of their labours with much joy and comfort," [21] there were those in London who could not but wonder at the neglect of the company's property and the failure of its revenue. They watched with alarm the growing dependence upon tobacco, not only because of the dangers they foresaw in an economic order resting so completely upon one product, but also because of the disrepute into which the whole enterprise might fall when, instead of serving the public ends for which it had been founded, it supported only a vice which they in common with the majority of their fellow countrymen condemned. And when the merchant leaders undertook no progressive program for the continued growth of the colony, and appeared to be actively interested in little more than the success of the Magazine ventures, it was easy to suspect them of having no interest but their own personal profit. Complaints of exorbitant prices in Virginia reënforced suspicions at home, and perhaps more than Sir Robert Rich felt " that the merchants who then swayed the courts affected nothing but their own immoderate gain, though with the poor planters extream oppression, as appeared by their magazine." [22]

The leading spirits in an opposition to the responsible officials of the company which developed out of these cir-

[21] Rolfe, *loc. cit.*, I, 105.
[22] This quotation is from a letter which with good reason has been attributed to Rich. — Brown, *First Republic in America*, p. 279; *Records* II, 404.

cumstances were Sir Edwin Sandys, the earl of Southampton, Sir John Danvers, and John Ferrar. These men, as we have seen, were representative of that part of the adventurers with whom the desire to render a public service was especially strong in their support of colonization. As they witnessed the sad state to which that worthy enterprise had sunk, they were not alone disturbed by considerations of personal profit and loss. There was in it something more than an ordinary business failure; there was also something akin to a betrayal of trust and a failure to measure up to the demands of a great opportunity to serve their country. Of such stuff were the men who were first aroused by the lethargy that had overtaken the company and by suspicion that its leaders had not done all they might.

They began with a demand upon the officers for an account of their stewardship, and proceeded then to plans for reform and reorganization that would enable them once again to present Virginia as an enterprise worthy of every Englishman's support. Their intention was to solicit new capital by removing those features which discredited the company. They were especially concerned for the reputation of the business, which depended so much upon success in meeting its public ends, because they were conscious of the reserve of strength and support that could be evoked by a patriotic and religious appeal. It was not difficult to win the sympathy of many discontented adventurers, especially among the minor adventurers. It is usually the small investor who is most easily aroused by the failure of a business or by suspicion of its leadership. Many of them had been practically beaten out by repeated disappointments, but they returned now to the courts in increasing numbers as the opposition led by Sandys gave promise of setting the business aright. Other allies were found in the numerous disgruntled persons always present in a failing business. Small merchants like Captain Bargrave, better known for his criticism of the company's government, who had tried to break the monopoly of trade reserved to the company without much success, added their voice to the general chorus accusing the merchant leaders of selfish exploitation. Thus Smith found himself confronted with a strong and growing opposition. It was composed largely of small adventurers of no great means or importance, but they were being welded into an effective party that threatened to assume control of the courts through the direction of one of the most astute political leaders of the day.

The growing discontent of these adventurers found definite expression after 1616. November of that year marked the end of a seven year period in which it had been decided that the stock was to be accumulated by a monopoly of trade and remain undivided. The profits of the company during these years, however, were so small that in 1616 the only recompense for the adventurers lay in a distribution of lands.[23] It was some time after this disappointing revelation of the company's condition that Sandys, Southampton, Danvers, and others, "after sundry private meetings among themselves," demanded that a special audit be made of the officers' accounts, and were responsible for the appointment by the court of Sandys, Danvers, and Messrs. Wroth, Abbot, and Abdey for this purpose.[24] *The Historye of the Bermudaes* explains this action as due to the fact that

. . . Sir Thomas Smith haueinge from yeare to yeare, for a long time bin continued in his treasurour-shyp of the Virginian Company, it was found that many and great sommes of mony collected and brought in for the vse and behoufe of that plantation wer so expended and lost, as a very smale growth and improvement of that colony could thereby be any way discerned; neither (as it was sayd) could ther euer be gotten any perfect or iust account of these disbursements. It

[23] Bruce, *Economic History of Virginia*, II, 279.
[24] Brown, *First Republic in America*, p. 279; Wodenoth, *Short Collection of the Most Remarkable Passages etc.*, pp. 5-6.

was nowe, therefore, with somewhat more life and quicknesse
than formerly, affected and required; . . .[25]

Differences arose in auditing the accounts, and these disputes spread into the company. The thoroughness with
which the auditors fell to their task carried implications
displeasing to Smith. He " believed they ment him noe
good by their earnest requires for all old bookes of account." He disliked their refusal to do the auditing at
his house, which hitherto had been used as the company's
office. And most galling of all were Sandys' repeated complaints in the courts that the auditors were not receiving
the proper coöperation from the officers, and that unless
they did it would be impossible " to attaine to any perfect account." [26] Smith's reply was that the fault lay in
the inexperience of the auditors, and he directed his attacks especially at Sandys. The result of these disputes was
a breach between Smith and Sandys that was never healed.
Parties formed on either side and there followed much
controversy and many accusations.

In these disputes over accounts many adventurers found
opportunity to express their discontent with the state and
management of the business. And around this rallying
point there grew a party of opposition which looked to
Sandys for leadership. Their attack was strengthened as
the conditions prevailing under Argall became better
known, and by 1618 there was a strong demand for certain important reforms. This demand was stronger by
virtue of the fact that several groups of adventurers were
now contemplating the settlement of private plantations
in Virginia — a movement which probably grew out of
the land grants of 1616. At any rate within two years
several groups were planning to settle plantations under

[25] J. H. Lefroy, ed., *The Historye of the Bermudaes*, Hakluyt Society, London,
1882, p. 128. Both John Smith and Nathaniel Butler have been accredited
with this work.
[26] *Ibid.*, pp. 128-129.

patents from the company with the hope of succeeding where the company had failed. Among these was one led by Sandys and Southampton for a plantation which was at first known as Smith's Hundred and later as Southampton's Hundred. Another was that headed by John Smyth of Nibley, the records of which have been preserved in the "Smyth of Nibley Papers" in the New York Public Library, and there were several others that began settlements in 1618. The population of the colony was increased from about 400 in April of 1618 to around 1000 by the following spring, and this growth was largely due to the arrival of settlers sent by private adventurers.[27]

The fact that an influential and important part of the adventurers were now planning to send large numbers of colonists in the near future with the idea of developing Virginia into a colony of numerous and prosperous plantations was one of the most important factors in effecting the reorganization of the business which occurred in 1618. The incentive for these new ventures may have come in some cases from the prospect offered by tobacco, but it is more likely that it was chiefly the conviction growing out of the attacks upon Smith that past failures had been largely the result of mismanagement and negligence. In the years immediately following the failure of the plantation type of colony many statements derogatory to the climate, fertility, and resources of Virginia found wide acceptance in England. John Rolfe had written his "Relation of the State of Virginia," probably early in 1617, to answer just such attacks and to show that "this cause, so much despised and disgraced," suffered from many wrongful imputations.[28] Now that the sustained attack on Smith and the other officers presented another explanation of previous failure, such arguments as those of Rolfe carried more weight. There followed a revived interest and enthusiasm among the stockholders which was based upon

[27] *Records*, I, 350.   [28] Rolfe, *loc. cit.*, I, 101-113.

a new belief in the possibility of a successful colonization of Virginia. And since this new confidence rested so much on the conviction that the chief hindrance in the past had been error in policy and management, it is not surprising that with it came a demand for the reform of certain conditions in company and colony which were necessary not only for attracting colonists to the new plantations but to the success of their efforts after arrival.

Partly in response to this demand, partly perhaps to ward off the attacks of Sandys' faction, and partly because of a sincere interest in the welfare of the colony, Smith undertook in 1618 genuine reforms which were to have a lasting effect upon Virginia's history. Smith's program so nearly conforms to the policies followed by Sandys after his election in 1619 that there can be no doubt that Sandys had been largely responsible for calling attention to the abuses and weaknesses demanding reform and had led in pointing the way to their remedies. He evidently cooperated with Smith in 1618, and perhaps to Sandys more than any other should be given credit for this work, but it is a mistake to attribute all the reforms to him and thus to neglect the important part played by Smith. Sandys was not yet in control of the company, and these reforms could never have been accomplished without Smith's support.

One of the first steps taken was the recall of Argall. To succeed him the adventurers chose Captain George Yeardley, who was one of the older colonists and had served as deputy governor from Dale's departure in 1616 to Argall's arrival the following spring. He was commissioned on November 18, 1618, and sailed the following January with important instructions for setting aright the colony's affairs. It is to these instructions of Yeardley that we must look for an indication of the conditions in the colony which had called forth the greatest criticism in the preceding years, and for a lead as to the policies which were to guide the company through the next six years.

CHAPTER III
REORGANIZATION AND REFORM IN 1618

THE reforms effected by the adventurers in 1618 are comparable to the reorganization accomplished in the period between 1609 and 1612 in their importance as marking a turning point in the company's history. Both reforms were preceded by a disappointing lack of progress in the colony. In each case the adventurers undertook to discover the causes of their failure and to provide adequate remedy by a suitable reorganization and restatement of policy. Both efforts were partly the product of, and partly the cause of, a new enthusiasm which inspired a more energetic attempt to achieve the original purposes of the business. And both were followed by disappointment and failure to attain their objective.

The acrimonious debates of two years had by 1618 clarified the opinion of the courts concerning the remedies necessary to the reëstablishment of the company's fortunes. There were sharp differences of conviction as to the responsibility for previous errors, but there was little disagreement on the policies now to be followed. It was clear enough that the alarming disposition of the colonists to devote their time almost wholly to tobacco must be checked, and that in its stead their efforts must be directed to the production of food and of a large variety of staple commodities for which the English market was dependent upon foreign countries. Such a policy would not only place the economic life of Virginia upon a more certain foundation, but it would save the reputation of the business from the damage that inevitably must accompany the production of nothing more than a " cloud of smoke." It was also expected to win for the colony a secure position in English trade and thereby support the revenues of the company, which was a matter of primary concern to the adventurers, whether viewed from the point of their own investment or in the light of plans for the further growth of the colony. For the increase of revenue it was also agreed that the public lands must be reoccupied. Both of these policies called for a considerable increase in the labor supply, and the company looked forward to a program of large scale colonization within the next few years.

Before inaugurating this program, however, it was necessary to reform certain conditions of life and labor in the colony. In the years since 1614 Virginia had drifted into a disorderly and unsettled state in which many uncertainties of a political, economic, and social character vexed the colonists' life. Economic conditions rendered uncertain their food and any benefits they hoped to derive from their labor, the severity of martial law made insecure both their rights and property and produced a general discontent, and there was need for the settlement of some definite and permanent policy regarding tenure that would define and guarantee their rights in the land. Complaints at these conditions had engendered faction among both adventurers and planters and had sadly reduced the "reputation of the business," which must now be restored to enlist the support either of new capital or of new colonists.

The courts of 1618 devoted their chief attention, therefore, to certain preliminary reforms of which the settlement of land tenure, the abolition of martial law, and the establishment of the Virginia Assembly are among the most important. The unusual attention devoted to the political side of these reforms has somewhat beclouded the real intentions of the adventurers. They had set for themselves an ambitious program and they were engaged in nothing more than an attempt to set their house in order with the hope of providing the most favorable circumstances for the success of that program. There was much talk of making Virginia into a regular and well ordered state. It had been the purpose of the company, read

Yeardley's instructions, " to lay a foundation whereon a flourishing state might in process of time by the blessing of Almighty God be raised." [1] While such statements, when considered alone and unrelated to the movement from which they sprang, can be given an interpretation that is especially political, to do so is to lose the full scope of what the London adventurers attempted in 1618. To attribute to them any idea of creating a body politic either politically or economically independent of the company and of England is to credit them with an idea that is compatible neither with contemporary theories of colonization nor with reason.

Political reform was merely one phase of a much broader reorganization of the company's affairs, and to seize upon it as the most important feature of this work is to neglect several other aspects of more immediate significance. The reforms in Virginia were followed by a similar setting in order of the affairs and machinery of the company. The rights and duties of all officers and official bodies within the corporation were restated and set down in a long document drawn up and ratified by the adventurers in quarter court.[2] Their desire was to reduce confusion to order, to replace uncertainty by certainty, and to settle upon definite policies which would serve not only as the foundation of an expanding and prosperous colony, but to eliminate all possible opportunities for disagreement and factional strife of the type that had for some time hindered the advance of the business. To one who thus surveys the whole field of attempted reforms in 1618, that year assumes its proper place in the history of Virginia as the period in which the company endeavored to clear the deck for action, and to prepare the way for the application of those economic policies whereon Sandys

---

[1] "Instructions to Governor Yeardley, 1618," *Virginia Magazine of History*, II (1894), 154.

[2] *Orders and Constitutions*, in Force, *Tracts*, III, No. 6.

in after years labored to build a prosperous and thriving colony.

The intended reforms in the conditions of the colony were put into effect according to several commissions, ordinances, and instructions prepared by the company and sent with Governor Yeardley to Virginia. While some of his instructions have been lost, the most important are still in existence and the remainder may be reconstructed by references in other papers, so that it is possible to give a fairly complete sketch of the general purposes of his commission. His first immediate task was to secure sufficient food supplies for the maintenance of the colonists and to " draw on " the many people who were preparing to go to Virginia but had been discouraged by the late decay of the public store. He was especially charged to stop " the excessive applying of Tobacco, and the neglect to plant Corn which of all other things is most necessary for the increase of that plantation." [3] In keeping with this policy patents for private plantations granted in England included provisions that the settlers should not devote all of their time to tobacco, but rather would develop other enumerated commodities. [4] And the first assembly, which enacted into laws of the colony many instructions that had been given to Governors Delaware, Argall, and Yeardley, passed several statutes looking to the protection of the food supply, the restriction of tobacco, and to preparations for the production of wine, silk, hemp, and flax. [5]

Other instructions, which likewise won the approval of the assembly, sought to remove certain abuses and grievances that had hindered the prosperous growth of the colony. Some of these were directed at idleness, gambling, drunkenness, and the wearing of excessive apparel, but the most important attempted to remedy some of the griev-

[3] P.R.O., Admiralty Court, Instance and Prize, Libels 80, No. 123.
[4] Smyth of Nibley Papers, 3 (4).
[5] "Proceedings of the Virginia Assembly, 1619," edited by L. G. Tyler, in *Narratives of Early Virginia*, New York, 1907, pp. 264-265.

ances arising from the administration of the Magazine. According to an order of October 26, 1618, at which time the adventurers in the company had come to an agreement on this sore question, the Magazine was allowed to continue through the four year term fixed at its organization. But in response to complaints of exorbitant prices the profit of Magazine sales was definitely limited to twenty-five percent., and to ensure the enforcement of this limitation the governor was to receive an invoice of all sales. The Magazine's monopoly of trade was to continue with but two exceptions, both of which presaged a future policy of free trade. For the encouragement of private plantations it was ordered that whatever commodities were raised upon any of them could be returned directly to the adventurers in the plantation, but the privilege extended only to goods of their own production and under no circumstances to commodities acquired by trade. Another exception was made in cases of merchants who offered for sale necessary commodities which the Magazine at the time could not provide.[6]

The assembly heartily endorsed these regulations of the Magazine, as also further instructions given Yeardley in December of 1618 which recognized tobacco, for the time being at least, as the medium of exchange and established a fixed price for its sale. Abraham Piersey, cape merchant or factor for the Magazine, was required to accept tobacco in return for his goods at 3s. per pound for the better grade and 18d. for the second. Thus by a limitation of the percentage of profit allowed and the establishment of a definite value for the colonists' tobacco an attempt was made to remove one of the chief causes of discontent among both planters and adventurers. The Magazine was to be protected, however, from having to receive worthless tobacco at these prices by the provision that when leaf of an especially low grade was offered the cape merchant

[6] *Ibid.*, pp. 263, 266-267.

might refuse to accept it after four men, two chosen by
him and two by the plantation from which the tobacco
came, had under oath declared it not vendible at 18d.
This was also intended to encourage the planters to give
their tobacco a proper curing, and for their better encouragement tobacco so refused was to " be burnt before
the owner's face." [7]

Of all the papers entrusted to Yeardley, however, the
one designed to effect the most important of these preparatory reforms has been enshrined in history as the
" greate Charter " — a term which was applied to it by
the burgesses of the first assembly. Curiously enough a
great deal of its historical fame has rested upon a misinterpretation of its character. Proceeding from the assumption that the chief significance in the events of 1618 was
the triumph of a political liberalism, the historians of Virginia have reasoned that it must have been a political charter. But unable to find among the surviving records a document which corresponded to the character thus given it,
they have assumed that it was lost, or, proceeding more
carefully, have concluded that the term referred to several different papers providing for political changes and
guarantees, important parts of which no longer exist. They
then allowed their imagination free play in its reconstruc-
tion, and placed in our history as the very cornerstone of
American liberty a document totally without historical
foundation. For the " greate Charter " of the Virginia
burgesses they substituted a Magna Carta as far removed
from the original as was the popular interpretation of
King John's famous grant from the feudal document
sealed at Runnymede.

The error is more interesting because the real Charter,
though unrecognized, has not been unknown. The Library
of Congress possesses a copy of it which will shortly be
published by Miss Kingsbury in a further volume of the

[7] *Narratives of Early Virginia*, pp. 260, 267-268.

company's records. It was published in a slightly muti-
lated form as " Instructions to Governor Yeardley, 1618 "
by the *Virginia Magazine of History* in 1894.[8] And it has
long furnished the basis for discussions of land tenure
and quit-rents in Virginia, the subjects with which the
Charter was almost exclusively concerned. The identification of this document is to be found in John Pory's account of the first Virginia Assembly, where the burgesses
examined the Charter in detail and made suggestions
for its change in several particulars. Indeed, L. G. Tyler
in editing the " Proceedings of the Virginia Assembly,
1619 " identified the well known " Instructions to Governor Yeardley " as the document to which the colonists
referred as the " greate Charter." [9] But it seems to have escaped the attention of later historians and it will not be
amiss at this point to examine in some detail the contents
of the so-called Virginia Magna Carta.

The Charter deals with the question of government and
political rights only in the most general manner. It opens
with a statement of the company's purpose to lay the
foundation for " a flourishing state," and charges the offi-

---

[8] *Virginia Magazine of History*, II, 154-165.
[9] *Narratives of Early Virginia*, note to p. 255.
The identification may be established by an examination of six petitions in
which the assembly prayed for certain changes in its provisions. If they be compared with Yeardley's "Instructions," it is found that they correspond both in
content and order with the provisions found in the first part of that document.
The task of examining the Charter was divided between two committees and
for the expedition of their work the document was divided into four "books,"
a step which has led to a strange error by some historians who have failed to
understand that "book" meant no more than a division and have referred to the
four books of Yeardley's commission as though they were four volumes. The
committee for the second portion of the Charter recommended no changes,
although the governor in private expressed the opinion that the provision for
allowing a distance of ten miles between private plantations might have dangerous consequences for the defense of the colony. And since there was, in the words
of Pory, "no further scruple in the mindes of the Assembly touching the said
great Charter of lawes, orders, and priviledges, the Speaker put the same to the
question, and so it had both the general assent and the applause of the whole
assembly." See *ibid.*, pp. 255-259.

cials to look after the necessary provision of corn and cattle. In support of this purpose it had been thought good to settle " a laudable form of Government by Magistracy and just laws for the Happy guiding and governing of the people there inhabiting like as we have already done for the well ordering of our own courts here and of our officers and actions for the behoof of that Plantation." [10] With this, however, the question of government, that is in its political aspects, was dismissed. The provision for the assembly was made in an entirely separate document,[11] and in fact the whole tenor of the brief reference to government and law indicates that these problems had been dealt with elsewhere.

The body of the Charter undertook instead the settlement of land tenure and of questions concerning the internal organization of the colony. In the first place, an attempt was made to ensure the orderly administration of the older settlements and to provide for the reëstablishment of the public lands in the hope of some financial benefit thereby for the company. The older holdings in Virginia were divided into four boroughs, to be known as Jamestown, Charles City, Henrico, and Kecoughtan, soon thereafter given the name Elizabeth City. In each of these a reservation of 3,000 acres was to be farmed for the profit of the joint-stock by tenants sent at the company's expense. All persons transported to Virginia at the company's charge since 1616 were to be settled on the

---

[10] *Virginia Magazine of History*, II, 154.

[11] Pory describes the occasion on which Yeardley presented the several documents comprising his commission to the assembly in 1619. The Speaker, he relates, "read unto them the commission for establishing the Counsell of Estate and the general Assembly, wherein their duties were described to the life. Having thus prepared them he read over unto them the Greate Charter, or commission of privileges, orders and laws, sent by Sir George Yeardley out of Englande." (*Narratives of Early Virginia*, p. 255.) The phraseology indicates clearly that the order for the establishment of the assembly was separate and distinct from the Charter. For the ordinance creating the assembly see below, pp. 73-75.

reservation at Jamestown immediately, and during the next two years several hundred tenants were provided for these lands in the hope of developing them into profitable plantations. The tenants were entitled to one half the profit of their labors. The remainder, after the deduction of a fifth of it for the payment of bailiffs and overseers, was to be the company's share.

Further reservations within each borough were to be made for the support of all officials charged with the government of the colony. At Jamestown 3,000 acres were set apart as the governor's land to be tilled by tenants sent for the purpose from England. They, like those on the company's land, were to be "tenants by halves," the governor receiving one half the products of their labor. In succeeding years several lesser officers were established in this same fashion with a grant of land to be farmed by tenants provided by the company. The same principle was relied upon in 1618 to provide for the support of magistrates and for all other costs of local government. In each borough 1,500 acres were to be set aside for this purpose. With an eye to the spiritual welfare of the people it was ordered that 100 acres of glebe land should be reserved in each of the four boroughs. And at Henrico the reservation of 10,000 acres for the endowment of a college in which Indian children might be trained in religion and in civil virtues is evidence that at least the company had some intentions of doing missionary work among the natives.[12]

Of greater interest to the planters were the provisions dealing with questions of land tenure. The problem of tenure was somewhat complicated by the necessity of recognizing the various claims of adventurers who were to receive dividends on their investment in the form of land, of the "ancient planters" whose sufferings through the earlier years entitled them to some special consideration,

[12] *Virginia Magazine of History*, II, 154-159.

of settlers already in Virginia but who had settled in recent years, and of those colonists whom they hoped to
attract in the near future. A distinction was made between
old and new planters which depended upon settlement
before or after Governor Dale's departure from Virginia
in the spring of 1616. The personal adventure of the old
planter, in so far as the number of acres allotted to him
by the Charter was concerned, was held equivalent to the
£12 10s. adventured by the stockholder. Thus, all those
who had settled at their own cost before Dale's departure,
and had remained in the colony for three years, received
on the first division a grant of 100 acres. In case they happened also to be stockholders of the company, they were
to receive an additional grant of equal size for each share.
There was no mention of a quit-rent, and these grants
were apparently unqualified.[13] Others who had settled before that date, but at the company's charge, were to be
granted, after their term of service on the public land had
expired, 100 acres to be held by them in return for an
annual quit-rent of two shillings.[14]

Those immigrants who had arrived after the spring of
1616 fell within a different classification both as to the
amount and terms of their grant. Those who came at their
own cost, in this case, received only 50 acres and were
also required to pay a shilling quit-rent. The same conditions held for any person who might settle in Virginia
at his own expense in the future, such a person securing
50 acres upon a first division, made after three years resi-
dence or upon death after taking ship, and an equal
number on a second division, allotted after the first was
occupied, with a reservation of one shilling annual rent
for every 50 acres after the first seven years of the grant.
Those who had been or should in the future be sent at
the common charge of the company were to complete a
seven year term of service on the company's land, during

[13] See note to p. 60.   [14] *Virginia Magazine of History*, II, 156-157.

which time they were entitled to one half the profit of their labor. At the end of their service the context indicates that their personal adventure would be rewarded by the grant of 50 acres with the regular reservation of a shilling rent. For the encouragement of all necessary trades it was ordered that any tradesman who preferred to follow his trade should be allowed a dwelling house and four acres of land to be held in fee simple so long as he, or his heirs, continued to ply their trade in the said house. A free rent of four pence was to be paid in return for this grant.[15]

The remainder of the Charter dealt at length with the status of one of the most recent features of the colony's development, private plantations established by associated groups of adventurers in the company to be farmed for their own benefit separate and apart from the projects of the common joint-stock. They were developed under special patents from the company conveying to the patentees large contiguous areas of land with the privilege of farming the grant as a private plantation. The earliest grant

---

[15] *Ibid.*, II, 157, 159-160, 164-165.

The accepted interpretation of Yeardley's instructions has been that no rents were due from the planters until after 1624, and that therefore the administrative problem of collecting them became a purely royal one. It is true that a postponement of collection for seven years was offered in 1618 as an inducement to new settlers, but in the case of earlier settlers rents were apparently due before 1625. Obviously, the seven year exemption for them would expire before that date. The Charter indicates that rents were due from planters settled prior to 1616 at the company's charge immediately upon expiration of the seven year term of service on the public land. It would appear, also, that no more than seven year's exemption was allowed those who had settled on the company's land after Dale's departure but prior to the fall of 1618, and that the same rule applied to those who had entered Virginia within the same period at their own cost. Such an interpretation of the Charter is supported by the assembly's petition in 1619 for the appointment of a resident treasurer in the colony to collect rents because of the difficulty of paying in England, to which was joined the request that they might pay their rents in commodity and not in money, "whereof we have none at all, as we have no minte." (*Narratives of Early Virginia*, p. 258.) It is more difficult to determine whether any rents were collected. But it is significant that one of the duties devolving upon George Sandys at his appointment to the office of treasurer in 1621 was the collection of more than a £1000 already owing the company in rents and dues. (*Records*, I, 450.)

of this type was probably one made to Captain Argall in 1616.[16] At any rate, the entire movement was apparently an outgrowth, on the one hand, of the introduction of private holdings which followed after 1614 and, on the other, of the necessity which the company found in 1616 of rewarding the stockholders by dividends in land. Thus at the same time that the future of Virginia came to rest so much upon the hopes of private initiative, adventurers were casting about for means of turning their land dividends to some practical use. Some of them encouraged perhaps by the prospects for tobacco plantations, and others caught up by the new optimism which preceded and accompanied the reorganization of 1618, came to consider seriously the possibility of developing their lands into profitable plantations. The leaders of the company encouraged them in these projects, for it would enable them more quickly to build up the colony's population and hasten the day when Virginia would be a prosperous commonwealth producing and exporting valuable commodities for English trade. The company had many things to gain and nothing to lose by the early occupation of large areas which it could hope to develop only very slowly by its own efforts.

And by 1618 several projects of this kind were under way, of which there were three general types. Individual adventurers in only a few cases had sufficient land or capital to promote a plantation by their own efforts. They resorted, therefore, to the practise of pooling their land and resources in one joint enterprise. Several "associations" of adventurers were formed in this way. A patent was then secured from the company granting them a large area of land lying in one place, the size of which depended upon the number of shares held jointly by them in the company's stock. The well known societies of Smith's Hundred and Martin's Hundred were of this group. In other

[16] *Virginia Magazine of History*, II, 163.

cases an adventurer associated himself with outsiders, and the new association, or company, then secured a like grant from the Virginia Company. Such grants were usually made in the name of the original adventurer who took the lead. Plantations of this sort were those of Captain Argall, Captain John Martin, and one planned by Lord Delaware before his death in 1617. Yet a third type was that of new adventurers who apparently took stock in the company chiefly to get the land grant, and then organized for the purpose of establishing a plantation. The plantation of Christopher Lawne was of this type, and in 1618 there were other similar associations planning such settlements.[17]

In the four years following Sandys' election in 1619 forty-four patents for private plantations were issued by the company, and six were declared to have been granted under Smith.[18] Seven such settlements were represented in the first assembly. Most of the grants made after this date were not developed, but the encouragement of private plantations remained a conspicuous feature of the company's policy. A large percentage of the colonists sent to Virginia in the years after 1618 went to these plantations, and some of the financial difficulties of the company may be partly attributed to the fact that so large a portion of the investments made by adventurers in the colony during these years was diverted from the projects of the company itself to the support of their own private interests.

Fortunately one of these private patents has been preserved, a grant to Sir William Throkmorton, Sir George Yeardley, Richard Berkeley, George Thorpe, and John Smyth of Northnibley, made on February 13, 1619, by which Berkeley Hundred was settled on the upper James.[19] There is, however, a copy of the form used for such patents, dated May 20, 1622, preserved in the British Museum.[20]

[17] *Ibid.*, II, 160.
[18] *Records*, II, 350.
[19] Smyth of Nibley Papers, 3 (4).
[20] Add. MSS. 14285, ff. 49-53.

And the Charter deals fully with the questions of land tenure and the relation of these plantations to the rest of the colony, so that by the study of these three documents it is possible to sketch the general character of these undertakings.

The amount of land comprising the plantation depended upon the number of shares held by the proprietors in the company's stock. For each share there was a grant of 100 acres upon a first division, and to encourage the settlement of this land there was a promise of as many more upon a second division to be made after the first was " sufficiently peopled." Thus there were conveyed to the patentees for Berkeley Hundred on the first division 4,500 acres in return for their forty-five shares in the common stock. Further to encourage the patentees to develop their land, the system of head grants was adopted. For every person sent to their plantation at the charge of the association within seven years after Midsummer Day, 1618, who remained there three years, or died after taking ship, there was to be an additional grant of 50 acres upon a first division and an equal number upon the second.[21] In

[21] Smyth of Nibley Papers, 3 (4); *Virginia Magazine of History*, II, 163-164.
Some question arises as to whether or not these grants to stockholders were made free of quit-rents. The author is inclined to believe that they were. The phraseology of both the Charter and the Berkeley patent is somewhat ambiguous on this point, but it is noticeable that in every statement concerning grants in return for shares in the company there is no reference to a quit-rent, while in every other case it is carefully specified except for the old planters who had settled at their own cost. Their personal adventure, however, was considered equivalent to that of a stockholder. And the fact that the provision for them contains no statement of a quit-rent obligation, while it is expressly stipulated that all old planters who had gone at the company's charge were to pay 2s. rent, is not perhaps without some bearing on the point. Moreover, the Charter in making provision for the 100 acres allowed on each share of stock and the 50 acre head grant for every person sent within seven years declared that these grants were to be held "without paying any rent to the Company for the one or the other." And while the phraseology here is sufficiently ambiguous to be interpreted as applying only to the first seven years, the absence of any stipulated rent in the Berkeley patent indicates that such grants were entirely and permanently exempt. The failure to specify a rent for these two types of grants seems more significant in view of the fact that the Berkeley patent carefully re-

this way it was possible for any of the associations to extend their holdings as the need arose, but the expansion depended upon a corresponding development of previous grants. Thus did the company avoid large grants of undeveloped land which might interfere with the normal growth of the colony.

The plantations established under these special patents were variously designated as Argall's Guift, Captain Lawne's Plantation, Martin Brandon, or Smythe's Hundred. But while no one name was given these divisions, the term hundred was most commonly used. The Virginia hundred has often been explained as a carry over from the English administrative division. This is possible, at least so far as the name was concerned, but it hardly seems likely in that there was little comparison between these scattered plantations of Virginia and the English hundred. It is a mistake to conclude that there was any attempt at this time to divide the colony systematically into subdivisions comparable to the English counties and hundreds. Rather the Virginia hundreds resembled much more closely the feudal manor, in that they were private estates scattered at various intervals along the James River and possessed of a certain economic and political independence which set them apart from the rest of the colony. In view of this and the fact that the term was not universally applied to all private settlements, it seems more likely that in origin it was a sort of colloquial designation of such plantations as had been given no definite name.[22]

---

quired in one place that a quit-rent be paid the company after 1625 by any person who contracted with the patentees to settle as a member of their plantation at his own cost. Such a person received 50 acres adjoining the Berkeley grant, and was to pay a shilling rent. It appears from this evidence that the company, acting on the theory that the grant to a stockholder was the dividend on his investment, or desirous of giving all possible encouragement to these private plantations, exempted such lands from the customary quit-rent payment.

[22] The term may have been suggested by the fact that these grants were made in units of 100 acres, or more likely, by the obligation to settle on the land so

Whatever may have been the origin of the name, the appearance of these semi-independent communities made much more complex the problems of internal organization and government. Consequently, the company in 1618 endeavored to settle upon a definite and uniform policy for their development, giving especial attention to their relation to the colony as a whole. The need for such action was emphasized by the confusion and faction that had grown out of one or two earlier grants, which apparently had been made according to no uniform or settled policy. In outlining the conditions under which these plantations might be established, therefore, the Charter declared the company's intention to allot to everyone his due shares and rights, but in such a way as neither to disturb the rights of others nor to interfere with the good form of government intended for the benefit of the people and the strength of the colony.[23]

The patentees were free to chose the site of their plantation with the advice and consent of the governor at any place not already occupied or chosen by English settlers. No plantation, however, was to be placed within five miles of any of the four boroughs, nor within ten miles of any other plantation, except when the two fell on opposite sides of a great and navigable river. Under such circumstances both were to enjoy equal rights to the use of the stream and all its products. The general purpose of this regulation seems to have been to avoid all possible conflict and to give room for the adequate expansion of these plantations. This so-called " straggling " of settlements was severely criticised after the Indian massacre of 1622, and there was some objection to it in 1619 because of the weakening of the colony's defense. However, within each particular plantation the officers were warned against " strag-

granted 100 colonists, which was apparently understood if not actually stipulated in the patent. See *Records*, II, 350.

[23] *Virginia Magazine of History*, II, 160.

gling " the settlers over a large area, and were required to settle them in one compact body. After the site chosen had been surveyed and its bounds limited, the company promised within seven years after the granting of the patent to convey the title to the patentees along with letters of incorporation under some fit name.[24]

The internal organization of these settlements was left largely to the proprietors. While the governor was ordered to furnish every aid possible in the work of settlement, the cost and responsibility rested with the patentees. The hundreds were very definitely private enterprises in which the proprietors undertook to realize a profit on their investment, and the company did not attempt to dictate in questions of tenure or of economic organization, except in such general considerations as the limitation of tobacco. Rather these private corporations enjoyed special privileges which left their economic life comparatively free from interference. The adventurers and all their tenants, servants, and any others they should contract with for employment in the service of the plantation were to be free to trade and traffic, to import and transport their goods and merchandise at their own will and pleasure paying only such customs and dues to his majesty as were required of the company itself. They were to be subject to no other taxes, impositions, burdens, or restraints except such as should be imposed by the grant and consent of the general colony or for the public service of the plantation itself. None of the settlers could be taken away from their employment by the governor or by any other authority upon any pretense whatsoever except for the necessary defense of the country, for the preservation of peace, or for trials of matters of justice by orders of the company thereafter to be established.[25]

These privileges and exemptions, however, were largely economic in character. In consideration of the unity and

[24] Smyth of Nibley Papers, 3 (4).   [25] *Ibid.*

general welfare of the colony as a whole, the company did impose important restrictions on the religious and political life of these plantations. Each was required to make the same provision for ministers and religious interests as had been made in the four boroughs.[26] And in the Berkeley patent an extra grant of 1,500 acres was made for the support of ministers, churches, schools, and other charitable works. More important were definite limitations upon proprietary rights of jurisdiction. The adventurers were incorporated with liberty to frame all ordinances and constitutions necessary for the government and ordering of all persons settled upon their land, but such orders and constitutions were required not to be repugnant either to the laws of England or to the government established by the company for the entire colony.

Politically, the colony was to be one unit with uniform law and government, and while the patentees were given a limited control over purely local problems the Charter was explicit in its requirement that their settlers should live under equal laws and orders with the rest of the colonists.[27] Appeals from the hundreds were to be heard in the " supreme courts." Each plantation was represented on a basis of equality with the boroughs in the general assembly, and the enactments of that body applied equally to all portions of the colony. One of the chief objections to Captain Martin's patent, which was a storm center in company and colony for four years, was a clause which apparently exempted him both from the laws established by the company and from such enactments as might be passed by the assembly.[28] By these regulations it is apparent that the private plantation, according to the company's policy of 1618, was to be a separate and distinct unit within the colony, but restricted in such a way as not to disrupt

[26] *Virginia Magazine of History,* II, 163.
[27] *Ibid.,* II, 160-161; Smyth of Nibley Papers, 3 (4).
[28] *Narratives of Early Virginia,* pp. 252-253.

the colony's unity nor the uniformity of its laws and institutions.

The provisions of the charter not only applied to all
future grants, but were also retroactive in their effect.
With the assertion that much damage had been done by
previous grants in " general words," the Charter required
that all former patents be submitted to the company within
a year, that they might be revised wherever objectionable
and replaced by new patents conformable to the company's
policy.[29] Such action was declared necessary because of
"various fraudulent and dangerous courses" entered
upon by several unnamed patentees. Among those at
whom it was directed was Captain Martin, whose patent
was objected to not only because of the exemption from
the full authority of the colonial government, but because of his claim to a division of 500 acres per share instead of the 100 set forth in the Charter.[30] There were
others who had sought to avoid the cost of transporting
their colonists from England by persuading settlers already in Virginia to take up divisions in these new plantations, which of course was a practise opposed to every interest of the company. Captain Argall seems to have been
held the chief offender, and the governor was especially
warned that the patent secured by him in 1616 was in no
way to be respected since it had been secured by slight and
cunning. Argall's plantation, located about a mile north
of Jamestown, was taken over by the governor to form a
part of the Jamestown public lands.[31]

Others in a conspiracy to defraud the king of his lawful
customs duties were declared to have made " grants of
association " to shipmasters and mariners who had no intent to inhabit in Virginia, but sought merely to take
advantage of the exemption from port duties allowed to

[29] *Virginia Magazine of History*, II, 161.
[30] *Narratives of Early Virginia*, p. 262.
[31] *Ibid.*, p. 276; *Virginia Magazine of History*, II, 162-163.

the goods of the company. There was yet another group composed of men outside the company who planned to establish plantations under similar grants of association secured from patentees of the company. It was ruled, therefore, that any person who settled without proper authorization from the company would be considered an occupant of the common land and required to pay one fourth of the produce of his land in rent until he received a regular grant. Members of the company who had settled without permission were required to secure a patent within two years or thenceforth be deemed settlers on the common land.[32]

The Charter was concluded with several general provisions requiring an accurate record to be kept of all patents given under the company's seal and of all colonists sent to Virginia, and commanding a complete survey to be directed by Yeardley for determining the respective boundaries of the various plantations. From beginning to end it is a document dealing with the most prosaic features of colonial life. But these are often the most important, and may well be considered the subjects of chief interest to the colonists in 1618. In a well established society political rights and privileges assume at times an importance out of proportion to their basic value in relation to other considerations, such as that of economic security. It is easy to forget, yea even for historians, that there have been many times when men have shown a greater love for peace and order, for security of economic tenure, and for those conditions of social organization that would enable them to build their homes upon a sure foundation. It was for guarantees of this sort, and not for the grant of representative government, that the Virginia burgesses after examining the Charter " professed them-

[32] *Virginia Magazine of History*, II, 162. The chief person affected by these provisions was Captain Warde who had established a plantation on the upper James. The right of his plantation to seats in the assembly in 1619 was questioned on this ground. See *Narratives of Early Virginia*, p. 252.

selves in the first place most submissively thankful to almighty god," and instructed the Speaker to return " their due and humble thankes to the Treasurer, Counsell and company for so many privileges and favours as well in their owne names as in the names of the whole Colony whom they represented." [33]

The work of 1618, however, was not completed without important reforms in the political life of the colony, of which the establishment of the Virginia Assembly is best known. There are few events in American history that have been more grossly misinterpreted than this part of Yeardley's commission. Virginians, writing in the light of what the assembly later came to be, have read into the history of this reform ideas which are not only unnecessary to its interpretation but are often inaccurate. It has been taken as the key to the whole history of the company after 1618, the clearest example of Sandys' liberalism and democratic policies, and as the chief bone of contention between the Sandys faction and the so-called court party under Smith and Warwick. So attractive did this idea become that it contributed to a complete misinterpretation of one of the most important crises in early colonial history.

The first essential to an understanding of this revision in the colony's government is to get away from the fact that the Virginia Assembly was the first popular assembly in the western hemisphere. It is not necessary to slight the significance of the fact in later American history, but if it may be temporarily forgotten, ample explanation will be found in the problems confronting the company in 1618. One who turns to that year, rather than to some later period, will note first of all that these changes in government were made by the authority and under the leadership of Sir Thomas Smith. And while the suggestion may have come from the Sandys side of the court, as apparently did so many of the plans of that year, the chief respon-

---

[33] *Narratives of Early Virginia*, p. 259.

sibility must rest with the treasurer who commissioned Yeardley and authorized his actions. Provision for the new government was incorporated in Yeardley's commission of November 18, 1618. He sailed in January, and arrived at Jamestown in April, 1619, at about the time Sandys was elected head of the company. The first assembly met on July 30, 1619. The reform in government was not the work of either party; both factions were committed to it, and it is impossible to regard it as the chief cause of contention between them. And despite all that has been written on the subject, there has not been unearthed one dependable piece of evidence to prove that the so-called " subservient tools " of James I objected to it.

In fact, the Virginia Assembly predates the establishment of a similar body in Bermuda by only one year. The adventurers of the younger company undertook in 1619 to reform some of the conditions in Bermuda of which complaint had been made by a program not unlike that adopted by the Virginia Company the preceding year. A significant feature of this program was the provision for a general assembly which met in its first session at the town of Saint George on August 1, 1620, almost a year before the Sandys faction was able to wrest control of the Bermuda Company from Sir Thomas Smith. In a sitting of four days a total of thirty-two measures were enacted, fifteen of which were returned to England for ratification.[34]

The political reforms in Virginia are properly to be regarded as merely one phase of the more general reform effected by the adventurers in 1618. The plans of that year were indeed ambitious; they required the investment of much capital, and it was but natural that the company should endeavor in every way possible to protect this investment by creating conditions in Virginia favorable to the success of its new program. It would have been surpris-

[34] Edward Arber, ed., *Travels and Works of Captain John Smith*, Edinburgh, 1910, II, 673-674; Butler to Rich, October 23, 1620, Manchester Papers, 284.

ing if the leaders in undertaking so extensive a program
had overlooked the necessity of reshaping the government
in a form more adapted to the colony's economic organization. For the economic welfare of any community must depend in no small part upon the peace and content which its
government affords. Moreover, the necessity of enlisting
additional supplies of capital and labor caused much attention to be given to the colony's reputation. And there
were few things of recent years that had done more to
bring the business into disrepute than the repeated and
loud complaints of martial law in Virginia. These complaints were a strong factor in discouraging Englishmen
from giving financial support to the enterprise or from considering Virginia a fit place in which to live. To remove
this blemish on the colony's reputation by some reform of
the government was an almost indispensable preliminary
to any effort at reëstablishing the company's fortunes.

It was because of practical considerations of this type,
rather than any idealistic scheme looking toward an independent and democratic state, that attention was turned
to political reform. It was natural that in framing the new
government the adventurers should be influenced by the
practises of the mother country, and in fact should endeavor to bring a greater conformity to the spirit of English institutions. For thereby, not only would it be easier
to attract English immigrants, but the colony would enjoy
a much better reputation among those to whom it must
look for support. The interpretation of these changes in
government has often presented them as a sort of revolt
against political conditions in England, but in fact they
were dictated by just the opposite motives. It is not without significance that the company later advertised to the
country that " the laudable forme of Justice and government used in this Realme " had been " established and
followed as neere as may be " in the Virginia colony.[35]

[35] Force, *Tracts*, III, No. 5, pp. 5-6.

The reform of greatest immediate importance was the abolition of martial law and the substitution of the English common law. The privy council was requested to assist the company in a compilation of English laws suitable to the problems of Virginia.[36] The Charter was especially careful to secure the equal enforcement of these laws in all parts of the colony, and to require that all laws for the government of purely local affairs within private estates should not run counter to English law. With the common law came also the English magistrate. The government of Virginia, according to Yeardley's instructions, was to be by " Magistracy and just laws," and provision was made for the support of these magistrates out of the proceeds from public lands.[37]

While these facts have not been unknown, they have been considerably overshadowed by the attention given the assembly, and it will not be amiss here to give them again their proper place in Virginia's history. Martial law had become the most objectionable feature of the old government, and there is good reason for the statement that the introduction of the common law was considered by the colonists the most valuable part of the political changes provided in 1618. Five years later when the Virginia disputes had been called before the privy council for settlement, the Sandys party secured the support of some of the colonists through the fear that the outcome would be a return to conditions existing before 1618. In papers submitted by colonists at that time their chief complaint of the old regime was the harsh and cruel law under which they had been forced to live, and their main argument in behalf of the new was the justness and mildness of its government.[38] Nor is the immediate importance of these reforms in the administration of justice the only

[36] *Records*, I, 394-395.
[37] *Virginia Magazine of History*, II, 154, 158.
[38] *Narratives of Early Virginia*, pp. 422-426.

consideration entitling them to a position of first rank, for they left a permanent impression on the course of America's institutional development. Certainly this step toward a judicial system founded upon the principles of the common law is an event deserving, at least, equal rank with the establishment of the first representative assembly.

The second main feature of political reform was the provision for a legislative assembly. This action was partly dictated by the same general motive that led to the adoption of the common law — the desire to bring a greater conformity to English institutions. But there were more specific considerations. One purpose that was served was to add much to the spirit and content of the colonists. There was a marked similarity between the government of the colony and that of the company after 1619, which suggests that the latter's organization may have been a model. The company was governed by a treasurer, council, and assembly of adventurers. In the public statements of the company, especially in appeals for colonists, there was much talk of Virginia's resting upon the support of two groups of adventurers, those in London who adventured their capital, and the planters in Virginia who adventured their lives and labor, both equally contributing to and enjoying the honor of its success. The establishment of the assembly may have been partly due to an effort to build up the spirit of the planters by the feeling that like the adventurers at home they too enjoyed a voice in the government.

Some idea of a further motive may be seen in the uses to which the assembly was put. At its first session a long list of instructions, touching all phases of colonial life, brought by the governor from London were enacted into laws of the assembly.[39] It is not unreasonable to suppose that the enforcement of these instructions was made much

[39] *Ibid.*, pp. 262-269.

easier through their ratification by the colonists themselves. They were no less the instructions of the company, but they gained an added force and facility of administration by this endorsement. In much the same way
as had Edward I found it easier to collect taxes after they
were granted by the knights of thirteenth century England, thereby taking an important step toward the development of the English parliament which in so many
ways was the prototype of American legislative assem-
blies, so now the company could more easily explain its
policy and thereby secure a greater coöperation in its enforcement. Such a representative body facilitated also
an understanding of conditions and problems common
to the entire colony, and restored to some extent a
political unity lost since the decay of the old company
plantation.

Finally, it helped in the correction of another fault
which experience had shown in the relations between
company and colony. Virginians lived under a dual authority, that of the company and that of those officials
into whose hands was given the execution of policies determined upon by the adventurers in London. Most of
these adventurers had never been to Virginia and had
only a very superficial knowledge of conditions and problems there. As a result many policies and instructions
which seemed wise in London proved to be impracticable
in Jamestown. This meant friction, delay, and often mis-
understanding, which proved a real impediment to the
progress of both company and colony. As Sir Francis Wyatt
explained to the privy council in 1624 after the dissolution
of the company had been decided upon:

Some inconveniences we have found by the strict limitations
of the Governor and Council by instructions out of England,
since in so far a distance and not perfect knowledge of the
Country that may seem good in advise, which may by accident
prove otherwise in execution, . . .

It was his plea therefore that " we may retain the liberty of our general Assembly, than which nothing can more conduce to our satisfaction or the public utility." [40]

There had been sufficient opportunity for the recognition of this difficulty before 1618, and there were at that time two possible remedies. The governor in Virginia might be given more authority and be made less subject to instructions from London, but there were obvious objections to this, objections which had been emphasized by the conduct of Argall. The experience of his administration argued against giving the governor too much power. But some restrictions of a general character might be placed upon him by a wider distribution of authority in the colony which at the same time would not impair too greatly the necessary unity in leadership. The old council had served this purpose. Now the assembly was added as another and larger council to serve something of the same purposes.

This suggestion is strengthened by an examination of the structure of the assembly. Provision was made for its establishment and its duties were outlined in " An Ordinance and Constitution for a Council and Assembly in Virginia." [41] The original of this document has not been discovered, but we are fortunate in having a copy of it dated July 24, 1621. On that date long instructions were dispatched to Yeardley ordering certain preparations for the arrival of his successor, Sir Francis Wyatt.[42] The governor and council were required to revive all commissions and instructions sent with Yeardley in 1619, and to see that anything in them that had not been followed was put into force immediately. For their guidance in this work copies of all papers comprising Yeardley's com-

[40] Wyatt to Privy Council, February 29, 1623-4, Bancroft Transcripts, Virginia Papers, II, 368-371.
[41] Miscellaneous Papers, 1606-1683, pp. 21-23.
[42] Manuscript Records of the Virginia Company, III. Part ii, pp. 11-14. (Hereafter cited as MS. Rec. Va. Co.)

mission of 1618 were now dispatched to Virginia. It is to this action that we owe the surviving copy of the ordinance for the assembly.

According to this document there were to be henceforth two councils in Virginia. First, a Council of State, the members of which were listed as chosen by the company in London, was to act as a permanent advisory body to the governor. The larger council, to be known as the General Assembly, was to consist of the Council of State and two burgesses chosen by the inhabitants from every town, hundred, or " other particular plantation." It was to be assembled by the governor once a year, and no oftener except upon " very extraordinary and important occasions." It had the power to treat and conclude " of all emergent occasions concerning the public," and to make, ordain, and enact such general laws and orders for the welfare of the colony as should from time to time seem necessary.

Thus the company shifted to a body more thoroughly acquainted with conditions in the colony the enactment of a large number of measures dealing with local problems, which taken singly do not appear of great importance, but in sum total comprise one of the most important functions of government. The little irritations often bring the greatest discontent in a social group. And many such irritations were avoided by placing the enactment of laws governing the colonists' daily life in the hands of their own representatives. But at the same time it did not diminish the authority of higher officials in company and colony, for the assembly was definitely limited by important restrictions. The burgesses were required to follow the laws, customs, and government of England as nearly as possible. The governor held at all times the right of veto over any measure of the assembly, and none of its laws were to have force unless ratified by a quarter court of the company. A last and very interesting provision, indicating more the desire to eliminate the difficulties which resulted from the adventurers' inadequate knowledge of Virginia rather than any expectation of establishing a free state, was the promise that after the colony had been well established the company intended to extend to the settlers the privilege of not being bound by the enactments of the company courts until they had been ratified by the assembly.[43]

At its work the assembly is shown again as a sort of greater council. It was much more than a legislative assembly. Questions of policy were considered, not only in the ratification of instructions from the company but by petitions suggesting the initiation of new policies or changes in those already decided upon at London, and important judicial functions were performed. The Virginia planters found in the assembly a high court, composed in part of their own representatives, to which they might freely petition for justice, thereby gaining a greater feeling of security than had been theirs when judicial powers remained largely in the hands of one man. They were quick to take advantage of the opportunity. At its first session Captain William Powell petitioned for justice against a servant who had neglected his business, had impudently abused the captain's house " through wantonnes with a woman servant," and had falsely accused his master of drunkenness and theft. It was the opinion of this worthy body that the offending servant should stand four days with his ears nailed to the pillory, and on each of those days be publicly whipped. The question of what satisfaction he should render for the neglect of his work was left to the governor and council. On the same day, August 13, another petition from John Rolfe against Captain Martin for " taxing him both unseemly and amisse of certaine

[43] Rather conclusive proof that this paper is a true copy of the original is found in a petition of the first assembly requesting that this last promise might be put into effect as early as possible. This refutes the suggestion sometimes made that this provision was added in 1621. See *Narratives of Early Virginia*, p. 278.

thinges wherein he was never faulty" and for casting aspersion upon the present government was also referred to the council.[44]

On the following day Captain Henry Spellman was degraded from his rank of captain and forced to serve seven years as interpreter to the governor for the confessed offense of having brought the governor and colony into contempt with the Indians through telling Opechancanough, a neighboring chieftain who later plotted the massacre of 1622, that within a year there would come from England a greater governor. There was then considered a petition from the inhabitants of Argall's Town that they might be discharged of bonds whereby they were bound to Argall for the payment of £600 for 300 acres of wooded ground and of £50 to Captain Powell for clearing and building houses thereon. The burgesses doubted their power to grant this prayer, but became humble suitors to the company that the bonds might be cancelled.

There were other instances in which the assembly meted out justice between planters, or imposed some punishment or obligation upon persons whose actions were considered dangerous to the colony. These cases usually dealt with problems arising in the relations of settlers with the Indians. Captain Martin had sent a shallop into the Bay for corn. A group of Indians had refused to trade, whereupon Martin's men had proceeded to take their corn by force giving them a few small trinkets in payment. The offended Indians had appealed to Opechancanough, who in turn complained to the governor. The incident was called to the attention of the assembly, and Martin was required to take leave of the governor on all such expeditions and to give security that his men would commit no such outrage.[45]

In many instances, as it may be seen, the burgesses simply

[44] *Narratives of Early Virginia*, pp. 268, 269.
[45] *Ibid.*, pp. 253-254, 274-276.

referred the case to the governor and council or to the company. Their right of action was as yet definitely limited by the superior powers of the governor. Yet the mere privilege belonging to the colonists of free petition to this body for the redress of grievances was a guarantee of their rights, of a more equitable administration of the new code of laws, and a security against any highhanded course by the governor such as some had felt to be one of their most legitimate grievances against Argall. It was one of the most valued privileges given the planter by the new government, and enabled the company to advertise in England that the " Governor is so restrained to a Counseil joyned with him, that he can doe wrong to no man, who may not have speedy remedy." [46]

There is nothing surprising nor especially radical about the establishment of the Virginia Assembly. Its functions were of much the same general character as those of the older council. The instructions and laws of the company were given greater force through their reënactment by representative colonists. A group of settlements scattered up and down the James River for over a hundred miles were bound into a closer political unit. The governor and company were enabled to acquire a better understanding of problems common to the colony. The difficulty of enacting detailed orders for plantations too far removed to allow the London adventurers an adequate understanding of all their needs was avoided without concentrating too much power in the hands of one man. And withal, the general satisfaction of the colonists was increased by their voice in a government conforming more closely to the spirit of English institutions. In no way can it be said to have brought any immediate weakness in the government. The governor's authority remained supreme. Nor did it interfere with the company's right to full control over the life and development of the colony. Important

[46] Force, *Tracts*, III, No. 5, p. 6.

questions of policy were still decided upon at London, and detailed instructions continued to issue forth from the London council. All enactments of the assembly were subject to the veto of the governor and the approval of the company. All important officials for Virginia were selected by the adventurers. In short, the " government of Virginia " still centered in the company, and its hand was only strengthened by a better understanding, a better spirit, and stronger coöperation on the part of the colonists.

The proper understanding of these changes in government can be had only by their study in connection with the much broader program of reform and reorganization of which they were a natural and integral part. A perspective, more suitable than that ordinarily used in examining this part of Virginia's history, may be had by a glance at the use to which the adventurers put these reforms in their appeals for popular support. On July 1, 1620, the company published *A Declaration of the State of the Colony and Affairs in Virginia,* in which the council endeavored at length to remove certain aspersions cast upon Virginia's climate and soil, enumerated its many commodities, as also the large number of persons who had gone to Virginia during the preceding year, and continued:

The care likewise that hath beene taken by directions, Instructions, Charters, and Commissions to reduce the people and affairs in *Virginia* into a regular course, hath beene such and so great, that the Colony beginneth now to have the face and fashion of an orderly State, and such as is likely to grow and prosper. The people are all divided into severall Burroughs; each man having the shares of Land due to him set out, to hold and enjoy to him and his Heires. The publique Lands for the Company here, for the Governor there, for the College, and for each particular Burrough, for the Ministers also, and for divers other necessary Officers, are likewise laid out by order, and bounded. The particular Plantations for divers private Societies, are settled in their Seates, being alotted to their content, and each in convenient distance. The rigour of Martiall Law, wherewith before they were governed is reduced within the limits prescribed by his Majesty: the laudable forme of Justice and government used in this Realme established and followed as neere as may be.

This orderly arrangement of the colony's affairs had given all settlers good heart, who had now fallen to building houses, to ploughing, to setting vineyards, and to producing many staple commodities. Nor should there be omitted the care for reducing all proceedings and affairs of the company to an orderly course of government and justice. There had been compiled a book of standing laws and orders " whereby both the company here, and the Colony in *Virginia,* have their businesse carried regularly, industriously, and justly." All of these reforms and consequent improvements led the council to feel that it would be greatly injurious to the adventurers " if we should not acquaint them with this seasonable time for the reaping of that benefit and reward which is due unto them." Then follows an explanation of the conditions under which they might secure patents for their own particular plantations, and thus enjoy the benefits of the prosperity awaiting the Virginia colony.[47]

The position of the Virginia Assembly in the history of the company should be the same as that given it by its founders, as merely one of many improvements made in the colony's life. When studied in connection with other reforms of 1618 it is unnecessary to read back into its history ideas and conceptions belonging only to more recent times. And while recognizing the great importance of the assembly's later history, the accurate historian must seek the explanation of its origin in contemporary conditions rather than in more recent developments. Nor does this procedure detract in any way from the credit due its

[47] Force, *Tracts,* III, No. 5, pp. 5-7.

founders. In fact, it is more to their credit that they were able to meet immediate and practical problems with a program that contributed some of the most admirable features of English colonization for all time, and that in its breadth and wisdom commands the admiration of any serious student.

CHAPTER IV

SANDYS INAUGURATES THE NEW PROGRAM

THERE was nothing permanent in whatever truce may have existed between the rival factions during the reorganization of 1618. Hardly had the leading questions before the company been settled than once more various disputes gave evidence of internal strife among the adventurers. Yeardley had been the choice of Smith, but bitter feeling arose between the two shortly after the governor's commission was issued because of a knighthood conferred upon him contrary to Smith's wish. It was not an uncommon practise to give in this way some added prestige to the governor's office, but Smith was greatly offended thereat and openly declared his displeasure. His opponents in the courts quickly rallied to the governor's support, whose interest and loyalty thereafter became closely identified with the fortunes of the Sandys party. Sandys, " thinking it unfit that the Treasurer of the Company and the Governor of the Colony should be at Variance," effected an apparent reconciliation before Yeardley's departure, but afterward Smith renewed his displeasure at the governor's " unduly procured knighthood " and another member muttered " matter of disgrace to his wife." The news of these attacks so incensed Yeardley that he demanded a release from his office, but the report of Sandys' election evidently persuaded him to continue. Sandys recounted the whole affair to Southhampton in a letter expressing his indignation at such treatment of a man " to whom they had professed friendship, who was chosen by themselves, and sent by them (in great part at his own private charges) to so difficult a service." [1]

These unpleasant exchanges, in which Sandys strongly supported Yeardley, signalled the revival of the factional

[1] Sandys to Southampton, September 29, 1619, Ferrar Papers.

strife which had only partially subsided in the months preceding the appointment of the new governor. Many of the points formerly in dispute had, of course, been settled in the courts of 1618. But though the majority of the adventurers seem to have agreed on the diagnosis and on the remedy, they were yet sharply divided on the question of placing responsibility for the company's troubles. Some were disposed to charge all blame to the directing officers and to demand their removal from office. The question of Smith's accounts, which had neither been settled nor forgotten, provided the rallying point, and from Yeardley's departure plans were shaping toward the treasurer's removal. Earlier suspicion had, through prolonged disputes over the auditing of the company's books, ripened into the conviction that public funds had been converted to private use. And as Smith's opponents looked forward to the inauguration of a program requiring heavy expenditure from the common treasury, they demanded of him a settlement of his accounts.

The treasurer's refusal to lend hearty coöperation in this effort to substantiate the charges against him convinced his accusers that there was no hope for a satisfactory auditing of the books so long as he remained at the head of the company. They decided, therefore, to attempt the election of Sandys. Their decision, as explained by them in 1625, arose from the "apparent misprosperinge of the Plantation, and the fowlnes of the Accounts here." [2] Support was recruited among the adventurers through the argument that some disinterested party should be selected for treasurer, if only for the time necessary to complete the auditing.[3] The adventurers, naturally, were not unprepared for the suggestion of a possible misappliance of funds, and it was easy to convince many of them

[2] "The Discourse of the Old Company," in *Narratives of Early Virginia,* pp. 445-446.
[3] *Historye of the Bermudaes,* pp. 129-130.

that a change of administration might bring a change in fortune.

Sir Thomas, however, had many friends and was a man of great influence. His following was especially strong among the merchants who formed one of the most powerful groups within the company. Sandys' support came largely from the minor adventurers, and his party was not strong enough in itself to overthrow Smith. There was promise, though, of winning the support of Robert Rich, recently become earl of Warwick, and of his friends, a large and influential group including Sir Nathaniel Rich, the cousin and close business associate of the earl. Warwick was at the time engaged in a bitter dispute with the East India Company, of which Smith was also head. Two ships of the Rich fleet had recently been engaged in a piratical expedition through the Red Sea. There in 1617 they had given chase to a large carack belonging to no less a person than the Queen Mother of the Great Mogul. The chance appearance of the company's fleet had alone prevented the capture of this ship with its wealthy cargo valued at £100,000. Sir Thomas Roe and others engaged in the attempt to establish the trade of the East India Company were emphatic in their description of the damage to English interests that would have followed. As Roe pointed out, there was no distinction made in that part of the world between one Englishman and another. Warwick's ships were seized and converted to the company's use, and much feeling on both sides accompanied the earl's attempt to secure from the company compensation for his loss.[4] There seems also to have been bad blood between the two men because of the recent secret marriage of Smith's son to Warwick's sister, Isabella, a union to

---

[4] The story of this dispute, which was not finally settled until 1628 before the house of lords (*Journals of the House of Lords*, III, 837) is found in the Original Correspondence of the India Company, V, 564, 586, 610, and in the minutes of the East India Company in Court Books, IV, VII, IX, and X preserved in the India Office at London.

which the father of the groom appears to have been strongly opposed.[5]

The most favorable circumstance for Sandys' purpose, however, was a dispute in the Bermuda Company over the selection of a governor for the colony. To follow the influence of this dispute on the Virginia elections in 1619, it is necessary to understand the close connections that existed between the two companies. The Virginia Company had in 1609 laid claim to the Bermuda Islands as lying within its grant, but had been unable to take any effective steps toward their development. Three years later, however, the more active members of the company purchased these rights and organized separately as the Bermuda Company, which received its charter in 1615. Thus it was that the membership of the Somers Island Company, as it was more commonly known at that time, differed very little from the active membership of the Virginia Company. Smith was treasurer and remained in control of the company until 1621. Furthermore, the two colonies presented many problems in common. Their economic development was much the same, tobacco becoming the chief product of both, and their geographic proximity was responsible for the feeling that in the problem of defense the two colonies were interdependent. The work of the two companies, consequently, was practically one, and a Virginia court was frequently converted into a

[5] Warwick's mother was the famous Penelope Devereaux, who had married Lord Robert Rich against her will in 1586 and had proceeded to live thereafter a most faithless and unhappy life. She became by 1595 the mistress of Charles Blount, eighth Lord Mountjoy. To Blount and Rich she bore ten children, five of whom she openly attributed to Blount. Among those five, however, were two girls whom Blount refused to recognize. There remained, therefore, a certain amount of doubt as to the parentage of Lady Penelope's two daughters, although they bore the name Rich. On the marriage with Smith's son, in which Southampton had been instrumental, see Brown, *Genesis of the United States*, II, 980. It may be noted that there is little justification for Mr. Brown's belief that there was considerable ill feeling between the two branches of Lady Rich's children which may have influenced Warwick in his later attitude toward Sandys. See *Cal. St. Pap., Dom.*, 1625-1626, p. 52.

Bermuda court merely by a change in presiding officers.[6] It is not surprising that under these circumstances the factions which split the older company found their counterparts in the younger body. From the beginning of Sandys' regime to its end, the differences among the Virginia adventurers were only one part of a larger fight extending to both companies. The motives of the two factions could be better understood if the records of the Bermuda Company were more completely preserved. As it is, it becomes necessary to rely chiefly upon sources recounting the problems and quarrels of the Virginia courts, in which the differences brought over from the other company are only partially reflected.

The dispute in the Bermuda Company, upon which Sandys relied to secure Warwick's aid, had arisen from the imprisonment in 1617 by Governor Tucker of Robert Rich, a brother of Sir Nathaniel and the agent in the colony for the Rich interests. Smith, disregarding Warwick's strong objections, had supported Tucker in this action, and there was thus added further cause for friction between them. When in the spring of 1619 the problem of selecting a successor to Tucker arose, Warwick was determined to secure the choice of a man friendly to the Rich interests. He accordingly advanced the candidacy of Nathaniel Butler in opposition to a Captain Southwell who was supported by Smith. Sandys took advantage of these differences between the two most powerful men in the company to enter his brother, George Sandys. The result was a three cornered fight over the appointment of a new governor for the Bermuda colony.[7]

Sandys saw an opportunity of turning this situation to his advantage in the Virginia Company. His supporters accordingly proposed to Warwick's group that if they

[6] *Records*, II, 38, 156-157, 273, 345, 367, 390.
[7] The *Historye of the Bermudaes*, gives a long account of these disputes on pp. 122-130. See also Scott, *Joint-Stock Companies to 1720*, II, 266-267.

would assist in the election of Sandys as head of the Virginia adventurers, " a point (as they sayd) of maine necessitye for the wellfare and stabilitie of that plantation," they would support Butler for deputy governor in Bermuda. After " some fewe meetings of the prime men on both sides" such an agreement was reached.[8]

There remained one other detail unattended to in the arrangements. It was known that several of the company who were willing to remove Smith were dependent upon him in other ways to such an extent that they dared not openly profess their opposition by the usual method of voting, " erection " of hands. For this reason the famous " ballatinge boxe " was brought in at the election.[9] Provision for it was made at a meeting of a committee composed of Sandys, Nathaniel Rich, Alderman Johnson, and two others appointed for the purpose of setting down the rules and regulations of the company governing procedure, elections, and official tenure. The committee met on April 27, and among other things provided that all principal officers in the company and colony should be chosen by the ballot,[10] a practise, it should be noted, not uncommon among joint-stock companies.

This innovation was probably not altogether due to a desire to facilitate the removal of Smith, but its introduction just at the time of the move for ousting him from office undoubtedly has some significance. The question arises as to how Sandys was able to accomplish this end at a time when Smith was still in the chair and therefore in control of committee membership. It is necessary only to remember that the advantages of the committee system invariably go to the most alert party, and there seems little doubt that Sandys and his cohorts were much more active in the preparations for the coming elections. More-

---

[8] *Historye of the Bermudaes*, p. 130.   [10] Manchester Papers, 245.
[9] *Ibid.*, pp. 130-131.

over, the proposal for the appointment of the committee on rules was made only two days before the election, at which time Smith may have already decided not to stand for reëlection. And finally, it should be recognized that the proposal was such as could not with good grace be opposed. But as feeling in the company increased after Sandys' election, the balloting box became to his enemies conclusive evidence of an underhanded conspiracy for private purposes, and it was openly charged, even by members of the Warwick party, that his whole purpose was to get control of the company in order to cover up certain crooked dealings in connection with the administration of the lotteries.[11] When in 1620 the balloting box was offered to the Bermuda adventurers for use in their elections, Sandys' enemies gave an effective demonstration of their feeling by confiscating it.

The well laid plans for the election were successfully executed in a quarter court held on April 28, 1619.[12] Smith, perhaps because of a knowledge of his opponent's strength, though expressing a desire on account of many other pressing duties to be relieved of the cares of office, declined to stand for reëlection. Sandys was chosen treasurer, while John Ferrar became deputy treasurer. And in May Butler was easily elected resident governor in Bermuda. At this point, however, the coalition between Sandys and Warwick failed. Smith defeated Sandys for the governorship of the Bermuda Company, and Alderman Johnson, his son-in-law, retained the position of deputy. The friction between the two factions thereafter was in no way relieved by the fact that one controlled the Virginia Company while the other dominated the Bermuda Company. As Chamberlain wrote Carlton, " the Virginia Company have displaced Sir Thomas Smith and made Sir Edwin Sandys their governor, but the matter is little amended when the next court or meeting they confirmed Sir

[11] *Ibid.*, 343, 344.   [12] *Records*, I, 212.

Thomas Smith in his presidentship of the Bermudas." [13]
It was two years before Sandys gained control of the Bermuda Company, and even then he experienced much difficulty by virtue of the fact that his enemies remained stronger in the younger company than in the older.

Sandys' election has been considered the turning point in the history of the Virginia Company. But while this is partly true, it must be pointed out that this administrative change brought no real change in policy. The adventurers had already decided upon the program for the ensuing years and had expended much effort in perfecting its details. Sandys was in full accord with the reforms of 1618, and was probably responsible for much that had been accomplished in the months preceding his election. The significance of his election, therefore, lies almost wholly in the change of administrative heads, whereby the problem of working out the program of 1618 was transferred into the hands of a new and more enthusiastic, though less experienced, group of officials.

Their task was already prepared for them. By wholesale reorganization and reform an attempt had been made to create conditions favorable to a program of colonization in full accord with the best opinion in England on the proper development of colonial projects. It was Sandys' job to demonstrate that upon this foundation there could be reared a healthy economic structure. And the chief importance and interest in his administration is to be found in an heroic attempt to work out the economic salvation of the company by building a few enfeebled and scattered settlements into a prosperous colony serving the ends of mercantilism and fulfilling the adventurer's hope of profit.

Questions concerning the political organization and welfare of the colony received only such slight attention as was necessary to the execution of the documents drawn up

[13] Chamberlain to Carleton, London, May 8, 1619, P.R.O., S.P. 14/109, 18.

in 1618. The news of the first assembly which met in July, 1619, was received by the courts at home with neither excitement nor objection, and the petitions of this famous body were acted upon in the ordinary routine of business.[14] In the following year the privy council was requested to assist the officers in the compilation of English laws suitable to Virginia,[15] but there is little else of political interest to be found in the official minutes of the courts. This absence of material relating to the colonial assembly in the court records, of which only those after 1619 are preserved, has served to confirm the opinion of some historians that Sandys was engaged in a program of political reform so advanced and opposed to the spirit of his time that it was necessary to guard his steps with the greatest possible secrecy. The true explanation, of course, is simply that arrangements for political reform had already been completed, and that the questions now confronting the adventurers were of an entirely different character.

The only major task of any political significance undertaken after Sandys' election dealt with the political problems of the company itself. It is not surprising that one part of the thorough attempt at reducing the whole business to an orderly state should have been a restatement of the rules and regulations of the company, and of the tenure and duties of all officers connected with the corporation. An agreement on these points, based upon precedent and the majority opinion of the adventurers, and incorporated in a constitution duly ratified in quarter court, would not only insure a smoother functioning of the machinery of business but might be expected to eliminate some of the faction and strife which had marked the courts. On points of order and official duties and privileges there would be at hand an authoritative document to which final appeal might be made.

This work, though begun in 1618, had not been com-

[14] *Records*, I, 310, 325, 336.   •   [15] *Ibid.*, I, 394-395.

pleted, and an order in a preparatory court of April 26, 1619, provided for the appointment of a committee composed of Sandys, Sir Edward Harwood, Sir John Wolstenholme, Sir Nathaniel Rich, and Alderman Johnson to set down the several offices and standing laws and orders of the company. The committee held its first meeting on the following day, at which time a preliminary draft, including the provision for the balloting box, was drawn up against the election of the morrow.[16]   After the elections, the committee went more thoroughly into its task. The report of its work was approved by the council and a preparatory court in the first week of June, and formally ratified by a quarter court on June 9.[17] It was published in 1620 as the *Orders and Constitutions, Partly collected out of his Maiesties Letters Patents, and partly ordained upon mature deliberation, by the Treasurer, Counseil and Companie of Virginia, for the better governing of the Actions and affaires of the said Companie here in England residing.*[18]

This document is a valuable source for any who would examine the machinery of a seventeenth century joint-stock company. It concerns us here, however, only in a few significant particulars, some of which indicate important causes of earlier discontent. The duties of the various officers from the chief to the lowest were taken up in detail. All offices, with the exception of seats on the council, were to become vacant each year with the quarter court of Easter Term, at which time the court was to proceed to the election of new officials. The most important business at this session, of course, was the selection of the treasurer and his deputy. The retiring head of the company was required to make a full report on the state of the colony and of the treasury, and to submit an account for the year's expenditures passed upon and approved by the auditors.

---

[16] Manchester Papers, 245.
[17] *Records*, I, 225.
[18] Force, *Tracts*, III, No. 6.

Seven auditors, two of whom were required to be members of the council, were to be selected each year to prepare a careful audit of all accounts, and in addition to this duty they were charged with the difficult task of straightening out all old accounts. It was hoped that in the future they might avoid some of the dissension over accounts that had plagued the courts of the past.

Certain new and additional qualifications placed upon candidates for the governorship of the company represent a further attempt to forestall the repetition of earlier troubles. It was believed by many that the numerous duties of Smith as head of several other companies, especially the India Company, had resulted in a damaging neglect of Virginia. It was therefore provided that, in view of the increasing weight of duties falling upon the treasurer, no man could be chosen for that office who at the time was governor of any other company, unless he agreed to resign the other and to devote his full energies to the interests of Virginia. An exception could be made only in case it appeared advisable that the governor of the Virginia Company should also lead the Bermuda adventurers. Another innovation was the limit of three years placed on the term of office for the treasurer and deputy. The intended benefits of rotation in office, however, were not actually secured, since with the division of the adventurers into two clearly defined parties the real leadership, regardless of the titular head, remained with party leaders. Sandys held office for only one year, and yet he was the guiding force in the company until its dissolution. For a freer expression of the company's will, the treasurer and deputy were to be elected by the use of the secret ballot. But other offices in the company were to be filled in the usual way.

The ballot was to be used, however, in the selection of all principal officers for the colony, who were listed as the governor, lieutenant governor, admiral, marshal, chief justice, and treasurer. This provision has been responsible for a rather ludicrous suggestion, found at times in chapters on Sandys' liberalism, that along with the representative assembly there may have been introduced into Virginia the secret ballot. Such a suggestion is evidence of an unpardonable carelessness, since not only do the *Orders and Constitutions* specifically state that all important offices in the colony were to be filled by a quarter court at London, but the least acquaintance with the history of the company shows this to have been the practise. Elections in Virginia were apparently restricted to the selection of deputies for the general assembly, and of the qualifications for that privilege and the procedure used we have no record. In naming the colony's council and all minor officers reserved for the company's choice, the voting in quarter court was by the customary procedure, unless the court desired for some reason to use the ballot. Officers for Virginia were commissioned for three years only, and their continuance thereafter was at the company's pleasure. A general limit of six years was to hold in all cases except that of the governor. The whole official roster in the colony was to be supported by the income from public lands.

With the exception of this important document, by which it was hoped that the company might have its business "carried regularly, industriously, and justly," the attention of Sandys was directed almost solely to working out the new economic policies. With characteristic energy and ability he mapped out a program that in its scope and embodiment of current ideas on the place of a colonial venture in the mercantile scheme of the mother country presents an unusually valuable study of the purposes and hopes which motivated seventeenth century adventurers. Sandys attempted to put into actual practise the principles and theories advanced by a host of pamphleteers and writers who preceded him in the advocacy of colonization. For many years Englishmen had been stirred to an interest in the new world by the possibility of securing there certain staple commodities for which England was dependent upon foreign countries. Many had pointed out the probability of valuable stores of ore, naval supplies, timber, and drugs, and had suggested the possible development of important products such as wine and silk. Some feeble efforts had been expended in an effort to tap these resources, but none of them had been so thorough and extensive as the plans now undertaken by Sandys.

In his attempt to work out this problem, Sandys presents an interesting study in that combination of public and personal interests which moved men of Stuart England to support colonization. To him the success of Virginia was measured by the degree in which it served the interests of English trade. His persistent devotion and service to the company cannot alone be explained by a desire to protect his own investment; important also to him were considerations of honor and public service. But this in no way eliminated the motive of personal gain. It seemed clear enough that the best guarantee of financial reward lay in the development of colonial products that would allow the plantations to fit into the mercantile scheme of English commerce. If Virginia could produce naval stores to relieve England of her longstanding dependence upon the Baltic, or silk and wine to compete with the products of Persia and France, a secure position in English trade would be the reward, and only by such a position, it was felt, could the adventurers hope for any real return on their investment. The market for tobacco, in view of the attitude of the government, was uncertain and insecure, and existed largely by sufferance. The prohibition of its sale in England at any time appeared to be a likely probability.[19] The fear of some such action by the government,

[19] Indeed, the house of commons in 1621 came very near passing a law prohibiting the importation of all tobacco into England, and were restrained from so doing only by the plea of those interested in Virginia and Bermuda that such an act would ruin the plantations. *Journals of the House of Commons*, I, 581, 582.

coupled with the general disapproval of tobacco, sorely handicapped him in any attempt to recruit new capital. It appeared obvious, therefore, that success or failure depended upon relieving the colony of its dependence upon tobacco by the substitution of other staple commodities.

With these considerations in mind Sandys outlined his policy for the development of Virginia in a three-fold criticism of conditions under his predecessor. He objected to the decay of the company land, to the inordinate growth of tobacco to the exclusion of other necessary and profitable commodities, and to the small number of colonists that had been sent over in recent years.[20] It was his purpose to remedy these defects.

The first essential seemed to be a rapid increase in population, in order that the public lands, from which was expected the bulk of the company's profits and the support of all officials, might be settled and a labor supply provided for the production of new commodities. The labor supply was hopelessly inadequate for the great program of expansion and development Sandys drew up on taking office in 1619. He declared that in April of the preceding year the colonists numbered only about 400, and of them only 200 were able to "set hand to husbandry." In the intervening year the settlement of private plantations had raised the total to nearly a thousand, but the public lands were still largely unsettled and there was need for a great many more laborers. The governor therefore devoted his attention to the task of selling Virginia to the English people as a home in which many might better their condition. His own personal efforts and those of other individuals within the company played an important part in this work, but its most interesting feature is found in the success with which he used the printing press. In the religious controversies of the sixteenth century Englishmen had learned the value of the printed word in influenc-

[20] *Records*, I, 266-267, 350, 519.

ing public opinion, and within two decades after Sandys had taken his final call on the English stage both Roundhead and Cavalier endeavored to advance their cause in the civil wars by the greatest flood of pamphlets and tracts yet seen in England. It is not surprising that the commercial companies falling within this period should also recognize the powerful appeal of printed propaganda.

It was especially valuable at this time when Virginia's reputation had fallen to a very low level. Several tracts were issued by the authority of the court during the succeeding four years, in which the advantages of Virginia were set forth in the best possible light. Typical of such documents is a double appeal for colonists and adventurers issued by the council on July 1, 1620.[21] At great length the authors attempted to dispel any idea that Virginia was unfit for colonization. Corrupt and ill disposed persons had attempted " to staine and blemish that Countrey, as being barren and unprofitable" by rumors both malicious and false, but instead it was declared to be a land of such fertility that it was capable of producing most of the " richest commodities" found in the world. In addition to many natural products, the colonist by application could produce a long list of commodities to add to his comfort and to bring him profit. There was an abundance of food in a land where cattle became " much bigger of body," and English grains flourished, and in fact were even surpassed in pleasantness and strength by the native maize. The woods were full of deer and other " beasts of sustenance," the seas and rivers of excellent fish, and both land and water yielded fowl in great quantity and variety. In short, it was a country " which nothing but ignorance can thinke ill of, and which no man but of corrupt minde and ill purpose can defame."

It was true that in the past God had suffered the " great

[21] *A Declaration of the State of the Colony and Affairs in Virginia,* reproduced in Force, *Tracts,* III, No. 5.

Enemy of all good Actions " to oppress this "noble action," but it had now pleased Him to bless and prosper their recent efforts to correct all defects and repair "all former breaches." A beginning had been made in the development of many new staple commodities, over 1,200 colonists had sailed for the plantations in the past year, and the care taken by instructions, charters, and commissions to reduce the people and affairs of Virginia "into a regular course " gave great promise for the future.

All this was but a preface to an appeal for adventurers to take advantage of the opportunity to reap some benefit by the settlement of private plantations, and an outline of the conditions upon which the company would enlist during the ensuing year 800 colonists for its own land. Each colonist would be landed in Virginia with full provision of victuals and cattle for a year, and a complete equipment of weapons, tools, and implements, "both of house and labour," at the charge of the company. He was to enjoy the moiety of all the profits resulting from his labor, and was to be bound by covenant to seven years' service upon the company's land, with free choice at the end of that period either to remain or move to some other land.

The success of this type of advertising may be seen in the fact that during a four year period when the colonists were undergoing the most rigorous suffering Sandys was able to secure the emigration of some 4,000 settlers. His success depended in no small part upon the unusually favorable picture of Virginia presented in the public statements and publications of the company. In 1623 his enemies charged him with having led hundreds of the king's subjects to their death by the spreading of false rumors through the publication of letters, books, and "cozening ballads." [22]

In the first year of Sandys' administration he was able to send a total of 1,261 persons, of whom 871 were trans-

[22] Manchester Papers, 347, 362.

ported at the charge of the company, although only 650 were settled on public lands.[23] The remainder went to private plantations at the charge of their individual proprietors. The apportionment to the public lands provided 80 tenants for the governor, 130 for the company land, 100 for the College, 50 for glebe lands, 100 apprentices for tenants, and 50 servants for the company. The list was completed by 90 maidens sent at public charge for wives of some of the older tenants. This latter was one of the most important features of Sandys' colonization, calculated to add to the general content of the colony and to provide for a natural growth of population that might in time relieve the company of the burdensome task of shipping its labor supply from England. It would be interesting to know the origin of these first ladies of Virginia. Unfortunately, there are no records upon which to base any conclusions, but it may be safely assumed that they came from a not too elevated position in English society. Another hundred were sent over in 1620, and many of the new settlers probably carried with them their own womenfolk. The plans for the second year also called for the transportation of 700 men at public charge, the distribution to be 400 tenants on the general land of the company, 100 tenants for officers, of which 10 were to be added to the 50 already settled on the glebe land, and 20 were to provide support for a physician, 100 boys to become apprentices to tenants, and 100 servants for old planters.[24]

Any statement as to the communities from which Sandys' settlers were drawn must be based largely on probabilities. It has been generally assumed with good reason that a majority were drawn from the poorer classes of the city of London. One of the services of the company, upon which there was based an appeal for public support, was

[23] *Records*, I, 351-352, 411-412, 492-493; Force, *Tracts*, III, No. 5, p. 10.
[24] Force, *Tracts*, III, No. 5, p. 14.

the relief of overpopulation. This pressure was felt chiefly in London where the company's headquarters were located, and at times the Lord Mayor coöperated with the company in providing for the transportation of orphans and other dependent children to Virginia. A subscription of £500 from charitably disposed citizens of the city was turned over to the company in 1619 to cover a part of the cost in settling 100 children, including some girls, on the plantation as apprentices and servants.[25] In 1620 another subscription of £400 was applied to the cost of transporting an additional 100 children to serve as apprentices for seven years and then as tenants for an additional seven years, after which they were to be allowed 25 acres apiece at 6d. quit-rent and to be free to dispose of their services as they desired.[26] In the same year an appeal was made to the justices of peace throughout the country to send to the company youths over fifteen who were burdensome to the parish, along with £5 to aid in the cost of shipping them to Virginia as apprentices and servants.[27] A goodly number of criminals and delinquents were also to be found among Sandys' settlers, some 50 drawn largely from the criminal population of London going in 1620.[28]

Sandys endeavored, however, to interest prospective settlers of good character in all sections of the country, and with some success. In reviewing the first year's accomplishments the council claimed that settlers of that year had been mostly choice men born and bred to labor and industry, the suggestion of course being that of a contrast with earlier practise. Out of 1,261, 100 men " brought up to Husbandry " had come out of Devon, above 110 were from Warwickshire and Staffordshire, about 40 from Sussex, and the remainder " out of divers Shires of the Realme." [29] In a public statement, however, the council

[25] *Records*, I, 270-271, 293, 300.
[26] *Ibid.*, I, 304-305, 355.
[27] *Ibid.*, I, 411-412.
[28] *Ibid.*, I, 212, 253, 259, 288.
[29] Force, *Tracts*, III, No. 5, p. 5.

would naturally present the most favorable front, and the actual figures given for the counties may possibly be taken as representative of the average proportion drawn from the country.

At the same time that these important steps were taken for increasing the number of laborers, much attention was given to the occupations at which they should be employed. Of first importance was an adequate food supply, and great stress was laid upon the necessity of producing sufficient quantities of corn. The neglect of this for tobacco was declared to be one of the chief causes for their suffering. In order to make the food supply more secure by the diversion of attention from tobacco, there was now a definite limitation on the amount of tobacco to be grown by each individual,[30] which was in addition to the general limiting clause included in all patents for private plantations. The plan was eventually to wean the Virginians completely from tobacco, and in the meantime to allow only so much as would avoid any too sudden change in the economic life of the colony.

The interim was to be used in building up a large variety of new commodities. Sandys looked upon Virginia as a place where there might be found in abundance the furs, " Cauiary," and cordage " which we draw from Russia," the masts, planks, boards, pitch, tar, potashes, soap-ashes, hemp, and flax " which now we fetch from Norway, Denmark, Poland, and Germany," iron, " which hath so wasted our English woods that itself in short time must decay together with them," the wines, fruit, and salt imported from France and Spain, the silks of Persia and Italy, " in no kind of worth inferior," and in addition a long list of natural commodities such as woods, roots, and berries producing excellent dyes, plants and other drugs " for physical service," sweet woods, oils, and gums " for pleasure and other uses," and " cotton-wool " and sugar

[30] Weldon to Sandys, March 6, 1619/20, Ferrar Papers.

cane.[31] Such hopes were by no means new, in fact Sandys asserted that three years before his election there had been returned from Virginia twelve separate commodities " to the great honor of the action and encouragement of the Adventurers," [32] and in a way he was merely trying to get back to the original purposes of the venture. But the thoroughness with which he attempted now to realize these hopes gives to them an unusual importance in the history of colonization.

Among all the projects planned and undertaken in the first two years of Sandys' control, that most favored and receiving the greatest attention was an attempt at the development of a successful iron industry. This looked not only to the provision of tools and all necessary hardware equipment for the colony, but to the production of iron products for exportation to England. The use of coal in the smelting process was yet a century and more away, and the rapidly disappearing forests of England had already brought a serious decline in the domestic industry. The virgin forests of Virginia offered an apparently unlimited fuel supply, and the leaders of the company, taking for granted an adequate supply of ore, decided upon iron as their chief project. It was undertaken at once and 150 persons were dispatched in the first year for the purpose of setting up three separate iron works, forty of which number, " all framed to Iron-workes," were recruited from Sussex.[33] The officers, of whom a Captain Bluett was chief, and " carpenters " for the iron works sailed in the spring of 1620, and arrived at Jamestown in May.[34] Within the next two years approximately £4,000 were expended in the support of this favored project, and thereafter the total investment was increased to the sum of £5,000.[35]

[31] Force, *Tracts*, III, No. 5, p. 4.
[32] *Records*, I, 266-267.
[33] Force, *Tracts*, III, No. 5, pp. 4, 10.
[34] Yeardley to Sandys, June 7, 1620, Ferrar Papers.
[35] *Records*, I, 472; II, 349.

Next in importance was an attempt to develop thriving industries in silk and wine. A species of the mulberry is common to the south Atlantic area, and according to some of the reports received from Virginia was considered to be as numerous as in Persia. It is not surprising, therefore, that much consideration should be given to the possible production of silk. The leaders were encouraged in this project by the unusual interest of the king. From the early years of his reign. James I had taken a peculiar interest in the development of a native silk industry. In 1609 he planted the famous Mulberry Gardens on the present site of Buckingham Palace for the encouragement of this particular industry, and at Oatland he maintained a nursery for cocoons under a French master.[36] To the Virginia adventurers he made numerous contributions from this store of cocoons, or " silkworm seed," the first in 1619, and another in 1620.[37] None of these survived the voyage, but James continued in his interest, and after 1621 more earnest efforts were put forth by the company.

The company went to greater expense in the first two years in forwarding the production of wine. England's climate has forced her sons for centuries to a dependence for wine upon countries more blessed with sunshine. The importation of this commodity for the tables of the English gentry formed an important item in England's foreign trade. The colonist in Virginia found a natural growth of vines common to the country, and it is not surprising that vineyard dressing was considered well worth the efforts of Sandys' settlers. Skilled " vignerons " were dispatched in 1619 with a supply of the best vines, and order was made for the transportation in the following year of additional vines and " vignerons " to be secured from France and the Rhineland.[38] Instructions for the setting and dressing of vines were provided by the company, and in May 1621,

[36] *Ibid.*, I, 543.
[37] Force, *Tracts*, III, No. 5, p. 11.
[38] *Ibid.*, pp. 11, 15.

George Thorpe was able to report from the college land that despite the disinclination of the settlers nearly 10,000 vines had been set.[39]

Added to these three major projects were many others. All colonists were to devote part of their time to the production of cordage and linen, for which, besides hemp, there was at hand "silk-grass," a natural growth in great abundance which was declared to make the best cordage and linen in the world. Instructions of 1619 required each householder to set 100 plants of "silk-grass," and the governor was reported in the following year to have set 5,000 himself. "Polackers" who had been sent to Virginia before Sandys' election were to direct the production of potash, soap, pitch and tar, and in 1620 it was planned to secure from "Eastern parts" other men skilled in the work of these products and of flax. The forests were to be drawn upon for naval stores in addition to pitch and tar. Men and machinery were sent in 1619 to set up sawmills for the preparation of masts, planks, and boards for shipbuilding, and in the following year skilled workmen were secured for this work from Hamburg. Plans were even on foot and skilled craftsmen secured for shipbuilding, although these plans apparently looked to nothing more than the construction of a small pinnance or two needed by Yeardley in local trade with the natives and fishing in the Bay. Salt works, which had decayed under Argall, were ordered set up again in order to supply the colony's immediate needs and later, it was hoped, the "great Fishings" on the Atlantic coasts. And finally, the plans for 1620 called for the production of oils from walnuts, found in great quantities in Virginia, and from olive plants which were to be provided from southern Europe.[40]

This completes a rather full list of the staples which

[39] Thorpe to John Ferrar, May 15, 1621, Ferrar Papers.
[40] Force, *Tracts*, III, No. 5, pp. 10-11, 15-16; *Records*, I, 372; Yeardley to Sandys, June 7, 1620, Ferrar Papers.

Sandys hoped would provide the main support for Virginia. But in addition to these commodities, which it was hoped would be produced not only for local use but for a profitable trade, his intention was to provide all possible necessary supplies for colonial life within the colony itself. All skilled in any art or craft were encouraged to follow their trade. The charter of 1618 had attempted to make favorable provision for the settlement of any who wished to do so. And in 1620 the company advertised for all sorts of tradesmen, besides those to be used in the major industries, in a list which included gardeners, brewers, bakers, carpenters, joiners, ship-wrights, boat-wrights, mill-wrights, plough-wrights, masons, brick makers, turners, smiths of all sorts, coopers, weavers, tanners, potters, fowlers, fishermen, shoe makers, rope makers, tile makers, edge-tool makers, leather dressers, lime burners, and many others.[41]

Such was the course charted by Sandys and his chief lieutenant, John Ferrar, in their first two years as pilots of the company's fortunes. Sandys devoted his full energies to the task, well aware that not only the fortunes of the company but his own and those of his party depended upon his success. It is here that we find the key to the company's history through the succeeding years of faction and strife to its final failure and dissolution in 1624. Had Sandys been successful in giving Virginia the desired place in England's trade, the bitter attacks of Smith and Warwick would have fallen with slight effect, but a dismal failure gave to his enemies the means of bringing about his ruin.

But though failure was Sandys' reward, it was not altogether due to fault in planning. There were of course some errors in judgment, the result largely of inexperience, but they were errors common to his day when in their earliest enthusiasm Englishmen expected too much of the new world, and Sandys should not be condemned

[41] Force, *Tracts*, III, No. 5, p. 17.

for not seeing farther ahead than his fellows. His plan to build for Virginia a secure position in the nation's trade by the production of staples for which there was a constant and steady market at home, the instructions issued to the colonists for carrying through this work, and the enlistment of skilled craftsmen from Poland, Germany, France, and England to direct these projects, are all parts of a program that commended itself to the best opinion of his day, and must also be regarded with favor by the student of seventeenth century colonization. His courage too in undertaking a task of such dimensions with a company divided in spirit and bankrupt in purse commands admiration, and entitles Sandys to as great a place in the history of American settlement as has formerly been awarded him on the basis of an alleged political liberalism. The fault lay in execution, in an overhasty desire for results, and in certain factors wholly beyond his control.

CHAPTER V
FACTIONAL STRIFE OVER ACCOUNTS, PATENTS, AND PIRACY

THE story of the London Company would be comparatively simple were it limited merely to a study of the
failure of Sandys' economic program. But although considerations of an economic character are fundamental in
the interpretation of these famous disputes, it is also necessary to consider all sorts of personal dislikes, jealousies,
and rivalries which arose from various causes to irritate
the proceedings of the company. There are numerous instances in which the opposition to Sandys was motivated
not so much by disagreement with his policies and sincere
alarm at the state of the colony as by the simple fact that
Smith and Warwick disliked Sandys and were anxious to
satisfy some longstanding grudge. At the same time a bitter
feeling of personal injury was developed in Sandys and
must be given due consideration in the explanation of
many of his actions. All of these things complicate tremendously the problem of the student who attempts to
write the history of the company, for few of the records
upon which he must depend are free from bias or feeling of some sort. There is perhaps no better proof in history that an economic interpretation cannot alone satisfy
the requirements of scholarship, even though the subject
be the vicissitudes and fortunes of a commercial company.

Sandys upon taking office spoke highly of Smith's efforts
in behalf of the company, and moved that twenty shares be
granted him in recognition of his services.[1] Such omens of
good feeling, however, were not of long duration. Within
two weeks the company was once again torn by severe factional strife. Robert Cushman, one of the agents for the
Leyden Puritans at that time in London on a mission to
make some arrangement with the Virginia Company for

[1] *Records*, I, 213-214.

their migration to America, wrote to his friends on May 8 that they were making no progress whatsoever because of the dissensions and factions within the company, "which are such as that ever since we came up no business could by them be despatched." His explanation was that after Smith's retirement he came to feel that he had lost "part of his honor," became angry, and set about to raise a faction "to cavil and contend about the election, and sought to tax Sir Edwin with many things that might both disgrace him and also put him by his office of governor." In these contentions they were still engaged, and were "not fit nor ready to intermeddle in any business." What the issue would be, he could not say, but his own sympathies are shown in the belief that Sandys would "carry it away; and if he do, things will go well in Virginia; if otherwise, they will go ill enough always." [2]

A more likely explanation of this factional strife is found in a renewed attack upon Smith's accounts. It was no doubt Sandys' hope that this troublesome question could be settled without further quarrel, but he had no intention of dropping it. The plans on foot for the colony's development called for heavy expenditures, and it was only natural that Sandys should be more determined than ever to bring a settlement. As he explained to the earl of Southampton, after outlining his plans for 1620, "this my good Lord cannot be done without great charge, which causeth the withdrawing of public money out of private hands, whence riseth this name of Accounts, so mortally hated." [3]

These differences came to a head in a court of May 12. At the April elections Sir John Danvers, John Wroth, John Ferrar, and Messrs. Essington, Briggs, Wiseman, and Chambers had been selected as auditors for the coming year, and were urged to give all possible expedition to

[2] Alexander Young, *Chronicle of the Pilgrim Fathers of the Colony of Plymouth,* 2nd. ed., Boston, 1844, pp. 68-69.
[3] Sandys to Southampton, September 29, 1619, Ferrar Papers.

their work.[4] Smith now requested that three of his friends, Humphrey Handford, later sheriff of London, and Anthony Abdey and Morris Abbott, both wealthy merchants, might be added to this number to see that no wrong was done to him. The request was granted but with an additional proviso that, in view of the greater experience of the old auditors, three of them, Sandys, Danvers and Wroth, should be necessary to a quorum at any session dealing with Smith's accounts and that nothing should be concluded without the consent of at least two of these three.[5] Thus were the labors of Sandys joined with those of the regular auditors in an attempt to settle one of the most perplexing problems confronting the new administration. He continued to be thereafter, as he had been before, the leading spirit in all efforts to audit old accounts. But since the three men selected for this all important rôle had been the most active adventurers in bringing charges against Smith's books, it is not surprising that Sir Thomas and his friends were left with the feeling that he had been dealt with unfairly.

Further difficulties arose in the quarter court of June 9, at which time the adventurers passed upon the *Orders and Constitutions*.[6] By this document the auditors were charged anew with the task of making a final audit of all "olde accounts," which included Smith's books covering the period from the beginning of the plantation to November 30, 1616.[7] Smith objected to this provision, and argued that it was unfair that three or four men should now contradict an account already approved by sixteen "worthy and sufficient men." He requested, therefore, that this account should stand and the present auditors proceed only with accounts since 1616, and, secondly, that in view of his "extraordinary business" and "disability in body" the auditing might be done at his own house. In conclusion,

[4] *Records*, I, 213.
[5] *Ibid.*, I, 217.
[6] *Supra*, pp. 89-91.
[7] Force, *Tracts*, III, No. 6, p. 11.

he protested that he would satisfy to the utmost whatever damage had been done the company by such officers as he had trusted, and desired a speedy conclusion to the business. This motion apparently caught Sandys unaware, and for the time being Smith carried the court with him. He was assured that the purpose of the article was not to deprive him of the benefit of the " said old Accompte," and it was agreed to let the *Orders and Constitutions* pass to the vote. After a while, however, there was brought into court a written answer to Smith's proposals drawn up by four of the auditors. Upon the reading of this paper Smith, " to give all men satisfaction," agreed that the auditors " should proceed with his Account from the beginning." The auditors also objected to meeting at Smith's house, arguing that it would be very inconvenient for Sandys. who was by his experience of much more value in the work than Smith. Again after much controversy Smith conceded the point and suggested that the auditors settle among themselves the place of meeting.[8]

But despite these concessions and the professed willingness of Smith to meet any discrepancies that could be rightfully shown, the auditors made almost no progress through the summer and their efforts served only to increase the feeling in the company. In September Sandys complained bitterly to Southampton: " Instead of thanks for my labor, I have reaped a mass of malignity, under which (had it not been by your Lordship's noble Justice) I might have quailed. But in affiance of the blessing of God first and next of your Lordship's Constancy, I will not faint in persisting to go on to do that without which this work cannot be done." [9] The following summer, however, found him no nearer a satisfactory audit, and at this time when the feeling in the company reached a greater height than at any time preceding 1623, he was forced to recognize

---

[8] *Records*, I, 225.
[9] Sandys to Southampton, September 29, 1619, Ferrar Papers.

that the "matters of Accounts" were the first cause of the "distractions of the Company by partialities and factions." [10]

He endeavored now to expedite the work of the auditors by dividing it into four parts, *viz.*, receipts from adventures, receipts from lotteries, receipts from fines, collections, and the sale of goods returned from Virginia, and finally Smith's disbursements. Each division was assigned to one of the four committees into which the auditors were divided, and the result of their labors in a joint report was to be presented to the fall quarter court. But this, as all other efforts, failed completely, and the burden of the November report was that very little had been accomplished. Sandys reported that he and Danvers, who were charged with auditing the records of adventures, found it " a most intricate and difficult piece of work " because of the "disagreement of the books themselves." Yet they hoped in time to arrive at some sort of conclusion to present to the company. The committee on lotteries reported simply that they had been able to find no books, and in fact a year later the company was still requesting of Smith the lottery books for the use of the auditors.[11] The third committee could find no record of any goods brought from Virginia, and a request for an explanation was forwarded to Smith. On his disbursements the committee was at a loss because they could find neither warrants nor any other records of the disbursement of money, " and having acquainted Sir Thomas Smith therewith his answer was that he knew not what was become of those warrants." "Notwithstanding all these difficulties," the earl of Southampton, who was now treasurer, urged the auditors to proceed " to the drawing of these Accompts to some head " since Smith "had so freely offered to be answerable for whatsoever they would charge upon himself and would be ready also to pay for his men's defaults." [12]

[10] *Records*, I, 387-388.   [11] *Ibid.*, I, 572.   [12] *Ibid.*, I, 417-418.

And yet, although Sandys did some work on the books in the winter of 1621 and 1622, the audit of Smith's accounts was not completed when the king interfered in 1623.

The dragging out of so sore a question over a period of four years added immeasurably to the feeling which divided the adventurers. The auditors in reply to all requests for reports merely complained of the inaccuracy and confusion of Smith's books, or charged that some accounts either had not been kept or were being withheld. Thus it happened that while Sandys was able to satisfy himself and his followers that Smith was much indebted to the company, he was never able to arrive at a sum for that indebtedness in which he had sufficient confidence to take action for recovery. This was his greatest error in handling the problem. Smith's books were undoubtedly quite unsatisfactory, and it seems likely that it was impossible to arrive at a complete and perfect audit. But even so Smith's greatest offense was probably carelessness and a tendency, because of his many interests and duties, to rely too much on his lieutenants; even Sandys recognized that Smith " neither kept the Accounts nor made them " and denied any intention of casting aspersion upon his reputation " further then of neglect and that through multitude of business." [13] And Sandys would have served both the company and himself better had he accepted the fact that the books were incomplete, and fixed upon some approximate sum by which he could have bargained with Smith. Sir Thomas time and time again professed his willingness to meet any deficiency that could be shown and to make good any loss that had come by officials who had been false to the trust in which he had placed them. Had Sandys named some approximate sum it seems likely that he and Smith might have at least agreed upon a compromise figure, which, done in the first year of his ad-

[13] *Records*, II, 260-261.

ministration, would have been worth far more to the company, by the removal of one of the sorest sources of irritation, than treble the amount three years later.

As it was handled, however, the question of accounts only multiplied Sandys' troubles. Members of his party went about London freely reporting that Smith refused to meet his indebtedness. This was particularly galling to all of Smith's friends because of his repeated offers to meet any deficiency and the company's refusal to make any definite charge or effort at settlement. One day in February, 1623, Sir Thomas chanced to meet with Sir Edward Sackville, who had become one of Sandys' most violent partisans, and charged him with circulating false reports of his indebtedness to the company. Sir Edward replied that he was responsible for such statements as he understood to be true, and Smith then protested that he "had divers times importuned an auditing of his Accounts, which by the space of three years he could never yet obtain, though for his part he had delivered in all his books" and inquired further "that if he were indebted so much as was imputed why did the Company that pretended necessity forbear thus long to begin to recover it, he being able to make satisfaction?" The argument and sincerity of the man so impressed Sackville that he returned to the next court to enter a plea that a final end be put "to this business by the liquidation of his Accounts," and argued that until that was done every man was "bound in Charity to hope the best and in honesty to condemn no man that that fairly puts himself to his trial." Such arguments were of even more force with Smith's closest friends. And their resentment was greater not only because the "old accounts" had received the approval of the regular auditors after 1616, but by the fact that the three auditors selected in 1619 to represent Smith had discovered and had even entered a report under oath to the adventurers declaring that in reality the company was actually indebted to its former head to the sum total of over £500.[14]

It was really an impossible situation, and the only hope of solution lay in some compromise settlement. But it was not until 1624, when the early dissolution of the company was practically certain, that Sandys decided upon £800 as the sum of Smith's indebtedness.[15] Had he done this four and a half years earlier he might have gotten at least part of it, but as he chose to handle it, he got none of it and added immeasurably to the difficulties of his administration, for the friends of Smith could interpret his action as leading only to an unjust slander of the reputation of one to whom the company was indebted for many years of faithful service.

The accounts of the Magazine proved to be as difficult a problem, and, because of the more violent character of its director, Alderman Johnson, as great a source of feeling. Sandys was firmly convinced that there were discrepancies in Johnson's accounts, and was determined to make a thorough audit of them. His concern was greater by virtue of the fact that some of the company's capital had been adventured in the Magazine. Johnson and Smith, probably considering the Magazine as simply a means of supplying the colony, and not able because of disappointing returns to attract sufficient adventures, had entered the company as adventurer to the sum of at least £800.[16] Dividends were to be paid adventurers according to the profits realized, but the expected dividends had not been declared and thus it was that capital of the company was still tied up in the stock of the Magazine.

There is no evidence upon which to base any conclusion as to the regularity of Smith and Johnson in this action, but Sandys was convinced that money of the company had been illegally converted to the use of the Magazine. He was in great need of this capital, and therefore

[14] *Records*, II, 259-261.   [15] *Ibid.*, II, 506-507.   [16] *Ibid.*, I, 235-236.

anxious to straighten out the accounts. It is not surprising
that the books of the Magazine presented some difficulties
and even discrepancies. The auditors complained especially of differences in the accounts kept at home and
those of the cape merchant in Virginia.[17] In fact, it was
a difficult problem to keep them together. The cape merchant sold his goods almost wholly for tobacco and other
commodities at as good a figure as he could secure, but
no doubt he often received tobacco at a figure considerably above what it was actually sold for in Europe, and it
is not to be wondered at that under these conditions two
sets of books kept at a distance of three months or more
apart should not tally exactly.

There were sufficient grounds no doubt to warrant
Sandys' demand for an audit, but he made the mistake of
approaching a task difficult enough in itself with the attitude of one seeking to confirm some suspicion of crooked
dealing. The effect was to antagonize Johnson and Smith,
and to make the necessary measure of coöperation impossible from the beginning. The Magazine came into discussion in the court of June 9, when the managers were
ordered to put into effect their promise of the preceding
April to make a division of "one Capitall," and to present
their accounts for the satisfaction of the company. At the
same time it was decided that all officers should be elected
thereafter for a term of one year only. Much time was consumed in other courts of that month in disputes about the
meeting place for the Magazine. Johnson contended for
Smith's house because of his infirmity and large adventure,
but Sandys steadfastly refused this request on the grounds
that it should meet at the regular meeting place of the
company which held also a very large investment. As in
the case of the similar disputes over the meeting place of
the auditors, Smith and Johnson were forced after much
heated argument to give in, and the court finally got

[17] *Ibid.*, II, 218-219.

around to the appointment of the auditors for the Magazine on June 28.[18]

The smouldering feeling built up through June broke in a court of July 7, when Sandys called for a report from the auditors appointed at the last court. Mr. Essington, who was chiefly responsible and also apparently a friend of Johnson, had absented himself and there was no report to be presented as ordered. Thereupon, Sandys " being some thing moved " that the company should be thus put off without the payment of the money due or an audit, spoke with some spirit to Johnson as director and threatened to complain to the privy council or to enter suit against him. Johnson then lost his temper, and considering the attack as personal replied in such sharp and " contemptible " words that he was subjected to censure for contempt of court by a special committee, on which sat his later allies, Warwick and Nathaniel Rich.[19]

This trouble consumed so much time that it was necessary to carry over until the next week the question of accounts. At this time the auditors for the company entered a long complaint, in which they charged that while Johnson was both deputy of the company and director of the Magazine great sums of the company's cash had been illegally converted to the use of the Magazine. They mentioned especially £341 used in May, 1617, to buy supplies, which according to the cape merchant's books had been returned with a profit of over £85, and another sum of £176 received by Johnson in October, 1618, as payment for the tobacco grown on the company's common land. Further they declared there was need for the settlement of " divers reciprocal demands made both by the Company and the Magazine for persons and goods interchangeably transported by each of the other." The auditors protested that they at all times had been anxious to audit and clear

---

[18] *Records*, I, 227, 235-238.
[19] *Ibid.*, I, 241-243; Manchester Papers, 250.

these items, but had found no disposition to coöperate among the Magazine officers " notwithstanding our often requests and divers orders of Courts, which they have neglected and broken and do so still persist." Some further action by the court was earnestly requested.[20]

Yet in November no progress had been made either toward the declaring of a dividend on the past year's magazine or the settlement of its accounts and those of the " old Magazine," and the council was now requested to take the business in hand. It was hoped in this way to bring some friendly end to these troubles which were considered " the cause of all dissentions that hath been amongst the Company." [21] But before the month was out the failure to complete the audit of these accounts and a report of the desperate state in which the Magazine then rested had again precipitated a dispute which this time turned on the larger question of whether to continue the Magazine or to dissolve it at the end of its four year license, now nearly expired. This question too was referred to the council.[22] Finally in December, Mr. Keightly, one of the auditors appointed for these accounts, reported that the books had been audited, and that they had " never found books in better order nor Accompts better kept, for not four pennyworth of goods is sent but is orderly set down, marvelling that as it appears there should be 2000 and odd pounds owing to the Adventurers and they continue £1000 to the Chamber of London besides — 5200 and odd pounds worth of goods remaining in the Magazine as it cost the first penny here." [23] These difficulties in accounts were never satisfactorily solved, and their chief immediate influence was to aid the decision to dissolve the Magazine, which was done in January, 1620.[24] Thereafter, the problem of supplies was handled through individual agree-

[20] *Records*, I, 244.
[21] *Ibid.*, I, 260, 263.
[22] *Ibid.*, I, 272-273.

[23] *Ibid.*, I, 286.
[24] *Ibid.*, I, 293.

ments, usually covering only one voyage, between the company and merchants.

But the old Magazine through its accounts remained to plague the courts. Early in 1623 Deputy Ferrar reported that the auditors were then engaged in checking up on the records which they had in hand, but he warned the adventurers to look for little comfort as they were likely to receive no more than half the principal, there being only £1,000 to divide among them, and he complained of the great difficulty in their work due to the difference between the books kept at London and those of the cape merchant. In March he was still engaged in this work.[25] There was much confusion and feeling in the courts at that time, and there is no record to show that any end was put to this business before Johnson and Warwick carried all of Virginia's troubles to the privy council.

So it was that the whole question of accounts was dragged along from year to year with no other effect than to multiply tremendously the bitterness which divided the company. There is no disposition on the part of the present writer to whitewash Smith and Johnson, although with the most meager bits of information, and that at second hand from their enemies whose feeling and bias was as great as any other, there is hardly sufficient grounds for the unqualified condemnation that has been passed on these two men by some of Virginia's historians. It is easy enough to understand Sandys' conviction " that no man carrying the face of an honest man could have been displeased with being called to an Account." [26] But it should be remembered that Smith's accounts at least had been passed once by qualified auditors, and this coupled with the whole attitude of suspicion and accusation with which Sandys undertook a second audit could account for any indisposition to coöperate. The only charge that can safely be brought

[25] *Records*, II, 218-219, 317-318.
[26] Sandys to Southampton, September 29, 1619, Ferrar Papers.

against these men is carelessness in the keeping of their records. And when Smith finally agreed to a second audit and frequently professed his willingness to meet any discrepancy that could be shown, he could not but regard the sweeping accusations of men who refused to bring any definite charges as base ingratitude for long years of service. This is undoubtedly the chief indictment to be made of Sandys' conduct in dealing with this touchy question. His pressing need for money and his desire to secure all that he believed the company's due is easily understood. There can be no doubt of his sincerity. Yet one cannot but wish that for his own sake he had seen the necessity of putting an end to these differences even at the cost of surrendering a part of what he considered the just due of the company. It was a grave mistake to inject into an atmosphere already fraught with resentment and bitterness charges of dishonesty which he was unable to substantiate.

Further faction arose in the company through disputes with two prominent adventurers in Virginia. One of these was Captain John Martin, the only member of the original council of Virginia left in the colony. For five years he argued with the company the legality of a patent secured by him before the enactment of the " greate Charter " in 1618. It will be remembered that this document was retroactive, and chief among those effected by it was Martin. His patent was one of the so-called grants in " general words " which the charter recalled with the promise of another conforming to the new policy regarding private grants.

Martin's patent was the subject of much discussion by the first assembly when it was found to be contrary to the charter on two counts. The first was a clause giving to Martin, his heirs, or assigns, the right to govern all persons on the estate " free from any comaunde of the Colony, excepte it be ayding and assisting the same against any forren or domesticall enemy." Upon the ground that this not only exempted him " from that equality and uniformity of laws and orders which the great charter saith are to extend over the whole Colony, but also from diverse such lawes as we must be enforced to make in the General Assembly," the two burgesses from Martin's plantation were excluded from the assembly, and Martin was ordered to appear personally in defense of his patent. When after two days Martin came before the burgesses and flatly refused to consider any change in the patent, his burgesses were permanently excluded, the assembly feeling it unjust that men should have a part in making laws by which they would not agree to be bound. The assembly then drew up a petition to the company asking for a rectification of this clause, should the adventurers join the burgesses in the belief that it was contrary to the charter and dangerous to the good government of the colony. They requested also the clarification of another clause allowing Martin to enjoy his land in as large and ample a manner as " any lord of any manours in England," which some feared might allow him to protect his men " from paying their debts and from diverse other dangers of lawe." A third petition presented the second main objection to his patent, a provision under which Martin claimed a 500 acre division per share rather than the 100 provided by the charter.[27]

It was four and a half years before this question was brought to any peaceful settlement. During that period Martin stubbornly defended his patent, and was able to secure considerable support in England through powerful friends, because of his long service to the colony, and by the argument that the company had no right to disallow by an ex post facto ruling a patent lawfully granted. The company replied with the offer of a patent equal to that of any other in Virginia, and defended its action by declaring his patent inimical to the peace and good govern-

[27] *Narratives of Early Virginia,* pp. 252-253, 261-262.

ment of the colony and on the grounds of a technical error in that it had been ratified by an ordinary court when only a quarter court had the authority to do so.[28]

While trouble with Martin began from the first year of Sandys' control, it was in 1622 that the greatest feeling arose from this dispute. Martin was in England that year, and brought to bear all the influence he could muster to force the company to recede from its position. His brother-in-law, Sir Julius Caesar, was an influential member of the privy council, and Martin was able to secure the support of several lords of the council who were joined by Sandys' chief opponents within the company, Warwick, Smith, Johnson, and Argall. With the backing of these powerful individuals he presented a petition to the king " which contained many scandalous suggestions as well against the whole Company, as some special Members thereof," and requested the settlement of the dispute by referees to whom he was willing to leave the decision. The company's answer, charging that the referees named by Martin were " suspected to have been the chief Abettors of Captain Martin in this business," was presented by Lord Cavendish to the king in June along with the names of certain other lords to whom the company would be glad to refer the decision.[29]

The government evidently took no action, however, for the company after some months more of recrimination and slander won out, and in November Martin was persuaded to surrender his patent for a new one. Apparently he hoped for a compromise settlement, for when the company issued to him a regular patent he was much discontented, and desired especially that he be allowed 500 acres for a share rather than the usual division. The company, blaming him much " for his impertinences and obstinacy," flatly refused, and Martin left the court " so ill satisfied " that once again he proceeded to " wrong " many worthy members "with his clamorous reports." [30] But finally in the spring he gave up all hope of any special grant, and on April 12 accepted a regular patent.[31]

This preceded by only a few days Johnson's famous petition to the privy council for a thorough investigation of the company, but the fact that Martin's dispute was settled when Johnson appeared before the lords seems to refute the suggestion that the royal investigation and dissolution of the company was the work of Sir Julius Caesar who hoped thereby to secure justice for Martin. Caesar's dislike of Sandys may have predisposed him to support Johnson's plea, but the chief importance of the Martin quarrel lies in the fact that Martin's loud complaints and attacks upon the company's officers and the support which he openly received from Sandy's opponents served both to increase and to advertise the dissension among the adventurers for Virginia.

The most violent dispute was that which broke the alliance between Sandys and Warwick. This union had never rested upon any stronger foundation than a mutual dislike of Smith, despite the gesture in behalf of a permanent alliance found in the elevation of Warwick, Nathaniel Rich, and Nathaniel Butler to the Council for Virginia in June, 1619.[32] The only hope of a permanent alliance was the possibility that Sandys might court the continued favor of Warwick by a few concessions to Warwick's particular friends and interests. But Sandys was not the man to make such concessions. His was a straightforward course designed for a definite purpose to which he was passionately attached, and whatever act the interests of Virginia seemed to demand he executed regardless of the cost. As in

[30] *Records*, II, 119-120, 126-127, 140, 145.

[31] *Ibid.*, II, 344-345. Some differences arose thereafter in the drawing of the final patent, but these were in time composed, and Martin departed the following February with a "very favorable letter in his behalfe" from the company to the governor and council in Virginia. *Ibid.*, II, 509-510.

[32] *Ibid.*, I, 226-227.

the case of Smith's accounts he was unable to make any concession or compromise so long as he saw the remotest possibility of making a final audit that would secure to the company all that he felt was its due, so now was it alien to Sandys' character to make concessions to Warwick on points affecting what in his mind were the proper interests of Virginia. While such steadfastness of purpose and character is admirable, it often happens that a more politic leader, who compromises at times with the devil for the sake of peace, accomplishes more in the end. It is not, however, the task of the historian to speculate on what might have been, but rather to record in this instance that Sandys in a short time crossed Warwick on two scores and forced him into a bitter opposition in alliance with Smith and Johnson. Later he was to suffer, and as he believed unjustly, from this antagonism.

The first break with Warwick came from Sandys' insistence upon calling Captain Argall to account. Much feeling against Argall had developed in the courts through 1617 and 1618, and many were disposed to hold him chiefly responsible for their misfortunes. Forced, as we are, to depend upon very unsatisfactory records, it is impossible to pass judgment on the man. The difficulties of his position were undoubtedly great, and, as John Rolfe insisted, there was much to be said in his behalf and many who played him false. Perhaps any other man in his position would have fared as badly. On the other hand, the persistence of men like Sandys in attempting to bring him to trial argues that there were some grounds for action, if no more than that, as John Pory expressed it, he " being rich, a bachelor, and devoid of charge, . . . excessively intended his own thrift." [33] Of one thing only can we be certain, that these differences bred much feeling in the company.

It was a problem already sore with much handling that

[33] Pory to Sandys, January 13, 1619/20, Ferrar Papers.

Sandys endeavored to settle in the first year of his administration. Warwick had set his face steadfastly against any effort to bring Argall, with whom his own interests were joined, to trial either in England or Virginia. Smith had incurred his wrath in 1618 by censuring the governor in the Virginia Council. When Yeardley reached the colony with instructions for an investigation of his administration, he found that his predecessor had taken French leave on a ship provided by his patron. John Pory, who accompanied the new governor as Secretary of State, had been engaged by the earl to look after his interests in the affair and to keep him informed. And Yeardley was the victim of damaging rumors circulated against him at Warwick's instigation. He "intercepted" several letters from Warwick to Argall and others from Pory to the earl which he forwarded to Sandys, declaring that he forgave them both anything contained therein tending to his own "private damage." [34] A letter from Pory in January, 1620, protested his loyalty to Yeardley, as also to Warwick, and declared that his purpose had been no other than "to nourish Sir George his due respect and worthy service towards his lordship" as "hath been your endeavor to maintain his lordship's favor towards Yeardley." [35] It was this affair, however, that was largely responsible for Pory's removal from office at the expiration of his three year term.

No sooner did Sandys undertake to bring Argall to trial on the basis of information returned by Yeardley than he too became the object of Warwick's wrath. For two years his every effort ended in a stalemate. Not only did Argall have the powerful support of the Rich group, but others of Sandys' enemies on the council embraced the opportunity to thwart him. The council became thus so equally divided that it was impossible to arrive at any decision. On June 26, 1620, Nathaniel Rich presented in Argall's name a petition

---

[34] Yeardley to Sandys, July 20, 1619, Ferrar Papers.
[35] Pory to Sandys, January 13, 1619/20, Ferrar Papers.

signed by several councillors in which he agreed to submit to a trial before a committee of the council selected by himself. But Sandys, although recognizing that he would procure " a good deal of ill will and malice " in so doing, strenuously objected and carried the court with him.[36] With the failure of this effort the council refused to make any further attempt at an agreement on Argall's trial, reporting to the court two days later that the question had become such an intolerable bother that they would be troubled with it no more.[37]

At the next court Sandys suggested an investigation by the court itself that he hoped would bring an end to this troublesome question, which in his opinion was second only to that of accounts as a source of faction and strife in the company. He divided the charges into three parts, each of which was to be investigated by a committee. Reports were to be made at the next quarter court and final judgment passed. But this effort was as futile as all others. By July, 1622, nothing whatever had been done, and although the committees were urged now once more to " proceed in that business with all expedition and diligence " the courts had become so wearied of the whole question that upon Argall's departure from England shortly thereafter the charges were dropped.[38]

Thus another dispute fraught with feeling was dragged out over four years. Sandys was never strong enough to overcome the powerful support which rallied around Argall, and as a result nothing came of the whole affair but fruitless charges and counter charges. Argall united with Smith and Warwick in attacks upon Sandys' government of the company, in the spreading of unfavorable reports, and in petitions to the privy council against the company. It was in vain that Sandys replied that the charges against Argall had originated with Smith and that he was only perform-

[36] *Records*, I, 375.
[37] *Ibid.*, I, 384.
[38] *Ibid.*, II, 40-56, 78-80, 405.

ing his duty as head of the company in continuing to press for a decision on Smith's charges. Argall and all his friends held Sandys personally responsible and bitterly assailed him whenever possible. And Sandys, never strong enough to bring Argall to bar, even in the company which he controlled, could only reply with equal bitterness that Argall escaped a just punishment " by means of his great friends."

A noticeable point in all these disputes is the peculiar helplessness and impotency of the company. So much of the time the machinery of the company, as may be seen in the refusal of the council in 1620 to make any further attempt at the settlement of the charges against Argall, was paralyzed by factional distrust and strife. Neither side had any confidence in the good faith of the other. Both were willing to put themselves to trial by their friends, but apparently had no hope of fair dealing in the hands of any other. The lack of coöperation from Smith, Johnson, and Argall, so often interpreted as a sidestepping of justice, may have been just as well a fear of entrusting their reputations and records to rivals whom they believed not so much disposed to do them justice as to vindicate charges of crookedness which they had already noised abroad. Perhaps if Sandys could have approached these problems at the first without the air of one seeking to confirm some foul suspicion, he might have secured a more hearty coöperation and a quick conclusion of these unpleasant questions. But his first step was unwise, though it may have been just, and in the turmoil of recrimination and abuse which followed, any real coöperation became an impossibility. The adventurers hated, abused, and sought revenge rather than any sane settlement.

Of greater importance in the break between Warwick and Sandys was the famous dispute between these two men over the use of the plantations as a base for piracy in the West Indies. There was a close connection between English piracy as it was developed by the Elizabethans and the colonization of America. Not only did it add tremendously to the wealth and marine power of the country, but it was the means of an increasing interest in the possibilities of the new world. The names of many who were active as privateers in the Spanish war are found on the rolls of the great colonial companies, which they supported with ships built for, seamen trained in, and money acquired by piracy. And while some of these had turned to colonization in search of a legitimate means of profiting by the new world after the Peace of 1604 had removed the legal excuse for their warfare on Spain, there were others who had no intention of relinquishing this profitable attack upon the hated enemy of England's religion, whom they also still considered the chief rival to their country's normal economic development. To such persons an outstanding advantage of an English settlement in America was the use that might be made of it as a base for operations against the neighboring Spaniard. Tobacco and " a fair war with Spain " were, in the opinion of Governor Butler, the only two " staple " commodities that were certain to return a profit to the Bermuda adventurers.[39] A general court of the Providence Island Company in 1636 was met to consider the settlement of the Island of Association, and among the reasons advanced in its favor was the " advantage it receives by a Neighbourhood to Hispaniola, the faire opportunityes of gayning by prizes." [40] This group formed an important and influential part of the membership in all the commercial companies of the seventeenth century.

The most active and important of all this group was the Rich family. Lord Robert Rich, fourth baron of Leighs and in 1618 first earl of Warwick, had as the grandson of the infamous Richard Rich inherited one of the largest

[39] Butler to Warwick, October 9, 1620, Manchester Papers, 275.
[40] P.R.O., C.O. 124/2, p. 279.

fortunes in England. In common with many other gentlemen of his time, he had seen in the warfare upon Spanish commerce an opportunity of picking up a quick profit, while at the same time striking a blow for his God, his queen, and his country. When Elizabeth left her subjects to the tender care of the peace loving James Stuart, Lord Rich had collected probably the largest private fleet in England and had added considerably to the family fortune. Rich and his son were chief among those who, despite the outspoken opposition of James I to piracy, refused to give up this profitable phase of their maritime interests. They were encouraged by the fact that the king's efforts to stamp out piracy were generally frustrated by inadequate facilities for policing the seas, the influence that could be brought to bear upon his officials by persons of wealth and power, and by the favorable attitude with which the public regarded such activities, an attitude which became more favorable with the growing unpopularity of the court's pro-Spanish policy.

When the elder Rich died in 1619, his son and heir, the second earl of Warwick, was already engaged in several ventures of this type set out jointly with his father, and he continued throughout a long life the greatest privateer in England. To him the spoiling of Spanish commerce was a legitimate, honorable, and patriotic part of his large commercial interests. He considered the use of colonies as a base for such activities a reasonable privilege belonging to one who had invested heavily in their establishment, and partly for this reason he regarded the more southern colonies as of the greatest value. He attempted to divert the Puritan migration to the Caribbean area, and led in the work of the Providence Island Company, its settlement off the Mosquito Coast becoming in the 1630's the most famous pirates' base in the West Indies, and he undertook single handed the settlement of Trinidad and Tobago. When at the outbreak of the civil war in 1642 parliament commissioned him lord high admiral, his fame as an enemy of Spain had become so great that his preparations of the royal fleet were viewed with sincere alarm by the Spanish ambassador for fear that his real intent might be some attack on Spanish America. In fact he did in that year send another fleet of his own with 1100 men who for three years scoured the West Indies for plunder, attacked and held for ransom important towns, and even captured and held for a year the colony of Jamaica.[41]

But not all adventurers in the commercial companies of his time regarded such activities in the same light as he. There were obvious objections which were more apparent to men who were not actively interested in these ventures. There was the possibility of some retaliation by Spain upon English settlements, and the equally serious and perhaps more probable risk of losing royal favor, not to mention the damage to the company's monopoly in trade through the sale of goods picked up as plunder by the pirates. Warwick, therefore, often found himself in open conflict with company officials, in which he enjoyed a position not altogether unlike that of an ordinary interloper. The earliest of these disputes had been with the India Company, the importance of which in the history of Virginia has already been noticed.

The most important of all was the dispute with Sandys over his famous ship, the *Treasurer*. This ship was one of several set forth by the young Rich under papers secured with his father from the Duke of Savoy. Savoy had been engaged in a quarrel with Spain, and in 1616 had sent an agent to England in search of money. This agent received much attention from Rich, and in return for a large money payment he secured a commission to prey upon

[41] For a general survey of Warwick's career as a gentleman pirate see W. F. Craven, "The Earl of Warwick—a Speculator in Piracy," *Hispanic American Historical Review*, X (1930), 457-479.

Spanish commerce.[42] It was in this way that Englishmen
were able to secure from foreign princes the papers giving
some semblance of legality to their depredations upon
their old enemy which their own government denied them.
While this practise was opposed by the government and by
companies who received injuries therefrom, it was not altogether unlike the time honored custom of recruiting
troops of mercenary adventurers from neutral states. The
difficulty of clearing an English port with a ship laden only
with powder and shot, which of course drew suspicion,
was obviated by securing from the government a license
to capture pirates. James had come to depend upon this
license as a chief means of policing the seas, but as Sir
Thomas Roe declared in 1617 it had become little more
than " a Common Pretence of beeing Piratts." [43] The Riches
had set forth three ships in 1616 with this license, two
of which had proceeded to plunder under the Savoy commission for two years in the West Indies,[44] and in the
same year the two ships which so involved Rich with the
India Company sailed from England under similar commission from Savoy and Florence and licensed by James
to rid the seas of pirates. The *Treasurer* sailed from England in April, 1618, under the command of Captain Daniel
Elfrith, a captain who was for many years thereafter in
the service of the Rich interests.[45]

The object of this voyage was a plundering expedition
in the West Indies, and he was allowed privileges of trade
and provisioning in the Virginia harbor by Governor
Argall. Shortly before Argall's departure the ship was re-
fitted by him and sailed from Virginia under pretense of
getting salt and goats for the colony. Elfrith called by
Bermuda and secured additional supply of corn from Cap-

[42] The mission of this agent and the attention shown him by Rich may be
followed in *Cal. St. Pap., Venetian*, vol. XIII.

[43] Roe to East India Company, February 14, 1617/18, O.C., V., 610.

[44] *Cal. St. Pap., Venetian*, XIV, 437; XV, 376.

[45] Pory to Carleton, September 30, 1619, *Narratives of Early Virginia*, p. 282.

tain Kendall, who was at that time deputy governor, and from thence proceeded to the West Indies. There he fell into consortship with a Dutch man-of-war, and the two after taking some small prizes set sail together for Virginia. They lost one another in passage, however, and the Dutch ship arriving at Virginia the last week in August, 1619, preceded Elfrith by three or four days.[46]

But during Elfrith's absence Argall had departed and Yeardley had succeeded him as governor. The *Treasurer* had sailed from England under suspicion, and Yeardley had carried with him to Virginia careful instructions for an investigation of its activities. In pursuance of these instructions he had informed the company shortly after his arrival that there was constant rumor " not without many apparent probabilities that this Ship had gone to rob the King of Spain's Subjects by seeking Pillage in the West Indies and that this was done by direction from my Lord of Warwick." Upon the receipt of this information Sandys assembled the council to ask their opinion therein, but, apparently anxious not to alienate the powerful Rich group or at least careful not to proceed to any open charges until rumors were confirmed, not without " having first blotted my Lord of Warwick's name out of these letters and anything that might directly touch him and so left the information to rest wholly upon Captain Argall."

It was the opinion of this meeting that the privy council should be acquainted with the letter, since by their oath they were required to make known all matters of importance to the state. But Sandys realized how deeply it might concern Warwick, not only in the loss of his ship but in his person, and so he sent for the earl and Nathaniel Rich. The result of two conferences with the earl of Southampton was a plan agreeable to both parties. Southampton, who was a member of the privy council, was to be present

[46] Rolfe to Sandys, January 1619/20, Ferrar Papers; Manchester Papers, 270, 279.

when Sandys presented the matter, and agreed to advise the lords in such a way as to quiet any further "search or stirring in the business." In addition, he was to see other members of the council beforehand to inform them of the business and to entreat their support in passing over the affair without investigation "as a complaint rather necessary in regard of our oath than a matter fit for their Lordships" to inquire into. Warwick himself was to approach certain friends of his to entreat their favor in "Captain Argall's behalf." [47] And thus the question was settled for the time being.

But while making this concession to good feeling in the company, Sandys wrote Yeardley on June 21, 1619, very heartily commending him for his proceedings in the case and concurring with him in the belief that it was of the utmost importance to Virginia. He was ordered to seize the ship immediately upon its return for an examination of her course and proceedings, and according to his earlier instructions to give full information at once to the officers of the company.[48] Elfrith, unaware of this correspondence, anchored at Kecoughtan several weeks later in considerable distress for water and victuals. Yeardley immediately gave order for his seizure, but the captain was able to make his escape and sailed for Bermuda. Shortly afterward the *Treasurer* arrived there "so weather beaten and torn as never like to put to sea again," and with a cargo of negroes, at first reported as twenty-nine but later as fourteen, two chests of grain, two chests of wax, and a small quantity of tallow, all of which, along with the men, were put to the company's use until the ownership could be definitely established.[49]

It has often been assumed that Elfrith disposed of some of his negroes in Virginia, but there is no evidence to

---

[47] Manchester Papers, 279.

[48] P.R.O., Admiralty Court, Instance and Prize, Libels 80, No. 123.

[49] John Dutton to Warwick, January 20, 1619/20, Manchester Papers, 261.

support this. He spent very little time there, not enough in fact to secure necessary supplies from the inhabitants of Kecoughtan who in their reception of him were anything but friendly, and had he disposed of any of his slaves they would certainly have been partly in exchange for supplies. Moreover, there is no mention of any negroes other than those with which he arrived at Bermuda. It seems certain, therefore, that the first slaves introduced into Virginia were not these aboard the *Treasurer* but rather those of the Dutch ship which arrived a few days earlier and according to the testimony of John Rolfe disposed of some twenty negroes in exchange for victuals from the governor and cape merchant. This man of war of Flushing remained for some weeks, received the entertainment of the colony, and sailed early in the fall bearing letters to friends and officials in England.[50]

In the meantime, steps were taken which led to some of the most severe feeling within the company. Elfrith at his departure, either because of his haste or for some other reason, had left behind in Virginia one of the ship's minor officers. Yeardley questioned this man under oath and he confessed that they had been robbing the Spanish. Sandys was at once informed of this confirmation of former rumors, and the steps taken by the council upon the receipt of this news caused as much bitterness as any other incident in the historic quarrel that split the Virginia Company. The effect was to throw Warwick and his friends on the side of Smith and Johnson in bitter opposition to Sandys.

Sandys assembled the council, without in this case giving previous notification to Warwick, made public the contents of Yeardley's letter, and declared it to be their duty in his opinion to notify the privy council. This notifi-

[50] Pory to Carleton, September 30, 1619, *Narratives of Early Virginia*, p. 282; Rolfe to Sandys, January 1619/20, Ferrar Papers. For further support of the belief that none of Elfrith's negroes were sold in Virginia see *Records*, II, 402.

cation was given on February 25, 1620, when Sandys appeared before the lords of the council and disavowed any connection of the company with the *Treasurer*. He also produced a letter to show that the Spanish agent in London had received full satisfaction as to the company's part in the affair.[51] This involved no little danger to Warwick, for not only did it threaten "suddenly ere he was aware a confiscation of his ship and goods," but it involved also a personal danger of no small consequence. There had been a break in Spanish influence at James' court since 1618, but the pro-Spanish group was now reasserting its control. Lord Digby, England's ambassador at Madrid who was in London at that time, was so strong in his denunciation of acts of hostility to Spain that he appeared in the eyes of his opponents to be nearer "the King of Spaines ambassador in England," [52] and the famous Count Gondomar was already on his way from Spain when Sandys appeared before the privy council.[53] Under these circumstances it is not difficult to understand the resentment with which Warwick regarded such treatment.

Nathaniel Rich, as his spokesman, complained bitterly of Sandys' action, and left a record of his feeling in notes evidently prepared for a speech in Warwick's behalf.[54] Rich declared that in the summer of 1619 he had heard of Yeardley's intention to examine Elfrith's crew under oath, and had complained to Southampton that this was unjust. Southampton apparently left the impression that he agreed with him, even going so far as to declare that it would be nearer the Spanish Inquisition than the law of England to make men thus accuse themselves, and he suggested that Sandys should be urged to instruct Yeardley to refrain from any such procedure. Sandys too had left the impres-

[51] *Acts P.C., Col.*, I, p. 30.
[52] P.R.O., S.P. 14/112, 104.
[53] Gondomar, the Spanish ambassador, had been out of England since the summer of 1618, but he returned in the first week of March, 1620.
[54] Manchester Papers, 279.

sion that he agreed with Southampton, and this of course had aggravated the injury to Warwick. Rich went further to claim that the company was not under obligation to report the affair. The requirement, as he interpreted it, was that upon complaint by any offended prince the company must make restitution as demanded by the king, and that if such restitution were not made in the allotted time the company would lose royal protection. Therefore, he argued, " we were not tied to complain against our own countrymen." Another grievance arose from the fact that Warwick had asked for the return of his ship and goods to England and had offered bond to be answerable for them. Sandys, however, alleged that it could not be done without first acquainting the privy council, which Rich felt " was a courtesy would not have been denied the meanest merchant in Town." Rich in fact could see nothing but ill affection to the earl in the whole of Sandys' actions, and complained that, had they been able to prove this business, Warwick would not only have been " in the mercy of our own king, but must have been brought under the clutches of the king of Spain which perhaps would not have been removed till he had crushed him to pieces, for God deliver me from the clemency of the Spaniard and from them that would inform for him, especially without warning."

This paper avoided entirely the question of Warwick's responsibility for Elfrith's piracy, and even declared that the ship had been sent with supplies and was intended to be used thereafter in trade to the north. Throughout the whole of this attack upon Sandys there runs the suggestion that the responsibility lay with Argall, and this interpretation has found favor with several historians who have implied that perhaps the *Treasurer* was not acting at Warwick's direction, but rather that Argall had taken advantage of his patron. There can be no doubt, however, of Warwick's complicity, and historians have been led into this error by relying entirely upon the report of the Historical Manuscripts Commission, which quotes from Document 261 of the Manchester Papers only the line reading, " it was Captain Argall's unworthy boldness to use your Lordship's name as a bolster to his unwarrantable actions." [55] A reading of the entire document leaves no doubt about Warwick's responsibility. It is a letter from John Dutton to the earl telling of the arrival of his ship in Bermuda, in which he continues:

. . . All which being before proclaimed yours by Elfrith and Thomas Foster, Mr. Rich's Deputy, were so received, the Governor and myself (till we know how far your Lordship would be seen in the business, in regard she was in question ere we left England) labored to control that received opinion, declaring it was Captain Argall's unworthy boldness to use your Lordship's name as a bolster to his unwarrantable actions, when you but only out of love, at his request victualled out such a ship, nor was it safe for any man from misreport to dishonor an honorable man; though indeed I, dealing with Elfrith and the Purser (who hath delivered in his book of accompts which is sent you by the Governor), found plainly how your Lordship was engaged in the business, which though I saw, I sparingly confessed how easy a matter it might be for Captain Argall, of whom you were so confident, to abuse so noble a nature in persuading things were that were not answerable. So that having drawn them almost to a seeming belief of what I said, I added that things standing as they did and Captain Argall standing bound to answer what the Treasurer should do, that your Lordship not mentioned, might through yourself and noble friends clear the business for them, which made a party you could not do.

Further evidence is found in a letter from Governor Butler to Warwick, in which he describes the crew of the *Treasurer* as dangerous tongued fellows, who had declared that if they were not paid to the utmost penny of their

wages they would go to the Spanish ambassador and tell
all. A postscript informs him that half of the fourteen negroes [56] in the ship did not belong to the *Treasurer* but
were stolen from a Dutchman, and that for fear of the company's finding it out and taxing him " for not informing
them of it " as well as " for fear of prejudicing your lordship," he was holding seven for the time being on the general land of the company. He added that if after a year he
had heard nothing from the company concerning them,
" I will (silently) deliver them over to your Lordship."
The closing sentence is of interest in showing how the
governors in the colonies might be persuaded to aid in
such private enterprises. The words are few but eloquent
in their testimony, " I humbly thank your Lordship for
my two." [57]

While Warwick's allies tried to cover up his part in the
affair, the fear of the consequences of its revelation only
increased their resentment. They proceeded to a bitter
personal attack upon Sandys, and their feeling in regard to
the *Treasurer* was soon joined with that arising from the
belief that Sandys was partly responsible for the failure of
another venture in which Warwick was deeply interested.
This was the abortive North expedition for the settlement
of Guiana. This part of Latin America had for a long time
held the interest of Englishmen, and repeated attempts
had been made at its settlement, the most famous of which
was Raleigh's ill-fated Orinoco venture of 1617. Despite
the unhappy ending of Raleigh's efforts, the break in the
negotiations with Spain in the following year seemed to
offer an opportunity for another expedition. Accordingly,
a company was organized under the leadership of Rich,
and a commission secured from the government. Captain
Roger North, a brother to Lord North, was put in com-

[56] Butler's number for the slaves on board differs from that of John Dutton
who speaks of 29 (Manchester Papers, 261). Butler's letter, written some
months later, is probably nearer correct.
[57] Butler to Warwick, October 9, 1620, Manchester Papers, 275.

mand of an expedition which sailed early in 1620 with 120 men.[58] Shortly thereafter, the renewal of negotiations for a Spanish marriage of Prince Charles, the return of Gondomar, and the consequent decline of the anti-Spanish party brought this venture to an end. On May 7 Warwick was ordered to deliver up his commission, a royal proclamation declared North had sailed secretly without permission and required him to return, and on May 23 Warwick surrendered the patent.[59]

The combined influence of Gondomar and Lord Digby had been responsible for this reversal of fortune,[60] but there were some of the Warwick group who held Sandys to be partially responsible. He was charged with having attempted to prejudice Gondomar against both Argall and North. Sandys denied the accusation, and even proved that he had been in the country at the time when the action was set on foot against the Guiana project, but the suspicion lingered on among his enemies.[61]

Sandys by the mere act of reporting the affair of the *Treasurer* had stirred the Warwick group to deep resentment, but this feeling became even more bitter when Sir Edwin determined to make the *Treasurer* the issue in a fight to stamp out piracy in the two plantations. Taking as an excuse the reception of Captain Elfrith in Bermuda after his expulsion from Virginia, Sandys charged that the Somers Islands were " infested " with pirates and in the spring quarter court of the Bermuda Company raised the whole question of piracy. His efforts, however, were foiled by the dominant party in that company. In fact, he was not even allowed to deliver his speech, but at the next meeting of the Virginia Company he did enter his com-

[58] Newton, *Colonizing Activities of English Puritans*, p. 27; Locke to Dudley, April 30, 1619, P.R.O., S.P. 14/108, 85.

[59] *Acts P.C., Col.*, I, pp. 36, 37-38; P.R.O., S.P. 14/187, 80.

[60] Chamberlain to Carleton, February 26, 1619/20, P.R.O., S.P. 14/112, 104.

[61] *Records*, I, 359-360.

plaint on the ground that it was a matter vitally affecting the safety of Virginia. It was Sandys' contention that so long as the Bermudas were safe from attack so also was Virginia,

but now as the case stands the Somer Islands is much frequented with men of war and pirates, with whom the inhabitants there are grown in great liking by reason of the commodities they bring unto them, in so much that by a letter from one of their ministers directed to Sir Thomas Smith and read in open Court the robbing of the Spaniards (as being limbs of Antechrist) is greatly commended. And the ship called the Treasurer after her robbing of the Spaniard . . . is there entertained and divers men of war set out to the same end are there refreshed, one Kerby, also a professed pirate as is reported, doth haunt those Islands insomuch as if there be not a strict course taken herein it will be made another Argier. . . .

The governor felt that such conditions constituted a question of state with which the privy council should be acquainted, and a committee was appointed for this purpose.[62]

At the same time Governor Butler was severely attacked for his part in the reception of these pirates. Late in 1620 he complained to Warwick that he had " received a company of scurvy letters from some of the petty chapmen of your Company, upon no other grounds than their foolish credulities. . . . I cannot devise what they ail to write so, unless it be the base fruit of faction in some that think I love your Lordship too well." [63] The reception of Elfrith was the main point in contention, but Sandys was concerned with the much broader question presented by the fact that the receipt of pirates was become a common practise in Bermuda. A Captain Kirby, an out and out pirate with no commission whatsoever, had frequented Bermuda in the months just preceding Butler's arrival, and Kendall,

[62] *Ibid.*, I, 367.   [63] Manchester Papers, 275.

his predecessor, had victualled him at the same time he did Elfrith. Even Butler considered Kirby a dangerous man. There were others who came under commission from the Netherlands, among them a Captain Powell to whom Butler had given the hospitality of the colony. For this also he was severely taxed by Sandys.[64]

Under such circumstances there was considerable justification for Sandys' stand. John Pory writing in 1619 expressed the general fear in Virginia of " some attempt of the Spaniard upon us, either by way of revenge, or by way of prevention; least we might in time make this place *sedem belli* against the West Indies." [65] And while this fear was probably greater than any actual danger, Sandys was obligated to make secure the safety of Virginia in every way possible. His judgment was sound too in the belief that the safety of the two plantations was one problem because of their geographic proximity. But perhaps the most important consideration was the possible loss of royal support at this time when James was once more drawing close to Spain. Regardless of what may have been Sandys' attitude on the pro-Spanish policy, his first regard as the head of the company was to avoid the severe blow to Virginia's fortunes that must follow the withdrawal of royal patronage. It is not surprising that he considered it necessary to the interests of both companies to stamp out piracy, and in all of his dealing with these questions to make certain that upon any royal inquiry the company should have a clean record to present. But while Sandys' motives were highly commendable, he received as reward for his endeavors little beside condemnation and resentment. He found himself in conflict with a large and powerful group in each company, the most violent wing of the anti-Spanish party, men who were anxious to grasp any opportunity for exhibiting their hatred of Spain, especially when with it

[64] Manchester Papers, 270, 275.
[65] Pory to Carleton, September 30, 1619, *Narratives of Early Virginia*, p. 283.

went the chance of some profit, and who considered that Sandys was unwarrantably interfering with a legitimate, even patriotic business.

Though Sandys was successful in securing from the Bermuda Company a prohibitory order in 1620,[66] Warwick was no less firm in his conviction that he was moved by personal spite. The earl was warmly supported in this opinion by Governor Butler with arguments which are of value, not only as an indication of the feeling in company and colony, but because they explain to a considerable extent the generally favorable attitude with which pirates were regarded in the colonies. With supplies uncertain and often inadequate the colonists welcomed chance ships which brought relief, and had little disposition to ask embarrassing questions. The governor, responsible both at home and in America for the welfare of his people and frequently haunted by the fear of famine, must often have welcomed the sight of any sail which offered the prospect of food and clothing. Under such conditions their exclusion by order from home was considered by some an act of oppression. " The people here," wrote Butler in 1620, " begin to talk that these strict courses against their admittance are only set on foot for fear lest the poor inhabitants here by getting some refreshments and clothing from them, should not be tied as hitherto to the cut-throat prices of the Magazine Ship."

There was also the fact that the governor was not always prepared to exclude these ships. The defenses of the colony were never too strong, and there was almost as much to fear from the hostility of the pirates as from the Spaniards. " In your general letters," argued Butler, " you seem to be in great fear lest the receipt of such as you please to term pirates should cause the Spaniard to attempt upon us, and why may you not misdoubt lest the exclusion of such as are our friends . . . may produce the same effect

[66] Manchester Papers, 284.

with them, and cause them to make the same war upon us that they do on the Spaniard in the West Indies, since the grounds are one and the same?" This difficulty was greater when a captain arrived and presented a commission from some foreign prince, for whether or not such a man was a lawful privateer or a pirate was a question still unsettled in England. It was on this ground that Butler vehemently defended his reception of Elfrith and Captain Powell. He inquired with some reason "by what spirit of devination I should take him for a pirate who had as lawful a commission to warrant his actions in these parts as these talkative tedious orators for their Church patrimony or gaudy and player-like laced cloaks." [67]

It was impossible for these two groups, with widely diverging opinions and interests, to come to any agreement on the question of piracy. Warwick could see nothing but ill will in Sandys' conduct, while Sandys, sure of his motives, could not but believe that the earl placed his own gain and interests above those of the company and colony. From this breach grew a feeling more bitter than that arising from any other of the famous quarrels, and it was of greater importance in the final disruption of the company. Warwick and Nathaniel Rich furnished the driving force behind the charges presented to the privy council in 1623, and Sandys at this time gave evidence of a greater resentment against these two than any other.

It is little wonder that the spring and summer of 1620, which witnessed the fight over piracy, the futile efforts at bringing Argall to trial, the first rumblings of the storm over Martin's patent, and the abortive attempts at settling accounts, was marked by the most severe factional strife in both companies before 1623. "I am sorry," Butler wrote in the fall of 1620, "that every ordinary passenger that returns from you seems to find occasion and to complain of

[67] Butler to Warwick, October 9, 1620, Manchester Papers, 275; *ibid.* to Rich, October 23, 1620, Manchester Papers, 284.

the continual brangles and perpetual disputes you have amongst you in your Court, which they say rather are Cock-pits whereby you conclude nothing, but rather seek to cross one another than to find out the truth." [68] One attempt at least was made at the settlement of these differences. In the Manchester Papers, where are to be found the papers of Nathaniel Rich, is a rough draft of certain propositions for restoring harmony among the adventurers. It was proposed that all business affecting Argall should be submitted to arbitration, that the Virginia and Bermuda courts should not "intermeddle" with the affairs and proceedings of one another, and that an order be made in each disfranchising anyone who thus attempted to disturb the peace, that Smith's accounts should be perfected within a month, and finally that all parties in any way interested in these differences, particularly Sandys, Southampton, Warwick, Smith, and Nathaniel Rich, should "at some Church in London receive Communion in confirmation of their mutual accord." [69]

This attempt at a "mutual accord," however, was of no avail. Smith, Johnson, Warwick, and Rich were all nursing grievances against Sandys which they could not forget. Sandys, on the other hand, in all honesty could see only that he had endeavored to the best of his ability to protect the interests of the company. It is not necessary to impugn the character of either party, nor is there sufficient evidence for so doing. To appreciate the importance of this factionalism in the company's history, it is necessary to understand that it was largely the product of conflicting interests, and not so much the quarrels of men of good intent with those of mean purpose. It must be recognized that widely divergent interests and opinions, introduced into an atmosphere already fraught with distrust and resentment, made it impossible for these men to view any ques-

[68] Butler to Rich, October 23, 1620, Manchester Papers, 284.
[69] Manchester Papers, 281.

tion dispassionately. Both sides, consequently, attributed to the other ill will and dishonest motives. The result was an irritation around which festered all the troubles of the Virginia Company for four years. Sandys' opponents were out to even the score, and were therefore more critical, more anxious to find fault, and were even so desirous of seeing his failure that at times they were not above placing some obstruction in his pathway. This, of course, gave Sandys a sense of personal injury equally great, and it explains the impossibility at any time after 1620 of healing the breach within the company.

The first act of Sandys' enemies was to remove him from the treasurership of the company. It was accomplished by the indirect means of an appeal to the king for interference. Far too much emphasis has been put upon James' dislike of Sandys, but there can be no doubt that his opponents had access to the royal ear and gained thereby an advantage denied to Sandys. His leading opponents were men of wealth, power, and influential connections, and it is not surprising that they made use of them in the Virginia disputes. Smith took the initiative in the move to prevent the reëlection of Sandys, as may be seen in the fact that at the time he was the object of the greatest resentment by Sandys' partisans. There was much talk of his unfair use of powerful friends of the bedchamber in effecting this end. But even so there is little reason to suppose that Smith's argument related to the political opinions of his opponent. Rather the evidence supports the belief that he based his objections on Sandys' inexperience and mismanagement of the company's business, objections which events proved to be well grounded, and argued that instead the care of the plantations should be entrusted to some merchant since, as James later contended when interfering in the elections of 1622, " Merchants were fittest for the government of that Plantation." [70]

[70] *Records*, II, 35.

When the election came in May, 1620, the king suggested to the company the selection of some merchant of experience and means, and mentioned particularly Smith, Sir Thomas Roe, Alderman Johnson, or Mr. Maurice Abbott. The message was delivered to the court on the 17th as an absolute prohibition of the election of any other. This breach of the liberties and privileges of the company created considerable excitement, and after much debate it was decided to postpone the election until the next quarter court. And since " it manifestly appeared that his Majesty had been much misinformed of the managing of their business this last year," a committee was selected to call upon the king and ask for a free election.[71]

In the meantime, the adventurers engaged in much acrimonious debate both within and without the courts, and Sandys made a special plea to the royal favorite, the duke of Buckingham, for support in his attempt to secure the king's consent to his continuance in office.[72] The suit,

[71] *Ibid.*, I, 348, 357.

[72] In a letter which throws some light upon the grounds for the king's interference, Sandys wrote:

"I understand by the later boastings of Sir Thomas Smith and his partisans of their sedulous endeavors, by a cloud of untruths, to make a fresh interposition between the most joyfull light of his Majesty's favor and the darkness where with my self and my service rest yet obscured, an attempt of strange malignity, which if I have deserved by any offer of the least wrong to him or his, I will bear it with patience, as the effect of just revenge, though not measured by justice. But if (being resolved by God's Grace to wrong no man) I have not so much as offended Sir Thomas Smith or his upholders, save only in one kind, in that I have not yielded to the abetting or cloking of those courses in managing the affairs of Virginia, which with derogation of his Majesty's authority, and contrary to his Royal Instructions (unworthily smothered) have been held from time to time, to the disheartening of all Adventurers and perpetual keeping down of the Plantation that it might not prosper; and on the other side to the enriching of themselves or some of them, by means so unlawful as the enhazarding of the destruction and utter expiration of the Colony. And in that it hath pleased God also to bless my late labours, that more hath been done in my one year with less than eight thousand pounds, for the advancement of that Colony in people and store of Commodities, than was done in Sir Thomas Smith's Twelve years, with expence of near eighty thousand pounds; as by view of both our Accounts (if yet his be an Account) doth manifestly appear. Then my good Lord I humbly tender to his Majesty's Princely Justice and to

however, was not successful, and the adventurers were given to understand that the reëlection of Sandys could not be allowed, although the king insisted that his messenger had misinterpreted his message to the company in that his purpose was merely to recommend certain men, but not to the exclusion of some other more suitable to the company. The company, upon hearing this report, voted its thanks to the king for the recognition of its liberties, and then proceeded to elect the earl of Southampton on June 28, 1620.[73] This, however, brought no change in the policies nor in the real leadership of the company. Southampton was in full accord with Sandys. He had supported him warmly through the troubles of the preceding year, and Sandys continued to be the leading spirit in the company until its dissolution.

An alliance with Warwick had been necessary to Sandys' rise to power in 1619, and an interesting question arises as to how he maintained control of the company after the defection of the Warwick group. Warwick's course is difficult to follow, but it may have been that the Rich group unwittingly gave their support to Sandys in the election of 1620. They seem at first to have held him personally responsible rather than his party. At any rate, Southampton retained for a while their good will. In a letter written several months after Sandys' removal, Butler agreed with Nathaniel Rich in his belief in the " justice

---

your Lordship's favorable mediation this equitable suit, that his Majesty upon this complaint against me may be graciously pleased to call me to answer before any indifferent Judges to be deputed by his Majesty. And if Sir Thomas Smith or his abettors be able to make good any one of their material accusations against me, or if his Majesty should please also so to appoint (though it be far from my disposition to be an Accuser of any man) that I be required to make good what I have here informed to Your Lordship and I fail in any one material clause thereof: I shall willingly submit myself to condign censures for both and from thenceforth make utter forfeit of all hope of his Majesty's favor, being that which of all worldly things I most earnestly desire."—Sandys to Buckingham, June 7, 1620, Bancroft Transcripts, Virginia Papers, I, 345-353.

[73] *Records*, I, 384-385.

and nobleness " of Southampton, and promised to remain " indifferent between factions." [74] They were not yet closely associated with Smith, although their common hatred of Sandys tended to draw them together, and it is quite possible that they voted for Southampton in 1620.

In time, however, it was bound to become apparent that Southampton was merely a screen behind which Sandys continued to direct the work of the company. But even so, a working understanding with the Smith faction seems to have come but slowly. The Rich group chose rather to express their resentment by dropping all connection with the courts and meetings of the council except when their own interests were involved, and while they joined with Smith at times to support complaints against the company such as those of Captain Martin, it was not until the tobacco fight late in 1622 that the two factions definitely joined forces with the purpose of overthrowing the Sandys party. There had been much feeling between Smith and Warwick, and the earl could perhaps see little advantage in removing Southampton only to have him replaced by Smith or Johnson. The tobacco contract, however, threatening the chief interests of both Warwick and Smith in Bermuda was sufficient to draw them together.

In the meantime, Sandys was safe in his control of the company, winning every election after 1619, partly because of Warwick's course, and partly because of a numerical increase in his party. The increased strength of Sandys' party was undoubtedly due in part to the approval won by his policies and his sincere efforts in behalf of the company's interests. There were many commendable features in Sandys' policies for the development of Virginia, and it would be unfair to charge that his continued hold upon the courts was due entirely to the manipulation of voting. A great deal of his strength, however, and in the end, that margin which enabled him to defeat the com-

[74] Manchester Papers, 284.

bined forces of Smith and Warwick seems to have come from the advantage taken by him of the rules governing membership and voting in the company. The method of voting was by head, not by shares, with the result that the holder of several shares had no more voice in the decisions of the courts than the possessor of a single share. Sandys was frequently accused of having admitted a large number of new adventurers, small stockholders having little stake in the colony, and admitted to membership for the sole purpose of giving Sandys such a majority that his opponents could not overthrow him. It was frequently the bitter complaint of both Smith and Warwick that those controlling the policy of the company were the smallest adventurers, men who had much less at stake than their opponents. And in 1623 Nathaniel Rich delared that these " new adventurers " of Sandys had not subscribed as much as £300 for the relief of the colonists, their only purpose and function having been to support their patrons by their presence at courts.[75] Such practises were considered a great injustice to the "old adventurers."

There was also an even more shrewd method of accomplishing this end. Sandys' partisans often increased their strength by distributing their shares among relatives and friends to hold merely for the purpose of voting. It should be pointed out, however, that Sandys was not alone in this practise, for on one occasion at least Warwick increased the number of his votes in the same way.[76] But in the use of this weapon the controlling party enjoyed a considerable advantage, since the admission of any new adventurer either by purchase or transfer of stock required the approval of the court, and the majority party might veto any transfer they wished.[77]

[75] Manchester Papers, 362.

[76] *Ibid.*, 273.

[77] An excellent discussion of the rules governing voting in the company and their manipulation by Sandys may be found in Scott's *Joint-Stock Companies to 1720*, II, 272-276, 278-281.

The dependence of much of Sandys' strength upon votes secured in this irregular way merely added to the resentment of his rivals. It was far more difficult to forget their injuries when it was felt that the power to inflict them came by an unfair manipulation of votes. And it is not surprising to find that they often complained of this " packing of Courts by turning over shares to their friends and confidants to compose their private ends." [78]

[78] Manchester Papers, 347.

CHAPTER VI
OVERHASTY COLONIZATION

IT was the failure of Sandys' economic policies that welded his enemies into an active opposition and gave them the means of bringing about his fall. Various grudges tended to draw the Smith and Warwick groups together and embittered the quarrel with the company's officers, but the prolonged duration and growing intensity of the struggle was due mainly to the miserable failure of Sandys' efforts to find for Virginia a profitable place in England's trade. The motives of those who called upon the king to interfere in 1623 may be interpreted in terms of spite, jealousy, or hatred, but a bankrupt company and a colony devastated by massacre, famine, disease, and death gave reason and justice to their case against Sandys.

Sandys had undertaken a very ambitious program in 1619, one that required the support of a vigorous and united company. Yet at no time could he rely upon more than a mere faction in the courts, and from the beginning of his administration the company was heavily indebted. Smith at his resignation reported that there were £4,000 left in the treasury, but Sandys was quick to show that this statement was misleading in view of outstanding obligations to the sum of £3,700 at least.[1] In time the indebtedness of the company was found to be even greater. By the spring of 1622 almost £5,000 had been paid out, " to the great exhausting of the common Treasury," on debts contracted by Smith. So great, in fact, had been the drain on common funds that it was now ordered that any further claims falling within Smith's administration which were not validated by the company's seal or by the court records should not be honored. Such claimants could seek satisfaction only from those officers who had been responsible for incurring the obligation.[2]

[1] *Records*, I, 216.

[2] *Ibid.*, II, 13.

The problem of financing Sandys' numerous projects was made more difficult by the fact that he alienated the most substantial element in the company and was forced to depend upon a party composed largely of minor adventurers. It is true that there were new adventurers, but few of them were for any considerable sums. The total revenue from this source, in fact, was so small that it was not even included in Sandys' estimates of expected income. And while some of his party invested rather heavily, especially those who were interested in Southampton Hundred, their investments were largely directed to the support of their private plantations. The adventurers were not so much interested in new adventures in the joint-stock as they were in realizing on earlier investments by a profitable development of their land divisions. This made all the more difficult Sandys' problem of financing the public lands, the iron-works, and other projects designed for the benefit of the company.

For these purposes he was forced to rely upon means of support which supplied neither a regular nor an adequate income. By far the largest portion of his revenue for two years came from the Virginia lotteries, which the government had licensed in 1612. Gabriel Barbor, the manager, was under frequent pressure from company officials. " I have written very earnestly to Mr. Barbor," wrote Sandys to John Ferrar in June, 1620, " do you also I pray the like." [3] Barbor, an energetic and capable manager, replied to such requests with reassuring promises. In October, 1619, he wrote from Exeter promising £2,500 by the following February and £1,000 more if necessary by March, and added that his business prospered " exceedingly in these western parts, where (I think) twill hold till Christide; I perceive small Towns and great markets doth exceed the best Cities, and might deserve a new survey through England and yet not return twice to any." [4] In

[3] Ferrar Papers.
[4] Ibid.

an estimate of the probable income for the fiscal year 1620–1621, Sandys reckoned upon the lotteries to provide £8,000 of a total budget of £17,800.[5] This may be taken as typical of his earlier budgets, for in providing for the auditing of lottery accounts in 1621 it was freely stated that the colony "hath in these latter years been chiefly supported by his Majesty's most gracious grant of the use of the Lotteries."[6]

In addition to the lotteries, there were three other main sources of revenue to which he looked. In his budget of 1620 he counted upon the collection of £5,300 of some £16,000 outstanding in subscriptions. The subscribers were divided into three groups, and committees were appointed to solicit each. But collections by these committees amounted to very little. In most cases they were met with receipts for payment or requests for time. Sandys also based part of his plans upon the expectation of £4,000 in payments resulting from the settlement of accounts, but the accounts of Smith and Johnson, from which the greatest help was expected, were never settled, and the income from this source was negligible.[7] The support for one special project, the college for the training of "infidell" children, was expected to come largely from collections by the Anglican Church. Sandys reported in 1620 that there were nine bishops who had made no contributions, and a committee was appointed to solicit "their Lordships" in the hope of securing £700 more.[8] But here, as in other quarters, the results were disappointing, and, while some few contributions were made in the next few years, the college land in common with the remainder of the colony suffered from a shortage of funds. Thus it may be seen that only from the lottery did he secure any considerable revenue, and since this fell far short of his actual needs, he labored from the beginning under the severe handicap of insufficient funds.

[5] *Records*, I, 390, 396-397.

[6] *Ibid.*, I, 492-493.

[7] *Ibid.*, I, 390, 397, 580.

[8] *Ibid.*, I, 391, 397.

Any weaker spirit would have admitted defeat at an early date, but Sandys actually believed that he could overcome these financial difficulties. Even after two disappointing years he was still firm in his conviction that Virginia could be built into a thriving commonwealth. This undue optimism was based upon the doubtful hypothesis that settlers sent from England could in a short time return by their labor a sufficient profit, both to cover the initial cost of their transportation and to provide an operating capital with which other laborers might be sent and new projects established. He explained his plan of finance to Southampton in the fall of 1619. He had sent 150 persons to be divided equally between the governor's land, the company's land, and the college land, and it was his plan to double that number during the ensuing winter. He expected the profit from the labor of these 300 settlers to come to no less than £3,000 a year, which would provide £1,000 each for the governor, the college, and the company, and he hoped "in short time double that sum," which would be "a fair ground whereon to reedify that state." [9]

The problem, it seemed, was to conserve and direct the expenditure of the limited funds at his command so that the largest possible number of planters could be settled in Virginia. If by the use of the money he could secure from lotteries, subscriptions, and old accounts, he could tide over the period necessary for the settlement of several hundred planters, he believed that thereafter the financial needs of the company would be met by the profit accruing from their labors. With this conviction it is not surprising that he felt it necessary to expend the major portion of his income in the shipment of that labor supply which was to provide the income of later years, and that he entered with great haste into a program of large scale colonization.

Another consideration in his plan to send a large number of settlers was his position in the company. He was from the first months of his administration under severe

[9] Sandys to Southhampton, September 29, 1619, Ferrar Papers.

attack by many powerful adventurers. To offset their attempts to overthrow him he had the support of a loyal and enthusiastic party, but their loyalty and enthusiasm rested in no small part upon their expectation of early success in Virginia. As an experienced political leader, Sandys was conscious of the necessity of showing some evidence of progress both to stave off the attacks of his enemies and to keep alive the interest of his own followers. The best case he could present was a large emigration to the colony, for the ability of the company to attract large numbers of English settlers was evidence both of the possibilities of Virginia and of the company's progress. Only in a favorable balance sheet in Virginia's trade could he find a better argument in his behalf. And how could a profitable trade be established without a large and strong body of colonists? His first emphasis, therefore, came to be upon numbers, and the number of colonists sent in the next few years gave such an illusion of success that not only were his contemporaries convinced, but many historians, though looking backward from the vantage point of three centuries, have been misled by figures on Sandys' emigration. Time and again Sandys, in replying to attacks by Smith and Warwick, quoted statistics on the migration to Virginia as evidence of the improvement brought by his administration, and historians in support of the same conclusion have quoted the same figures in words that are often taken almost verbatim from the governor's public statements.

Yet an examination of available records proves conclusively that this impatience of Sandys for quick results through a rapid increase in population was his greatest blunder and one of the chief causes of his ultimate failure. The transfer of several hundred people from an old world to an undeveloped colony is a serious undertaking, requiring much expense and care in providing for them during the period of their settlement and adjustment to a new environment. Many things should be considered. They cannot be expected to be self-supporting for some time after their arrival. For almost a year they must of necessity be so many more mouths to feed without being of any real help in providing that food. There is also the question of shelter and clothing, and numerous other questions of less importance. Sandys' colonization of Virginia shows little evidence of a careful consideration of these facts. Within one year he more than doubled the population of the colony. It would tax the facilities of any modern community to provide for double its population in so short a space of time, and it was much more difficult in a frontier community which was still to a great extent dependent upon a base three thousand miles away. The problem became increasingly difficult as each year brought new shiploads of settlers until by 1622 the number had reached some 3,500, most of whom had arrived unexpected by the governor, who was prepared neither to give them adequate shelter nor to make up the deficiencies in the supply of food, clothing, and equipment sent with them from England. A careful and well executed program of colonization might in time have brought the reward of a profitable trade. Sandys' haste, however, multiplied immeasurably the mistakes of inexperienced officers and the toll exacted by disease, famine, and death, with the result that his colonists were landed in Virginia so far from being prepared to enter into the work planned for them as to be instead a positive liability.

The failure of Sandys' plan of colonization is fundamental in explaining the larger failure of his whole program. Under the circumstances it was necessary to stake all on this one hope, upon which depended the development of new commodities, the establishment of a healthy trade with England, and the rehabilitation of the company's finances. The failure in this effort is rightly considered the first factor contributing to the final collapse of the company.

In examining Sandys' unsuccessful efforts at colonizing Virginia, it is necessary to consider many things for which he was in no way to blame, but the most important single factor contributing to the failure of his plans was the faulty execution encouraged by his overhasty desire for results. To begin with, most of his colonists sailed from England poorly equipped for the task that faced them in the new world. For though Sandys spoke often in his public statements of the care to select colonists well endowed by nature and training for the peculiar needs of Virginia, there can be no doubt that in his desire to effect a rapid growth of population he often compromised with these sound principles and sent a large body of inferior colonists. This seems to have been especially true of the first shipments, for several warnings from the colony in 1620 urged that he be more careful in the selection of his people. Governor Yeardley, John Pory, and William Weldon, of the college land, all insisted upon the necessity of sending " true laborers," men " brought up to labor " and of twenty to thirty years of age, since, as Weldon added, old men either died or lived to be of little service to the colony.[10] The popular interpretation of such phrases as " men brought up to labor " as an indication of the gentlemanly quality of Virginia's first citizens deserves, of course, little serious consideration. They apply with even greater force to vagabonds and paupers, and are merely the earliest of many complaints registered by colonists for centuries afterward at the disposition to unload England's undesirables on the colonies. In Sandys' behalf it should be noted, however, that there is less of this complaint to be found in the later years of his administration, which may indicate a greater care in the selection of colonists, although it may also mean that other and greater grievances merely crowded this particular one into the background.

[10] Yeardley to Sandys, June 7, 1620; Pory to Sandys, June 12, 1620; Weldon to Sandys, March 6, 1619/20, Ferrar Papers.

Even more disastrous in its effect upon the fortunes of the colony was the fact that most of the settlers sent from England were so poorly equipped and supplied by company officials with the necessities of life, that many who might otherwise have done well were denied a fair chance. The desire to send the largest possible number of colonists at the least possible cost was a temptation to load their ships with settlers when they were not able to provide them with the necessary supplies of food, clothing, arms, tools, and household equipment. Rather than send a smaller number of people properly equipped, as sound judgment should have directed, the company's officials far too often gambled on the chance of Yeardley's ability to make up the deficiency in supplies after the ships landed in Virginia.

The responsibility for this, one of the gravest errors of the Sandys administration, while resting ultimately upon the treasurer, falls especially on John and Nicholas Ferrar, who served as Sandys' deputies, the former until 1622 and the latter from that date to the company's dissolution. The deputy treasurer was charged with the actual task of arranging for all shipments of colonists and supplies — a task which included making arrangements with ship captains, buying provisions, recruiting emigrants, deciding the number of persons to be sent in each ship, and apportioning the supplies for each individual. A committee of sixteen men chosen by the court annually with a change in one fourth part of the membership each year, formed the administrative machinery through which the deputy attended to this work. Like the Magazine, the committee and deputy met in courts of their own, and were responsible to the company for a careful account of their transactions.[11]

Sandys' failure was due in no small part to the faulty execution of his plans by the Ferrars and the members of

[11] *Orders and Constitutions*, Force, *Tracts*, III, No. 6.

the committees which worked under their direction. Their important duties might have been performed far better had Sandys been able to give more personal attention to this part of the work, but he was a man busy with many responsibilities both within and without the company. The first year after his election most of his time was given to the abortive efforts at auditing accounts, at settling disputes within the company, and in the search for an adequate revenue. In 1621 he was busy with many responsibilities attendant upon his leadership in the house of commons, and through 1622 his attention to the work of the company was made more difficult by the extended illness of his wife, who suffered a miscarriage in 1621 and was on the point of death for another year. During that period Sandys was most of the time at his home, Northborn in Kent, and while he corresponded frequently with the Ferrars and made hurried trips to London when the occasion demanded it, the responsibility for carrying on the business from day to day was left largely to the Ferrars.[12] It is they who must answer for a large part of the privation, sickness, and death suffered by Virginia through the four years of Sandys' control.

Numerous complaints extending over the whole period of Sandys' administration show that emigrants were far too often set forth by the Ferrars without adequate provisions. In November, 1619, the *Bona Nova* arrived in Virginia with 100 men in good health, but the supply of victuals brought with them " fell so short " that Yeardley was forced to put out half of them for a year as servants on private plantations, where they were to receive their keep and three barrels of corn and fifty-five pounds of tobacco per man.[13] Fifty of this number had been sent to Captain Weldon for his use on the college land, and these circum-

---

[12] Sandys to J. Ferrar, October 1, 1621; Sandys to J. Ferrar, October 13, 1622, Ferrar Papers.
[13] Rolfe to Sandys, January, 1619/20, Ferrar Papers.

stances which caused him to lose their services for at least a year led him to send a bitter complaint to Sandys. Ferrar had promised him three suits of apparel for every man, full equipment of arms, and competent provision of "household stuff." But it was found upon their arrival in Virginia that there were only two suits for a man, and one of them so mean and unserviceable that it gave poor protection against the extreme cold they had suffered since landing. There were but 30 muskets, 5 iron pots, and one small kettle for 50 men. And the provision of victuals, not to mention the promises of kine and other things which he still hoped would be performed, was so short of their needs that when the governor and cape merchant saw his invoice they protested he had not a competent supply for more than four months, there being only $32\frac{1}{2}$ hogsheads of meal and a small quantity of oil, and neither butter, cheese, rice, oatmeal nor any other English victuals. "In regard whereof," he wrote, "the Governor and Council thought it fit to put out the one half of my Company for their victuals this year and a proportion of Corn and Tobacco to victual and apparel them the next year, which I was constrained to do to my own great grief and the no small discontent of my whole Company." He concluded with a plea that in later shipments of settlers the company should above all have regard for adequate provision of food and clothing, for these necessary provisions could not be secured in Virginia upon any terms whatsoever.[14]

The immigrants who arrived the following spring, however, were even more scantily provided. The governor in order to fill out their provisions was forced to resort to buying food from Mr. Shaw, master of the *London* then at Jamestown, from whom he took 5 hogsheads and 5 barrels of peas, 12 barrels of oatmeal, and 1,000 biscuit. He charged the bills of exchange to Sandys whom he hoped would not take it ill since he had found " this

[14] Weldon to Sandys, March 6, 1619/20, Ferrar Papers.

variety of victual to be much to the content and health of
the people." This unexpected arrival of three shiploads of
settlers just after planting season sorely perplexed Yeardley to provide for the unusual deficiencies in their supply,
and caused him to enter the most urgent and bitter protest of his three years as governor.

I protest before god [he wrote] I run my self out of all the
provision of Corn I have for the feeding of these people looking . . . for no recompence, the provision now sent being but
one thousand and eighteen bushels of meal, which at a bushel
per month, being the least I can give them, will but serve them
for ten weeks, whereas Mr. Ferrar sayeth he hath sent 6 months
provision. Mr. Ferrar is my worthy and loving friend, but
herein I must blame him in casting up so short Allowance.
Also for Clothes they come very short. Wheresoever the fault
is I know not, it behooves him to look to it. The people are
ready to mutiny for more affirming that more by him was
promised. What shall I say? All I have or can make means for
I am willing to offer for the performing and making good your
promises there made, but, Sir, I beseech you be not offended if
I deal plainly respecting the honor and reputation of my
friends and suffer me I pray you to advise you that you do not
run into so great matters in speedy and hasty sending so many
people over hither and undertaking so great works before you
have acquainted me and have truly been informed by me of
the state of the Plantation and what may be done here. If you
do not observe this rule I shall and must fail in the executing
of your projects.

In conclusion, he begged Sandys that if he sent any more
men before Christmas to provide them with six months
supply of food at least, allowing a bushel of meal a man
per month.[15]

But warnings of this type apparently had little influence
with the company officers, who continued to send colonists with inadequate provisions. Over a year later the

15 Yeardley to Sandys, June 7, 1620, Ferrar Papers.

council informed Yeardley that nine patents had been granted under which 1,000 persons were to be taken to Virginia in the spring of 1622, and requested that due provision be made for their food " in regard that through the great raise of grain here, they are like to come slenderly furnished hence." [16]

While the fault in execution was largely that of the Ferrars, the policy which encouraged this error was that of Sandys. And curiously enough, despite all the complaints and warnings received from the colony, he never seemed able to understand the seriousness of the problems arising from this practise. After the massacre in 1622, when the company had been informed that the colony suffered much for want of arms, food, and shelter and even faced the prospect of starvation during the winter, the council replied that they were unable to send sufficient supply but were happy to inform them that there " go now over in this Ship, and are immediately to follow in some others many hundreds of people." It was most essential that they should be given every assistance possible in settlement that " others by their welfare may be drawn after them " since " in the multitude of people is the strength of a kingdom." [17] And this to a governor who only by the most heroic efforts could hope to prevent the starvation of the people already in Virginia!

Further evidence of the carelessness of responsible officials in attending to this most important feature of their work is found in the failure to take any effective steps before the summer of 1623 to see that settlers shipped for private plantations carried adequate provisions. The shortage of food among any settlers, whether upon public or private land, placed a responsibility on the governor to provide for them. In the last two years of Sandys' control emigration at the company's expense declined because of a lack of funds, but the problems of the governor were as

[16] MS. Rec. Va. Co., III, Part ii, 21a.   [17] *Ibid.*, III, Part ii, 23a-25.

perplexing as ever on account of the large number of poorly equipped colonists sent for private plantations. Certainly it was the company's responsibility to see that these prospective planters sailed with ample equipment, for otherwise not only would private adventurers suffer loss, but the whole colony would be burdened by an extra drain upon its limited resources. Yet the administration was content merely to issue a published declaration for the " direction and advice " of those sailing for Virginia which listed the supplies necessary to each individual. It was not until June, 1623, after Nathaniel Rich had indicted Sandys on this count before the privy council, that the court in response to several recent and urgent complaints from Virginia decided it was necessary to take some action to " constrain " emigrants to abide by the published directions of the company.[18]

Sandys' emigrants had not long to wait after they left the shores of England before feeling the effects of this inadequate preparation. The voyage to Virginia, usually lasting from two to three months, even under the best circumstances was often one of severe hardship. On board vessels fitted out by the Ferrars the ordinary discomfort, sickness, and tedium were made much worse by the fact that ships were frequently overcrowded and the food provided was unsatisfactory both in quality and in quantity. The result was that the toll of sickness and death left many shiploads sadly depleted when the long crossing was finally ended. Even those who survived were often so weakened by the rigors of the voyage that they died in a short time or lived to be of little service.

Much attention was therefore given in letters from Virginia to ways and means of reducing the disastrous effects of the voyage itself. Governor Yeardley and other prominent colonists quarrelled first with the company's practise of making their shipments in the spring, and insisted rather

18 *Records*, II, 439-440.

upon fall sailings. The disadvantages of the former were obvious to anyone acquainted with conditions in the colony. The sickened condition of most newcomers was aggravated by the summer heat. And even those who arrived in good health could only in a few instances get settled and acclimated before the planting season had passed. As a result they were entirely dependent upon supplies from England, or any surplus the colony might be able to provide, until the passage of more than a year had brought another harvest toward which they could contribute their labors. On the other hand, by timing their arrival for the early fall they found a much more favorable climate, and the time through which they must be supported by the company and colony was shortened by some several months.

It was in 1620 that the effects of the spring sailings were most severely felt. The *Jonathan,* the largest of three ships arriving in May, had lost its master, three mariners and 25 passengers out of a total of 200. And on the other vessels there had been a heavy mortality which increased after they had anchored. It was the landing of these men, all of them poorly provided and most of them sickened, that caused Yeardley to enter the strong protest to Sandys quoted above, in which he also declared that " had they arrived at a seasonable time of the year I would not have doubted of their lives and healths, but this season is most unfit for people to arrive here, and to tell you the very truth I doubt of much sickness for many of them to the number of 100 at least came some very weak and sick, some crazy and tainted ashore, and now this great heat of weather striketh many more but for life." [19] John Pory joined Yeardley at this time in insisting upon fall sailings, and his argument was strongly supported by the sharp contrast between the voyage of the *Jonathan* and that of the *Bona Nova* which had reached Virginia the preced-

[19] Yeardley to Sandys, June 7, 1620, Ferrar Papers.

ing November with all of its 120 passengers "lusty and healthy." [20]

Complaints of this sort were not without effect, for most of the sailings after 1620 were timed for the late summer or early fall. In January, 1622, the council in Virginia was happy to inform the company that none of the passengers on the nine ships arriving there the past fall had died by the way and that since then they had enjoyed excellent health, which seemed to them sufficient justification for their insistence upon fall sailings.[21] By following this advice the company lessened considerably the ill effects of the crossing, although at times the officials fell into their old practise of setting forth ships in the spring.[22]

But no crossing, regardless of the season, was free from many difficulties and hardships, and the problems of the passage continued to hold the attention of colonial leaders. They attempted especially to decide upon the most favorable route to be followed by the company's ships. There seems, however, to have been no distinct advantage to either of the two main routes, one by the West Indies and the other referred to as the "northern passage," for there was not the same agreement of opinion found in the case of seasons. In the first years of Sandys' administration experienced colonists favored the West India passage. Both John Rolfe and John Pory in 1620 argued that the northern route was preferable only in the spring and summer, the seasons most unsuitable for the landing of colonists in Virginia, whereas in the fall the southern passage proved more refreshing to the passengers and had the additional advantage of being the shorter. Yet neither was entirely satisfactory, and it was hoped that the master of the *Swan* who returned to England via the Bermudas that

---

[20] Pory to Sandys, June 12, 1620, Ferrar Papers.
[21] MS. Rec. Va. Co., III, Part ii, 1.
[22] *Ibid.*, III, Part ii, 21a.

summer would find a better passage.[23] His effort apparently resulted in no helpful discovery, but company officials did thereafter accede to the colony's insistence upon the southern route despite their preference for the other. By 1622, however, colonial leaders had changed their opinion, and after the loss of some valuable seed by the heat of the passage through the West Indies, the council in Virginia advised the use of the northern route.[24]

There were but few of Sandys' settlers who landed in Virginia prepared either in health or in equipment to take up without great difficulty the problem of adjustment to their new life. Weakened and diseased and inadequately provided as they were, however, their situation would not have been so serious had the colony been prepared to receive and care for them. But this was not the case. Sandys' haste gave the governor little time in which to make ready for the great influx of new settlers which followed year after year. His first difficulty was that he had neither sufficient time nor warning to prepare for the reception of the host of colonists, who arrived in most cases without warning. Thus in May, 1620, three shiploads, to which reference has already been made, surprised Yeardley and left him "not a little" puzzled to provide for them. In writing to Sandys he acknowledged his zeal for the "hasty and speedy erecting this good work," but felt constrained to add that "had not your zealous desires over hasted you and the passage at sea been so unfortunate to the duty, whereby I had no warning at all given to provide for these people, I should have been able to have done much better than now I can." Having recounted all his difficulties in getting them settled, he begged Sandys not to send colonists thereafter until he had been fully informed by him of conditions in Virginia and of the number for which

[23] Rolfe to Sandys, January, 1619/20; Pory to Sandys, June 12, 1620, Ferrar Papers.
[24] MS. Rec. Va. Co., III, Part ii, 1.

provision could be made. Upon no other condition could they hope for success.

What think you that I am able to perform [he continued] it being but yesterday to speak of since my first coming the colony was in election of starving left so by Captain Argall. I have done what I can do and will do still to utmost, but I pray sir give me both time to provide means and to build and settle before you lay one load, if you will but take my advice hence I will inform you truly and do to the utmost, . . . what I can and am able to do if you will have patience I will from time to time inform you, and doubt not but to give you full content, but both you and I must give leave to time.[25]

This request, however, carried little weight with Sandys. During the whole of Yeardley's term he never enjoyed a sufficient breathing spell in which to put things in order for the proper reception and settlement of new colonists. The nearest to a notification usually given him was a letter with the first ship sailing to inform him that others followed shortly afterward. Sandys' finances were on so uncertain a basis that plans could not be made far ahead, and the urgency he felt to keep things moving did not allow for the passage of several months while he wrote and received reply from Virginia. The policy of fall sailings was of some help, but it gave to the governor little idea of the actual number to expect.

The colonists who arrived thus unexpectedly were not able to turn at once to the production of their own food. And since they rarely brought a sufficient supply with them, the governor was forced to draw upon any surplus that could be provided by the labor of the older planters. But even in the best years this often fell short of actual needs. It was no easy task to make a living in Virginia, despite Sandys' highly colored accounts of its climate and fertility. He was a fortunate man who by dint of hard labor could produce enough corn to meet his needs from

[25] Yeardley to Sandys, June 7, 1620, Ferrar Papers.

one harvest to another, and enough tobacco to purchase a few clothes and other necessities. With the best of luck he could hope for little variety and certainly little surplus. " I assure you," wrote Captain Thomas Nuce, who in 1620 had been commissioned to manage and direct the company's land because of the governor's pressing duties,[26] " the world goes hard with many even at this time. The labor is infinite that they are here put to for Corn yearly. In so much that it takes up at least three parts of our hands." [27] Under such circumstances it is not surprising to find Yeardley writing Sandys in 1620: " I pray think it not strange I should write thus to send victuals with your people for you may be pleased well to conceive that if such numbers of people come upon me unexpected, and that at an unhealthful season and too late to set corn, I cannot then be able to feed them out of others' labors." [28]

There were many difficulties in addition to those of nature. Efforts at growing English grains often failed because of bad seed. Nuce observed in 1621 that Virginia's soil could be expected to produce anything grown in England, "and yet have we very little of your corn or other grain, and I guess the reason to be for that seldom any of our seeds come kindly or seasonably hither." That spring he had planted several varieties of garden seed, but none of them had come up.[29] In the following winter the colonial council informed the company that their chief difficulty in growing English grains came from the bad seed sent from home. They urged care in selecting " new seed," and advised that they be sent between the decks and not in the hold of the ship where they had so often been spoiled by the heat. By following these directions and tak-

[26] *Records*, I, 371.
[27] Nuce to Sandys, May 27, 1621, Ferrar Papers.
[28] Yeardley to Sandys, June 7, 1620, Ferrar Papers.
[29] Nuce to Sandys, May 27, 1621, Ferrar Papers.

ing the cooler northern passage they hoped for a solution
of the sore problem of seed.[30]

Another problem arose from the shortage of domesti-
cated animals. With the 1200 and more colonists who went
to Virginia within the first year after Sandys' election there
were sent only 112 cattle.[31] The disproportion becomes
more significant when it is recalled that Captain Argall
had left the stock of cattle sadly depleted. The company
in 1618 had wisely provided for the enclosure of certain
parts of the public lands for the preservation and breeding of an adequate stock of cattle, but Sandys failed to
follow up with provision of the stock necessary to carry
through the plan. During the whole of his administration
there was a shortage of live stock. William Weldon upon
his arrival late in 1619 was sorely disappointed to find
Ferrar's promise of kine unfulfilled, and Peter Arondelle,
who landed two years later, entered an almost identical
complaint. In the same year, Nuce pointed out their great
need in the colony for more cattle " both for plough and
payle." [32] In August a ship loaded with cattle sailed from
London under the command of a Captain Gookin. But
while he carried the recommendation of the company, the
colonists were warned against taking more than a few cows
at the company's charge because of the exhausted state of
its treasury.[33] With this exception, their greatest effort was
to advise in July against slaughtering any cattle for food,
and to instruct the governor to follow the instructions of
1618 for fencing land on which cattle, swine, and poultry
might be preserved for breeding.[34]

The arrival of so many ill-equipped settlers and the inability of the old planters to provide for them would not

[30] MS. Rec. Va. Co., III, Part ii, 1.

[31] *Records*, I, 351-352.

[32] Weldon to Sandys, March 6, 1619/20; Arondelle to Sandys, December 15,
1621; Nuce to Sandys, May 27, 1621, Ferrar Papers.

[33] MS. Rec. Va. Co., III, Part ii, 18.

[34] *Ibid.*, III, Part ii, 12.

have been so serious had the company followed up with shipments of supplies. But instead, ships which should have been laden with supplies came too often merely with another load of colonists, and the whole colony suffered from a shortage of provisions. Weldon complained in 1620 that it was impossible for him to make up the deficiences in the supply of victuals and apparel for his men in Virginia, although he had " both spoken and sent and written to the Capemerchant." [35] The next year, Nuce informed Sandys that the half year for which they had been victualled had almost expired " and yet we hear of no supply." Had it not been for some corn fetched from the Bay by the master of a ship at that time in Virginia they would have been in great distress, he added, for " your provisions fall exceeding short, which is not my complaint alone." [36] George Thorpe, the governor's deputy for the management of the college lands, at the same time informed Ferrar: " The country will be generally in great distress for all manner of apparell against winter, many men wanting already wherewith to cover their servants nakedness. I beseech you therefore be mindful of us in that kind." [37] In response to these warnings the company with great difficulty provided a private magazine for their relief, but warned them that if they expected any further help, they must be sure that a profit was returned on this venture, since the company was not financially able to support a magazine itself.[38]

More commonly, however, Yeardley was forced to fall back upon trade with the natives. This recourse was the solution of his problems in 1620, though not at all a satisfactory solution since the trade supplied little beside the famous Indian maize, which did not allow for much

[35] Weldon to Sandys, March 6, 1619/20, Ferrar Papers.
[36] Nuce to Sandys, May 27, 1621, Ferrar Papers.
[37] Thorpe to J. Ferrar, May 15, 1621, Ferrar Papers.
[38] MS. Rec. Va. Co., III, Part ii, 15a.

variety in food. But even here he was sorely handicapped by the lack of small shallops for plying the trade in the Bay, where the most favorable conditions for native trade existed. Several efforts to send boatwrights for the construction of these small boats failed because of deaths. One man was sent in 1620, but that "silly fellow" died soon after landing and left the governor with "no means so speedily to set up the new shallop for transporting the people and their provisions that had I not a shallop of my own to employ that way I know not what to do." [39] Yeardley continued to urge this need upon the company, and in December, 1621, he was informed that despite the exhausted state of its stock several adventurers had agreed to underwrite the sending of shipwrights whom they hoped to ship in April. It was not until June, however, that they sailed, and then it was too late for them to be of much service.[40] The governor got along as best he could with his one shallop, and at times of extreme need persuaded captains of ships arriving at Virginia to undertake trading voyages for corn before their return to England. This expedient solved his problem in 1621 when a "good and free trade" with the natives on Chesapeake Bay was established, and after the massacre in 1622 it probably saved the colony from absolute starvation.

But even at the best, with an occasional supply from England and the help of native corn, the Virginian's food was an inadequate and unbalanced diet which kept him in a weakened state. The effect was greatest on those who landed in a sickened condition, for their recovery was made doubly difficult by the food they were forced to live upon. A diet consisting chiefly of bread, peas, and oatmeal will make inroads upon the strongest constitution. And while to these staples there was added at times the game of fisherman and hunter, newly arrived colonists were

[39] Yeardley to Sandys, June 7, 1620, Ferrar Papers.
[40] MS. Rec. Va. Co., III, Part ii, 21, 23.

none too adept at this means of livelihood even when they were well enough to undertake it, and the endless work of crop season often kept the older settlers from the streams and woods. Colonists arriving in 1620 were supplied only with meal which Yeardley considered " very harsh for them to feed upon being new comers," and for " variety's sake and in regard also the proportion out of England sent with them would nothing near hold out," he contracted with a merchant in port for a further supply of peas, oatmeal, and biscuit.[41] Many others, however, were not so fortunate as to enjoy even this variety. Nuce wrote in the same year that " the people live very barely for the most part, having no other food but bread and water and such manner of meante as they make of the Maize, which I would to God I could say they had in any reasonable plenty." [42]

It was not merely the insufficiency and lack of variety from which they suffered, but the quality of their food often did even greater damage. Much of their food was damaged during the long voyage by the heat of the ship's hold. The makeshift utensils which they used in the preparation of food were considered another main cause of their suffering. As late as 1621 George Thorpe wrote that the people were forced " to sift their meal in sifters made of leather burned full of holes with a hot iron," which made their bread very unwholesome and was in his opinion " a great cause of their fluxes." He urged that some sieves be sent for trial.[43] It was not till that year that an effort was made to establish a corn mill for grinding meal. In instructions to the colonial council it was advised that corn mills should be erected and public bakehouses in each borough, but there is no record that this was ever done.[44]

---

[41] Yeardley to Sandys, June 7, 1620, Ferrar Papers.
[42] Nuce to Sandys, May 27, 1621, Ferrar Papers.
[43] Thorpe to J. Ferrar, May 15, 1621, Ferrar Papers.
[44] MS. Rec. Va. Co., III, Part ii, 12.

The result was that even those who had survived the voyage without any severe illness soon became victims of diarrhea, commonly referred to as the " fluxes." The strongest rarely survived the period of adjustment without some sickness of this sort. " Seldom any escapeth little or much," wrote John Rolfe.[45] Diarrhea quickly saps the strength of its victim, and those who were weakened in this way were far more susceptible to many infectious diseases. Many came down with severe and burning fevers, which may have been related to the malarial fever that has infested the southern seaboard in modern times. Leading colonists attributed this infection largely to their lack of good drink. There was some supply of English beverages, but much of it seems to have been of an inferior quality and like their food often damaged by the long voyage. A load of " stinking beer " was accounted one of the chief causes of the great mortality during the winter of 1622–1623.[46]

While there is mention of much drunkenness, most of the settlers apparently were forced to depend upon water as their chief beverage.[47] The drinking of water is not necessarily harmful, but the water consumed by Sandys' planters was probably very injurious to their health. The water supply of the South Atlantic coast has undermined the health of more than the first generation of its inhabitants. In the low and level coastal plains water veins run close to the surface, and only recently have public education and regulation of community sanitation tended to check the spread of disease through wells and springs infected by large quantities of surface water. Little of this was understood by the seventeenth century Virginian, and while he guessed that part of his trouble came from the

[45] Rolfe to Sandys, January, 1619/20, Ferrar Papers.
[46] MS. Rec. Va. Co., III, Part ii, 6–6a.
[47] One man in 1620 proposed the manufacture of "artificial wine" in Virginia in answer to the loud complaint of a lack of drink. Smyth of Nibley Papers, 30.

water, he adjudged the cause to be that he was forced to drink water instead of beer or mead. Thorpe in an endeavor to solve the problem acquired for himself an interesting place in history as probably the first manufacturer of corn whiskey, later to become one of the South's most famous products. In 1620 he wrote a friend in England that he had " found a way to make so good a drink of Indian corn as I protest I have divers times refused to drink good strong English beer and chosen to drink that." [48] But probably only a few were privileged to, or could, enjoy this drink. It can hardly be considered a fit substitute for water. And with the miserable failure of the colonial wine industry, the colonists were left dependent upon a poor and inadequate supply of drink from home.

The suffering and spreading of infection was increased by inadequate housing facilities. Many diseases were brought by newly arriving colonists, and the general infection of the colony was greater because there were no special provisions for the housing of new arrivals. The company at an early time recognized the imperative nature of this need and gave instructions for building " guest houses " in each borough. But either through neglect, or lack of time, tools, and skilled hands, the repeated and urgent requests of the company bore no fruit. None were built in the first year of Yeardley's administration, and early in the second summer Pory explained that nothing could be done until winter because all hands were busy with crops and sap made the timber unfit. During the following winter there was built the only guest house provided in Sandys' administration. This structure was raised on the college land by Jabez Whittaker. A large number of men for whom he was " ill provided " arrived in the fall of 1620, and he was kept busy through the entire winter caring for them. Finding six in a house to be too many for their comfort and health, he built enough new houses

[48] Thorpe to John Smyth, December 19, 1620, Smyth of Nibley Papers, 33.

to accommodate his men three to a house, and for the reception of new arrivals thereafter he constructed a guest house of forty by twenty feet.[49]

Whittaker was highly commended by the company, and instructions to the council urged similar preparations in all other plantations. A letter from London spoke at length on the subject, and with some strength expressed the belief that this work would already have been done if half so much care and time had been taken in doing it " as hath been spent in giving reasons to the contrary." The officials at home refused to accept " the plea of impossibility." The colonists' excuse, they assured themselves, was " rather a bug-bear than an essential cause of forbearance." [50] The pressure continued, and in notifying the colony of the sailing of several ships that fall, the council could not " but apprehend with great grief the sufferings of these multitudes at their first landing for want of guest houses wherein they might have a while sheltered themselves from the injuries of the air in the cold season; which omission and defect we hope and very earnestly desire you will supply by a courteous and Christian entertainment of them in your own houses, till they may conveniently provide themselves; and that against next year you will have erected in the four several Boroughs as many guest houses capable to receive these great numbers." [51] One wonders why Sandys could not see the necessity of giving the colony time to build guest houses and to make other general provisions for the reception of colonists before sending them on in such large numbers. The urgency of the need was again dwelt upon in a letter to the colony of December, 1621, when it was promised that carpenters would be sent by April.[52]

[49] Whittaker to Sandys, May 1621, Ferrar Papers.
[50] MS. Rec. Va. Co., III, Part ii, 15a-16.
[51] Ibid., III, Part ii, 17.
[52] Ibid., III, Part ii, 21-21a.

But despite all the attention given the subject in the company's letters there was not at any time adequate provision for housing newcomers. It was necessary to provide for them in the homes of older settlers, thereby making more acute the ill effects of a general deficiency in housing facilities which some considered a primary factor in the colony's suffering. The consequent overcrowding, the spreading of infectious diseases, and the dangerous exposure resulting from a lack of adequate facilities in the average household to care for extra persons are all objectionable features of this practise that require no comment.

It is little wonder that under such circumstances there was much suffering and sickness. Some of the more strongly constituted recovered from the first attack, and after becoming acclimated continued to enjoy good health. But many others were not so fortunate. An appalling number of them died, and scores of those who survived recovered only slowly and were for a long time thereafter unfitted for work. Many probable causes were suggested in letters home. Some of their misfortunes they attributed to improper selection of colonists, some to the hardships of the voyage and the season of arrival, some to their drink, some to exposure, and all agreed upon the shortness and badness of their food as one of the major factors. Captain Nuce was at a loss to understand in 1621 " how so many people sent hither of late years have been lost . . . unless it be through water and want, partly of good food, but chiefly of good Lodging, which have been the only causes of the death of so many as came with me." [53]

Some suggested that psychological conditions were partly responsible. Nuce thought that " the conceipt of their 7 years servitude " caused many to lose heart, and suggested a shorter term of indenture. And Thorpe, a keen observer, was of the opinion in 1620 " that more do die here of the disease of their mind than of their body

[53] Nuce to Sandys, May 27, 1621, Ferrar Papers.

by having this country's victuals over-praised unto them in England and by not knowing they shall drink water here." [54] One can readily imagine the effect upon colonists, who had been enlisted by the most highly colored picture of Virginia and the prospect of improving their position in the new world, when they arrived to find a country only in the first stages of development, their supply of food, clothing, and other equipment inadequate, and then to be seized with an attack of diarrhea, crowded into a household where their presence was probably resented, and to lie there for days under the scourge of a severe fever. There must have been little in the stern reality that fulfilled the glowing anticipations with which they had sailed from England. It was enough to make them despair, and to leave those who survived neither in a mood nor in a condition to promote with enthusiasm those " public ends " for which they had been sent.

The amount of sickness and death varied from year to year, and from one plantation to another, according to varying conditions of time and place. But there was no year from the first to the last in which the colony was entirely free from this scourge, nor was there any plantation which escaped. According to John Rolfe there was much suffering during the first year after Sandys' election, when he rushed with such ill-advised haste into his plans for colonizing Virginia. Of all newcomers those of Martin's Hundred located at Argall Town with good and convenient houses fared best. Many of them died, but the mortality there could not be compared with that of other plantations.[55] All told, some 300 colonists were reported to have died during the year.[56] The immigrants who reached Virginia the next year were a poor lot of whom the governor despaired from the first; and the ensuing winter witnessed

[54] Thorpe to John Smyth, December 19, 1620, Smyth of Nibley Papers, 33.
[55] Rolfe to Sandys, January, 1619/20, Ferrar Papers.
[56] *Records*, I, 320.

much privation and death. In 1621 even greater suffering was avoided only by trade with the natives and a privately financed magazine from home. So far was Sandys at this time from success in his program of colonization that Yeardley was removed from office, and an entirely new beginning was made by the company in a last great effort to put into practise contemporary theories on colonization.

Sandys was not entirely to blame for these disasters which contributed so much to the final ruin of his hopes and ambitions. One cannot read through the records of the company without recognizing that colonization was yet in the experimental state when many errors were altogether unavoidable and inexperience still exacted a heavy price. But a heavy burden of responsibility must rest upon him for his ill-considered measures. Had he proceeded with greater care, sent fewer colonists and more supplies, and given the governor time to make preparation for their reception, there would have been a different story to write.

CHAPTER VII

FAILURE IN VIRGINIA AND
BANKRUPTCY AT HOME

THE conditions resulting from Sandys' methods of colonization explain in great part his failure to find for Virginia that profitable place in England's trade, upon which depended his whole plan for building both the company and colony into a prosperous and happy state. Failure in his program of colonization was accompanied by failure in the attempt to establish new staple commodities, and by the collapse of the company's finances. When the government completed its investigation in 1624, it was found not only that the net increase in population was merely 275 souls but that these people were still largely dependent upon tobacco, and that the company itself was bankrupt.

An essential feature of Sandys' program had been the restriction of tobacco with a view to diverting the planters' attention to more wholesome commodities. Experience proved, however, that it was easier to decide upon such limitations in London than to make them effective in Virginia. Since the development of other commodities on a profitable basis was a long process which offered to the colonists no immediate prospect of a livelihood, it was especially necessary that they be well provided with the requisite supplies of food and clothing, in order that they might have both the time and will to devote their labors to Sandys' newly projected industries. But instead, his plans were foredoomed to failure by his policy of leaving to the colony the responsibility in the all important question of supply. From the first to the last, the chief and most urgent concern of the Virginian was an immediate supply of food and clothing. The production of a variety of new staples might be advisable for the future welfare of the colony, but there was little time to think of the future when the provisions for the next year were a pressing and imperative question of the moment. As a result most of their time was given to corn, from which must come their food, and to tobacco, the only crop offering any promise of ability to purchase clothes upon the arrival of the company's magazine. There was thus, of course, little time left to experiment with new staples. Captain Nuce explained to Sandys in 1621 that if he would consider the great labor they were put to for food, he would " not wonder that so great works as you expect to be done have so slow progress." [1]

Typical of the efforts of Sandys' agents to carry out his instructions was the experience of William Weldon. His men upon landing in the fall of 1619 found their supplies so inadequate that Yeardley was forced to put out half of them as servants for a year. And although this caused much discontent among the men, they bore it all patiently until Weldon acquainted them with the restriction to be placed upon their growth of tobacco. At this they complained bitterly that they had no other means of furnishing their apparel for another year and might even, if the restraint held, be faced with starvation. So far as Weldon could see, they " spoke the truth," and he decided with the approval of Yeardley to remove the restriction for a year, although he promised that he would attempt to limit the amount as far as was possible by " enjoining them to set as much corn as they could attend." [2]

Under such circumstances it is not surprising that efforts at reducing the production of tobacco failed completely. No better evidence of the failure can be found than the continued and repeated attempts of the company to devise some effective method of achieving this end. Two years after his election Sandys was still searching for some means of restricting that " smoky weed," declaring that the pres-

[1] Nuce to Sandys, May 27, 1621, Ferrar Papers.
[2] Weldon to Sandys, March 6, 1619/20, Ferrar Papers.

ent growth was displeasing " to the king and scandalous unto the Plantation and unto the whole Company." A court in June, 1621, tried to cope with the problem by an order definitely limiting the amount of tobacco planted to not above 100 weight the head,[3] and instructions to the colony a month later insisted that this order be strictly observed according to his majesty's advice and the desire of the whole state.[4] But this was no more successful than were earlier regulations, and Virginia remained so dependent upon tobacco that Sandys found it necessary to give his attention in the last months of his control almost entirely to arrangements for its profitable disposal in England. It is impossible to read through the records of the famous fight over the tobacco contract in 1622 and 1623 without recognizing that even Sandys had accepted the company's dependence upon tobacco. From the first of his administration to the last, despite all that he could do, the chief interest and energy of the Virginia planter was devoted to his tobacco crop.

The factors contributing more particularly to the failure of his plans for new staples may be followed through the fortunes of his most favored projects. For two years his chief interest was in an attempt at the production of iron. Here, as in so many other instances, Sandys exhibited a tendency to rush with too much haste and enthusiasm into plans that were not well thought out, and for which the necessary preliminary study and preparations had not been made. There was not at the time evidence of a sufficient store of ore to justify the investment made in the project, and there were those who pointed this out to Sandys. In 1620 John Pory in writing of the iron-works suggested that so important a work " should have taken more time of deliberation there in England." He felt especially that some skilled men should have surveyed the country for a year at least to make certain of " some abun-

---

[3] *Records*, I, 480.   [4] MS. Rec. Va. Co., III, Part ii, 11.

dant iron mine and fit places to work it in," for the small quantities of ore found on the surface in late years did not at all guarantee a store that could be worked with profit.[5] This warning, however, came too late to be of any use, for the occasion of Pory's letter was the landing of the first "carpenters" for the iron-works in May, 1620. The voyage to Virginia had already struck a heavy blow at this favored project, for the "chief men for the iron works" had died at sea, and there was little prospect that the survivors could accomplish much toward the establishment of the industry. Little "or nothing will be done therein this summer," the governor informed Sandys, "it being a hot and heavy work, if this summer with all the means I have to help them I can but build lodgings and transport their materials I shall think I have done well."[6] Within a few months their short supplies, the summer heat, diarrhea, and fever had fulfilled Yeardley's fears for the lives of that year's settlers, and the investment in the iron-works was a complete loss. Before the winter was passed all the principal officers and men for the iron-works had died.

Much the same fate met all other projects launched by Sandys between 1619 and 1621. Silk, which had seemed so promising and in which the king had taken a great interest, failed because of unsuccessful efforts to send cocoons. Two successive contributions by the king in 1619 and 1620 were lost in the long passage across the Atlantic.[7] Nor had there been anything accomplished by 1621 in the production of wine. The people were reported as loath to follow the company's instructions for the setting and cultivating of vines. The greatest progress had been made on the college land where 10,000 vines were set, but they as yet were bearing no fruit.[8] In the same year the company

---

[5] Pory to Sandys, June 12, 1620, Ferrar Papers.

[6] Yeardley to Sandys, June 7, 1620, Ferrar Papers.

[7] Force, *Tracts*, III, No. 5, p. 11; Pory to Sandys, June 12, 1620, Ferrar Papers.

[8] Thorpe to J. Ferrar, May 15, 1621, Ferrar Papers.

upbraided the colony most severely for its failure in the production of salt, pitch, tar, soap, and ashes. In spite of the great charge to which the company had been put in sending men and materials for these works, they still received complaints at the shortage of these commodities for the use of the colony itself.[9] It was partly due to a lack of time and interest on the part of the colonists, but it was also in part a justification of Pory's judgment in 1620 that there was no hope for profit in some of these products. He doubted the value of pitch and tar especially, for although these products were found in Virginia, the trees from which they came were so scattered that the cost of production would make impossible any competition with Poland where the trees were found in compact groups. His opinion was the same on timber, of which there was a plentiful supply and such as would serve the colony well, but in his opinion the freight to Europe would increase the cost to such an extent that the profit would be almost nothing.[10] There had been no progress in the production of flax, hemp, and "silke grasse," all of which the company had held to be of great hope, and officials in London attributed entirely to negligence and inexperience reports from Virginia that the difficulties of these industries were too great to be overcome.[11] Nor had any steps been taken toward the development of fishing and shipbuilding industries such as later proved the salvation of New England.

Thus it is seen that by 1621 Sandys' whole program had met with failure at every point. He had gambled all on the ability of his settlers to return a quick profit on their labors. But many of them had died, the remainder had suffered severe privation and sickness, and none of their projects for new staple commodities had succeeded.

The disastrous condition of the colony was reflected

---

[9] MS. Rec. Va. Co., III, Part ii, 13.
[10] Pory to Sandys, June 12, 1620, Ferrar Papers.
[11] MS. Rec. Va. Co., III, Part ii, 3.

in the equally deplorable state of the company's finances. The profit which Sandys had expected in 1619 had not materialized. The only returns from Virginia had been a few shiploads of tobacco. But while this tobacco had been of some help to the colonists, it had proved just the opposite to the company, which suffered consistent losses in the sale of its tobacco in Europe. There were several conditions in this trade which operated to the disadvantage of the company. One difficulty came from their inability to make satisfactory arrangements with the farmers of the government monopoly of tobacco for the importation of Virginia's crop into England. In fact, the conditions of importation were so unsatisfactory that in 1620 the company resorted to sending its crop direct to Holland. Further losses were suffered because of the very poor quality of tobacco produced in the colony — a condition due in part to the unsatisfactory methods used by the colonists in curing their leaf. George Thorpe entered a second and very urgent request in 1621 for lines to use in the " sweating " of their tobacco, and warned the company that, unless something were done to give them " speedy remedy " in this, it would prove the undoing of the colony and " the crop of this year will as it were utterly perish." [12] In the same year, the company's factor in Holland warned that unless the next consignment of tobacco were better than that of the previous year there was no hope at all for its sale, " for albeit it passed once yet the wary buyer will not be again taken." [13]

Even greater loss resulted from the stabilization of tobacco prices in Virginia. In 1618 an attempt had been made to meet some of the complaints from the colony at excessive prices charged for the Magazine's goods, by establishing the price of tobacco in exchange for the goods of the cape merchant at 3s. per pound for the better grade

[12] Thorpe to J. Ferrar, May 15, 1621, Ferrar Papers.
[13] MS. Rec. Va. Co., III, Part ii, 19.

and 18d. for the second, and by placing a limit of twenty-five percent. on the profit allowed to the Magazine.[14] A falling market, however, had resulted in a considerable loss to the company and its magazines, since the market value of tobacco in England was not equal to the price set in Virginia.

The council explained this situation to the colony in 1621. From the old Magazine, closed out in January, 1620, they had no hope for more than half of the £7,000 invested, and to date they had not received " any one penny." To make matters worse the supply sent in 1620 had been returned with a loss of the principal itself. Of some 40,000 weight of tobacco, over half had not yielded 17d. per pound and the remainder not above 2s. The market by the summer of 1621 had fallen even lower, and in setting forth the magazine provided that fall by private capital, the company insisted that the manager should be absolutely free in determining the price to be allowed for tobacco received in return for his goods " according to the prices and instructions he hath here given unto him by the Adventurers, whose unanimous resolution and charge is not to accept of tobacco at 3s. per pound." There were certain difficulties in this change affecting economic relations within the colony itself, where tobacco at 3s. had become the standard medium of exchange. Some planters, therefore, had proposed that the standard price be allowed to hold but that the magazines should increase the price of their commodities sufficiently to meet the difference between this artificial value of tobacco and its actual market value. The company, however, flatly refused to entertain the suggestion lest " we should maintain the Colony in their overweening esteem of their darling Tobacco to the overthrow of all other Staple Commodities, and likewise continue the evil will they have conceived there, and the scandalous reports here spread of oppression and exactions from the

[14] *Supra*, pp. 50-52.

Company selling all their Commodities for three times the value of what they cost, upon which found and unjust surmises they think it lawful to use all manner of deceit and falsehood in their tobacco that they put of the Magazine." [15]

Even more disastrous to the common treasury than the losses on tobacco was the termination of the lotteries in 1621. From them had come by far the greater portion of the company's revenue for the past two years. In fact, Sandys had drawn upon this one dependable source of income to such an extent that he made of the Virginia lottery a general nuisance to the kingdom, and thereby brought about its dissolution. The lottery, with its doubly effective appeal to the gambling instinct and the philanthropic spirit of the people, had rendered valiant service to the company, but there was a limit to the total revenue that could be derived from this source. And Barbor by two years of energetic " surveys through England " had wellnigh reached that limit. The minutes of the courts record in November of 1620 that " the Lotteries were allmost spent." And the leaders were greatly concerned because of an increasing chorus of complaint and criticism directed at the administration of the lotteries, which threatened the loss of those small sums that might yet be expected to aid in tiding them over to the next year, when there was hope of relief from Virginia for their sore financial problems. On November 4 Sandys suggested to the court the advisability of a " printed publication " setting forth several things, the second point thereof " to be in the behalf of the Lottery now of late very much disgraced that it may be delivered of many foul aspersions unjustly cast upon it by malignant tongues." [16]

Sandys' enemies in the company were probably responsible for some of these " aspersions." During the investiga-

[15] MS. Rec. Va. Co., III, Part ii, 19-19a; *Records*, II, 480.
[16] *Records*, I, 410-412.

tion of 1623 they were violent in their attack upon the administration of the lotteries, charging fraud and mismanagement and declaring that the lotteries had been a means of robbing and deceiving his majesty's subjects. They were especially severe in their indictment of Barbor as " a man of a poor and weak estate, who appointed his substitutes at his own will and pleasure men unknown to the Company and unsworn to deal therein." Their chief charge was that he had converted seven or eight thousand pounds to his own use, and had avoided being called to account by bribing the auditors.[17] Any statement at this time was probably highly colored, and Sandys' enemies were perhaps merely making use of the general ill repute into which the lotteries had fallen. It is safe to conclude, however, that the usual abuses attendant upon lotteries were present from 1619 to 1621, and that in this case they were aggravated by Sandys' tendency to overwork this source of income. Objections to the lotteries found expression in parliament, and the license was withdrawn by an order in council of March 4, 1621, which explained that the order was given in response to the complaint of parliament.[18]

Sandys was thus left from 1621 without a single source of revenue upon which he could rely for any considerable sums, and from that date there is increasing evidence of the serious state of the company's finances. Shares in the joint-stock of a nominal value of £12 10s. were selling in May for 40s. and 50s.[19] In June the Deputy explained that his accounts for the preceding year could not be presented because there was not yet money enough in the treasury to discharge his indebtedness. He was given a respite until the debts could be met, and late in the fall this respite was extended indefinitely. Nor had Sandys by this date cleared

[17] Manchester Papers, 344.
[18] Bancroft Transcripts, Virginia Papers, I, 357-358.
[19] *Records*, I, 469.

the accounts for his first year's administration.[20] The effect of these conditions on the morale of the company was such that in October Ferrar felt called upon to exhort the adventurers

not to be discouraged for that he hoped God had still a hand in the protection of Virginia who turned all things for the best when divers former Projects in their first appearance seemed to tend towards the very destruction of the Plantation; and therefore hoped that having put their hands to the Plough they would not now look back nor be weary of well doing for the Action itself was such as he knew no man but confessed it to be the most Christian, honorable and glorious, and of high consequence unto this commonwealth, and though they might seem to some to have cast their bread upon the waters, yet after many days he doubted not but they should find it again to their great comfort.[21]

It is a tribute to Sandys' courage that he did not give up now, but instead proceeded with even greater determination to map out plans for another effort to carry through his original program. One of the steps taken was the removal of Yeardley. The events of two years had bred considerable dissatisfaction on both sides of the Atlantic. Letters from the company had already assumed the caustic note which characterized them for two years thereafter, and Yeardley, while complaining about the haste and lack of care in preparations at home, had expressed a desire to be relieved of the unhappy duties of his office. As the end of his three year term approached he requested permission to surrender his place to Captain George Thorpe, a man whom he considered worthy of the position. He hoped that he could then be free to give his attention wholly to Southampton Hundred, the plantation in which he with the leading members of Sandys' party were the chief adventurers, and which he felt, partly through his absence, had " so much miscarried." There

[20] *Ibid.*, I, 487, 557-558.   [21] *Ibid.*, I, 537-538.

was little satisfaction in looking backward over his administration, but as relief from his duties drew near he was not disposed to find comfort in criticism of mistakes at London so much as in submission to the will of God.

What am I that I should be able to do anything against which the Lord of Lords hath otherwise disposed, [he wrote Sandys] or what are we all that we should gainsay the Allmighty, and although as I do acknowledge all things have been most effectually and wisely projected, yet if the Lord will lay his hand upon us and cross us with sickness and mortality, and so appoint in his providence a longer time for the bringing those matters to pass which are by man determined of, what then shall he say unto these things but that it is the Lord, let him do what he please, and although he kill yet still to trust in him, not doubting but there is a time wherein he will be merciful, for my part as I know my conscience to be clear from any neglect in me of what I have been able to do to the utmost of my power, so will I not justify myself but that my sins and unworthiness have gone together with the rest both of the people here and the company at home.[22]

In accord with his wish and the best opinion of the company, he was not pressed to continue in office. And Sir Francis Wyatt was chosen in the summer of 1621 to succeed Yeardley at the expiration of his term on November 18.[23]

Lengthy instructions preceded the new governor to the colony. Copies of all commissions and instructions drawn up in 1618, including the " greate Charter " and the ordinance providing for the assembly, were forwarded with directions to revise all features of the colony's government and organization which were not in accord with these documents. More important, however, was a lengthy document outlining the company's economic policies with detailed instructions for the coöperation of the colony in

---

[22] Yeardley to Sandys, Ferrar Papers.   [23] *Records*, I, 440.

their execution.[24] The colonists were once again exhorted on the question of tobacco and on the necessity of producing ample food supplies. Much stress was put upon the great need for guest houses, and Dutch " sawmill men " had been secured to provide more fully the materials necessary to meet the housing problem. The council was instructed to restrict the excessive fees charged by officers, of which there had been much complaint, to superintend the building of corn mills and bakehouses, and to make proper provision for the care and breeding of cattle. But chief attention was given to new and more elaborate plans for the development of staple commodities. The company expressed its great disappointment in the general failure of previous efforts, and upbraided the colonists somewhat for their negligence and lack of interest in this most important work. It was hoped that their hearty cooperation in the plans now on foot would lead to more satisfactory results.

Sandys' unfortunate experience with colonial tobacco had strengthened his conviction that the only hope for Virginia lay in a healthy production of a wider variety of staples. And with the single but all important exception of looking to the condition of the colonists in matters of food, clothing, and health, he once again mapped out plans that were admirable for their scope and completeness. Once more he attempted the establishment of an iron industry, and sent John Berkley to have charge of this work and a new group of twenty skilled men who accompanied him.[25] But from this time on the company, disappointed in its last effort and probably influenced by the opinion of the king, came to consider silk the product most worthy of their attention, and so informed the colonial leaders. Several supplies of cocoons secured from

[24] Council to Governor and Council in Virginia, July 24, 1621, MS. Rec. Va. Co., III, Part ii, 11-14.

[25] *Records*, I, 472, 475-476.

France, Italy, and Spain were forwarded at various intervals through the year,[26] and the governor was instructed to see to the planting of mulberry trees in every plantation. A large number of "excellent books" on the culture of this product were sent for the instruction of the colonists, and to direct the work the company secured "at great cost" experienced men from France.[27] The cultivation of vineyards was again especially recommended and officials of the colony were charged with providing for French "vignerons" who were being sent at considerable cost to the company. A new project was undertaken in the sending of Italians skilled in glass work to set up under the leadership of Captain William Norton furnaces for glass beads and pottery.[28] In addition to these four major projects, the company again laid great stress on the possible production of naval stores, "silke grasse," hemp, and flax. They were commanded also to search for mineral dyes, gums, drugs, and "the like." And finally all "artsmen" were to be held to their work, apprentices were to be trained in useful trades, and none of them were to be allowed to quit them for tobacco or any other such "useless commodities."

The most significant provision of this document, however, was for the establishment of a new office in Virginia to have general supervision over all these projects. The council explained that "there hath been in these late years great fault or defect in not putting in execution our orders of court and council for the setting up and upholding those staple commodities . . . which hath happened in part by our charging the Governor with too much business." They had therefore chosen George Sandys, brother to Sir Edwin, to hold the new office of treasurer in consideration of his faithfulness and knowledge of "our intentions and counsels whereunto he hath been from time to time privy."

[26] *Records*, I, 431, 483, 510.
[27] *Ibid.*, I, 432, 459-466, 543.
[28] *Ibid.*, II, 375.

To his care was committed the "execution of all our orders, charters, and instructions tending to the setting up, increase, and maintaining of the said Staple Commodities." In addition, he was to attend to the collection of all rents and dues belonging to the company, of which £1,000 were already due, but his chief function was to oversee all newly projected industries. Fifteen hundred acres were allotted to the support of this office and fifty tenants, of which twenty-five were sent then and the rest were to follow in the spring.[29]

The Indian massacre in March, 1622, disrupted the whole life of the colony and cut short this second attempt of Sandys before his plans were given anything like a fair trial. But even so, there seems only a small probability that he would have been rewarded with any great success. Some of his projects, notably silk, were doomed to failure from the very beginning simply because the climate of Virginia was not suitable. A more important factor to consider, however, was the inability of the company because of its financial stringency to give to this program the vigorous support from London that was so necessary under any circumstances. Even had responsible officials at home benefited by two years' experience, which is not at all certain, they were not now able to make any practical use of these lessons. Once more as in 1619, the company proceeded in all of its plans from the assumption that the colonists could be self-supporting and begin at once a large number of profitable enterprises.

It is clear enough that from the summer of 1621 the company was for all practical purposes bankrupt. Every crop since Sandys' election had been sold at a loss, every magazine had been returned without profit, the deputy had incurred a considerable indebtedness in the performance of his office and in the following spring was still behind to the sum of £1,400,[30] the lotteries had been dis-

[29] *Ibid.*, I, 449-450, 464-465, 468.   [30] *Ibid.*, II, 19.

solved, and a greatly disheartened body of adventurers could be counted on for no large contributions. In the company's efforts after 1621, therefore, it was necessary to resort to all sorts of makeshifts which provided neither regular nor adequate support for the colony. The initial expense involved in several of the favored projects, such as wine and silk, was not necessarily heavy. The problem was to divert the attention of settlers already in Virginia from tobacco to these new industries, and the chief costs came in providing vines, silkworms, and a few foreign specialists to guide and direct the colonists in their efforts. By applying what small revenue the company could command to the purchase of supplies and by resorting to fishing licenses to cover the cost of transportation the company was able to meet the heaviest charge in this work.

A license to fish in all parts of the Virginia coast between 33 degrees and 45 degrees northerly latitude, with full rights to land, dry nets, etc., was issued to Captain John Huddleston, master of the *Bona Nova,* in November, 1621, in return for his agreement to carry to Virginia forty-five persons and their provisions. On the same day a similar license was granted to Daniel Gates, master of the *Darlinge,* for performing like services.[31] And there were two other commissions issued to Captain Smith of the *Hopewell* and Captain Jones of the *Discovery.*[32] By such means the company was able to send a few settlers for public lands, for its officers, and for the direction of its industries, but large scale emigration at public charge was no longer possible.[33] In August a request from a band of Walloons and French for permission to plant in Virginia received favorable action by the council, but it was necessary to append the statement that the company's stock was "so utterly ex-

[31] Add. MS., 14285, ff. 74a-75, 75a-76a.

[32] *Records,* I, 554, 562. For use of fishing commissions to cover the cost of transporting settlers after 1621 see *Ibid.,* II, 116, 156, 262, 449.

[33] Of the 1000 settlers sailing after the summer of 1621 only about 100 went at public charge. *Ibid.,* I, 538.

hausted by these three last years' supplies, as they are not able to give them any further help in that kind than only in point of advice and counsel for the cheapest transportation of themselves and goods." [34]

For more expensive projects it was necessary to fall back upon an extension of the practise of subsidiary joint-stocks. It was in this way that the newly projected glass-works were financed. Captain Norton proposed in June to take his family and personal servants to Virginia at his own cost and to carry with him six men skilled in the glass trade, provided the company would grant him a seven year monopoly of the industry and pay the cost of equipping and transporting the laborers. A bargain was accordingly agreed upon whereby Norton secured 400 acres of land and the requested monopoly in return for one half the profits accruing from the glass-works, whereof one fifth was to be remitted to Norton in reward for his services. It was found, however, that the company could not provide the £150 necessary to cover the transportation of the six men and their families, eleven persons in all, without going into debt, and when upon further calculation it was discovered that another £80 would have to be added for materials and equipment the company was forced to surrender the plan. [35] It was then offered in joint-stock to private adventurers at a capitalization of £500, the joint-stock to take the bargain upon the same terms and the company to enter for one fourth part of the adventure.

In addition the rolls of four other joint-stocks were opened for subscription by the adventurers that summer and fall, one to provide for ship-builders to be sent for the construction of shallops, one for a fur trade with the natives, another for apparel, and another for the shipment of " 100 maids to be made wives." [36] Although Sandys and

[34] State Papers, Colonial, James I, Vol. I, No. 55.
[35] *Records*, I, 484, 493, 498-499, 500-501, 507.
[36] *Ibid.*, I, 513-514, 557, 565-567.

Southampton led the way with liberal subscriptions of £200 a piece in testimony of their "zeal and constant resolution to advance the Plantation," [37] the rolls were underwritten but slowly, and it was only by the energetic efforts of company officials that the subscriptions were finally completed. By November the stocks for the glass-works and for a magazine of supplies were closed out at £500 and £1,800 respectively, but the adventurers were still being solicited for subscription to the three remaining rolls the following January, although £800 had been secured for the matrimonial venture and £900 for the fur trade.[38]

By such emergency measures the administration was able to tide over the difficulties of 1621, but they faced the next year with much apprehension. Beyond the fact that a dependence upon subsidiary joint-stocks offered little chance of rebuilding public revenues, there was serious concern for the future welfare of the colony because the ability of the adventurers to send further supplies and necessary equipment depended almost entirely upon the outcome of the present year's private ventures. With the public stock "utterly exhausted" and the company left with "no means of supply but from private purses," [39] the colony was now dependent for future supplies upon a method in which the hard question of profit and loss would be the determining factor in its continuance.

Especially serious was the question of food and clothing. There was considerable trouble in securing the underwriting of these essential supplies in 1621 because of the general dislike of subscriptions to be "paid in smoke," and should this venture fail, the problem another year would be almost insolvable. Officials at home were well aware of the seriousness of the situation when in dispatching the supply of 1621 they warned the colony that, should this

[37] *Records*, I, 522-523.   [39] MS. Rec. Va. Co., III, Part ii, 21.
[38] *Ibid.*, I, 576-577, 583.

venture fail as had the former, " it is vain ever to hope for like supplies from hence: for want whereof if the Colony fall upon any calamity or misery, theirs be the shame and guilt whose fault it is; as for us, it will be our comforts neither to have failed in abundance of charities hitherto, nor in timely advice and warnings now given." It was their hope that this evidence of the company's interest would lead them to make a profitable return of the stock now sent and " not as hitherto evil and disgraceful words for our zeal of their welfare, and nothing at all or at least less than the principal laid out." Their insistence came only from a love of the colony and the hope that by a good return of this venture the colonists might " encourage and confirm the good minds of the old Adventurers, by many losses almost beaten out, and draw in many men into the Company, and which most of all perhaps concerneth the Colony, establish a constant and large trade with them, whereby not only all their wants, but even their desires, will be at all times plentifully furnished." [40]

It was a hopeless situation. Tobacco alone was produced in sufficient quantities to offer any possibility of payment for these supplies, and its poor quality together with marketing conditions at home offered little prospect of profit. The only hope seemed to be in other commodities, and yet the company was not able, except through this trade of which Sandys wrote, to provide the supplies and conditions of life in Virginia necessary to their development. The situation in the colony was essentially the same as before 1621. Settlers sent now by the company were, as in the first two years, poorly provisioned and equipped. Peter Arondelle's complaint in December, 1621, is the same as that of earlier settlers. Mr. Deputy Ferrar had promised him " provision for a whole year beforehand, a house ready built, and Cattle; which proved far defective." For food his men had only a pint and a half of " musty meal for

[40] *Ibid.*, III, Part ii, 19-20.

a man a day," and he was told by the deputy there that there had come with them " scarce enough for half a year's provision." As for promises of other necessary provisions there was " not one observed." [41]

In truth, the only hopeful feature of the company's finances was its inability to send colonists. This would have proved a real blessing to the colony had it not been that a large emigration continued to private plantations at the charge of individual associations of adventurers. Officials gave even more encouragement to these enterprises now that the company was forced to abandon any extensive colonization of its own. Plans in the fall of 1621 called for the transportation of 1,000 settlers the following spring under the terms of several patents issued to private associations, and the company warned the colony that these people would go " slenderly furnished hence." [42] The carelessness of officials in checking up on the provisions of these private settlers, as also the impression deliberately encouraged by the company that new arrivals could quickly become self-supporting, must be considered one of the major factors contributing to the great suffering which followed the massacre.

These conditions and the short time before the massacre allowed for little progress in the new industries. A number of mulberry trees were set out, and steps were taken for the care of vines.[43] One small sample of Virginia wine was sent home early in 1622, but its " musty cask " and the long voyage had so spoiled it that the council considered it more a " scandal " than a credit to the company. The curt request to send some " good wine " speaks well for its quality.[44] Nothing had come of the glass-works by the following summer,[45] and after the massacre the colony was

[41] Arondelle to Sandys, December 15, 1621, Ferrar Papers.
[42] *Records*, I, 537-538; MS. Rec. Va. Co., III, Part ii, 21a.
[43] MS. Rec. Va. Co., III, Part ii, 1.
[44] *Ibid.*, III, Part ii, 22.
[45] *Ibid.*, III, Part ii, 23.

in sore need of almost all products of iron.[46] Exportations from Sandys' staple industries seem to have been confined to this one sample of wine and the famous " fire-shovel and tongs and a little bar of iron," which his enemies scornfully proclaimed the only fruit of an expenditure of £5,000 in the iron-works.[47]

And yet leaders in the colony seem to have been more optimistic during the winter of 1621–1622 than at any time before. The colonists arriving the preceding fall came in better health, and there are fewer references to sickness during the winter. It is true that many newcomers suffered from the customary shortage of provisions, but the fall magazine, while disastrous to the adventurers, relieved the colony of any immediate danger, and the older planters were becoming better acclimated. The company in replying to a letter of that winter was happy to know of the good " entry " made in the iron-works and other staples.[48]

Any causes for optimism that may have existed, however, were completely removed by the Indian massacre of March, 1622. A colony composed of widely scattered and poorly defended groups of planters, whose economic life was yet to be placed on a secure footing, were visited by murder and pillage, forced to abandon over half of their settlements, and, unable to provide for themselves, were left dependent upon a bankrupt company. The inability of the company to provide adequately for an emergency due in part to its own mistakes was responsible for one of the most miserable stories of suffering and death in colonial history.

On March 22, 1622, the long standing peace with the natives was suddenly broken by an attack on the Virginia settlements resulting in the massacre of over 300 men, women, and children. This treachery seems to have taken the settlers almost entirely by surprise. There had been

[46] *Ibid.*, III, Part ii, 3a.   [48] MS. Rec. Va. Co., III, Part ii, 22-23.
[47] Manchester Papers, 362.

some warning of an approaching conspiracy against the whites in the preceding year, but authorities had failed to find any proof, the Indians had denied all such imputations, and the colonists, as the passage of time seemed to confirm these denials, allowed their vigilance to lapse.[49] As a result they were quite unprepared for the blow when it fell.

In addition to the element of surprise, there were several other factors which explain the great damage wrought by the Indians. The most severe criticism of the company, both in the colony and at home, after the massacre was directed at its policy of " straggling " plantations. The planters had been strung out in small settlements over a comparatively large area, and their defense against any general attack by the natives was thereby greatly weakened. Their situation might not have been so precarious had more of Sandys' immigrants lived to provide in each plantation a good body of healthy and able-bodied men. But the ravages of disease and death had left in far too many settlements only a small band, weak in numbers and in provision for defense. To add to their difficulties there was an astonishing shortage of arms and munition. Nor was it possible for these dispersed settlers to withdraw with speed and safety at the first alarm to any centrally located place of security, where they might find adequate provision for their maintenance and defense. The difficulty of accomplishing such a withdrawal was increased by the absence of a sufficient number of shallops to be used in the transportation of settlers and their goods.[50]

Regardless of all difficulties, however, they were forced to undertake a partial withdrawal of the colonists to Jamestown. Four settlements, Charles City, the Iron Works, the

---

[49] MS. Rec. Va. Co., III, Part ii, 4-5a, 23a.

[50] The sending of ship-builders, for which subscriptions were solicited through several months after the summer of 1621, was not accomplished until the summer of 1622.

College Land, and Martin's Hundred were entirely abandoned to the natives who proceeded to do further destruction on their forsaken houses and cattle. And according to communications from the colony, an even larger number of settlements would have been abandoned had it not been for the difficulty of retiring from so many " dispersed and straggling " plantations with any hope of saving the people with their goods and cattle.[51] But the withdrawal of these persons was only of slight help in solving the problems growing out of the massacre. In fact, officials were faced now with many serious questions arising from the congested conditions of life in Jamestown and the other settlements to which they still held. The ever present shortage of food and provisions was made more acute by the unavoidable abandonment of some of their stores. To replace these stores in Virginia was no easy task. The hostility of the natives required the time and labor of many men in guard duty. It was impossible to avoid some reduction in the acreage of crops and a postponement of the planting season now almost upon them. All told, the colony's plight was more serious than it had been at any time since Sandys had taken control.

At the first opportunity, which was in April, a letter was dispatched to the company acquainting them with the " treachery of the Indians " and the disastrous state in which they had left the colony.[52] Two things were urged upon the company as of especial consequence to the safety of the entire colony. Most important of all was the question of fortifications and defense. This had been a pressing problem since before Sandys' election, the solution of which had been frequently urged upon the colony by the company and in turn by colonial officials upon the leaders in London. Governor Argall had repeatedly urged the necessity of attention to this need during his term of

[51] MS. Rec. Va. Co., III, Part ii, 3, 23a-25.
[52] Ibid., III, Part ii, 3-3a.

office, and his successors continued to do so after his removal.

These requests were prompted not so much by a fear of the Indians, however, as by the general apprehension of some attack by the Spanish. This fear of the Spaniard was a very real thing both with the company and in Virginia, and the apprehension of the colony had been increased considerably at the time of the *Treasurer's* affair by the possibility of some retaliation for the depredations of English pirates in the West Indies. In fact, Captain Elfrith had brought with him from the West Indies rumors of an intended attack in the following spring. This report had "much disheartened the people," who had no place of retreat, and John Rolfe felt called on to press upon Sandys at great length the weakness of their defenses and to urge that he consult with Argall concerning the best steps to be taken for their immediate strengthening.[53]

For three years, however, the company did nothing further than give advice. The instructions preceding Wyatt in 1621 directed that no offense should be given any foreign prince or people by the reception of pirates, and required of the governor and council " serious Considerations for the speedy erecting of fortresses or Blockhouses at the mouth of the river as also for all other manner of Needful fortifications in all places." [54] A new office, that of marshal, to have supervision over all fortifications, arms, and armed forces of the colony, was also established in 1621, and conferred upon Captain William Nuce, who was well recommended to the company as a man of judgment and experience in military affairs. In accord with the usual practice, 1,500 acres were allotted to the support of this office with 50 tenants, and £400 were to be appropriated to cover the charge of settling these tenants.[55] But

[53] Rolfe to Sandys, January, 1619/20, Ferrar Papers.
[54] MS. Rec. Va. Co., III, Part ii, 11.
[55] *Records*, I, 453, 454, 464–465, 468, 482–483.

due to various hindrances, of which financial difficulties were probably the greatest, Nuce did not sail until late in 1622.

Thus it may be seen that no really effective steps had been taken by the adventurers prior to the massacre. The financial condition of the company forbad any real help from home, and in December, 1621, the council had advised the governor that although they had " labored diligently in the matter of fortifications " they could as yet promise nothing. Until the company could find some relief from its financial embarrassments the colony must make up for lack of strength by care.[56] This letter was crossed in passage by another from the colony insisting once again upon the urgency of immediate relief. They asked especially that engineers might be sent and for permission, should it be found advisable, to remove the principal city to some more secure location.[57] But though this letter prodded officials at home to the first actual preparations for sending men and materials, they had been awakened too late, and the massacre found the colonists no stronger in their defenses, and in some ways even weaker, than they had been at the time of Argall.

The bitter experience of the massacre demonstrated to the colonists that their first care should have been for defense, " by the neglect whereof the Plantation, though it hath seemed to go on in a hopeful and flourishing course, yet hath all this while gone but so much out of the way." It was a matter now in which they could afford no further delay. Authority was requested for the assembly to pick the best location for building the chief defenses of the colony, and permission was again asked to remove the principal town to the site so chosen. Further help would be required of the company in the sending of engineers skilled in fortifications along with a great store of spades, shovels, mattocks, pickaxes, and other tools, of which there

[56] MS. Rec. Va. Co., III, Part ii, 21a.   [57] *Ibid.*, III, Part ii, 1a.

was a shortage in Virginia. A matter of no less moment was a supply of arms and munitions, of which there was so great a want that at least a third of the men able to bear arms were " utterly unprovided thereof." In the meantime, the problem of immediate defense made it necessary for them to unite in more compact settlements and to be content with less land, and it was their hope that no patents would be granted in England for any plantation "to seat where they want to," but that the place and proportion of land for such grants would be left entirely to the direction of the governor in Virginia.

No less urgent was the problem of food. These precautionary steps taken for defense made their need even more distressing. Not only were two thirds of the survivors women, children, and other " unserviceable " people, but many of the able-bodied men would now be required to devote much of their time to guard duty for the protection of the people, cattle, and crops from further attack. This produced a shortage of labor, which together with their inability to protect more than a limited amount of land made necessary a reduction in the acreage of corn. And to all of these difficulties was added the fact that they were of necessity thrown late in their planting. Their only other resort in Virginia was to secure food by trade or force from the natives, but while they were willing to exert every effort in the attempt it was an uncertain and hazardous undertaking. They were compelled by these circumstances, therefore, to look to England for supply, and the company was warned that " there was never more cause to fear the miserable ruin of the Plantation by a relapse into an extreme famine than at this time, unless our want be supplied from home." They begged a year's supply of corn and that the company would send no " new comers " without adequate supplies for a full year.[58]

This plea of a stricken colony came to a company which

[58] MS. Rec. Va. Co., III, Part ii, 3-3a.

was in no wise prepared to offer any immediate and sufficient remedy. For a year the company's leaders in every
communication to the colony had been proclaiming its
bankruptcy and calling attention to the disappointment
and waning interest of its adventurers. They had seen no
hope for the future except in a profitable trade with the
colony, and had quite definitely shifted the responsibility
in this upon the shoulders of the planters. With the supply
of the previous fall had gone the warning that should this
fail as had all former supplies, they could hope for no
further aid from England. When this magazine arrived in
Virginia, however, the tobacco crop had already been disposed of to numerous independent captains in return for
some food but also a large proportion of drink, sweets, and
other commodities which were of little help in relieving
the needs of the colony.

Here was another factor operating to defeat efforts at
supplying the necessities of life from England — the policy
of free trade adopted in 1620. And after the experience of
1621 there was some discontent among the leaders of the
colony with this policy. They explained the failure of that
year's magazine by the fact that there had already come
into Virginia so many private merchants " equally recommended " that five times the crop of that year could not
have satisfied them, there being not above 60,000 weight
of tobacco in the whole colony. Many of their commodities, such as sacks, sweet meats, and strong liquors, were so
attractive to the people that unless officials denied free
trade " contrary to your orders " these men could not be
prevented from taking much of their tobacco, thereby
leaving not enough to provide for necessary food and
clothing.[59]

There is apparent no disposition on the part of the
administration to change its policy, however, and when
the magazine of 1621 was returned with the usual loss,

[59] *Ibid.*, III, Part ii, 4-5a.

officials were content in their last communication to the colony before the news of the massacre reached England to confirm their warning of the past year that little in the way of future supply could be expected of them. The council was very solicitous of the company's many debts, and once again insisted upon the absolute necessity of the colony's attention to their debts and revenue. The remedy was the same. Profitable commodities must be produced for export from Virginia that by the " good proceeds of their adventures " the members might be encouraged to continue the supply of their wants, " which by the delay of one year is set so much backward, whereof the damage is the Colony's, and ours the discontent and grief, who would willingly have continued our yearly supplies, if we might have been answered as was fit with yearly returns." [60]

Thus it may be seen that the company leaders had practically washed their hands of all serious consequences that might befall the colony. As they explained later in the year, " to speak plainly we shall never believe nor dare to attempt anything of great engagement and hazard, till by real example of some extraordinary work by you effected, we may have proof of the sincerity of your intentions and assurances not to be deluded and frustrated, as we have hitherto been in so great and chargeable undertakings." [61]

It is not surprising, therefore, that all attempts at the relief of the colony were both weak and inadequate, not merely because of the financial weakness of the company but because of the grudging and resentful manner in which they were undertaken by the company's officers. They would have been more than human had they not found a certain satisfaction in the justification of their previous warnings in the present plight of the colony. It was August before a reply was sent to the colony's letter, and

[60] MS. Rec. Va. Co., III, Part ii, 22-23.
[61] *Ibid.*, III, Part ii, 25a-27.

the council could not forbear to preach at great length of the shortcomings of the colonists as the chief explanation of this catastrophe. " We have to our extreme grief understood of the great massacre executed on our people in Virginia," the council wrote, " and that in such a manner as is more miserable than the death itself." To fall by the hands of men " so contemptible," to be surprised in a time of known danger, to be deaf to all warnings of conspiracy, even " to be made in part instruments of contriving it, and almost guilty of the destruction by a blindfold and stupid entertaining of it, which the least wisdom or courage sufficed to prevent even on the point of execution " were circumstances which added much to their sorrow. Through it all was apparent the hand of Almighty God in punishment of their sins. " Whence the evil therefore spring the remedy must fast begin," and an humble reconciliation with the " divine Majesty " was earnestly advised. In particular, it was necessary that a speedy redress should be made " of those two enormous excesses of apparel and drinking, the cry whereof cannot but have gone up to heaven, since the infamy hath spread itself to all that have but heard the name of Virginia to the detestation of all good minds, the scorn of others, and our extreme grief and shame." It was in these faults and in the neglect of divine worship that the Indians had prevailed, rather than in their weakness.

And since no strength of " situation " could save them without the protection of God, it was the opinion of the council that there was no point in moving their principal city. It was felt that they could make themselves as secure there as in any other location, and they were therefore so wholly to " abandon the thought thereof, as in this point not to return us any answer." The council was equally arbitrary in over-ruling the better opinion of the colony on the necessity of drawing the people closer together for purposes of defense. The leaders of Sandys' party, more

than ever conscious of the importance of the colony's reputation now that their own funds were exhausted, declared
the withdrawal from four plantations to be not only a
matter of discontent to them but of " evil fame," and insisted that they be replanted at once " lest the best fire
that maintains the action here alive be put out." Martin's
Hundred could be left to the adventurers of that particular plantation, but all others must be restored without
delay by the officials of the colony. And with all the prodigious labor involved in this assignment, they must find
time for a severe and satisfactory revenge against the
natives by the use of all methods of warfare. Finally, their
counsel was concluded with another sermon on staple
commodities, " the want whereof hath been the truest
objection against the succeeding of this plantation." [62]

As usual, the company was free in advice and counsel,
but in its response to the two most urgent requests from
Virginia, the council demonstrated its failure to realize
the true seriousness of the colony's condition, as well as
its inability to take any strong steps for relief. A petition
was made to the king for the use of a stock of old arms in
the London Tower, and with this was joined another asking for 400 young men " to repair with advantage the number that is lost, to set up the public revenues of the
Company, and satisfy the deserts of worthy persons in the
Colony." The first of these, after some delay, received
favorable action by the privy council, but the second met
with a flat refusal.[63]

Beyond these petitions, however, the council did no
more in the matter of defense than to proceed with plans
which had been formulated in March for the construction
of fortifications in the following spring. Repeated requests
from the colony, extending over several years and accompanied in the winter of 1621-1622 by offers to bear all

[62] MS. Rec. Va. Co., III, Part ii, 23a-25.
[63] *Records*, II, 351; Bancroft Transcripts, Virginia Papers, I, 481-482.

costs if only the company would provide engineers and tools, had finally stirred the council to action just at the time of the massacre. A Captain Each proposed to erect a fort on the "Oyster banks" by March of 1623 through the labor supplied by the colonists, members of his crew, and twelve carpenters he intended to carry with him, upon assurance of 60,000 weight of tobacco as freight on the return voyage at 3d. per pound. Sandys agreed to the proposal on the understanding that the full charge was to be borne by the colony and that Each was to be subject to the directions of the governor in Virginia. The preparations for his departure proceeded slowly through the summer. The colony was acquainted with these plans in June, when the company took some credit upon itself for having raised £300 for tools and other necessary equipment despite an indebtedness of near £2,000, a charge which the colony must also bear "for whose safety and security" it was done.[64] The news of the massacre, however, resulted in no acceleration of these preparations, and officials continued with their original plan.

Their response to the demand for food was even less satisfactory. "The fear of your want of corn doth much perplex us, seeing so little possibility to supply you," so wrote the council, "the public stock being utterly as you know exhausted, and the last year's Adventures made by Private men not returned, as was promised, we have no hope of raising any valuable Magazine." In fact, so uncertain was the prospect of a supply from England that "we cannot wish you to rely upon anything but yourselves." And while everything possible would be done, it was hoped "that the danger of this extremity will henceforward persuade you not to commit the certainty of your lives to the uncertainty of one harvest; and that at last you will understand it is as fit and necessary to yield the return

[64] MS. Rec. Va. Co., III, Part ii, 22-23; Sandys to J. Ferrar, April 30, 1622, Ferrar Papers.

of Adventures yearly as to receive them." [65] With this last thrust the company was content to leave the planters entirely to their own resources.

This disregard of the earnest plea from Virginia could be pardoned had there not been added to it the most colossal blunder of Sandys' party through four years marked by many errors in judgment. With almost the same breath that they lamented their inability to send food, the councillors were happy to inform the colony that there were to go " now over in this Ship, and are immediately to follow in some others many hundreds of people." And to these plans the administration stubbornly clung, despite the fact that later letters from Virginia brought a fuller realization of the true state of the colony. No factor contributed more to the suffering of the colonists through the ensuing winter, and nothing can show more clearly Sandys' failure to appreciate the most fundamental problems of colonization. These settlers of course went to private plantations at the cost of individual associations of adventurers, and they therefore constituted no drain on public funds. But while it is easy to understand how he accomplished this, the question why is more difficult. It is true that the colony's request that no settlers be sent without full supplies for a year could be taken as evidence of the governor's agreement to continued colonization. But the emphasis in this request was clearly upon the qualification, and the officers of the company, instead of paying heed, followed their usual policy of careless disregard for the supplies of private emigrants, and allowed these men to sail with such glaring deficiencies in their provisions that they added tremendously to the burdens of the stricken colony. [66]

The explanation of such action, beyond the general inability of Englishmen to appreciate the true conditions of life in America, must be sought in the fact that Sandys and his followers had not yet given up hope, and that de-

[65] MS. Rec. Va. Co., III, Part ii, 23a-25.   [66] Ibid., III, Part ii, 4-5a.

spite many discouragements they were still determined to carry on—a determination that may have been in part a stubborn refusal to admit defeat to their enemies. Just at this time negotiations with the government for the monopoly of tobacco importation gave hope of removing one of the chief difficulties that had stood in the way of reëstablishing the company's revenue. The ability to enlist these emigrants is in itself evidence of a continued interest in private settlements, and it must have seemed to Sandys that there was yet hope of success in his original program if he could hold things together until the tobacco negotiations were successfully completed. In the meantime, any discouragement of private enterprise, on which the company must rely until its own revenues were reëstablished, must be carefully avoided. As the council explained, " as we here think ourselves bound to give the best encouragements for their going in regard (that in the want of a public stock) there is no way left to increase the Plantation, but by abundance of private undertakers; so we think you obliged to give all possible furtherance and assistance for the good entertaining and well settling of them, that they may both thrive and prosper and others by their welfare be drawn after them." [67]

Further explanation must be found in the failure of Sandys and Ferrar to catch the full import of the colony's messages. The massacre caused no stir in the courts before the return of Captain Butler in the spring of 1623. Beyond the ratification of the petitions to the king for arms and a troop of young men, references to it are only incidental. The management of relief was of course in the hands of the council, which by the practical withdrawal of the Warwick party and the infrequent attendance of Smith's supporters had now become little more than a steering committee for the dominant party. It may have been that the council, for fear of the effect upon the nego-

[67] *Ibid.*, III, Part ii, 23a-25.

tiations for the tobacco contract, or of the use to which this news might be put by Sandys' enemies, not to mention the influence on public opinion and therefore on the support of the company, labored to present to the courts and public the most favorable account possible.

Certain it is that they considered the effect on Virginia's reputation and endeavored to belittle the importance of the attack in *A Declaration of the State of the Colonie and Affaires in Virginia* published in 1622.[68] This tract contained the familiar propaganda concerning the fertility of soil and the variety of commodities promised by Virginia. The transportation of 3,570 persons to the colony during the past three years and the use of 42 ships was pointed to with pride as evidence of the strength of the business. The massacre was referred to as no more than a temporary reversal, and was declared in truth to have done more good than harm, since the planters would naturally be more careful for their security in the future. What great state had not had its troubles and reversals? In short, Virginia was presented again as a great undertaking full of hope and worthy of the support of all men. The success of such measures may be gauged by the failure of Sandys' enemies to make any capital of the massacre until a year after the event. But despite this precautionary attempt to control public opinion, it is difficult to believe that even the responsible officials in the council were at any time aware of the true proportions of the disaster which threatened Virginia, although communications which arrived in the late summer and early fall gave to them a clearer understanding than they had possessed in August.

The plight of the colony had become more serious with the approach of summer. It had been necessary to abandon even more of their plantations, and the congestion within the small area they were prepared to defend had

[68] Edward Waterhouse, London, 1622.

become so great that Governor Wyatt had seen no hope
except by the immediate removal of a part of the people
to a new settlement farther up the Bay. Accordingly,
on June 20 he commissioned Yeardley to go in search of
some fit location for a new plantation. His instructions explained that the dispersal of settlers in recent years had
made impossible proper provision for common safety, and
that with the massacre it had become necessary to quit
most of " our habitations." And " such places as we now
hold in this River being already filled," it seemed advisable for Yeardley to levy a sufficient number to embark
upon a voyage of discovery along the western or eastern
shores of the Chesapeake Bay, " or any other of our Sea
Coasts which shall seem best to you within the limits of
33 and 40 degrees of Northerly latitude." There he was
to find some convenient place for a settlement of three or
four hundred men. On the site so chosen he was to begin
a new plantation, giving to all men four acres of land for
their particular employment. Full command and authority over the expedition was given to him, as also power to
make war or peace with the natives as occasion demanded.
John Pountis, Vice Admiral and Councillor of State, was
to be joined with him in command of this expedition and
settlement.[69] The project was never carried out, but the
news of it together with other information from Virginia
stirred officials in London to more active steps for relief.

Sandys had continued to direct the policies of the company, but he had been forced for some time by the pro-
tracted illness of his wife to leave the actual management
in the hands of the Ferrars. And while the ultimate responsibility is his, the first responsibility for the conduct
of affairs at this crisis in the colony's history, as in the matter of provisions for new settlers, must rest with the Ferrars.
Sandys, however, came up to London whenever there was
urgent need and the condition of his wife permitted. In

[69] MS. Rec. Va. Co., III, Part ii, 38.

October, as he hastened up from Northborn in answer to a summons from the lord treasurer about the tobacco business, he was exceedingly troubled by Mr. Ferrar's last account " of the desperate state of Virginia if I knew all." [70]

A week before his arrival in London a letter written in terms which showed not a little bitterness had informed the colonists of steps taken now for their relief. The council sharply opposed any abandonment of older settlements, considering it " a Sin against the dead to abandon the enterprise till we have fully settled the possession." They still entertained hopes of receiving from his majesty the means to restore public lands and to provide tenants which they understood to be wanting on the land of the governor and of other officials " not only to our grief, but wonder." The adventurers for Martin's Hundred had set forth a supply of people to repossess their plantation, an action which gave great encouragement to them all. Instead of surrendering their lands to the savages they must begin at once to avenge themselves upon those " bloody miscreantes." To aid them in discharging this public duty, as well as in their defense against future attack, they were now to receive a supply of arms graciously contributed by the king. Their lack of arms was a surprise to the company which could be explained only by an " unanswerable neglect." In the larger question of defense, the company was proceeding according to its original agreement with Captain Each. Almost all adventurers having men in Virginia had agreed that a fifth of their men should be assigned to this work, and it was incumbent upon all other colonists to show an equal willingness to coöperate. They could not overemphasize the necessity of providing the proper amount of freight according to their agreement with Each, nor of guaranteeing the payment advanced for his materials, since this money had

[70] Sandys to John Ferrar, October 13, 1622, Ferrar Papers.

been advanced by private individuals because of the inability of the company to raise any funds of its own.

They had been able to provide a "scant supply" of food by private subscription, but it must be understood that even this would have been impossible had the pawn been any less than the preservation of the colony, or had the diligence of those at home been any less than indefatigable. It was therefore of especial consequence that not only this but all other magazines should be returned with due profit to the adventurers. Their plea was made not so much in the interests of the company as of the colony. The adventurers might expect that God would repay them in some kind " if you do not, but for you, we cannot conceive but that as you justly deserve you will be clean left and abandoned from any supplies hereafter." The danger of such an event was sufficiently evident by their " present necessities," and it was hoped that experience had now taught them " what on the credit of our words you would not learn." Once again the company felt that the development of staple commodities was the solution of all problems. Thus they might keep an adequate supply of shipping in Virginia, for the danger and poverty of all merchants was such that the promise of freight on the return voyage would invite shipping in abundance. In this alone was there any hope, for everything demonstrated that " things are at the bottom except the current be again restored from Virginia. . . . The Company's great poverty and many debts keep us infinitely perplexed, and the more because there are daily inevitable occasions of expence and no ground or hope of Revenues except from Virginia." [71]

Let this be a lesson to you — such was the gist of the company's letter. Even at this late date the council quite obviously underestimated the colony's needs. And even

[71] MS. Rec. Va. Co., III, Part ii, 25a-27.

had the councillors possessed a fuller understanding, it is very unlikely that they would have been able to do any more than was done. The company was in no position to meet the emergency, and with the exception of one small supply and a shipment of outworn arms, the colonists were left, as they had been warned in August, to their own resources.

And these resources were not at all adequate to the need. True to predictions made in Virginia just after the massacre, the shortage of labor, the restricted acreage, and the problem of defense made impossible the production of a sufficient food supply, with the result that from late summer the colony suffered a severe shortage. As early as the 10th of September, Yeardley was commissioned by Wyatt to undertake a voyage into the Bay to secure food with all possible speed to relieve their great want of corn.[72] From a later employment of the same sort he returned with a thousand bushels of native corn, and through the winter continued to perform valiant service to the colony. But in addition to his efforts, it became necessary for the governor to fall back upon special commissions under which captains of ships arriving in Virginia were sent into the Bay, up the Potomac, and elsewhere in search of food to be taken either by force or trade. Four of these commissions have survived, two dated in October, one in November, and another in January.[73] It might have been possible by such emergency measures to have made fair provision for the colony's needs had it not been for the company's lack of judgment in sending large numbers of new and poorly provided colonists. In issuing the last of these commissions to a Captain Tucker, the governor explained the necessity by their great want of food which became steadily worse " in regards our numbers do daily Increase, whereof some arrive meanly provided." And a letter from the gov-

[72] MS. Rec. Va. Co., III, Part ii, 38a-39.
[73] Ibid., III, Part ii, 36, 39, 39a.

ernor and council in January declared that the "multitudes of people scantily or utterly unprovided" which had been sent to Virginia constituted the "Chief cause of our scarcity." [74]

To add to their suffering from want of food "such a pestilent fever" as had never before been known in Virginia swept over the colony. This sickness was attributed to the arrival of the *Abigall* with a load of immigrants who had been poisoned en route "with stinking beer" supplied by a Mr. Dupper of London. With many on the point of death at landing, and others fearfully sickened and "everywhere dispersing the contagion," their admission to the colony was quickly followed by a general epidemic.[75] All the factors which had contributed to sickness and death through the past four years — congested conditions of life, inadequate housing facilities, and scant supplies of coarse and unpalatable food — were now present in more acute form than ever before. The contagion spread rapidly and brought upon Virginia a winter of unprecedented sickness and death. The death rate was especially high among new arrivals. Captain Each reached Virginia, but he was dead before there was any chance to reveal his plans for fortifications. His men were returned to England in the spring and the colony made plans to build their own fort as soon as they were able. A Captain Barwick, sent for the purpose of building shallops, was greatly hindered by the death of many of his men and he himself suffered a violent illness. Sir William Nuce, who came to assume the duties of his new office, did not survive the reading of his patent two days. And the people who came with him were sickly, ragged, and altogether without provision.[76] In no place did the settlers escape much sickness and many deaths. All told, some 500 persons met their deaths that

[74] *Ibid.*, III, Part ii, 4-5a.
[75] George Sandys to Mr. Ferrar, March, 1622/23, Manchester Papers, 318.
[76] MS. Rec. Va. Co., III, Part ii, 4-5a, 6-6a.

winter, and according to George Sandys there were scarcely as many left, so that the living could hardly bury the dead.[77]

It was inevitable that a disaster of such proportions should be given much publicity in England. Sandys, for reasons which seemed to him good and sufficient, had labored diligently to control the accepted opinion at home concerning the state of affairs in Virginia. This policy extended not merely to the publication of tracts and pamphlets for circulation, but even led him to a strict censorship of the information presented to the adventurers themselves. As early as 1620 he was charged in the courts with concealing the true status of the colony.[78] And one of the most telling arguments of his opponents in 1623 was that he had received through private letters information from Virginia which contradicted official statements both within and without the company, and that, while through these letters he had sufficient warning of the dangers in his methods of colonization, he had proceeded in absolute disregard of these warnings by a deliberate falsification of facts presented to the public. A serious charge this! And yet, although the point has been generally ignored in Virginia's history, the charge is not without foundation. One has only to read through the official statements and minutes of the company and then to turn to the Ferrar Papers, where he may find the private correspondence with leaders in the colony, to recognize that the impression gained from these two sources of conditions in the colony are quite contradictory. One of the major criticisms to be made of the company's history as it has been written is that it has been based too much upon official records without due regard for the material in private papers.

Admirers of Sandys may marshal numerous explanations

<hr />

[77] George Sandys to Samuel Wrote, March 28, 1623, Manchester Papers, 319.

[78] *Records*, I, 329-330.

in justification of this policy, but the important consideration here is that the public in general and a large part of
the company were not able to get at the true facts concerning Virginia prior to 1623. Of course it was impossible to
avoid the bearing of tales by seamen and friends of the
opposing party. Unfavorable rumors were undoubtedly
one of the factors in the opposition of Smith and Warwick,
and in their repeated contention that merchants were more
fitted to manage such a business. But reports of this sort
could easily be attributed to the personal pique of Sandys'
enemies, and they could be refuted by a convincing array
of figures concerning shipping and the numbers of colonists sent, or merely by the reading of letters from the colonial council, which were always more moderate in their
tone than those written privately.

Nathaniel Rich charged that Sandys had a regular system of " double and contradictory " letters, one written for
public reading and another for his own private information.[79] Whether this be true or not, the officials of the company were at least able to count upon colonial leaders,
through their loyalty to Sandys, to use discretion in communications home. Peter Arondelle, for instance, after
writing to the council in December, 1621, gave a more complete account of his affairs to Sandys, concluding: " Were
you not one of them known wise and best affected in the
action, I would not discover unto you the danger we are
in, for I will always do what I may to hide our defects and
encourage any to the furtherance of this Christian Plantation; neither do I complain upon any particular Officer,
knowing it is easier to find faults than to amend them. I
leave to your Judicious search for to discover from whence
they proceed, and to repair them to the relief of us all." [80]

After the winter of 1622–1623, however, leaders at home
could no longer rely upon this spirit among the colonists.

[79] Manchester Papers, 330, 347.
[80] Arondelle to Sandys, December 15, 1621, Ferrar Papers.

The great suffering they had experienced, and more particularly the stinging rebukes contained in the company's letter, had given rise to a much different feeling. " The extreme sickness I have suffered, the heartbreaking to see the ill success of your affairs, want of all things necessary for life, my debts in supplying your scant provisions, the Company's not performing their contracts and approaching poverty, I should esteem as nothing," so reads a letter from George Sandys, " if our incessant toil and best endeavors could but preserve your good opinions, but all we can do can purchase us but undeserved infamy." [81]

Although this resentment was short-lived and was quickly replaced by older partisan loyalties at the threatened overthrow of the Sandys party, it is of great importance in bringing to light the failure of Sandys' policies and in the decision of his enemies to attempt his defeat by use of this information. A host of letters, written not only to officials in the company but indiscriminately to friends and relatives, brought to England in the spring of 1623 news of Virginia's plight.

George Sandys and Captain Berkley planned to return to England in order that they might present more adequately the distressing need for relief, and they were preceded by a long letter, punctuated with many bitter phrases, from the governor and council. They could not but resent the company's heavy censure " as if we alone were guilty " of the massacre, and asked for due consideration of the many instructions they had received " to win the Indians to us by a kind entertaining them in our houses, and if it were possible to Cohabit with us, and how impossible it is for any watch and ward to secure us against secret Enemies that live promiscuously amongst us." They were willing to confess that their sins were in part responsible for their affliction, but they could not but wish that the company had not so far forgotten its own responsibility

---

[81] George Sandys to Mr. Ferrar, March, 1622/23, Manchester Papers, 318.

as to add sorrow to this affliction by wounding their reputations.

They had suffered much too by the company's refusal to heed their advice and warning. The project for removal to the eastern shore had been abandoned. James City had then been repaired and all men invited to build there — a work that had proceeded cheerfully until letters from England required once more the dispersal of their men. They would obey the company's command, but they wanted it understood that the " unanimous voice " of all colonists agreed that they should " seat together " in two or three great bodies. Such a policy would have led to the building of fortified towns, whereof they now despaired although they still held it to be the better plan. Their justification for quitting so many plantations was simply that it had been " absolutely necessary." It had been impossible for them to retain any other plantations and at the same time have a sufficient force for defense or for parties to send in search of corn. Their weakness in numbers could be demonstrated by the fact that no less than 300 men were considered necessary to attack their enemies, and yet they had not been able to levy for this purpose above 180 men, of whom 80 at least were of no service except to carry corn. And even by this small levy " the Plantations we held, especially by reason of the sickness of our people, were left as weak as was in any sort Justifiable." Nevertheless, they would try to remove the company's " causeless suspicion " by attempting to reëstablish all plantations, " provided that we be not charged from home with such multitudes of people scantily or utterly unprovided."

The shortage of food from which the colony had so frequently suffered was attributed to two conditions which the company might well remedy. The first of these was the " scant and bad provisions sent over with new comers," and the second was the inability of " tenants at halves " to feed themselves by their own labors for more than three months in the year. Freemen generally had plentiful provisions. And if remedy were provided in these two points, they were confident there would be no cause to entreat help in supplying corn or other provisions further than voluntary adventures. If the company would look to these points, as also not to burden them with new officers to command "where experience instructs more than any other sufficiency," they felt that the company's revenues would be no longer a source of worry.[82]

Even more bitter were letters from private individuals. Of these none spoke in stronger terms than those of George Sandys, who, apparently abandoning his plan of returning to England, in a series of letters through the spring presented as complete a condemnation of the company's policies and practises during the preceding years as was ever drawn by Nathaniel Rich. To Samuel Wrote in March, he suggested that some person of "judgment and integrity" be sent to inquire into the true state of Virginia where they suffered from "extreme sickness and unheard of mortality." There was a shortage of the absolute necessities of life, and colonists from England came "so famished to halves" that they made "a dearth of a plentiful harvest." Their suffering had been increased by instructions from the company which forced the responsible officers to act altogether contrary to their own judgment. As an instance, he cited the order to disperse their settlers rather than have them seated in well fortified groups. This led to a weakening of the colony's defenses when already 180 men, of whom 80 were not fit "to carry burdens," were all that could be had against a thousand of the enemy.[83]

To his brother, Sir Samuel Sandys, he wrote to the same effect, declaring that tenants who had been sent

---

[82] MS. Rec. Va. Co., III, Part ii, 4-5a.
[83] George Sandys to Samuel Wrote, March 28, 1623, Manchester Papers, 319.

" on that so absurd condition of halves were neither able
to sustain themselves nor to discharge their moiety, and
so dejected with their scarce provisions, and finding nothing to answer their expectation, that most gave themselves over and died of melancholy, the rest running so
far in debt as left them still behindhand, and many (not
seldom) losing their crops whilst they hunted for their
bellies." In conclusion, he attributed Virginia's miseries
to "vain glory and presumption" at home.[84] A letter to
another brother, Sir Miles Sandys, was of the same nature,[85]
and to Deputy Ferrar he complained that "these slow
supplies, which hardly rebuild every year the decays of
the former, retain us only in a languishing state and curb
us from the carrying of enterprise of moment." [86] He had
already related his "poor condition" to Ferrar, as also
the loss of four men by the Indians and nineteen through
sickness. "Be not offended that I speak the truth," were
his closing words, " you know but little, and we not much
more, for what can be discovered without means, or with
such an handful of people so dispersed?" [87]

The same grievances were presented by other colonists,
such as William Capps who wrote Ferrar in March.[88]
And Richard Frethorne, a recent arrival in Virginia, expressed the feelings of colonists other than responsible
officials, when he wrote his parents that he had often
" eaten more in a day at home " than he had there in a
week, and had often seen them give more to a beggar than
he was allowed for a day. A penny loaf of bread must supply four men, and he himself had eaten nothing " but
pease and loblolly (that is water-gruel)." " Oh! that they
were in England without their limbs . . . though they

[84] *Ibid.* to Samuel Sandys, March 30, 1623, Manchester Papers, 320.
[85] *Ibid.* to Sir Miles Sandys, Manchester Papers, 321.
[86] *Ibid.* to Ferrar, April 8, 1623, Bancroft Transcripts, Virginia Papers,
II, 45-60.
[87] *Ibid.* to Mr. Ferrar, March 1622/23, Manchester Papers, 318.
[88] Capps to Ferrar, March 31, 1623, Manchester Papers, 322.

begged from door to door " was the cry of the people day and night. " Sickness and death, except that one had money to lay out in some things for profit " were all that a man could find in Virginia. Half of those who had come with him were already dead, and the sailors told him that two thirds of the 150 they had brought over had died between Christmas and March.[89] Another settler, John Baldwin, informed a friend in Bermuda that: " It hath been a very hard time with all men they had like to all starve this year; there was them that paid forty shillings a bushell for sheld Corn. But howsoever, they die like rotten sheep no man dies, but he is as full of maggots as he can hold. They rot above ground." [90]

It has been too often overlooked in explaining Johnson's appeal to the government for interference in Virginia's affairs that not only had all of Sandys' plans failed completely, but that this failure had brought with it a bankrupt company, the weakness of which had been clearly demonstrated by one of the major catastrophes of England's colonial history. It was not unnatural that a condition affecting so large a number of his majesty's subjects should be carried to the government. And it would have been indeed surprising if Sandys' enemies had not decided upon some move against him at this time. There was at hand now a wealth of information from which they might draw material for an indictment of his policies and administration.

[89] Manchester Papers, 325.
[90] J. H. Lefroy, *Memorials of the Bermudas*, London, 1877-1879, I, 264-265.

CHAPTER VIII
THE TOBACCO CONTRACT

IN order to understand the influence of the course of events in Virginia on the fortunes of the Sandys party, it is necessary to take cognizance of the state of affairs in the company when the full effect of Sandys' maladministration was for the first time revealed. The adventurers had spent the entire winter in the most heated factional struggle, one that for bitterness and hatred surpassed even their earlier performance of 1620. Court after court had passed in lengthy disputations, in open charges of dishonesty, and in slandering many honorable reputations. The lie had been given and returned in absolute disregard of gentlemanly honor, and outside the courts members had vied with one another in spreading rumors and accusations maligning the motives and characters of leaders on both sides, until the strife within the Virginia Company had become a leading topic of gossip throughout the city of London. There were numerous causes for this rekindling of factional feeling, among them several long-standing disputes, but by far the most important was the tobacco contract negotiated with the government by Sandys in the preceding fall.

Tobacco had been the company's sorest problem for several years. The absolute prohibition of its growth would perhaps have been the accepted policy of the adventurers as early as 1618, had not their decision been governed by the fact that the colony produced no other marketable commodity of any real value. As it was, their policy became one of limitation and regulation looking to the development of such other staples as would in time relieve the planters of their dependence upon this one commodity. In the course so planned, however, there were many serious difficulties which the company was never able to overcome. Every indication suggests an almost complete failure in the attempt to reduce the acreage of this crop, although it is difficult to estimate the actual amount of tobacco exported from Virginia after 1618, because so much of it was never entered at English ports. But though this failure in a major policy is not without real significance in the company's history, it is of much less importance than the fact that the adventurers lost heavily and consistently on the sale of their tobacco in Europe.

There were several conditions in the tobacco trade that operated to the disadvantage of the adventurers. In the first place, they were bound by their own ruling to accept a crop of very poor quality at an artificial price of 3s. for the better grade and 18d. for the poorer, and to sell it in a falling market which offered prices much lower than the scale obtaining in Virginia. Of recent years there had been a rapid development of tobacco plantations in the West Indies, and the increasing quantities imported into Europe brought a quick decline in prices.[1] So ruinous was the effect of the court order of 1618 that it was reversed by the company in 1621 and a lower schedule of prices established.

They continued to suffer, however, from the strong competition of Spanish tobacco, which, with a good start on its English competitor and offering a commodity of far superior quality, threatened to capture the home market completely.[2] A discrimination in customs duties in favor

[1] Nathaniel Rich in certain proposals to the privy council in 1623 regarding the tobacco contract declared: "The quantitie of Tobacco (by reason of the late excessive planting thereof in the West Indyes and in the new plantacions of Guyana and Brazill) is like to bee so greate that all theis partes of Christendome wilbee glutted with it, and the price of Tobacco brought soe lowe that in probabilitie it will not bee worth so much a pound as his Majestie hath now for Custome."—Sackville Papers, p. 752.

[2] Between 1614 and 1621 there were imported into England 685,030 pounds of Spanish tobacco and only 309,569 pounds from Virginia and Bermuda. And while these figures are misleading as to the problem that faced Sandys, since they include earlier years when tobacco culture in Virginia was yet in its infancy, it is significant that in the three years between 1618 and 1621 the 238,562 pounds imported from the English plantations was little more than half the

of the two companies would appear to give them at least an advantage in the English market. But on the contrary, the unusually poor quality of their leaf placed them at a distinct disadvantage. The adventurers were loath to admit that in "wholesomenes" the Spanish tobacco was in any way superior, but they were forced to recognize that in "strength, tast, and estimacion" it far excelled their own.[3] Because of this inferiority, colonial tobacco could compete only with the lowest grades of the Spanish, and a large portion of the Virginia and Bermuda crops was reëxported each year for sale at low prices in Turkey, Barbary, and other foreign markets where taste apparently was not so discriminating as in England.[4]

The most serious problem in the disposal of colonial tobacco, however, was the making of favorable arrangements for its importation into England. Just when it was becoming of real importance as a money crop, innumerable difficulties in regard to customs duties and regulations for its sale arose to harass the responsible leaders of the company. The plantations from the first had been established with the understanding that they were to be outside the English fiscal system, and therefore subject to the general duties levied upon foreign goods. In practise, though, a distinction had been made between foreign states and the colonies by certain exemptions and preferential treatment which would serve to give them an advantage in the home market, while at the same time providing the king with revenue sufficient to repay him for the responsibilities assumed in their support. The regular customs duties were of two kinds: tonnage and poundage, popularly known as the subsidy or customs and granted by parliament at James' accession for life, and secondly,

411,917 pounds entered from Spain. There is also evidence that much foreign tobacco was smuggled into the country.—Sackville Papers, pp. 526-527, 754.
[3] Ibid., pp. 752-753.
[4] Ibid., pp. 750, 754, 758.

an additional duty levied by royal authority alone known as the impost. Each of these duties roughly approximated 5%, although the actual levy depended upon rate books which arbitrarily fixed the value of commodities for purposes of the tariff. By their charters the two companies were exempted from all duties for seven years, and after that time from any tariffs in excess of the parliamentary subsidy. The total exemption expired for the Virginia Company in 1619, and according to agreement should have run three years more for Bermuda tobacco. Nevertheless, from 1619 both companies were required to pay duties in excess of those provided by their charters.

This violation of their charters is explained in part by the fact that at the time of their issuance there was little reason to expect that imports from the plantations would be composed almost entirely of tobacco. Yet by 1619 such was the case, and the government's policy was influenced considerably by the desire to avoid all possible encouragement to the growth of this commodity. Knowledge of the king's attitude, as well as of the general disapproval of tobacco, left the companies so insecure in their position that they were unable to stand firmly upon their patents, and were instead disposed to submit to impositions in direct violation of their chartered rights. His majesty was also influenced by the loss in revenue resulting from these exemptions at a time when the royal income was a consideration of paramount importance.[5] And while this point probably would not have loomed so large in the deliberations of the government had the products from the plantations been any other than tobacco, neither the king nor his ministers were in any way disposed to contribute from

[5] The allowance made to the farmers of the subsidy for the goods of the two plantations imported from 1612 to 1618, a sum deducted from his majesty's rent, amounted in all to £2,215. The significant point is that £1,988 of this defalcation had been made mostly for tobacco brought in since 1616. And the large abatement of £1,332 for 1618 gave promise of increasingly heavy losses to royal revenue in coming years.—Sackville Papers, pp. 497-498.

the royal purse to the encouragement of this pernicious weed.

By the rate book issued in 1608, leaf tobacco was valued at 10s. per pound and roll at 6s. 8d., at which valuation the 5% subsidy came to 6d. and 4d. respectively per pound.[6] The Virginia Company, accordingly, should have been liable for the 6d. and 4d. subsidy after March, 1619, and the Bermuda planters should have been free of all duties for three years more. But instead, not only did the farmers of the subsidy collect the 5% customs from the tobacco of both companies, but the collector of the impost required another 6d.[7] The Virginia adventurers entered a strong protest and were favored with an opinion from Attorney-General Yelverton recognizing the legality of their claim.[8]

But this did not imply any intention on the part of the government to retreat from its demand that Virginia tobacco should pay duties amounting in all to a shilling. It was quickly followed by an attempt to secure the company's consent to the payment of higher customs duties, and through an ingenious bit of bargaining the grudging agreement of the adventurers was finally won. The privy council offered as an inducement to the company the tobacco farm and the promise of the absolute prohibition of tobacco planting in England and Ireland. The order prohibiting domestic tobacco planting was already drawn up and dated as of December 30, 1619, and would undoubtedly have been issued regardless of the company's reply.[9] And although it was of some influence in securing

---

[6] Patent Rolls, 6 Jac. I, July 28, 1608; *Records*, II, 37, 58. The printed rate book so frequently referred to was issued in 1611, but with no changes affecting tobacco duties.

[7] *Records*, I, 245, 248, 276, 277.

[8] *Ibid.*, I, 281-284.

[9] *Cal. St. Pap., Dom.*, 1619-1623, p. 107. Its issuance was fully in keeping with the government's policy of restricting the production, sale, and use of this commodity. Moreover, the high figure demanded for the tobacco farm, for which negotiations with Abraham Jacob had already begun at a proposed rental of £8,000, made such a step necessary. Jacob insisted upon it as a condition to

the capitulation of the Virginia court, the deciding factor
was a message from the king which served both to emphasize his determined opinion in the matter and to relieve
him at least technically of violating their chartered rights.
It was an easy matter to increase the actual rate of taxation involved in the 5% subsidy by merely revaluating the
commodity for purposes of the tariff. This had been done
frequently in the past, and especially when determining
tobacco rates where the policy was to evaluate it at the
highest price secured in the English market. Since 1615
foreign tobacco had been paying 18d. impost and 6d. subsidy, or a total of 2s. per pound.[10] In January, 1620, accordingly, the company was informed that it had been thought
advisable to raise the customs on their tobacco to 12d. since
Spanish tobacco had at times sold for 20s. per pound.[11]
By thus evaluating tobacco at its highest price, 20s., rather
than the 10s. established for customs in 1608, the 5%
subsidy due from Virginia tobacco would of course amount
exactly to the 12d. requested of the company. Some measure of reason was given this argument by the fact that, even
with the proposed increase, their tobacco at 1s. duty would
be paying only half the 2s. required of Spanish tobacco,
and would therefore continue to enjoy a preference in
the same ratio to foreign tobacco as provided by their
charter. It could well be argued that by their charter they
were exempted from only half the usual duties, and according to the proposed arrangement they would continue to
enjoy that exemption.

His majesty's proposal was occasion for much debate in
the court, where it was answered that Virginia's tobacco

---

the contract, and the high rental paid for the farm and monopoly by Sir Thomas
Roe, to whom the two were later granted, argues that he would have insisted
upon it had not the step already been decided upon. See Sackville Papers, pp.
523-524.
[10] Sackville Papers, pp. 523, 526; Beer, *Origins of the British Colonial System*,
pp. 108-109.
[11] *Records*, I, 290.

had never brought more than 5s. in sale, at which rate they felt there was due the king no more than 3d. Although there was much justice in this claim, the adventurers were in no position to defend their rights, and the general tenor of the king's message, implying that the higher duty would be imposed regardless of their answer, argued for a graceful submission to the inevitable. The offer of the tobacco farm was rejected, but it was agreed that in gratitude for the prohibition of tobacco planting in England there should be added 9d. more to their duties for five years, which would bring the total to 12d., "being in full of his Majesty's demand though not in the same form." [12] Thus within a year after Sandys' election the adventurers not only became liable to the expected 6d. customs, but were forced to submit to a levy of double that amount upon all tobacco imported by them into England. [13]

Further difficulties arose from the government's attempt to regulate the tobacco trade. It was a common practise to provide for the inspection at port of certain goods with the purpose of protecting the king's subjects from inferior or adulterated products, and in 1619 a patent for the inspection, or "garbling," of tobacco was issued to two patentees for the annual rental of £100. [14] While the fee collected for this inspection added further to the burden borne by colonial tobacco, it was not so serious to the com-

[12] *Ibid.*, I, 290-292.

[13] Some difficulty in following the history of this extra tax arises from the manner of its farming. The original 6d. subsidy, commonly referred to as the "old custom," was collected by the farmers of the subsidy. But the 6d. added in 1620, religiously termed the "increase of subsidy," was farmed along with the regular impost of 18d. upon foreign tobacco, and for all practical purposes constituted an impost collected on Virginia tobacco. (Sackville Papers, pp. 523, 525-526, 751-752, 762-763.) It is difficult to determine the final settlement made with the Bermuda Company. That the government intended to collect at least 6d. on its tobacco is certain. (*Ibid.*, p. 523; *Records*, I, 283.) And it is likely that the adventurers were not let off entirely in the plan to increase the revenue from tobacco. Of course, not before 1622 did they become liable to the full imposition borne by the Virginia crop.

[14] *Cal. St. Pap., Dom.*, 1619-1623, p. 47.

pany as the application of the monopoly system to the tobacco trade. The fundamental motive here was perhaps revenue, but it too was a policy of regulation looking to the control of the importation and traffic in this commodity. Such grants of sole importation — the phrase most commonly used at the time — gave the patentees the exclusive privilege of importing a specified commodity, and in consequence, a control over its sale within the kingdom. A tobacco monopoly had been established as early as 1615. And five years later it was granted, along with the farm of the impost on foreign tobacco and the 6d. " increase of subsidy " on the English product, for one year at a rental of £16,000 to a group of men headed by Sir Thomas Roe.[15]

A monopoly of this type created a vested interest anxious to realize as much as was possible above the rent paid the king, which in this case proved to be excessively high. The monopolists' revenue came from the collection of the impost and from their control over the retail market in England, in regard to either of which there was a disposition to give the advantage to Spanish tobacco over that from the plantations. Duties on the former were considerably larger, and being of much better quality it could be sold for much higher prices. The company, recognizing the great danger to its interests in the establishment of such a monopoly, protested strongly on July 7, 1620.[16] Nevertheless, they were able to secure permission to bring into the English market only 55,000 weight of tobacco from both plantations, which was considerably less than the amount imported by them in the preceding twelve months.[17] The Virginia adventurers, therefore, decided that the full proportion of 55,000 weight should be allotted to the younger company, and that they would make ar-

[15] *Cal. St. Pap., Dom.*, 1619-1623, p. 170; Journals of the House of Commons, I, 586.

[16] *Records*, I, 398.

[17] *Ibid.*, II, 68; Sackville Papers, p. 526.

rangements to send their own tobacco direct to Holland. They were able within a short time to arrange with the town of Middleburg for the importation of Virginia tobacco at a halfpenny per pound.[18]

But while they were able to secure far better terms for importing their tobacco into Holland, the plan was not at all satisfactory as a long term policy. It was in flagrant violation of the economic theories dictating government policy, and at any time they might be forced to bring all their goods into English ports. And unless they were able to make more satisfactory arrangements than had been possible in the summer of 1620, such a requirement would mean that the payment of English import duties would constitute a direct tax on a commodity which they would still be forced to sell in a foreign market.[19]

The company, therefore, did not relax its efforts to secure some change in the policies and conditions affecting the home market. The prominence of several adventurers in the Parliament of 1621 suggested the possibility of relief from that source, where the grievances of the company fitted well into the commons' attack on monopolies and their anxious inquiries concerning the " decay of our money " by the drainage of specie in payment for foreign commodities. It was not difficult to win support for Sandys' attack on the tobacco monopoly and his demand for the exclusion of Spanish tobacco, but the debate came dangerously near getting out of hand when a counter proposal to exclude all tobacco, including that of the plantations, was sympathetically received in several parts of the House. Sandys, Ferrar, Sackville, Smith, and Rich, however, were able to convince the commons that the colonists had no

[18] *Records*, I, 405-406, 422, 526-527.
[19] It is possible that they might have been able to secure some abatement on duties paid upon reexporting the tobacco. In 1623 in an offer made for the farm of Spanish tobacco and the impost on English, it was agreed that 3d. per pound should be allowed on all tobacco of the plantations "as shalbee shipped out againe and not vented in this Kingdome."—Sackville Papers, pp. 751-752.

other means of subsistence for the time being at least, and the bill as passed was restricted to the exclusion only of foreign tobacco.[20]

Although the measure failed of passage in the house of lords, it did serve as a strong expression of the commons' opinion and was probably of some weight in the decision of the privy council, that fall, to limit the importations of Spanish tobacco. Sir Thomas Roe's patent was surrendered at its termination in September, and a new patent was granted in December to Abraham Jacob at £8,000 for the impost and right of sole importation of 60,000 weight of Spanish tobacco, the Virginia and Bermuda Companies to be left free to import their tobacco without restraint after paying through his majesty's collectors the regular impost of 6d.[21] The company's efforts, therefore, had not been entirely in vain. The limit placed on foreign imports of tobacco represented a large reduction from the importations of the preceding year, and it may be taken as a valuable concession to the companies and a significant step in the development of a policy of colonial preference in the home market.

Yet the arrangement, though better than that of 1620, was not at all satisfactory to the companies. There had been no reduction in the tariff duties, by which they continued to be taxed at rates fixed upon a valuation of 20s. per pound for a product that had never brought more than 5s. And of recent years Virginia's tobacco had fallen considerably below that price. On the crop of 1620 sales had averaged 2s. for the better grade and 17d. for the second, and the company's factor, Arthur Swaine, did not expect even that much for the next year.[22] Moreover, the position of the Virginia adventurers gave greater concern because

[20] *Records*, I, 442-443; *Journals of the House of Commons*, I, 552, 581-582, 586, 605, 622, 627.

[21] Goodman, *Court of King James the First*, II, 211, letter from Cranfield to Buckingham quoted in note to Sackville Papers, p. 528.

[22] MS. Rec. Va. Co., III, Part ii, 19-19a.

the government had on October 15 taken them strongly to task for shipping their tobacco to Holland. The privy council, being not at all satisfied with their plea of absolute necessity, had then followed up with a sharp order of the 24th requiring them to bring all their tobacco direct to England and to carry it elsewhere under no circumstances until the customs duties had been paid.[23]

It is not surprising that the leaders of the company were ready to entertain a proposal in 1622 that the two companies should undertake the tobacco contract upon the expiration of Jacob's patent. The joint effect of the heavy taxation and monopoly of importation established in 1620 had been one of the major factors in the bankrupt condition of the Virginia treasury. The combined blow of the loss of the lotteries in 1621 and the heavy deficits on all its magazines had left the company with no appreciable source of income and an indebtedness which in the summer of 1622 still amounted to £2,000.[24] The one hope for the future lay in some arrangement for a profitable disposal of tobacco. In 1621 the company with almost no public funds had been able to launch a large and expensive program by an extension of the principle of subsidiary joint-stocks. Yet only one of these, the matrimonial venture, had returned any profit to the adventurers. All others ended in loss.[25] As a result, it was only with the most extreme difficulty that the officers were able to enlist private funds for the relief of the colony after the massacre. There was thus little prospect either of reëstablishing public funds or of promoting their many enterprises by private capital without some relief in marketing conditions at home. There was not even much chance of relieving the colony of its dependence upon tobacco unless in the meantime that tobacco could be sold at sufficient profit to pro-

[23] *Records*, I, 526-528; *Acts P.C., Col.*, I, pp. 48-49.
[24] MS. Rec. Va. Co., III, Part ii, 22-23.
[25] *Records*, II, 15. The best discussion of these subsidiary joint-stocks is to be found in Scott's *Joint-Stock Companies to 1720*, II, 276-277.

vide for the support of the new staples which were to take
its place. The importance of these considerations may be
seen in the fact that from the summer of 1622 to the day
of Johnson's famous petition for the king's interference
in April, 1623, the courts of the company were concerned
almost exclusively with the question of tobacco.

On the 5th of June, 1622, Sandys reported to a Virginia
court a proposal from the lord treasurer, Lionel Cranfield,
that the two companies enter into a contract with the
government for the tobacco monopoly. Cranfield, who by
demonstrated ability and loyalty had risen to a high place
in the king's council, was one of the older adventurers in the
company, had formerly been an active member of the Virginia Council, and as surveyor-general of the customs since
1613 had been in close touch with the affairs of the two
plantations. He was appointed to the privy council in
1619, after having qualified by a marriage into Buckingham's family, was elevated to the peerage in July, 1621,
and upon Mandeville's fall in October took office as lord
treasurer. A year later he became the first earl of Middlesex, by which title he is most commonly known. The settlement of questions regarding customs duties and the tobacco monopoly had been largely in his hands, and it was
with full knowledge of the past history of the company's
difficulties in importing its tobacco that he approached
Sandys, with whom his relations had not been altogether
unpleasant,[26] on the possible undertaking of the monopoly
by the companies.

Although changed in detail many times through the
ensuing months, the suggested plan remained essentially
the same: that the companies should have a monopoly of
the right to import all tobacco and should pay in return
a substantial rent which would secure for the king the expected revenue from this commodity. Cranfield demanded
an annual rental of £20,000, but Sandys, considering that

[26] Sandys to Cranfield, September 9, 1619, Sackville Papers, pp. 498-499.

tobacco "was founded only upon a humor which might soon vanish into smoke," proposed that instead of a fixed sum the companies should allow the king one fourth of all tobacco imported by them and thereby be freed from all other charges. The lord treasurer agreed in principle, but replied that no less than a third could provide the necessary revenue, and that as for other charges it would be impossible to relieve them of the 5% subsidy as it was already farmed. The negotiations had reached this stage when Sandys reported the proposition to the adventurers, who decided to entertain the proposal and selected a committee from each company to negotiate, subject to their approval.[27]

The companies' representatives, among whom Sandys was the leading spirit, made every effort through the several weeks of negotiation which followed to secure the most favorable terms. It was necessary, however, to yield to the government's demand for an absolute grant of a third of the crop for the king. They were also forced to submit to a strict requirement to import not less than 80,000 pounds of Spanish tobacco within two years, a provision which the company bitterly contested for four months without avail.[28] Nor could they secure relief from the payment of the 6d. subsidy in addition to a third of their tobacco. In return for these concessions they received little more than an agreement that the king would bear the 5% subsidy on his share of the imports and a third of the cost attendant upon the execution of the contract, although the adventurers were forced to shoulder the charges for freight on both their own and the king's tobacco. The weakness of the company's position, due to its bankruptcy, to the importance of tobacco as a source of revenue for the king, and to his care to avoid all unnecessary encouragement to its growth, left the committees almost helpless in the negotiations. They could do little more than accept the pro-

[27] *Records*, II, 35-38.   [28] *Ibid.*, II, 61-63.

posals of the government, and were forced to surrender their hopes of a really effective monopoly of the home market.

It was, therefore, an unhappy choice which Sandys submitted to the courts in the form of a preliminary draft on July 1. They might accept the government's proposals, or they might do worse and return to previous arrangements, as Sir Edwin frankly explained to the adventurers. Under his persuasion they decided upon what was hoped to be the lesser of two evils, and the committee was instructed to continue the negotiations.[29] The final drafting of the bargain was delayed for several months while both parties sought agreement on certain desired emendations to the preliminary draft.[30] It was not until November that final agreement was reached. The contract was then submitted to the adventurers, who, after one final and vain attempt to alter the obligation to import a set quantity of Spanish tobacco, agreed to accept it " not as good meat well sauced but of a portion necessary for their health being willing *devorare molestiam* of this bitter pill." [31]

The execution of the contract, however, was still held in abeyance by the government. On February 12, Southampton informed both companies that the contract " which had so long hung in suspence was now again sent signed by the Lord Treasurer" and approved by the privy council with no alterations from the copy ratified by the adventurers in November.[32] Notwithstanding, in a few

[29] *Records*, II, 67-69, 85-88, 97-98.

[30] Some light on the causes for this delay may be found in marginal notes made by Cranfield on a copy of the preliminary draft which indicate the points at issue. Cranfield's notes are published in the Sackville Papers, pp. 741-742.

[31] *Records*, II, 138-140, 142-144, 147-148. A copy of the contract signed by Middlesex may be found in the Sackville Papers, pp. 742-745. This copy was signed on February 12, but is identical with the draft agreed to on November 27 by the two companies. The Virginia quarter court of November 20 approved the document with exception of the provisions regarding Spanish tobacco, giving power to an extraordinary court to meet with the Bermuda quarter court on the 27th to conclude the matter.

[32] *Records*, II, 264.

days they were ordered to stay all proceedings in the business for a time, the whole question was reopened and debated before Middlesex and the privy council through March, and the contract was finally abandoned the last of that month. This delay and the final abandonment of the bargain were due largely to the outbreak of a violent dispute within the companies over the terms and management of the contract.

The terms of the tobacco agreement had not been concluded without strong opposition in the courts. It is true that the vote in the Virginia court of November 27, at which time final ratification of the contract was given, is reported as unanimous. But few of those who later were so outspoken in their opposition were present at that court. For some time Sandys' leading opponents had dropped regular attendance at courts, taking an active part in the company's affairs only as their own interests or those of their friends were affected, and they were frequently charged in succeeding months with having completely abandoned the courts except upon occasion of trouble. During the tobacco negotiations they seem not to have been greatly concerned, and it was only with the announcement of plans for the management of the new monopoly that they returned to raise their voices in the most bitter denunciation of the provisions for management and later of the contract itself.

It was provided in the contract that the administration of the monopoly should be vested in officers selected by the adventurers. A committee of both companies had been appointed on November 18 to draw up the necessary plans, and this committee in session with the council had decided upon an appropriation of £2,500 to cover the cost of management. A fifth of this sum was to be held as a reserve fund for emergencies, £180 was for rent of warehouse facilities, and the remainder was appropriated to the salaries of officers charged with the direction of the tobacco business. The chief officers were a director at a salary of £500, a treasurer at £400, and eight members of committees drawing a total salary of £400. The rest of this large sum was divided among a number of lesser officers. It was to be raised by an imposition upon the tobacco imported, Spanish leaf bearing a rate double that of English. A third of the burden would, of course, fall upon the king, and the balance was to be borne equally by the two companies.[33]

It is not surprising that there should have been strong opposition to these salaries. For they represented an extraordinarily large sum, amounting to £500 more than the company's total indebtedness, which was large enough in itself to cause the greatest worry to the adventurers.[34] It would entail an additional burden on the tobacco of the plantations, which in the minds of its opponents was not only unnecessary but a burden the planters were not able to bear. Within the next few months numerous counter proposals designed to reduce the cost at least by half, and some even more, were pressed upon the courts with the utmost vigor by lieutenants of Warwick and Smith.[35] This excessive compensation to the managers seemed proof enough that the leaders of the dominant party had endeavored to allocate to themselves all the benefits expected from the contract.

And this was the cause of their deepest grievance. The manner in which the appropriation had been passed gave grounds for the chief complaints of Smith and Warwick, whose spokesmen quickly and loudly declared the measure had been carried "foully and surreptitiously" by those who were to benefit thereby. The salary schedule had been decided upon by the Sandys faction in committee, and there was no mention of the sum to be allowed until the

[33] *Records*, II, 129, 151-153.

[34] Professor Scott has compiled some interesting figures on contemporary sums to demonstrate the exorbitance of the tobacco salaries. *Joint-Stock Companies to 1720*, II, 278.

[35] *Records*, II, 225-227, 269-271; Manchester Papers, 300, 315.

extraordinary court of November 27 when both the contract and salary were ratified. Even in a court in which many of their opponents were not present the schedule was not confirmed without opposition. Several were of the opinion that there were "divers gentlemen and other sufficient men that for conscience sake would do the business for far lesser rewards," but after much debate the appropriation was confirmed.[36] Proceeding from this sudden introduction and forcing of an immediate passage by Southampton to the fact that all the officers were selected from Sandys' partisans, it can be seen that the repeated accusation of self-seeking and unfair dealing was not without probable foundation. Sandys became director, John Ferrar treasurer, and all lesser offices were distributed as patronage to their loyal supporters. The charge of self-seeking was of course vehemently denied. Sandys on one occasion resigned because of the pressure from the opposition, but he quickly reaccepted the office upon the court's request and after the conventional protestation of his many duties. And in view of the exorbitant salaries provided and the fact that Sandys at the time was in sore financial straits,[37] it is difficult to avoid the conclusion that he and his supporters were moved by something more than an altogether unselfish concern for the welfare of the plantations.

On December 4, at the first court after the approval of the contract and salary, Samuel Wrote, a member of the Virginia Council, and Alderman Johnson expressed in a most violent manner their opposition to the arrangements concluded at the preceding court. Their chief attack was directed at the salary, which they did not quibble to term an ordinary graft. The minutes of the court record page after page of disorderly dispute. As the debate progressed Wrote spoke with increasing fervor until, beside himself

[36] *Records*, II, 153.
[37] Sandys to John Ferrar, November 22, 1623, Ferrar Papers.

with passion, he became so free in his accusations and slan-derous charges of dishonesty that it took the Virginia courts all of two months to agree on just what he had said and what punishment was due his contemptuous words. Through the whole of January all business was set aside while the adventurers endeavored to verify the minutes of December 4. Final sentence was not passed until February 5, at which time Lord Cavendish declared that his offense was not " out of present passion and heat, but upon pre-meditate intention to raise a Combustion," in which be-lief he was " more confirmed therein because at that Court he observed divers whom he had not for a long time before seen in Courts and was generally known and ob-served not to appear or show their faces but against a storm and Tempest." The offender was forever excluded from the council and suspended from the company for a year, to be readmitted only upon proper submission.[38]

Both the Warwick and Smith factions had rallied to Wrote's support, and in the heat and bitterness of his trial party lines were drawn hard and fast. There had not been hitherto any strong alliance between Smith and Warwick. They had embraced every opportunity to express their common dislike of Sandys, and had united to bring about his fall from office in 1620. But though a mutual hatred of Sir Edwin provided the basis for a coalition of these two groups, their union seems not to have been cemented until they joined hands in an attempt to overthrow the tobacco patent. The plan of management affected deeply their chief interest in the American plantations, which was Ber-muda tobacco. Their heaviest investments since 1619, when Sandys gained control over the destinies of Virginia, had been in the Somers Islands, where their interests now far outweighed those of their opponents. From a study of the tobacco fight it is apparent that most of the tobacco from the younger plantation belonged to members of the Smith-

[38] *Records*, II, 255-256, 258-259.

Warwick coalition. On the other hand, the chief interest and investment of the Sandys party was undoubtedly in Virginia. It is true that they had controlled the Bermuda Company since 1621, but this control was desirable for reasons of convenience arising from the close connections between the two plantations in matters of defense, including the suppression of piracy, and in their economic interests, among which common problems in the marketing of tobacco were of paramount concern. Few of the Sandys party were large shareholders in the company or had made any considerable investment in the colony.

Thus the tobacco question, despite the control of the same party over both courts, became in part an issue between the two companies. It seemed to men like Nathaniel Rich that Sandys was using his position in the Bermuda Company to exploit the younger plantation in the interests of Virginia. Next to the size of the salaries, their chief objection was to the provision that the tobacco of the two colonies should bear equally the burden of this appropriation. Time and again they argued that Bermuda tobacco was of lower market value, and that the salary imposition should be proportionate. " Before I yield to the salary," so read some rough notes by Rich, " these things to be considered: " and then follow certain queries as to how much the charge will come to upon the pound of tobacco, whether the Somers Islands shall stand upon equal terms with Virginia in payment of this imposition, and whether if Virginia tobacco outsell " ours " it be reasonable that " we should pay equal salaries." [39]

After the disposal of Wrote's case, the Virginia court turned its attention to a reconsideration of the salary schedule. The reopening of this question, however, came as no more than a formal concession from Sandys and Southampton, for all chance of compromise or coöperation was long since passed. A real concession to the demand

[39] Manchester Papers, 304.

for lower salaries could not have been made without implying some justification for the damning charges of Wrote and Johnson. Through the bitter quarrels of two months the salary schedule had thus become a matter of policy on which the Sandys party must either stand or fall. The prolonged debates in which the adventurers passed the month of February, therefore, served no purpose except to clarify the position of the two parties and to pile one upon the other the most vitriolic expressions of hatred and mutual distrust. Both sides brought to the fight all the resentment accumulated through four years of slanderous charges and counter charges, and the ensuing struggle for revision of the contract and salary added fuel to the fires of faction that had been lighted in earlier disputes over accounts, patents, and piracy.

There was no disposition in either party to yield, and in the end the issue hung on the question of which party could assemble the largest vote. Nathaniel Rich, who led the fight, elected to make the final test in the Bermuda Company. He and his supporters steadfastly refused to vote one way or the other in a Virginia court, thereby accounting for the large number of unanimous decisions recorded in the minutes of the courts for the winter of 1622–1623. Of course the contract and any provision for its management required approval by both courts. And in the younger company Sandys' enemies not only had greater interests at stake but much more chance of victory. They have been frequently represented as a fractious and irresponsible minority of obstructionists. This, however, is not true. They were hopelessly outvoted in the Virginia court, although Sandys' plurality there has at times been overestimated.[40] But in the other company the division was much

---

[40] In the spring of 1623 Rich listed 84 adventurers "that dislike the present proceedings of business in the Virginia and Somers Islands Companies," and while this list probably includes some whose votes were not certain, it serves to show the division of the company was closer than has been believed. (Manchester Papers, 327.) The largest vote polled by the Sandys party was in the

closer. A decisive vote of November 27 had been carried for the administration by a margin of only 21 to 20.[41] Warwick's group had not been present, and their subsequent union with Smith and Johnson apparently should have given Sandys' opponents the chance of a small majority.[42] Indeed, it is reasonable to suppose that they would have gone immediately to the king, as they promptly did after their defeat in the court, had it not been for some prospect of victory.

The month of February, therefore, in addition to its heated debates, was one of active vote getting. Every known device for manipulating the franchise was employed. The suspension of Wrote was merely one instance of the use of a tried and proved instrument of power, and by the spring of 1623 a total of thirteen active stockholders had been suspended from the Bermuda courts. It may well be imagined that the greater part, if not all, of this number were supporters of Smith and Warwick.[43] There seem to have been also many transfers of shares to friends and relatives to hold for purposes of voting. The passage of

---

election of 1622 when the king's interference probably contributed to a total of 117 votes cast for Southampton. (*Records*, II, 29.) The mistaken estimate of the opposition's strength is based upon Cavendish's reference to their number as only 26. (*Ibid.*, II, 352-362.) He was able to do this because the refusal of the opponents of the contract to vote in the Virginia court meant that the vote in the Bermuda Company, which was much smaller, represented the only recorded vote against the agreement.

[41] *Records*, II, 159-160.

[42] Professor Scott by an analysis of various extant lists of stockholders (*Records*, II, 159-160; Manchester Papers, 302, 305, 310, 357) concludes that the maximum poll of eligible voters was approximately 70, and by adding to the recognized supporters of Sandys all those who cannot be identified as members of the opposing party he estimates the full voting strength of his party at 33, leaving a possible 37 for Smith and Warwick. See *Joint-Stock Companies to 1720*, II, 278.

[43] Manchester Papers, 308. The belief that most of them were opponents of Sandys is supported by the fact that their names or references to them appear on lists compiled by Rich as estimates of his party's strength. Furthermore, the fact that the number of votes controlled by Rich at the final division on the salary, 24, is exactly 13 less than his list of the 37 opponents of the contract and salary may be of some significance. See *ibid.*, 310.

certain shares in a Virginia court of February 3 was occasion for one of many turbulent outbursts and caused Sir Henry Mildmay to remark that his majesty " wonders that so many are willing to give over their shares." [44] When the final test came in a Bermuda quarter court of February 20, Smith and Warwick controlled 24 votes, but fell short of the majority necessary to defeat the salary.[45] Their frequent complaints to the privy council in the next few weeks of their grievances " by votes assembled " bear witness to the feeling that on this, as at other occasions, they had been cheated of a victory rightfully theirs.

The defeated minority at once fell back upon their last resort, an appeal to the king. It was yet possible to secure a reconsideration from the other party to the contract. Their attendance at courts became less and less regular, but the fight was continued with even greater bitterness before the privy council. In explaining this, as well as the later appeal to the king on all questions affecting the plantations, it should be borne in mind that such a course was not decided upon until a determined effort had been made at a satisfactory settlement within the companies. There was now no longer any hope in that direction, and after their defeat in February Smith and Warwick made no serious attempt to contest an issue in the courts of either company. But though recognizing their defeat, they were less disposed to accept it because of the circumstances surrounding it. Their resentment was also greater by virtue of the fact that they had much more at stake in the settlement of the tobacco question than their more numerous opponents. In the minority were found the larger number of the heaviest investors, men who in number of shares held a decided majority, but who were outvoted by the smaller stockholders. Had the franchise been based upon the share rather than the head, Smith and Warwick would have controlled a clear majority. A list of the 37 opponents of the

[44] *Records*, II, 216.   [45] Manchester Papers, 302.

contract compiled by Rich carried an item after each name indicating the number of shares held in the general stock, the purpose being to show that a large majority of the active shares in the Bermuda Company were opposed to the contract.[46] It is not to be wondered at that they regarded with some resentment their recent defeat. It is significant too that it was in this contest over tobacco that the charge of democratic government was raised for the first time by Sandys' opponents as a serious criticism of the company's machinery.

Within two days after the defeat of Smith and Warwick the contract was suspended upon their complaint, and on the morning of February 24 the leaders of both parties, along with the customs officials, of whom Sir John Wolstenholme, a Virginia adventurer, was chief, were called for a hearing before Middlesex.[47] At both this and a second hearing before the privy council a few days later, the settlement of the important questions at issue was much delayed by the unusual vigor with which the irate adventurers attacked one another. At first the king's ministers seemed disinclined to revoke the contract, and Middlesex even instructed Southampton to proceed with plans for receiving the incoming crop since he felt these turbulent differences could in time be amicably settled.[48] In three weeks, however, the privy council decided to rescind the contract, and the Warwick party came away victor in the longest and most heated fight of the company's history.

Of some importance in the final decision was the revelation of the fact that the adventurers had for two years continued to send tobacco into Holland in flagrant violation of the council's order of 1621. For this bit of damaging news the Sandys party were chiefly indebted to their opponents, who at the earlier meeting with Middlesex had taken delight in professing their desire that all tobacco

[46] *Ibid.*, 310.
[47] *Records*, II, 294, 296-298.

[48] *Ibid.*, II, 298.

should be brought into England in accord with his majesty's wish.[49] At the subsequent hearing before the privy council Sandys, Cavendish, and Nicholas Ferrar were sharply taken to task for this violation of the council's command, and on March 4 an order in council was issued requiring strict obedience to the order of 1621.[50]

The deciding influence, however, seems to have been the arguments of Nathaniel Rich, who as spokesman for his partisans endeavored to persuade the privy council that the contract would be ruinous to the plantations and of little advantage to the king. In the Virginia and Bermuda courts he and his cohorts had waxed most eloquent on the exorbitance of the salary and the alleged irregularities in its passage, but now, as their opponents observed, "they dismasked themselves, and unanimously professed that they were against the very body of the contract."[51] The burden on the Bermuda plantation was so great that Rich foresaw a revolt of the planters through which England would lose a valuable foothold for the advancement of her interests in the new world. The least that could be expected would be that they would send their goods into foreign markets to the damage of English trade. The burden of the contract, he argued, would prove of equal damage to the adventurers at home. The planter was allowed 2s. 6d. for his tobacco in Bermuda, and, taking into consideration that most of the tobacco from the plantation could not be sold for even that much, to surrender a third to the king in addition to paying other heavy levies for customs, freight, and salary left no chance of profit for the adventurer. They would be seriously handicapped in settling their land, and emigration to the plantations would be greatly reduced, for the masters of ships upon calculating the increased cost on tobacco taken by them as freight would demand twice their former prices of £5 or

[49] *Records*, II, 298.   [51] Sackville Papers, p. 759.
[50] *Ibid.*, II, 305, 321.

£6 per head. These considerations were of special importance for the younger plantation, where the people produced nothing of profit save tobacco, and where those at home who must bear the public charge were few in number, many of whom by "maintaining a place of so great consequence without charge to his Majesty" had suffered great damage to their private fortunes. According to Rich, there were twenty adventurers who were out of their purses £20,000 for the support of the Bermuda plantations.[52]

In addition to these certain and heavy charges, their estates were placed in great hazard by several objectionable features in the plan of management. Two joint-stocks were to be created, one for the importation and sale of English tobacco, another for the Spanish, and these subordinate organizations were to have full control over all tobacco after it entered English ports. In Rich's opinion, it was a dangerous and unprecedented practise to allow a mere plurality of voices to place the goods of other men without their consent in joint-stock " coming home " when the adventure " outward " was by particular men and not in joint-stock. It would mean the utter ruin of trade, and add greatly to the already too heavy burdens of the contract. For men could not, under such an arrangement, have their money readily, but instead must await the sale and accompt of the joint-stock, a proceeding often entailing great delay. Their tobacco would be liable for the debts of the joint-stock, and more than this, they must suffer the delay and loss attendant upon frequent suits, intricate accounts, and the general confusion involved in such a method of control. One man's tobacco, he continued, was of better quality than another's, but according to the pro-

---

[52] *Ibid.*, pp. 755, 757; Manchester Papers, 316. Sandys' argument that the monopoly would provide some relief from these conditions by increasing the retail prices of tobacco was held invalid by Rich on the grounds of the encouragement given to smuggling by such an arrangement.

posed plan either it would be sold with that of lower grade to the owner's great loss, or if every man's lot was kept apart, he must still remain entirely dependent upon the good will of the company agents.[53]

And members of the Warwick group found no comfort in leaving their interests to the tender mercies of the "salary men" to whom they made strong objection, "some of them for want of skill, some want of estate, some of them no way interested, and other continually maintaining and raising quarrels and bitter contentions against sundry good Adventurers whose goods must come to their hands and possession to be disposed, Against which sundry of the Adventurers do protest as to men unfit to manage these affairs." [54] Here, one feels, was the heart of Rich's objection to the contract. It is also evidence of the extent to which party and factional bitterness had crippled the companies, for successful prosecution of corporate business must ever rely upon mutual confidence between officers and stockholders. There was now no such understanding possible between the officers of administration and a large body of men whose products they were to handle. It was unthinkable to Rich that he should surrender the control of his tobacco and the free right to sell it to the best of his advantage into the hands of bitter enemies, which was altogether aside from the irksome necessity of submitting to a heavy charge for salaries provided again by plurality of voices "of such as are least interested." [55] It was in vain that Southampton and Cavendish pointed to the ample security for faithful performance of duties required of all officers,[56] for would not the ultimate judge of their faithfulness be the very courts in which Rich and his party were already denied an effective voice?

Almost as great was their resentment at arrangements for importing Spanish tobacco. There was an obligation

---

[53] Sackville Papers, pp. 756-757.
[54] Ibid., pp. 758-759.
[55] Ibid., p. 756.
[56] Ibid., p. 761; Records, II, 284-288.

written into the contract and bound by the companies' seals to bring in 80,000 pounds, a heavy penalty operating in case of failure to perform. Yet despite the security given under the seals of the two courts, the companies were really to profit nothing by the importation. All benefits went to the subscribers of the joint-stock, although the companies must stand to make good any default in the fulfillment of the requirement. Rich with some justice held it a thing " of great danger and hazard for particular men's estates " to be thus engaged to his majesty by the seals of the companies for the performance of a contract that might " lie as a perpetual charge " upon the estates of all men free of the courts, " although they never received one penny benefit by their freedom." [57]

The hazards and uncertainties of these conditions, when added to the certain and heavy charges of his majesty's third, of the salary, and of the subsidy, would be so great as to bring the utter destruction of the plantations, to the damage not only of the planters and adventurers but to the trade of England and the king's revenue. Rich argued further that, aside from the probable ruin of the colonies' trade, the king had little advantage in revenue to expect of the contract — certainly not enough to warrant the risk of killing the goose that laid the golden egg. He calculated that the revenue which the king expected from Bermuda tobacco under the terms of the contract was not much larger than he might secure from a 6d. impost, and that the company by a saving of over £500 in salaries would certainly lose nothing by such a change.[58] It is obvious that by this date his fear of the contract was such that almost any other arrangement was preferable. Even a shilling duty, though heavy, had the merit of leaving each man full control over his tobacco with some certainty as to the " uttermost " of his charges. He really hoped, however, for another solution of the problem, and endeavored to

[57] Sackville Papers, p. 755.   [58] Manchester Papers, 315.

persuade the king to establish a government monopoly of tobacco patterned after the French *gabelle* and the Spanish monopolies of pepper and tobacco.[59]

The final settlement, though, was neither a return to the 12d. duties nor the establishment of a government monopoly. By the third week in March the privy council decided to rescind the contract and informed the adventurers of their lordships' willingness to consent to easier terms.[60] And within the week the plan of a contract with the companies was completely abandoned. The initial step toward a final settlement was taken by the farmers of the customs, who some time before the 19th had offered to abate 3d. of the subsidy upon English tobacco without demanding any defalcation therefor from his majesty's rent.[61] The explanation of this step, whether because of their anxiety to avoid the contract, which they had vigorously opposed, or because of the hope of coming out on the rent by the aid of an anticipated increase in importations from the colonies,[62] must remain uncertain. On March 24 Lord Cavendish reported the decisions of a final hearing before the privy council. The agents for the Sandys party had presented their proposals for a new contract, being roughly the same terms they had sought in the negotiations of the preceding summer. Rich, however, strongly objected to another contract and insisted that instead the adventurers should pay customs duties in money. The customs officials, who were also present, renewed their former offer to reduce the 6d. subsidy to 3d. In the end, after prolonged debate and many "contestations" it was decided that for the present colonial tobacco should be brought into England subject to the payment of duties amounting in all to 9d. per pound.[63]

Already a shipload of Virginia and Bermuda tobacco

[59] Manchester Papers, 315; Sackville Papers, pp. 752-754.
[60] *Records*, II, 329-330.   [62] See *ibid.*, II, 297.
[61] *Ibid.*, II, 332.   [63] *Ibid.*, II, 335.

had arrived in London, where it was held by customs officials pending a decision on the contract. On March 25 the lord treasurer issued instructions to the farmers and officers of the customs and to the collectors of the impost ordering its release. The privy council had after due deliberation, he wrote, considered the contract " prejudicial unto the Companies," and the tobacco was now to be delivered to the several proprietors after having paid 3d. per pound for the subsidy, " which the said farmers are contented to accept of *without demanding any defalcation from the King,*" and 6d. for the impost. It had been ordered that all tobacco from the plantations should henceforward be brought directly into England, and the adventurers had promised obedience. This paper, he concluded, was sufficient warrant to govern their collections of customs duties until further order was given.[64]

Thus it may be seen that the actual dissolution of the contract came the last week in March rather than late in April, the date most commonly given.[65] The only important question unsettled was that of Spanish tobacco. The chief concern of the adventurers thereafter was a fear lest the market might be left open to free importation of foreign tobacco. In April they petitioned at Rich's suggestion that Spanish tobacco might be limited to 40,000 weight and all other tobacco excluded except that from the plantations. The privy council acted favorably upon this request, and Middlesex offered the farm of 40,000 pounds of Spanish tobacco at £6,000 to the companies.[66]

So was the long, wearisome tobacco question finally concluded upon the most advantageous terms enjoyed by the

[64] Sackville Papers, pp. 762-763.   [66] *Records*, II, 365-366, 387-388.

[65] An order of the privy council dated April 28 has frequently been mistaken for the first formal dissolution of the contract. This was nothing more, however, than a restatement of the government's position on tobacco after the failure of the companies to include an account of the settlement in letters to the colonies which they were required to write after the first hearing before the privy council on April 17 of Johnson's petition for a royal investigation of the companies' affairs. See Lefroy, *Memorials of the Bermudas*, I, 293-294.

Virginia Company since 1619. All tobacco from the plantations was to be brought into England, and after the payment of 9d. duties was left to the free disposal of its individual owners. In addition to the benefits of reduced tariff rates, the tobacco of the plantations was to enjoy a virtual monopoly of the home market except for a limited quantity of Spanish tobacco. The credit for these more favorable terms belongs to Nathaniel Rich as spokesman for the Warwick party, and as Professor Beer concludes, the new plan " largely justifies their opposition to the agreement made in 1622." [67] The governor and council in Virginia expressed their appreciation the following winter, and only the defeated partisans of Sandys, recognizing the importance of this reversal in the final overthrow of their party, continued to regard with resentment the defeat of the old contract.

It was a decisive defeat for the Sandys party, and must be considered an important factor contributing to their fall. Many old wounds had been opened and new ones inflicted, with the result that a more or less passive and divided opposition was suddenly welded into an alert and active party with more determination in its resistance to Sandys than had existed since 1620. His enemies were still a minority, but the successful appeal to the king on the tobacco question suggested the possibility of an appeal on even broader issues that might result in the destruction of Sandys' power. Moreover, the king and his councillors were more favorably disposed to such an appeal because the events of recent months had demonstrated the hopeless factional division of the adventurers, and had therefore given support to the contention that the companies were no longer able to direct with expedition and success the important affairs committed to their care. It is little wonder, with this state of affairs at home, that the news of Virginia's sufferings through the preceding winter led almost immediately to a royal investigation.

[67] Beer, *Origins of the British Colonial System*, p. 133.

THE decision of the Smith-Warwick coalition to carry to the king the larger questions of Virginia's welfare and the condition of the company came in April, 1623. In explaining their action it is necessary, first of all, to recognize that in this step they were in complete accord with the tradition and custom of the English constitution. The crown, whether represented personally by the king or by his council, was the accepted agency for the settlement of those grievances which could not be righted through ordinary courses. And any suggestion that the appeal to the king is in itself evidence of an affinity in political convictions between James and the enemies of Sandys is to demonstrate a failure to understand the workings of the English government.

The motives which prompted this appeal for royal interference were born not of one consideration alone, but of a strange mixture of personal jealousies and dislikes with an honest concern for the welfare of Virginia. It was to them both a duty and a labor of hate. There can be no doubt that these men were intent upon evening several scores with Sandys. All of them, Warwick, Nathaniel Rich, and Alderman Johnson, the three who took the initiative and pressed the fight before the council, had long standing grievances, the memory of which had been quickened by the bitter invective of the tobacco fight. Smith and Johnson had been unhorsed by Sandys in 1619, and had suffered ever since under accusations of mismanagement and fraud noised about to the slander of their reputations. Their resentment sprang not only from an ancient wrong; it carried as well the full strength and bitterness of a fresh injury, for insult had been added to injury by slanderous reports not yet two months old. So recently as February had Smith entered his most bitter protest against what he considered an unwarranted damage to his name.[1] And the Rich family had neither forgotten nor forgiven the treatment they had received at the hands of Sandys in 1620.

Supporting and strengthening these major grievances were numerous lesser grudges, some of them in no way connected with Virginia, and others, arising from minor disputes in the conduct of business or in the debates of courts, that were of relative unimportance except that in an atmosphere charged with suspicion and hatred they added to the sum total of feeling. And back of all individual grievances was the more general resentment of a minority group excluded from the direction of the business. This resentment was of more than ordinary depth because of the unfair methods by which Sandys had maintained a majority in the courts, and because in the minority so excluded there were to be found some of the oldest and most substantial adventurers, men of greater experience, greater means, and, in their opinion, of greater right in the government of the company. Their repeated complaint to the privy council of the means by which Sandys had forced out " the ancient upholders of the Plantation " to replace them " by new comers without experience, to the great injury of the colony," [2] is not without significance in explaining their presence before that board.

These grievances, however, were closely interlocked in their minds with Sandys' failure as manager of the company. The severe criticism with which he had taxed his predecessors was made no easier for them to bear by the failure of his own efforts. There was probably some satisfaction for Smith and Johnson in the collapse of Sandys' program, but this left them in no wise more charitably disposed toward him; rather it served to burn deeper in their memory the strictures from which they had suffered. The same was true of the Riches, though probably to a lesser degree.

[1] *Records*, II, 259-261.   [2] Manchester Papers, 329, 346.

Aside from all considerations of feeling, however, these men were also prompted by a sincere concern for the present and future state of the company and colony. None of their contemporaries showed more devotion to the cause of colonization than did Smith, Warwick, and Nathaniel Rich, nor were there many whose investments in the Virginia Company were as heavy. Although Sandys' policies were in the main a faithful statement of contemporary ideas on colonization, his opponents had very early entertained certain objections to the policy in general,[3] and, more especially, had found serious grounds for quarrel with the hasty and unsound manner of its execution. It was this objection that prompted their frequent suggestion to the king that merchants were better fitted by experience to manage a business of such importance. They had made an earnest, though unsuccessful, effort to gain a voice in the company that would enable them to direct its administration according to sounder policies. Had they been able to outvote Sandys, they would have been satisfied, but any hope of this sort had been placed beyond the realm of possibility by the hardening of party lines in the disputes over the tobacco contract. Now with the company bankrupt, and their earlier fears more than justified by conditions in Virginia demanding such drastic steps for relief that, to judge by the performance of the past year, they could not be provided by the controlling administration, their only resort was to the crown. Of course, the fact that in looking to the interests of Virginia they were enabled to strike at their rival made them no less anxious to answer the call of duty.

Certainly in the state of both company and colony there was sufficient cause to justify the appeal for royal interference, and in the bitter factional feeling among the adventurers there is ample reason to explain it. When within the company itself there may be found reasons suffi-

[3] *Ibid.*, 275.

cient to account for the actions of every individual concerned, it is unnecessary to search outside the company's
affairs for evidence, which necessarily must be of doubtful
historical value, to prove an underhanded plot with
James to overthrow Sandys from purely political motives.

While the tobacco fight had multiplied factional bitterness and the successful appeal to the crown on the question
of the contract had probably suggested the same course in
all other problems of the company, the news of Virginia's
suffering after the massacre was the final factor in their
decision. In this connection, the return to England of
Captain Nathaniel Butler early in the spring of 1623 is
of great importance. Captain Butler had been the governor of Bermuda since 1619. His election to that office
had come from the strong support of Warwick, and he
had remained the earl's closest friend and partisan in
America. For this friendship he had suffered many severe
attacks from Sandys during the latter's attempt to stamp
out piracy in the two colonies. But although Sandys had
pressed his fight so forcefully that Butler was censured by
the Bermuda court, he was allowed to remain in office
for the full three year term which expired in 1622. His
grievances against the Sandys party, it may be guessed,
were as great as those of the adventurers at home. And on
his return trip in the fall of that year he made a special
visit to Virginia, probably at the suggestion of his co-
partisans in England, with the purpose of investigating
the state of affairs in that colony. He was there in the winter of its most severe trial, and returned to England full of
information and with his hatred of Sandys augmented by
the affronts of colonial leaders who regarded him as something of a busybody and spy.

He proceeded at once to relieve his feelings by spreading the news of Virginia's ills, and finally incorporated
his major criticisms of the controlling regime in the famous
" Unmasked Face of Our Colony in Virginia as it was in

the winter of the Year 1622," [4] which was presented to the privy council in support of the charges against Sandys. [5] Butler argued in this paper that conditions in the colony were so much worse than the adventurers and public had been led to believe that they presented a problem with which the company was not at all prepared to cope. There was, of course, much partisan coloring to Butler's picture. It was a long time since members of either party had been able to express opinions free of bias. Allowing a due margin for exaggeration, however, it will be found upon examining his charges that they were essentially true, and therefore deserve more than the summary dismissal commonly accorded them as an interesting example of the absurdly false evidence used against Sandys.

Opening with certain objections to the unhealthy location of James City, he proceeded to point out the weakness in the colony's defenses. Fortifications were so inadequate that a small boat might sail up the river without suffering damage to itself, and having anchored, " beat their houses down about their ears." He had found upon arrival neither guesthouse, inn, nor any other " like place " for the housing of newly arrived colonists, and the houses

---

[4] *Records*, II, 374-377.

[5] The first reference to Butler's paper is dated April 23, when a copy of it was sent to the company for answer. The phraseology of the court minutes indicates, however, that it was submitted to the king either with or shortly after Johnson's petition, which places its date much earlier in the month. Whether or not it was drawn up before this for circulation among members of the opposition party is not clear. At any rate, since it represents the opinions circulated by Butler upon his return to England, it falls chronologically within the period before the appeal to the crown. The exact date of his return is unknown, but there is little doubt of his presence in England prior to Johnson's petition. Letters from Virginia fall by date into two groups, the first written in January, and the next late in March, and taking this as an indication of his opportunities to secure passage home, it seems likely that he sailed from the colony in January, since the March sailing would not have permitted him to be in England at the time of writing. This conclusion is also supported by the fact that he left Bermuda in October, and considering conditions in Virginia, as well as his general unpopularity there, it is reasonable to expect that he took an early opportunity to leave.

in general were " the worst that ever I saw," a factor which
he considered of great importance in the death of many
settlers. " Expecting according to their printed books a
great forwardness of divers and sundry Commodities at
mine arrival," he continued, " I found not any one of them
so much as in any towardness of being." In common with
all other persons who had been to Virginia, he objected
to the " dispersal " of settlers, and argued that their scattered
settlements had given the Indians every advantage at the
time of the massacre. It was not unnatural that he should
call attention to the abandonment to the natives of some
of the best plantations, nor that he should dwell at length
on the severe shortage of food during the past winter. The
want of food had been greater because many of those in a
position to trade with the natives had used this advantage
for their own profit. With a few other complaints, such as
the charge that he found the government there in some
particulars not according to the " excellent Laws and Customs of England," he concluded:

There having been as it is thought not fewer than Ten thousand souls transported thither, there are not through the
aforenamed abuses and neglects above Two thousand of them
at the present to be found alive, many of them also in a
sickly and desperate estate: So that it may undoubtedly be expected that unless the confusions and private ends of some of
the Company here and the bad executions in seconding them
by their Agents there be redressed with speed by some divine
and supreme hand that instead of a Plantation it will shortly
get the name of a slaughter house and so unjustly become
both odious to ourselves and contemptible to all the world.[6]

Not only is the main outline of these criticisms fully
corroborated by the correspondence with leading colonists
preserved in the Ferrar Papers and in the Manuscript
Records of the Virginia Company, but it is possible to
substantiate the essential points in Butler's indictment by

[6] *Records*, II, 380-387, 397-399.

the detailed reply, composed largely of excuses and explanations, rather than actual denials, prepared by the company. It was easy to condemn this "false and scandalous" libel on the colony's good name, but when it came to an actual refutation of Butler's arguments it was impossible to avoid several damaging admissions. It was agreed that nothing had been done to provide guesthouses, but a partial excuse was found in the fact that the massacre had interrupted plans to remedy this defect at an early date. The company sought refuge in the massacre on many other counts, among them the complete failure of all projects for staple commodities, and endeavored as far as was possible to remove from the adventurers any responsibility for the causes or effects of the native conspiracy. It was true that there were no "artificial" fortifications for the colony's defense, but this lack was remedied to some extent by trenches which served the same purposes. They refused to recognize that any weakness resulted from their plan of settlement, for the people in Virginia enjoyed well built houses from which they might easily withdraw in time of emergency. The price of food during the preceding winter was greatly exaggerated, and the charge of profiteering among prominent colonists was branded absolutely false, although less than a year before the council had made the same accusation in a letter to the colony.[7] The abandonment of so many plantations was indeed regrettable, but it was hoped that they had already been rebuilt according to order.

Several of Butler's criticisms, especially his references to the government, were attributed wholly to personal pique at having been refused the privilege of sitting with the council, a privilege to which he had no right whatsoever. In conclusion, the company objected to his figures on the death rate under Sandys, but even so it was necessary to concede a very high rate of mortality. The estimated num-

[7] MS. Rec. Va. Co., III, Part ii, 4-5a.

ber of persons sent to Virginia since 1607 was given here as 6,000, rather than 10,000, of whom approximately 2,500 had gone under Smith, and the population of the colony at the time of writing was at least 2,500 instead of the 2,000 claimed by Butler.[8] This rebuttal of the "unmasked Face" was written and presented to the privy council as part of the company's defense against the charges brought before that body by the Smith-Warwick party.

Early in April Alderman Johnson had submitted to the king a petition requesting a thorough investigation of the company's affairs.[9] Johnson began with the assertion that, by God's assistance and the gracious encouragement of his majesty, the colony had prospered for many years under the discreet leadership of Sir Thomas Smith, the planters had lived in peaceful harmony with the natives, and a variety of staple commodities had been returned as the product of their labors to the honor of all parties concerned. Since 1619, however, although vast numbers of his subjects had been sent to Virginia,

the fruits of that work are withered and do not appear as in former times, our unity and peace at home is turned to rival discord and dissension amongst ourselves, and to massacre and hostilities between the Natives and our Colony in Virginia. The Ancient Adventurers and others conceive themselves injured and abused by unjust scandals and reprooffull censures, and as well by slanders divulged as upon records in Court, of which intolerable wrongs while they seek relief amongst themselves, their grievances by votes assembled are more increased, by which this faction and schism is grown to bitter malice and

[8] A group of mariners, masters, and "ancient" planters, who had often been to Virginia or had lived there at some time, prepared answers to most of Butler's accusations, and laid them before the court on April 30 (*Records*, II, 380-387). The governor and company completed the work by replying to those points dealing with Henrico and Charles City, the criticisms of the government, and Butler's figures regarding mortality. The whole was confirmed by a court of May 7 (*Records*, II, 397-399).

[9] An extraordinary court of both companies was called on April 12, at which time Lord Cavendish informed the adventurers of Johnson's action (*Records*, II, 346).

contention one against another, to the high offence of Almighty God, to the hindrance of your Majesty's royal and gracious intentions of both plantations and to the utter discouragement of such as with single heart intend the public good to prosperity of that worthy enterprise. And for that we find it impossible to cure and heal these breaches without the help of a more supreme hand, nor hold it fitting to trouble your sacred ears with our particular wrongs, we are come, not for malice nor revenge, but for remedy to appeal unto your most excellent Majesty.

The petitioner then prays for the appointment of a royal commission to inquire into and determine the true state of the plantations at the close of Smith's administration, and, proceeding from that point, to discover what funds since that time had been collected, by whom and from what sources, and how they had been expended — all with a view of deciding "what after the expence of so much money is the true estate and condition of those plantations at this present." He wished also an inquiry into all abuses and grievances arising from the conduct of the business, as well as all wrongs and injuries done to any adventurers or planters. And he hoped that after this thorough investigation the commission might "propound how the same may in time to come be reformed, and how the business of those plantations may be better managed, so that all contentions and differences being reconciled, the Authors thereof being punished, unity and peace resettled, and the form of governing and directing those affairs being better established, that work may prosper with a blessing from heaven to your Majesty's great honour and profit and to those religious and public ends for which they were first undertaken." [10]

Upon receiving news of this petition, leaders of the Sandys party called an extraordinary court for both companies on April 12. At this joint meeting Lord Cavendish,

---

[10] Manchester Papers, 328; *Records*, II, 373-374.

governor of the Bermuda Company, informed the adventurers of Johnson's appeal to the crown. It had been impossible to secure a copy of the petition, but Sir Edward Sackville was acquainted with the general substance thereof and outlined its points briefly. Although neither Warwick, Rich, Johnson, nor Smith was present, there were among the assembled adventurers several of their partisans who contended that the petition was not directed against the company itself and urged that definite action by the court should be deferred until a full copy of the paper was available. A majority of the stockholders, however, agreed that the complaint was against the company and that preparation of its defense should begin at once. Upon a vote taken, it was found that the court " liked very well " the " issue of the Petition itself," and it was ordered that another petition from the company should be presented to the privy council joining Johnson in his request for a thorough investigation of the company's affairs " that their Innocency or guiltiness might be cleared or punished." [11] For his majesty's information in the meantime, two papers defending the company against many accusations recently made were approved by the adventurers.[12] Lord Cavendish then took the chair, thereby converting the assembly into a court of the Somers Islands Company, and the agreements arrived at in the Virginia court were formally ratified by the younger company.[13] In establishing the machinery for a royal investigation, therefore, the privy council was acting in compliance with two separate petitions representing the expressed wish of both parties to the Virginia disputes.

The active interference of the government which followed was not an entirely new departure. From the first experiments in colonization there had been a close connection with the government, for although these ventures

[11] *Records*, II, 346-348.
[12] *Ibid.*, II, 348-351, 351-362.
[13] *Ibid.*, II, 363.

were supported by private capital, they were of a public character that made some dependence upon the crown inevitable. From no other source could adventurers obtain a secure title to their land, the authority to establish a government for their peoples, or the protection that was necessary in view of the territorial claims of other states. And there were numerous exemptions from laws governing emigration and customs duties, as well as other special privileges, such as a monopoly of trade, that were often essential to the financial success of their efforts. On the other hand, the responsibility assumed by the king in granting these privileges, and the fact that the progress of the companies involved the welfare and protection of a large body of his subjects, entitled him to certain privileges in the direction of their affairs. The first evidence of this close relationship is found in the royal charters under which the companies existed.

For eight years after obtaining the charter of 1612 the Virginia Company was left comparatively free from governmental interference, largely because there were few questions arising which required the government's attention. By 1619, however, certain changes were taking place in the state of Virginia that made it necessary for the king and his ministers to take a more active interest. The rapid development of tobacco had given the colony a product for exportation at about the same time that privileges of free importation into England had expired. Certain problems arose, such as securing the shipment of all of Virginia's exports to England, making arrangements whereby the king would be assured a proper revenue from the company's tobacco, and at the same time establishing safeguards against the overdevelopment of this objectionable product. There followed an increasing correspondence between the privy council and responsible officials dealing mainly with these aspects of the company's business.

Just as these developments were bringing problems in

which the council could not but be interested, the internal troubles of the company itself were becoming a hindrance to the advancement of a business in which the king now held a very real interest. The fights among the adventurers were from the first public property, but James' attention was especially directed to them by the repeated complaints of Smith. The ex-governor and his associates not only complained of their personal grievances against Sandys, but severely criticised the policies of his administration. James, in no wise loath to entertain criticism of Sandys, so far acceded to Smith's wishes that he secured Sir Edwin's removal from office in 1620. And again in 1622 he interfered in the company's elections, sending word to the adventurers that, although it was not his wish to restrict their privileges, it would please him if they chose their two chief officers from an appended list which included neither Southampton, Sandys, or either of the Ferrars. The company, very happy at not having its liberties infringed, decided to vote on three for each office, two of which should be taken from the king's list and one nominated by the company. Of course the nominees of the company were completely victorious, after which a deputation was selected to call on the king and express their appreciation for his interest, as also to explain that the old officers had been reëlected because of the great prosperity that had attended the administration of the past three years.

His majesty, however, was not at all pleased with this report, and expressed the opinion that merchants were better suited for such employment in view of " their skill and abilities for raising of Staple Commodities, and instancing Sir Thomas Smith in whose times many Staple Commodities were set up which were now laid down and only Tobacco followed." Whereupon, Lord Cavendish, who headed the company's deputation, replied that " in this point as likewise in many other particulars " his Majesty " had been much misinformed." The sole de-

pendence on tobacco and the neglect of all other commodities were in reality the fruit of Smith's administration.
In sharp contrast was the policy of the past three years, in
which no labor had been spared to promote iron, wine,
silk, and many other commodities " whereof they hoped
very shortly to give his Majesty good proof." The contrast
between the past and present administrations might be
seen in the fact that " the Colony had grown almost to as
many Thousands of people " as Smith " left hundreds." [14]
And with this interview the matter was dropped.

Shortly thereafter, the negotiations for the tobacco contract were opened, in which the government endeavored
to make satisfactory arrangements for the economic relations of the colony with the mother country. James followed these negotiations, and later the violent disputes in
the companies, which delayed for months the settlement of
questions that, aside from all considerations for the welfare of Virginia, were of real importance to the government. Throughout the winter he watched a quarrel that
brought all business to a standstill while the adventurers
fought among themselves and condemned one another in
virulent expressions of hatred. On more than one occasion
he sent word advising that they leave off their " verbal
differences " in order that their business might proceed. [15]
If by this observation he came to feel that it was impossible
for the adventurers to settle their differences among themselves, and to doubt the ability of an organization so torn
by feud and strife to provide a successful direction of the
affairs of Virginia, he was certainly not alone in such
opinions.

Thus it may be seen that the king's dislike of the management and progress of the company was not of recent
growth. With the exception of occasional advice and two
attempts to use his influence in elections, however, he had

[14] *Records*, II, 28-29, 31-32, 35.
[15] *Ibid.*, II, 216-217, 248, 252-253.

allowed the adventurers to pursue their course free from interference. But several considerations predisposed the king and his council to more decisive steps in 1623. For three years the council had experienced considerable difficulty in enforcing its requirement that all exports from Virginia should be shipped directly to England. Sandys' policy of sending the colony's tobacco to Holland had called forth a sharp reprimand in 1620, and yet it had been necessary so recently as March to issue another warning to the company's officers because of violations of this express order in council. This was a point in government policy on which there could be no dispute, and the flagrant disregard of the council's command undoubtedly operated heavily against responsible officials.

Another factor of great importance, which has not received due emphasis, was the government's attitude on tobacco and the so-called staple commodities as fit products for the colony. The one was held to be generally worthless and wholly to be condemned, while the degree of success in the other was considered a proper measure for judging the progress of the colony. For the great emphasis given this point in 1623 Sandys had himself in part to thank, since no man had done more to advertise the disadvantages of tobacco and the importance of substituting other products. Were the king and council to accept his words at face value, the same standard by which Sandys condemned Smith served now also to demonstrate his own complete failure.

James had followed these projects with real interest, especially attempts at silk culture, and no one recognized better than Sandys the disadvantage resulting from their lack of progress. In August, 1622, the Virginia Council in one of its numerous exhortations to the colony expressed the belief that the failure to produce staple commodities had been " the truest objection against the succeeding of this plantation, and the greatest hindrance and impediment (as we conceive) that his Majesty and the State have not set to a more liberal hand to the furtherance thereof." [16] Again in May, 1623, the adventurers in a letter to Virginia declared the failure of staple commodities, especially because of "His Majesty's resentment therein," to be a matter of great disgrace and damage to both the company and the colony.[17] If James was of the opinion that four years was long enough to show some proof of progress, so also was Sandys. The significance attached to the total collapse of his numerous projects may be seen in Johnson's petition, in the many references to it in the argument presented before the royal commission by Nathaniel Rich, and in the company's determined efforts to defend itself on this point.

It seems likely, however, that the deciding factor in the government's decision to act was the news of Virginia's suffering through the preceding winter. Regardless of all former prejudices, the report of so great a catastrophe affecting a large body of the king's subjects was alone sufficient to demand investigation. When with this news came a petition supported by some of the most substantial adventurers in the company, the king was but performing his duty in granting their request. Hardly any government could have avoided some responsibility in a crisis of this sort. That the government would respond to Johnson's petition was more probable because there had been differences and difficulties running through four years. Any doubts or fears that James may have entertained, either at Smith's suggestion or of his own initiative, appeared now to be well grounded. The impression gained in the preceding months of the company's hopeless division raised the question of its ability to meet the emergency now confronting the colony. And doubts of this sort were strengthened by reports of a complete failure to cope with similar

[16] MS. Rec. Va. Co., III, Part ii, 23a-25.
[17] Ibid., III, Part ii, 27a.

problems after the massacre. Even if it be admitted that the controlling factor in James' decision was his prejudice against Sandys, the presence of evidence to justify his proceedings assumes a place of no less importance.

While summing up the influences that determined the king's policies in 1623, it would probably be a mistake to disregard altogether the fact that Sandys did not enjoy royal favor. James hardly found the performance of his duty any less pleasurable because it involved some procedure against a man he thoroughly disliked. It is also quite likely that Sandys' opponents relied in part on his political disfavor as a persuasion with the king. Men in a fight governed by passion are seldom above using any weapon that comes to hand. But to interpret the whole affair in the light of political differences is to advance a thesis incapable of proof and to ignore completely conditions in the company and its relations to the government which offer a sufficiently adequate explanation.

Indeed, the degree of James' personal participation in settling the troublesome questions of Virginia, either before or after the establishment of the royal commission, is rather uncertain. Of his personal interest in the colony there can be no doubt, but the attention given by him to its problems has probably been exaggerated. He was never noted for constant application to business, and here, as with so many other problems of his reign, his attention was probably only fitful and spasmodic. The actual work involved in hearing and deciding upon the petitions from the adventurers, in setting up a commission for investigation, and in directing its labors devolved upon the lords of the privy council. Of course there are numerous references to the king's opinion, "his Majesty's wish," etc., but in these one may easily be led astray by the broad terminology of English constitutional practise.

The leaders of the two parties were called before the privy council on April 17, where there was exhibited "much heat and bitterness between them at first, fitter to perplex than to settle the business."[18] Sir Edward Sackville carried himself so insolently that the king "was fain to take him down soundly and roundly," but by the aid of the lord treasurer he was able to make "his peace" the next day.[19] Despite this feeling, the lords of the council were finally successful in bringing an agreement on two points. In the first place, it was agreed that there should be established a commission headed by Sir William Jones, Justice of the Court of Common Pleas since 1621, and composed of Sir Nicholas Fortesan, Sir Henry Bourchier, Sir Henry Spiller, Sir Francis Gofton, Sir Richard Sutton, and Sir William Pitt, to conduct a thorough investigation into all the questions now so hotly disputed. As a concession to the demand of the Sandys party, their examination was to begin from the very first of Smith's administration, rather than in 1619. But while they were thus "to examine the carriage of the whole business," their chief duty was to determine the present state and needs of the plantations and to suggest in what ways their affairs might be better managed. Secondly, in order that the planters in the two colonies might not be discouraged by any information proceeding from "factious humors or private ends," it was decided that letters from adventurers should contain no information except that absolutely necessary to the direction of their private business. As a further safeguard against false and biased reports, the companies were required to meet the next morning and agree on one general letter to be sent the colonists. This letter was to be approved by the council, and the lords themselves were to send another acquainting the colonists "with His Majesty's Pious and Princely care of them and the course in hand to provide better for them, whereby to unite their resolutions and give them encouragement

[18] Middlesex to Conway, April 18, 1623, P.R.O., S.P. 15/43, 10.
[19] Chamberlain to Carleton, April 19, 1623, P.R.O., S.P. 14/143, 22.

and constancy to go on cheerfully in the work they have in hand." [20]

This latter communication was finally dated on April 28, and carried the information that his majesty had now taken into his gracious consideration the welfare of the colonies with the purpose of establishing " fit directions and orders for the future, whereby all indirect courses, misunderstandings and dissentions may be prevented." It was hoped the good effect of this action would " both advance the public good and also redound to the particular contentment and benefit of every honest person." In the meantime, the colonists should not be discouraged by " loose advertisements " proceeding from factious humors, but rather should find comfort in attending the fruits of that good work which was now in his majesty's care.[21]

The commission for the investigation was drawn up by April 24, awaiting the approval of the council,[22] and it was finally issued under date of May 9. The commissioners were authorized to go through all patents, letters, and records of the two companies, and to examine witnesses under oath or by other lawful means, in order to discover any infringement of patents, any fraudulent practise, or anything else that had occasioned the hindrance or decay of the colonies and their commerce. This, with a careful auditing of all financial transactions, was to lead them to some decision as to the past and present state of the colonies.[23]

Johnson's petition and the instructions to the commissioners indicate clearly the economic nature of the questions at issue, but a still better indication of their true character may be found in the arguments presented by both parties in behalf of their respective cases. The whole

[20] Order in Council, April 17, 1623, Bancroft Transcripts, Virginia Papers, II, 69-73; Middlesex to Conway, April 18, 1623, P.R.O., S.P. 15/43, 10.
[21] Bancroft Transcripts, Virginia Papers, II, 93-96.
[22] Middlesex to Conway, April 24, 1623, P.R.O., S.P. 14/143, 60.
[23] Official Papers of the Pitt Family, Add. MSS. 29975, f. 63.

of the evidence laid before the royal commission by Sandys' opponents was an attempt to prove that the company's indebtedness and bankruptcy, both in morale and finances, the disasters suffered by the colony, and the high mortality of its inhabitants were all due to the mismanagement of the past four years. On the other hand, Sandys and his associates labored to refute this indictment of their administration and to prove that the colony's state at present was full of promise. Anything to the contrary they attributed as far as was possible to the faults of the preceding administration.

The preparation of the case against Sandys was undertaken by Nathaniel Rich. Although neither Johnson nor Smith was inactive, the broad condemnation of Sandys' policies and administration that carried so much weight in the deliberations of the commission was the work of Rich who, as spokesman for the Warwick faction, was indefatigable in collecting letters from Virginia, interviewing returned seamen and planters, and drawing upon all other possible sources of information. Of his labors voluminous evidence has been left to posterity in his private papers preserved in the Manchester Papers. Here may be found letters, scraps of paper on which notes were hastily scratched as a record of conversations or for reference in intended speeches, and most valuable of all, long documents summing up the contents of these letters and notes, which by their form and a more careful preparation indicate that they were to be presented to the royal commission. It is among these papers of Rich that the historian must search for the most accurate index to the motives which prompted the attack upon Sandys and the arguments which were prepared in its support. That the Warwick party, with Rich as its mouthpiece, was the most active in pressing the fight against Sandys, as in fact it had been in warring upon the tobacco contract, is proved not only by the material in the Manchester Papers but by the increasing bitterness with which this group was assailed by Sandys' partisans. Before the investigation had proceeded beyond its earliest stages Sandys' lieutenants had recognized in Warwick their most determined and dangerous foe.

And well they might, for the charges of this group were indeed many and serious. Prefacing their attack by the erroneous, though necessary, statement that the colony had made good progress under Smith's leadership, they attempted to prove that due to the sundry errors and abuses of Sandys this happy progress had been stopped and the colony reduced to a " miserable and most desperate estate," while the company languished under a heavy indebtedness of between six and seven thousand pounds. It was by foul means, of which the famous " ballatinge box " offered best proof, that Sandys came into control at a time when there was great hope of prosperity, argued Rich, and since then the company " by his and the two deputies' means hath been brought into great debts without any apparent means, to discharge the same factions have been bred and nourished amongst us." [24]

Disbursements during the four preceding years were estimated at between eighty-five and ninety thousand pounds, and for this vast outlay of capital only the most insignificant results could be shown. There were in Rich's mind several explanations, among others the planting of new officers in the colony with an " excessive proportion of tenants," a policy which had been the subject of much dispute in the preceding fall and had called forth strong objection from the colonial council during the winter.[25] Of course there were charges of crooked dealing, and an impartial auditing of all accounts was especially urged. In this connection the magazines came under heavy fire, and the commissioners were desired to be very careful " to examine the magazines of these last four years, and the

[24] Manchester Papers, 344, 362.
[25] Ibid., 347, 362; MS. Rec. Va. Co., III, Part ii, 4-5a.

prices thereof here and in Virginia, and who made the benefit of them." Even stronger was their denunciation of the administration of the lotteries and of the company's agent in this business, Gabriel Barbor, who was openly charged with the embezzlement of several thousand pounds.[26]

But while giving much attention to charges of fraud, graft, and embezzlement, most of which were hardly supported by anything more than rumor and suspicion, Rich got down to the real heart of the matter when he asserted that the company's indebtedness, as well as the unhappy state of the colony, was largely the result of ill advised and reckless expenditure. He took occasion here to condemn Sandys' "vast and wild projects," many of which should never have been attempted and all of which by their poor administration had constituted a heavy drain on public funds. He instanced especially the iron-works, which it was claimed, had prospered under the former regime but during Sandys' direction had served only to consume £5,000 of the public funds while returning to the company not even the principal invested.[27]

This criticism in no way prevented him from capitalizing the colony's complete dependence upon tobacco. It was a good point, Sandys had made it so, and it could be used with telling effect before almost any contemporary body of Englishmen, especially before one selected by the author of a *Counter-Blaste to Tobacco*. And yet it is doubtful if, beyond its value in the attack on the company's administration, Rich and Warwick were as greatly concerned about the rapid development of tobacco as were most of the adventurers. Rich's papers give far more attention to other features of the colony's affairs, and their interest through the preceding years seems to have been primarily in two things: tobacco plantations and piracy. The stubborn fight they made on the contract may be taken as some

[26] Manchester Papers, 330, 331, 334, 347.   [27] *Ibid.*, 330, 362.

evidence of the heavy stakes at issue for these two men. And Governor Butler's response to an inquiry of Warwick in 1620 that if "any staple commodity besides tobacco and a fair war with Spain prove real here, it will be the making of silk"[28] suggests that his patron had early entertained certain doubts as to the practicability of Sandys' program for producing a wide variety of staple commodities to take the place of tobacco. But although there must remain some uncertainty as to the real attitude of the Warwick group regarding the relative merits of tobacco and other products, there can be no doubt that they used the failure of Sandys' plans in every way possible to discredit him — both to criticize him for undertaking an unsound program and then to strafe him for having failed in it. It was a two-edged sword, and Rich wielded it well.

His most serious criticisms, however, were directed at Sandys' hasty and reckless program of colonization. It was on this ground that the administration since 1619 was most thoroughly and heatedly condemned. Rich demanded to know upon "what good and warrantable grounds the Company adventured to send such multitudes of people these four last years," and asked the commissioners to determine "whether the sending of so many people hath not indiscretely wasted the whole public stock, and been a means to cast away the lives of many of his majesty's Subjects and therefore to inquire what men have been sent and how many have died."[29] Not only had there been far too many colonists sent, in his opinion, but the conditions of their shipment had added immeasurably to the misery and suffering of both old and new planters. There was something more than his own personal interests that prompted Rich to condemn

The pestering of Ships with such a multitude of passengers and store of goods *for private gain* (in which the two Mr. Ferrars were sometimes sharers) by which means and the short allow-

[28] Manchester Papers, 275.   [29] *Ibid.*, 331.

ance of food to the passengers, they landed half starved, and brought with them their own deaths and infection of others in the Country so that in three years there died near upon 3000 persons, for which mortality no other cause can truly be shown but the want of houses, pestering of ships, shortness and badness of food.[30]

He pointed out the doubly disastrous effect of this policy upon the colony. Ships that should have carried provisions were loaded with settlers, who, in addition to bringing disease from their "pestered" ships, added many more mouths to be fed out of provisions already inadequate enough. This policy of sending settlers when the need was for supplies had often added greatly to the colony's want and consequently to its suffering. As an indication of the carelessness of officials, Rich asserted that only 192 head of cattle had been sent by the company in contrast to thousands of human beings.[31] Not content with showing a shortage in supply, he went further to maintain that when the company did awake to its responsibility the scant provisions sent were often unfit for consumption. A point was made of the poor quality of meal provided, and he could not overlook the fact that the committee which " provided that meal was both buyer and seller himself vzt. Mr. Caswell the baker." [32] As would be expected there were many references to the exorbitant prices of food and clothing in the colony.

Such accusations were serious enough in themselves, but they were made even more so by Rich's attempt to prove that Sandys had received frequent warnings from Virginia of the dangers in his overhasty attempts at colonization. Instead of paying heed, however, he had proceeded on his course in absolute disregard of these warnings, and worse still, had been able to continue this large emigration from England by a deliberate concealment of the true conditions in America. He accomplished it, according to Rich,

[30] *Ibid.*, 344.   [31] *Ibid.*, 362.   [32] *Ibid.*, 344.

by a regular system of "double and contradictory" letters, having the leaders in the colony compose one letter for public reading at courts and another conveying to Sandys the true facts. Through this practise many people had been "allured" to go to the colony on "false pretences," and Rich wanted the commissioners to force Sandys to produce under oath all letters from Virginia persuading or dissuading the sending of so many colonists,

And upon oath to inquire whether about one and the same time from some one or the same person or by some other of good Credit, there were not private letters written to some chief men of the Company concerning the true estate of the colonies, contrary or diverse to those that were read in public, whereby the Courts were deluded and drawn to consent to the vast Propositions of some, who it is feared again to obtain the same of sending great multitude of people in so short a time, could not or would not see the danger of the move they took to arrive at that end.[33]

The same purpose had been served by spreading false rumors and by the use of printed books and ballads describing the "happy estate of the Plantation, which was most unreasonably put in practice this last Lent, when the colony was in most extreme misery." [34]

When this charge of falsifying reports from Virginia was substantiated by lists of over two dozen letters,[35] some of them in Rich's possession, proving the state of the colony to have been quite different from that pictured in the public statements and correspondence of the company, Sandys was placed in a position difficult to defend. It was one thing to be presented as a man whose errors were due to inexperience, and another to be condemned as one whose fault was a willful and foolhardy proceeding in the face of facts. Rich pressed this argument for all it was worth, perhaps to the point of an unfair advantage. Yet

[33] Manchester Papers, 330, 331, 347.
[34] Ibid., 347, 362.
[35] Ibid., 338, 339.

he was uncomfortably near the truth. No one can read through the Ferrar Papers, the letters there from Yeardley, Pory, Nuce, Weldon, and others, without feeling that Rich's charge was not altogether unjustified.

To this chief cause of the colony's unhappy state, Rich added others. Officers had been appointed by favor, and as a result control had been placed in the hands of inexperienced and unskilled men. Old planters had been removed from their positions of security, and by the policy of granting fifty acres to each colonist the settlers had become dispersed, and the defense of the colony had been otherwise weakened.[36] The massacre was consequently more terrible in its effects. Heavy responsibility for that attack and for its dire consequences was fastened upon the officials both in England and in America.[37]

Since Johnson's petition had resulted in part from the inability of the Smith-Warwick group to wrest the control of affairs from Sandys, it is not surprising that there were attacks on the means by which he had gained and kept control of the companies. Rich complained loudly of the practice of

buying up old shares, for a trifle, of such as had left the business or else had their freedoms freely bestowed upon them, so that the face of the Court (as Mr. Ferrar professed it should be ere long) was quite changed, and composed of a number of friends, allies, and confidants ready to assist with their votes what by this faithful Treasurer should be projected.[38]

Courts had also been packed by transferring shares to friends who would hold them merely for purposes of voting. And the will of the old adventurers had been obstructed at times by prolonging the courts until so late an hour that Sandys' opponents were overcome with weariness, and after their departure he had pushed through important measures. There were other similar accusations,

[36] Ibid., 331, 347, 362.   [38] Ibid., 346.
[37] Ibid., 330, 331, 362.

among them that Sandys had even resorted to bringing into courts great persons whose presence served to awe those who would speak against him.[39] By such means, Rich declared, the Sandys party carried forward their designs " against the ancient upholders of the Plantation, only to reap a benefit to themselves and to wrong the Rest of the Adventurers." [40]

There were of course complaints of the " late pernicious contract " and the " exorbitant salary " which had been contrived for the benefit of only a few persons, particularly Sandys and Ferrar. The bitter aspersions cast upon Sandys' opponents in this fight had caused nearly all the adventurers most conversant with the affairs of the plantation to " desert the business." [41] Now the company was left bankrupt, its most able and experienced members unjustly excluded from its councils, and the colony by the direction of inexperienced and incompetent men was on the verge of complete ruin.

Such was the character of the testimony presented by the Warwick party in support of its request for some reorganization of the Virginia Company. From beginning to end it was an indictment of Sandys' management of the economic interests of the company and colony. It is natural to conclude that had there been a political struggle underlying this dispute, Sandys' enemies would not have hesitated to attack him on account of his so-called democratic ideas, and would have at least incorporated some of their objections to his political opinions in their private papers. The complete absence of any record of such an attack, or of such objections, in the papers of Nathaniel Rich is a fact therefore of considerable importance.

In the entire collection there is only one reference to Sandys' political opinions. This is found in a note, made apparently by Nathaniel Rich, of a conversation with Cap-

---

[39] Manchester Papers, 347, 360.   [41] Ibid., 347.
[40] Ibid., 329.

tain John Bargrave on May 16, 1623,[42] more than a month
after the Virginia disputes had been taken to the king.
Bargrave had come with a paper he had written concerning the "present Government of Virginia," which
Rich "only read and delivered to him again." The two of
them "being then all alone in the great Chamber of my
Lord of Warwick's house," there followed a conversation
to which several historians have attached great importance.
Bargrave began by declaring that he was afraid to discover
some of the things he knew about Sandys' proceedings in
the Virginia business, many of which he believed Sir Edwin would attempt to hide "under the name of the Company." He then told Rich

that by his long acquaintance with him and his ways he was
induced verily to believe that there was not any man in the
world that carried a more malicious heart to the Government
of a Monarchy than Sir Edwin Sandys did, for Captain Bargrave had heard him say that if our God from heaven did constitute and direct a form of Government it was that of Geneva.
And he hath oft times reprehended Captain Bargrave that in
some written tracts of his, and in his discourse he seemed to
dislike the constitution and frame of the present Government
of Virginia as that which inclines unto, if not directly being, a
popular Government, he telling Captain Bargrave that his intent was to erect a free state in Virginia and other words to
that purpose.

Sandys had even asked the Archbishop of Canterbury for
permission to send Brownists and Separatists to the colony.
In conclusion, Bargrave declared that if the charter which
Sandys had sent into Virginia, "in which is a clause (as he
says) that they shall have no Government put upon them
but by their own consents," [43] and his other proceedings
in the business of the plantations, "especially such as con-

[42] *Ibid.*, 368.
[43] The reference is to the last clause of the ordinance for the assembly. For
its content and meaning see pp. 74-75.

cerned government, were looked into, it would be found that he aimed at nothing more than to make a free popular state there."

Historians looking for evidence in support of a political interpretation of the Virginia disputes have made much of this document. Several considerations, however, rather discount its worth in explaining the motives of the Rich party. Its date, over a month after Johnson's petition, and the fact that it stands alone in a mass of material relating to economic conditions lead to the conclusion that, instead of representing the essential argument in the case against Sandys, it was merely an additional point which may have been used because of its probable weight with the king. There is no evidence, however, to prove that it was actually used even in this way. In none of the longer documents prepared by Rich for presentation to the royal commission is there any reference either to this conversation or in any other way to Sandys' political opinions. Furthermore, the manner in which Rich recorded this conversation is of some significance. One gets the impression that here was a new suggestion for him, one which he was ready to accept, it is true, but nevertheless a new angle on Sandys' work in Virginia. The secretiveness of Bargrave, the care with which his words are written down, and the frequent interposition of "as he says" or "as Captain Bargrave affirmed to me," hardly imply that the conversation dealt with facts that had been rather generally known, and for which Rich and his associates had for some time planned to call Sandys to account. When Bargrave suggested that if Sandys' proceedings in Virginia "were looked into it would be found that he aimed at" establishing a free popular state, he was apparently suggesting a new weapon to be used against Sandys. Such phraseology does not indicate that Rich had given the attention to the government in Virginia that would be expected had his objections to Sandys been political.

Another consideration in determining the value of this paper is Bargrave's relation to the company's affairs. He comes into prominence because of an extended dispute with Smith and Johnson arising out of certain rights of trade in Virginia which he had secured with Captain Martin during Smith's administration. It was his claim that in 1618 these rights had been violated by Smith. He eventually entered suit, and the case was under consideration in 1622.[44] Alexander Brown points to Bargrave's warnings to the royal courts at this time of the dangers in the popular government of Virginia as evidence of the political character of the dispute within the company.[45]

An examination of the records on Bargrave's case, however, shows that his statements have been entirely misinterpreted. It seems to have been forgotten that while making these criticisms he was engaged in a suit against Smith and Johnson, the enemies of Sandys, and not against those who had brought about Smith's fall and were then in control of the company. Bargrave had no quarrel whatsoever with Sandys; his grievance was entirely with Smith and his administration. He felt that Smith and Johnson had used their position as officers of the company to wrong him for their own private interests. It was for this reason that he became interested in the form of government by which they had attained power, and was led to suggest several reforms. To prevent a recurrence of such wrongs, he argued that the joint-stock plan, which was a popular form of government in that motions were carried by the majority vote of stockholders whose actions were comparatively free from royal interference, should be changed, since by it a few were able to combine in a party sufficiently strong to control the company and exploit the colony for their own private gain. It was in part the age-old dispute, common to all companies at this time, between individuals

[44] P.R.O., C.O. 1/2, 4, 4 I, 4 II.
[45] *English Politics in Early Virginia History*, p. 41.

who desired free trade with the colonists and controlling officials who recognized that the financial needs of the company required a monopoly of trade. Smith and his associates having "by practice and faction . . . framed a Company which being able by most voices to carry the government as they list," had according to Bargrave "thereby made a monopoly of the plantation and the labor of all the planters there."

One is not surprised that his remedy was a closer connection with the crown in order that there might be some means of preventing such abuses. Back of the proposal was the hope that in a crown colony all subjects would enjoy equal rights of trade. Although he recognized that the government was now in good hands, Bargrave felt that "nothing but the altering" of its form could make his majesty's subjects secure in the future. He therefore urged the privy councillors to help him in securing an examination of the company's affairs, in order that its government might be settled in such a form "that doing right to all parties interested in the plantation, it may fix the government of Virginia in a dependency on the Crown of England." [46]

It should not be overlooked that Bargrave emphatically denied that his criticisms were in any way directed at the government as administered by Sandys. The occasion for this denial came in April, 1622. In the preceding February his suit had been heard in Chancery, where the Lord Keeper found that although Bargrave had a legitimate grievance, the fact that the act had been done in the name of the company made it a matter of state, and he was sent for redress to the privy council. [47] He appeared before that body on April 12, and asserting that he had found "the popular government here to be the cause of great mischief to the plantation," he submitted a paper in which he had drawn suggestions for its reform, and petitioned for the

[46] P.R.O., C.O. 1/2, 4 I.   [47] P.R.O., C.O. 1/2, 4 II, 7 I.

appointment of a commission " to examine the abuses, and rectify the said government, which being not suddenly done the plantation will be undone." [48] This petition with his other papers was ordered sent to the governor and council for the company with a request for a written answer.

The company was naturally roused to action, and Bargrave was persuaded to present another paper to the council in which he protested that his objections were grounded only upon

the abuse of the Government as it was ordered in the time of Sir Thomas Smith, when taking to himself absolute power of governing both the Plantation and the Company according to his will, when no laws were made to prevent faction and parting of Courts, nor no order kept of managing businesses in public Courts lawfully assembled, but they were carried by private partings, the then Secretary framing, leaving out, adding and entering the Orders of Court with other acts that concerned the Company, as he was guided by the Combiners, for which he was since displaced. No assurance given to the planter either of his Estate and Liberty; Nor no Orders made to avoid the engrossing of trade into few hands, nor no Course taken to prevent oppression of single Planters or small bodies of Adventurers by plurality of voices of great numbers interested in any difference.

Since that time, however, he had found upon due examination that these things had been corrected, partly by laws established for the government of the company, and partly by charters and privileges confirmed for the colony. He was therefore anxious to disclaim any imputation upon the government of the past three years, and to declare that in his opinion the business of the plantations could not have been better managed. And whereas he had written five treatises advocating a closer union with the " Sovereignty of England," he " would burn them all together

[48] P.R.O., C.O. 1/2, 4.

with the hand that writ them, rather than they should be the means to hinder the going forward of so noble a work." [49]

A year later Bargrave is found attacking Sandys in his famous conversation with Nathaniel Rich. Yet in a few months he is back on the other side. In a letter to the lord treasurer he regrets the dissolution of the company and makes the statement, so often quoted, that the idea was "hatched at Alderman Johnson's house at Bow at the King's being there." He explains the king's action in doing what he himself had so often advised by the assertion that James had been "pressed to it by Sir Thomas Smith's friends of the Bedchamber to conceal the falsehood of his accounts and the grossness of their government from His Majesty's knowledge." [50] His temporary attachment to the Warwick party may have arisen from the hope that by giving this information against Sandys he would be rewarded with a settlement by Smith. Any such hopes as he may have entertained were apparently futile, for at the same time that he complained of the dissolution of the company, he carried his old suit against Smith and Johnson to the house of commons. [51]

Obviously, too much credence has been given the statements of a man whose words and actions were so contradictory. It has been overlooked that all of his criticisms of the government, with the exception of his ambiguous statements to Nathaniel Rich concerning Sandys' political sympathies, were directed at the machinery of the company in London, "the popular government here," rather than at the Virginia Assembly. And even in his famous conversation with Rich, his criticism of Sandys must in part be measured by an ulterior motive arising from the hope of enlisting Warwick's aid in his suit against Smith. It is not impossible that he entertained sincere objections

[49] P.R.O., C.O. 1/2 7 I.
[50] Manchester Papers, 402.
[51] Ibid., 401.

to the government resident in Virginia. But far more important were objections to the government as it was directed at London. This is also true of all others who figured prominently in the events of 1623. The records upon which we must base our conclusions lend little support to the idea that criticisms of representative government in the colony were of any great importance in the proceedings which led to the company's dissolution. The "popular government" to which strong objections were made was really that of a joint-stock company. To Americans looking backward over three centuries the "government of Virginia" is a clear reference to the governor, council, and assembly in Jamestown, and it is therefore easy to overlook the fact that this distinction between the officials and machinery of government residing in the colony and the authority and control in England was one slow in the making. It came only as Virginians came to think of themselves as Virginians, and Englishmen to regard them as other than Englishmen. There was no such clear-cut distinction in the reign of James I, and when an Englishman of that time referred to the "government of Virginia" his first thought was of a corporate body in London where resided the real power of governing the colony's affairs.

Bargrave was not alone in objecting to the organization of the company, for there were those among Sandys' leading opponents who objected to its democratic and popular character. Their objections, however, were not due to any fear of a political threat to the state, but to a belief, not unnatural to a minority group, that such an organization gave the majority too much power over the interests and rights of other adventurers. Bearing in mind their recent defeats on the tobacco question, Smith and Warwick condemned the government as "Democraticall and Tumultous and therefore fit to be altered and reduced to the hands of some few persons." The clearest proof of their meaning is to be found in Lord Cavendish's reply.[52]

He endeavored to refute the charge first by showing that the government was no other than that prescribed by the charter of incorporation. In the next place, he denied that the company exercised a jurisdiction independent of the state, since it was accountable to the king and ruled under his laws. This was demonstrated by the fact that the company did not enjoy absolute power over its own people. For when one of them committed an offense and escaped punishment in the colony, he could " outface " the company at home, which was left with no means of redress " but by appealing to higher Justice." It was impossible to describe a government as democratic "where the King only hath absolute power, and where the people swear Allegiance only to him." It was true, he admitted, that there was some show of democracy, but this was no more than just

because these Plantations, though furthered much by your Majesty's grace, yet being not made at your Majesty's charge or expence, but chiefly by the private purses of the Adventurers they would never have ventured in such an accord wherein they interest their own fortunes, if in the regulating and governing of their own business their own votes had been excluded.

It was the most profitable form of government, he continued, because the great supplies necessary for the colonists could be provided only by a large number of people, who would not venture thus if the control were in the hands of a few.

And whereas they cry out against Democracy, and call for Oligarchy, they make not the Government thereby either of better form or more monarchical. And to discern what is the judgment of a Company if there be not unanimity, there is no way

[52] Manchester Papers, 360; *Records*, II, 352-362.

but by plurality of voice, and if plurality of voice were not, there would scarce at any time in any point be unanimity in any assembly.

These objections were a clear proof to him that the real purpose of the opposing party was none other than " to draw all things into their own power."

It is difficult by any stretch of imagination to suppose that this argument concerned anything further than the organization and rules of government in the company, except the single suggestion that the company enjoyed a jurisdiction too independent in character. The attack and reply center around the procedure in the courts, a quite different type of democracy from that read into the history of these disputes by nineteenth century historians.

The defense of the Sandys party is to be found in four papers prepared by officials, which were openly read and approved in the courts of the company, and formally presented to the king or to his commission. The first steps in the preparation of this defense were taken at the extraordinary court for both companies held on April 12. Having agreed upon a petition joining Johnson in his request for an investigation, the court considered two papers which had been drawn for his majesty's information. The first of these had been written the preceding Christmas at Southampton's order by several of the council as a comparison of the present state of Virginia with conditions in the past. It was now read and debated point by point, and was finally ordered to be presented to the king as " A Declaration of the present State of Virginia humbly presented to the King's most excellent Majesty by the Company for Virginia." [53] The second was a paper prepared by Lord Cavendish, entitled " A Relation of the late proceedings of the Virginia and Somers Islands Companies, in answer to some imputations laid upon them, together with the discovery of the grounds of such unjust objec-

[53] *Records* II, 348-351.

tions, and a Remedy proposed for better avoiding the like inconveniences hereafter; Humbly presented to the King's most Excellent Majesty by the said Companies." [54] It was also debated and confirmed in every point.

It was impossible to proceed any further until they had secured more complete information concerning the charges of Smith and Warwick, and the court was accordingly adjourned. The Virginia court met next on April 23. In the meantime, representatives of both parties had been before the privy council, the Jones Commission had been established, and full copies of Johnson's petition and Butler's "Unmasked Face" delivered to the company. Several of those present who had been to Virginia were called upon to aid in the reply to Butler. For preparing the general defense before the royal commission it was agreed that the entire court, excepting those who joined Johnson in his accusations, should become a "great committee," which, working through numerous sub-committees, was to draw up an answer to all of Johnson's charges. Johnson, who was present, agreed to this proposal, and with several of his partisans immediately withdrew from the court.[55]

Those who remained formed the largest body of the company's active membership, and not without reason regarded their will and action that of the company. Johnson's idea had been some sort of proceeding against the responsible officials of the Sandys party, and not against the company. Although he had not been present at the court of April 12, some of his party were there who protested that the petition was not directed at the company, but they had been overruled by a majority vote which held that the complaint was "against the Company itself." [56] And so the issue was joined from the beginning

<hr />

[54] *Records*, II, 352-362; Manchester Papers, 360. The portion of this paper dealing with criticisms of the company's government has been dealt with above on pp. 283-285.

[55] *Ibid.*, II, 376-377.

[56] *Ibid.*, II, 346-347.

as between the company and its accusers, Warwick, Smith, Johnson, and Rich — a fact of some importance in the final outcome of the struggle. There is little reason to believe that these men contemplated an attempt to overthrow the company, but partly by this decision and partly by the very nature of the fight, they were unavoidably forced into the position of opposing the company while opposing Sandys, and in this way they contributed greatly to the company's fall.

Thus it was to the defense of the company that the "great committee" set its hand late in April. Most of its work was completed within the fortnight. On May 7 the court confirmed "An answer to a Petition delivered to his Majesty by Alderman Johnson in the names of sundry Adventurers and Planters of the Virginia and Somers Islands Plantations,"[57] and on the same day the reply to Butler was completed and approved.[58] The material in these two papers, which with the two approved on April 12 comprised the company's case, was as completely economic in character as were the indictments made by Nathaniel Rich. It was an attempt to show that there had been much improvement since Sandys' election, and that the condition of the colony, contrary to their opponents' claim, was now more than hopeful.

In undertaking to defend the administration of the past four years the committee faced a difficult task, for the truth is that the facts were on the side of Warwick and Smith. Only by comparison with the years before Sandys' election, could one regard with any degree of satisfaction the years that followed it. The company, therefore, attempted to direct attention to the preceding administration, and consumed much time and ink in a sweeping refutation of Johnson's laudatory claims for Smith. The "true estate of the said mild and Discreet Government" of Sir Thomas Smith was pictured as one of oppression, suffering, and

---

[57] *Ibid.*, II, 393-397.   [58] *Ibid.*, II, 397-399.

want in Virginia and of neglect and bankruptcy at home.

In sharp contrast to the former administration had been the history of the past four years. A well ordered government had borne the fruit of quiet and contentment among the adventurers, of whom there had come in twice as many in four years as in almost double that time before, "so that whereas in former times there were sometimes hardly got Twenty to keep the Quarter Court there are now seldom less than two hundred and sometimes many more." [59] It was true that the courts had been divided at times by discord and dissension. One dispute had been caused by Johnson "being called on for his Accompts for which in regard of his place he was very moderately censured," and Mr. Wrote, "upon other private discontent," was responsible for another. There had also been a faction in the council because of the support given by some of the members to Argall, whose government had been very detrimental to Virginia. But there had been no other dissension of note, and it should not be overlooked that all the trouble had been caused by the parties who now attacked the company, the "greatest number of whom are seldom seen in the Courts, but upon occasion of a Storm and to nourish Discord and Faction." Their clamorous claim of injury to the old adventurers was entirely false, for the company had dealt in justice with all alike. The massacre alone had given excuse for their accusations, and had it not been for this unhappy event "these opposers must have been mute having nothing else wherewith to disgrace the Plantation." [60] For the business had proceeded with steady improvement, as might be seen in the grant of forty-four land patents for private plantations in contrast to about six such grants in the previous administration, and in the employment of forty-two sail of ships as opposed to not above twelve. Their good work had also been frequently attested to by benevolences amounting in all to £1,500.[61]

The well ordered government of the company had been reflected in the prosperity and happiness of the colony. The content and peace of their people in America had "raised here at home so great a fame of Virginia that not only men of meaner estates, as at the first by necessity, but many persons of good sort out of choice and good liking have removed themselves thither and are daily in providing to remove."[62] God had laid his hand heavily upon them, it was true, but despite their many mortalities there were still alive twenty-five hundred colonists, who had been sent at an expenditure of only £30,000 to the company, beside the charge of particular societies and planters. The cattle now numbered above a thousand in addition to goats and swine "of infinite number."[63] And through the first three years of the present government there had been no hostility whatsoever with the natives, of which they would not boast, however, for it had "lulled the English asleep in too great security and consequently gave opportunity to the late bloody Massacre."[64] For the future protection of the colonists order had been given for the erection of a fort at some good location.[65]

The company's case was weakest in its effort to show some progress in the development of commodities other than tobacco. None of their projects had been successful, and all that they could possibly do in their defense was to recount those efforts, take refuge in the massacre as an excuse for having nothing to show for their work and expense, and express a hope for the future. During the past four years £5,000 had been spent on the iron-works, "which work being brought in a manner to perfection was greatly interrupted by the late Massacre, but ordered to be restored again with all possible diligence." Vineyards had

[61] *Ibid.*, II, 350, 351.
[62] *Ibid.*, II, 350.
[63] *Ibid.*, II, 348.
[64] *Ibid.*, II, 395.
[65] *Ibid.*, II, 351.

been planted, and had it not been for the massacre they could now show some of their fruits. Silk culture was of great promise, and although it had been difficult to send cocoons, they yet hoped in time to see this industry prosper. At great charge skillful men had been secured from Germany to set up sawmills, several English shipwrights had been sent to build ships, and men skilled in saltworks and other commodities had been planted in the colony, "the good effect" of which steps "we doubt not will shortly appear." His majesty had only to examine the company's records to see plainly what steps had been taken to limit the production of tobacco and to encourage the development of other products.[66]

"Having thus given answers to the seeming most material scandals and imputations," the company through Lord Cavendish endeavored "to discover the true causes" of this effort to disgrace the government of the plantations.[67] The first cause of their "malice," his lordship declared,

proceeds from the ill affection of the old Officers of the Companies, out of whose hands (the Plantations having not well thrived under them) the Government was necessarily taken, and the prosperity of the same since appearing and the benefit of that removal implying a proof of their misgovernment, hath affected them, that now they endeavor the better to cover that fault by public disturbance and private practice and consideration to hinder the present prosperity and hopeful increase of the Plantations.

In presenting the second explanation, he pointed out that the principal members of the opposition had held offices under the old régime, either in the companies or in the plantations. These officers had not cleared their accounts, "some of which are very suspicious," and being pressed to give account they had done all in their power to stir up prejudice and disturbance, "by that means to shroud themselves from a due and quiet examination."

[66] *Records*, II, 349-350.   [67] *Ibid.*, II, 352-362; Manchester Papers, 360.

In the third place, he attempted to explain the presence of the earl of Warwick in the opposition, declaring that

some other of those opponents and of other rank have had their hand partly in spoiling the Plantation of Virginia, and setting out a ship called the Treasurer for robbing into the West Indies, and partly in abetting and protecting those that have so done, and that with violence, to the great offense, scandal and loss of the Company, and their ends not fully answering their hopes hath caused them to abandon the Courts for Virginia save only in point of procuring their trouble, and by that means do keep the Company from leisure to call such offenses into question.

Such was the composition of the opposing party, according to Cavendish, with the addition of their servants or those who were otherwise necessarily dependent upon these leaders, and of certain men who had wronged the company and found protection from just punishment by joining with Smith and Warwick.

Thus we see that Sandys' defense was largely a condemnation of his predecessor, an expression of his own hopes for Virginia, which despite the passage of four years were still chiefly for the future, and a disparagement of his opponents' motives.

Regardless of other opinions that may be formed by the careful student of this evidence presented to the king and his commission, there can be no doubt that above all else the opposing parties were fighting over the economic policies of the Sandys régime and their effect upon the colony. The argument of both sides centers on this point. It is true that their argument was affected by hatreds acquired in disputes only indirectly connected with the company's policies, but these did not alter the central theme of their contentions. No one can read through the evidence cited above without arriving at the conclusion that the dispute which disrupted the Virginia Company was fundamentally a fight over economic problems and the policies for their solution.

CHAPTER X
THE DISSOLUTION OF THE COMPANY

MANY hypotheses have been advanced in explanation of the government's decision to recall the charter of the Virginia Company. Some of them deserve little serious consideration. Others merit more than a summary dismissal because they present factors which may at least have contributed to the company's fall. Although there was apparently no advantage to be gained for Spain in the transfer of the Virginia colony to royal control, it is not impossible that Count Gondomar's efforts to prejudice the king against Sandys may have indirectly influenced James in his dealings with the adventurers. Nor again, is it altogether improbable that the powerful friends of Captain John Martin, notably Sir Julius Caesar, used their weight to tilt the scales against the company. For though the questions of his patent were settled before the annulment of the charter, the acrimonious disputes attendant upon their settlement had left a residue of bitterness and ill feeling. It may have been, too, that Sir Ferdinando Gorges and other leading spirits of the New England Council, which included Warwick, were moved to support the action against the London Company on account of their conflicting claims to fishing rights along the New England coast.

Gorges had in 1620 attempted to revive the moribund North Virginia Company with the purpose of colonizing New England by funds secured in part from a monopoly of the Cape Cod fisheries. A patent was secured in November granting to the New England Council the desired monopoly of trading and fishing in the territory and adjoining seas lying between 40 and 48 degrees north with the privilege of collecting fees from all fishermen.[1] It occasioned an immediate protest from the London adventurers,

[1] Hazard, *Historical Collections*, I, 103.

who, in fact, had already entered several objections to Gorges' claim before the privy council.[2] It was a matter of grave concern to the company, for the lotteries were already well-nigh exhausted as a source of revenue, and their termination at the request of parliament within the next few months left the adventurers almost solely dependent on fishing licenses for the transportation of their people and goods. In a petition to the government setting forth that fishing was " the onely means lefte (now the Lotteries were allmost spent and other supply began to faile) to enhable them to transport their people and susteyne their Plantation," they besought a revisal of the monopolistic clause in Gorges' patent on the ground that the original charters granted the two companies gave each equal freedom to fish within the other's grant. The petition was successful. His majesty declared that anything in Gorges' patent detrimental to the interests of Virginia had been included without his knowledge, and he promptly gave an order that it should be held without seal for examination in this particular.[3]

Meanwhile, Southampton, who was also a member of the New England Council, undertook to reach an agreement with Gorges. Plans were on foot for securing a new patent for the Virginia Company, and Gorges for some reason was desirous of a revision in his own grant. The point was left for agreement therefore in the discussion attendant upon the drawing of the new charters. Southampton reported to the privy council on November 15 that since both parties were anxious to secure a renewal of their patents " by mutual advice with the council," it was believed that some accord on the question of the fisheries might best be reached at that time. Their lordships accordingly postponed the settlement of the issue. Gorges' patent was ordered to be held undelivered in the mean-

[2] *Records*, I, 277, 285, 321-322, 329, 339-340, 397.
[3] *Ibid.*, I, 410-411, 416.

time, and the Virginia Company was instructed that in accord with his majesty's express command they might continue to enjoy the free privilege of fishing conveyed to them in their original patent.[4] The new charter for the London Company was never issued, nor was the requested revision in Gorges' patent effected. But the company, either by understanding with Gorges or by order of the king, continued thereafter to enjoy the desired privilege of free fishing.

The extent to which the existence of this privilege may have persuaded the leaders of the New England Council and its friends to support the action for the dissolution of the London Company is highly problematic. But the quarrel over fishing rights probably did contribute to the unfavorable attitude of the privy council toward Sandys. For in the Parliament of 1621 he placed himself at the head of the fishing interests, who strongly opposed every effort at colonization both in New England and Newfoundland, and led a bitter attack upon Gorges' patent. Secretary Calvert and other spokesmen for the council essayed the difficult rôle of holding a balance between the two groups with the hope of obtaining a compromise settlement that would best serve the national interest. He met with little success in the house of commons, however, for Sandys and the powerful fishing interests secured the passage of a bill for free fishing.[5] The measure failed of passage in the house of lords, but Sir Edwin's strong support of special interests in opposition to the sounder considerations of national policy supported by the government was hardly forgotten in 1623.

Certain it is that Sandys' lack of favor with the leaders of the government, both on this count and many others wherein his position in the commons was not always dictated by a fair consideration of national interest so much as by his own private concerns, must be considered an im-

---

[4] *Records*, I, 428.   [5] *Journals of the House of Commons*, I, 626.

portant factor predisposing the councillors to a favorable reception of charges against him and his administration. So also must it be recognized that the influence and connections of his powerful opponents were factors of great importance.

The evidence in support of these conclusions, however, is so incomplete and so largely circumstantial, that there is little reason for believing that the fundamental consideration with the government was any other than the demonstrated failure of the company and its doubtful ability to reassume the responsibilities of management. The council was guided in every step by the findings of the Jones Commission, which through May and June conducted a thorough investigation into all phases of the company's affairs. Its report was based upon information acquired chiefly from three sources. Of first importance was a careful perusal of official documents and records. An order of May 15 required the officers of both the Virginia and Bermuda Companies to submit for examination all letters, patents, proclamations, commissions, warrants, records, orders, books, accounts, and other writings of record held in their custody relating to the plantations or to the affairs of the two companies.[6] In the study of these documents special attention was directed to the financial status of the companies and the effect of their policies on conditions of life and labor in the colonies. There seems to have been more interest in letters from the planters and in a comparative study of them with the official utterances of the companies than in any other line of their investigations.

The commissioners also made use of any information that could be acquired from mariners, former planters, or other persons likely to be informed on the problems of the colony. Among those solicited for their opinions was Captain John Smith. And while he naturally was disposed

[6] *Records*, I, 431-432.

to use the opportunity to draw an unfavorable comparison between recent practises and those of his own day in Virginia, several of his criticisms were sound and thoroughly justified. The chief defects in the government of Virginia were, to his mind, the "multiplicity of opinions here, and officers there." The first of these faults had come from the tremendous increase in the number of those having some word of authority in the direction of Virginia's affairs. There had been originally but six patentees, now there were more than a thousand; then but thirteen councillors, now not less than a hundred. Any man who would adventure but £12 10s. was given a voice equal to him who had sixteen years earlier invested the same amount. Thus were the old adventurers who had often suffered heavily in their fortunes forced to give way to new adventurers for the "trial of more new conclusions."

As for the officers selected by these inexperienced stockholders, Smith was of the opinion that had they managed their own estates no more ably than they had the affairs of Virginia they would have long since become bankrupt. Yet it was noticeable that few of the officers in England had lost their estates or had exhibited any desire to relinquish their offices. The reason was that these great men who controlled the company were insensible to the petty losses entailed in the collapse of the common stock, while they enjoyed many opportunities of profit from the freight for colonists and supplies sent in their ships. The freight rates of £6 per person and £3 per ton of goods had encouraged them to overload their ships, thereby occasioning much sickness and many deaths. For though all passengers died they were still sure of their freight, "and then all must be satisfied with Orations, disputations, excuses and hopes." The letters of advice from England and the replies to them from Virginia were so well worded that one was led to believe that all was well with the colony, an error to which the adventurers had always been subject. Yet such was not the case. It was altogether un-reasonable to expect that the planters in Virginia would be prepared to care for the great numbers of poorly pro-vided immigrants sent by the company, " for who here in *England* is so charitable to feed two or three strangers, have they never so much; much lesse in *Virginia* where they want for themselves."

There had been as much ado about the government of Virginia, according to Smith, as if it were the Kingdom of Scotland or Ireland. The company had erected as many stately offices provided with tenants as there were laborers in the country, " where a Constable were as good as twenty of their Captaines, and three hundred good Souldiers and laborers better than all the rest that goe onely to get the fruits of other mens labours by the title of an office." It was both absurd and a waste of the common stock to main-tain 100 men for the governor, 100 for the two deputies, 50 for the treasurer, 25 for the secretary, and more for the marshal and other officers who had never been to Virginia nor had adventured any great sums but had been selected only by favor " to be Lords over them that broke the ice and beat the path, and must teach them what to doe."

The massacre had resulted from the lack of discipline, the dispersal of settlers, the inadequate provision for de-fense, and the possession of arms by the natives. He esti-mated the cost of immediate relief at £5,000 for the send-ing of soldiers, laborers, and all sorts of necessary supplies. Permanent remedy for Virginia's ills, however, could be had only by a return to something of the original organiza-tion through a greater dependence on the crown. The officers there should be made responsible to an authorita-tive body in England, and that body in turn directly responsible to the king. He suggested a small poll or chimney tax throughout England to provide funds for a garrison and a sufficient supply of laborers. He felt that many able men of quality would gladly go to Virginia if transportation were offered in return for nothing more than allegiance to the Crown of England. As for the company's patent, there should be no more difficulty in annulling it than there had been in the recall of the first patent at the instance of those who now controlled the company. They had promised to do great things, and had cast many aspersions on the earlier leaders of the colony. But for all that Smith could see, " had we remained still as at first, it is not likely we could have done much worse." [7]

The last, but by no means least, source of information were the papers presented to the commission by the two parties of adventurers. In the evidence drawn up by Rich to support the charges against Sandys and in the documents provided in defense of the company, there was to be found much material pertinent to the commissioners' deliberations.

The leading figures on both sides also appeared to argue their case in person. We are fortunate in having a brief account of one sitting of this body which throws light on the manner in which the investigation was conducted. It is found in a few notes by a Mr. Gibbs forwarded to Sandys as a report of a day's proceedings before the commission.[8] Gibbs had according to instructions presented the charges against Smith's accounts, to which Sir Thomas, who was present with counsel, replied that he had submitted all books of accounts to the auditors. To this it was answered that his original cash books were yet missing. But in the general disputation which followed, the Sandys party was somewhat embarrassed in pressing the charges against Smith by the fact that their exceptions to his accounts were entirely too general in character. The debate was ended by a request from the chair that they offer some proof in support of their charges, especially a statement of the extent of Smith's alleged indebtedness to the company.

[7] Arber, ed., *Travels and Works of Captain John Smith*, II, 615-620.

[8] Mr. Gibbs to Sandys, "Notes of Proceedings Before Lords Commissioners," Ferrar Papers.

Lord Cavendish then offered Butler's " Unmasked Face " for examination. But here again, certain difficulties arose for the Sandys group from the fact that the paper had not been presented as a part of the complaint against the company. The commissioners were willing to accept it as evidence only on condition that the original under Butler's sworn hand were submitted. Sir Edward Sackville strongly objected to this ruling on the ground that it was a document of great damage to the plantation and, therefore, quite properly to be considered by the commission. The objection was promptly overruled, however, and it was declared impossible to accept the paper as evidence unless Butler agreed to submit it as a part of the regular charges of his party. Their reasoning seems to have been that their commission extended only to an examination of the company's affairs and the charges against its officers, whereas Cavendish's effort to introduce the document was in the nature of an attack upon Butler for his defamation of the colony's good name. This not only lay wholly without their province, but threatened the introduction of personal attacks contrary to his majesty's strict command.

With these two storms passed, the commissioners devoted most of their time to examining correspondence to and from Virginia. Smith and Rich urged great care in noting all points of difference between public and private letters, and called attention to all references to lack of health and scarcity of provisions. They also made frequent inquiries after a " Black Box " in which they declared much information concerning the lamentable state of the colony was being concealed. The commissioners read with special care letters from George Sandys and Sir Francis Wyatt, but reserved all opinions until they had opportunity to make a more careful study of the correspondence at hand. And so they rose.

It would be an impossible task to pass final judgment on the mass of contradictory evidence presented by the two parties to the royal commissioners. It is a mistake to conclude that either party was wholly in the right. Inevitably the feeling with which both sides prepared their cases led them to overstatements and the inclusion of charges which had no foundation other than rumor. One cannot envy the commissioners their task of unravelling this tangled mesh of spite, slander, rumor, and fact.

Several points, however, can be fairly definitely established. In the first place, Johnson's effort to prove that the company and colony under Smith had been prosperous and happy can hardly be regarded as successful. On the other hand, Sandys' supporters had no more success in showing any great improvement by their control. They had good intentions and well meaning efforts to recount, but little more. A defunct treasury and a heavy indebtedness could not be talked away, and this subject was studiously avoided. They could present nothing more than a hope for the development of a wider variety of commodities. For tobacco still ruled in both company and colony to such an extent that an attempt to arrange for its profitable importation and disposal had only recently tied up the business of the company for months. On one point alone, in the policies Sandys so hopefully outlined in 1619, had he been successful, and that was in attracting larger numbers of English emigrants to Virginia. But even here he had blundered miserably, and his affirmations of prosperity and happiness found by them in a new home were completely refuted by the fact that most of them were dead.

The accusations of the Warwick party were undoubtedly filled with many exaggerations, but there was no exaggeration in their charge of an appalling death rate among the Virginia colonists. The company's own statements prove the truth of this indictment. Sandys' supporters estimated that a total of 6,000 persons had been sent to the colony since the organization of the company, and that of this number not above 2,500 had gone under Smith.[9] According to these figures, 3,500 represents the number set forth since 1619. And these figures seem to be a fairly accurate estimate. The number sent in the first year was 1,261, of which 871 were sent at public charge.[10] Plans for 1620 called for the transportation of another 800 at the company's cost,[11] and in view of the fact that for another year it was possible to draw upon the lotteries for revenue, it seems likely that these plans were carried through. Considering the increasing interest in private plantations, it is safe to conclude that a proportion of private settlers equal to that of the preceding year accompanied these public tenants. Although colonization by the company declined rapidly after that year, there continued a large emigration at private charge. It was expected in the fall of 1621 that no less than 1,000 settlers would cross within the next few months to take up the claims of private associations in England.[12] And in the summer of 1622 the council declared the total emigration to Virginia since Sandys' election to have been 3,570.[13] Allowing for a certain exaggeration in a public statement of this sort, and counting in several shiploads of colonists who crossed in the fall of that year, it is safe to assume that the total number of emigrants who left England for Virginia between the spring of 1619 and the spring of 1623 was somewhere between 3,500 and 4,000. The population of the colony when Sandys assumed control was frequently given by him as 1,000, and so the total population for the four years was approximately 4,500 to 5,000. Yet in the spring of 1623 officials admitted that there were not above 2,500 of these left alive,[14] which means that according to the company's

[9] *Records*, II, 398.

[14] *Records*, II, 398-399.

[10] *Ibid.*, I, 351-352, 411-412, 492-493.

[11] Force, *Tracts*, III, No. 5, p. 14.

[12] MS. Rec. Va. Co., III, Part ii, 21 a.

[13] *A Declaration of the State of the Colonie and Affaires in Virginia*, Edward Waterhouse, London, 1622.

own figures almost half of those who had set forth for Virginia, or had been living there since Smith's governorship, had perished either on the way or after arrival. A death rate of approximately forty-five percent. was alone sufficient warrant for the charges of the Warwick party and for the investigation by the king.

But there was even more justification for condemning this side of Sandys' administration than perhaps even Warwick knew, for the company's figures did not tell the whole story. A considerably higher death rate was revealed in a communication to Nicholas Ferrar from Christopher Davison, a member of the colonial council, written from the colony in February, 1624. In the preceding April he had promised to send a list of all those who had died, or had been slain by the Indians, since the massacre, and in addition a list of those remaining alive. This information was supplied in a detailed census of each plantation at the beginning of 1624.[15] The number of dead was given as 370, of which number fifteen had been killed and two lost. The total population of the colony was only 1,275, a figure 800 less than Butler's estimate and about half that claimed by the company nine months earlier. When it is considered that over 300 of this number had migrated to Virginia so recently as the summer and fall of 1623,[16] it will be seen that seventy-five percent. is a more accurate index to the mortality during Sandys' direction of the company. And if it be assumed that the older planters, who had settled in earlier years and had become inured to their environment, were a hardier lot better equipped to resist the inroads of disease, exposure, and poor food, it must follow that the death rate among the settlers actually sent by Sandys was even higher.

This appallingly high death rate cut the ground from

[15] *Cal. St. Pap., Col.,* 1574–1660, pp. 43, 57.
[16] From May to November a total of 340 persons shipped for Virginia. *Records,* II, 496.

under the whole case for the company, and gave to its opponents their strongest point. It alone was sufficient to establish the basic truth in their charges of mismanagement, negligence, pestilence, and starvation. It was impossible for officers, who were forced to admit that more than half the population had died, to prove that their people had led a happy and prosperous life.

How far the difficulties of the Sandys party were due to the disasters of the massacre is a question on which there may be some difference of opinion. The company frequently took refuge in this catastrophe, and there can be no doubt that the colony's misfortunes could in part be attributed to the destruction and disorganization following in its wake. Sandys' argument, however, that the massacre provided the only excuse for the damaging charges of his opponents can hardly be considered valid. Failure so complete as that of the London Company cannot be explained by any one cause. The massacre can account directly for no more than four hundred deaths. The usual number given for those slain is three hundred and forty-seven. And even if the suffering and death that scourged the colony in the following winter may be attributed chiefly to the disorganization and confusion resulting from this disastrous attack, that in itself is evidence of weakness and mistaken policies in the earlier conduct of the business. Had sufficient provision been made for defense, the economic organization been more sound, and the company in a position to send prompt and adequate relief, the colony would have been better able to withstand this shock. Moreover, there is good evidence of much suffering and many deaths in Virginia prior to 1622. Sandys had overdone his whole policy of colonization, and the massacre is more correctly regarded as revealing the extent of Sandys' failure, rather than as the chief cause of that failure.

In an investigation so thorough as that conducted by Sir

William Jones and his associates, the facts of the company's maladministration could not long remain hidden. There could be little argument on the points of the company's insolvency, the failure of all its plans, the mismanagement of the colony's affairs, the exceptionally high rate of mortality among its settlers, and the poverty-stricken state of the colony. The result of the investigation was practically a foregone conclusion. The commissioners continued their work for several months thereafter, but they were prepared to make a preliminary report by the end of June. His majesty was informed that while there had been only a short time for inquiry into all points mentioned in their instructions, it was already apparent, especially by letters recently come from Virginia, that the colony's state was most "weak and miserable" and such that unless prompt steps were taken for the better ordering of the business the whole plantation lay in danger of ruin. Only a few of the colonists sent in recent years remained alive. Although it was impossible at this date to get accurate statistics, it was admitted by the company's officers that there had been 1,000 persons living in Virginia at the expiration of Smith's term of office and that since then there had been sent 4,270 settlers. But there were only a few of these left and they were in great want. Their poverty and famine could be relieved only by sending corn and other provisions, "not by way of merchandise, as had lately been used, to take advantage of their necessities by making them pay most unconscionable prices, but either of free gift or at reasonable rates." It would also be necessary to send able and experienced commanders to deal with the natives. Their relation of the company's state implied a doubt of its ability to cope with these problems. Though the common stock had benefited much by lotteries and more than £30,000 had been brought into the public treasury, it was now "entirely exhausted" and the company heavily indebted.[17]

[17] Manchester Papers, 382.

These facts concerning the company's past performances and its present weakness must be considered the first factor in the government's decision to provide some reform of the colony's management. There was little apparent reason to expect that it could in the future provide a safe and sound direction for so important a work involving the lives and fortunes of many of his majesty's subjects. Any doubts that existed as to the company's ability to reassume its great responsibilities were further strengthened by the hopeless factionalism which divided the adventurers and was now more bitter than ever before. Not only was the company bankrupt, not only had its management failed miserably, but it was apparently foredoomed to the fate of the house divided against itself.

The submission of the dispute to the privy council had stirred the feelings of the adventurers to a white heat. Warwick, Rich, Johnson, Smith, and Butler were all assailed with unparalleled bitterness as traitors by leaders of the dominant faction. On Easter Eve they attempted to "steal a court" on their opponents, but news of the intended meeting reached some of Warwick's friends who "presented themselves unwelcomed." Sir Edward Sackville openly termed the petitioners traitors to the company, and scored Nathaniel Butler for having given writings concerning Virginia to the king without first acquainting the court. His attack was especially directed at Warwick, and equally as vehement as Sackville in denouncing the earl was Lord Cavendish. "They blurred upon my Lord of Warwick in the point of the Treasurer, and according to their wont were braving, loud, and violent," wrote Butler to Nathaniel Rich.[18]

Not content with this, the officers of the two companies "contrived and set down in writing and caused publicly to be read a long and impertinent declaration, consisting for the most part of bitter and unnecessary invectives and aspersions upon the person of the Earl of Warwick and

[18] *Ibid.*, 355.

others whom they styled his Instruments and Agents." [19] It was presented by Lord Cavendish to a Virginia court of May 7 as "A Declaration made by the Council for Virginia and principal Assistants for the Somers Islands of their Judgments touching one original great cause of the dissentions in the Companies and present oppositions." [20]

The paper is a long and malicious indictment of Warwick's activities in the two colonies for the preceding six years, laying upon him the chief responsibility for the factional strife within the courts. Not being satisfied with a "lawful and orderly benefit" from his investment, this nobleman had sought to take all unto himself by the exploitation of both plantations. He had endeavored to gain control of the courts at home by every known device, from buying up the shares of old adventurers who had quitted the business to distributing these shares among his friends and relatives. Although failing to control the courts, he had managed to secure the appointments of Argall and Butler, and with the latter his influence was so great that the orders of the company carried almost no weight at all "if they came once to be countermanded by any mandate from his Lordship." By the aid of these two agents, both of whose records were branded as thoroughly bad, Warwick had stopped at nothing short of violence in his oppression of the planters. And in the case of the *Treasurer* he had even resorted to "threats of blood" in an attempt to prevent Sir Edwin Sandys from acquainting the privy council with the affair. All attempts at bringing Argall to trial for his many offenses had failed because of Warwick's protection, and in order "to draw unto himself some show of a party" every enemy of the company had received his support. Butler, not satisfied with the damage he had wrought in Bermuda, had gone to Virginia "in an ill season of the year towards the extremity of Winter, and in worse time otherwise after the late Massacre, where

[19] P.R.O., C.O. 5/1354, 79, pp. 205-206.   [20] *Records*, II, 400-409.

. . . he fed his eyes with the miserable spectacle of a Country overrun with a late Treacherous war." Finding upon his return to England that the companies were full of trouble by "factious spirits," he had joined hands with his patron in a tireless effort to disgrace "with all kinds of Calumnies and slanders" the present government of Virginia.

This disingenuous and distorted account of Warwick's activities in the colonies constituted a severe indictment of his character and record as an adventurer, and naturally aroused him and his friends to great wrath. They immediately petitioned the privy council to command Cavendish, Sandys, and the two Ferrars to appear before their lordships with this paper, which they described as "full of most grievous calumnies and reproachful accusations tending to the defamation of the petitioners in general and in particular of the Earl of Warwick." The injury was made more unbearable because "many strangers placed in a latticed gallery," some of them ladies, had been brought into the court to hear this slanderous attack and to spread the report thereof. The whole affair, they maintained, had been contrary to the council's order that all "matters of controversy and difference" be forborne in the companies and referred to the privy council.[21]

Such bitter and personal attacks in no way helped the commissioners with their difficult task of ascertaining the true state of the colony. And as Warwick claimed, the reading of the paper had been a flagrant violation of the council's order that both sides

should inform the . . . Commissioners of such abuses and grievances either in point of government, misemployment of monies or the like, whereof either side might have any just Cause of Complaint with express Charge and Command, nevertheless, from this Table that in the preparing of the Information each party should go directly to the matter, and

[21] Manchester Papers, 366.

avoid all bitterness and sharpness of style, or other impertinent provocation tending rather to revive and kindle former
heats and distractions between the said two Companies, than
any way conducing to the work and service intended.

The four offenders, accordingly, were on May 13 "restrained of their Liberty, and confined to their several
Lodgings or Houses, as persons guilty of a Contempt
against the directions and comands of this Table, where
they are to remain until His Majesty or this Board shall
give further order." [22] This was followed by another order
expressly charging that no complaints were to be brought
before the commissioners "which tended only to defamation." [23] Sandys and Cavendish objected that such an order
would exempt from any complaint the very persons who
had been most flagrantly guilty of violating his majesty's
directions, of oppressing and ruining the plantations, and
of "other outrages of very high nature committed by roving and robbing on the Spanish territories in the West
Indies." [24] Nevertheless, the order held, and the offending parties continued for some time confined to their
lodgings.[25]

The opposing parties were thus prevented from making
formal charges of a slanderous character, but there was no
way to keep them from giving full expression to their
hatred when they met on the streets and in the meetings
of the companies. As the summer advanced the two courts
became more turbulent and factious than ever, and the
citizens of London by street quarrels and reports of even
more bitter encounters in the Virginia and Bermuda
courts were treated to conclusive proof of the impossibility
of healing the schism between these famous factions. The

[22] P.R.O., C.O. 5/1354, 79, pp. 205-206.
[23] Manchester Papers, 372.
[24] Ibid., 376.
[25] Sandys secured his release somewhere about the third week in June
through the intervention of Lord Treasurer Middlesex. Sandys to Middlesex,
June 19, 1623, Sackville Papers, p. 510.

climax came in July at a meeting of the Bermuda adventurers, when Sandys "fell foul of the Earl of Warwick." Cavendish strongly supported Sandys, and in the ensuing dispute Warwick passed the lie to Cavendish. The compliment was returned with a challenge which was quickly accepted.

The two lords set forth from London on July 17 for Holland, where it had been agreed they should meet on August 1. Their departure created a considerable stir, for duelling had never become so common a practise in English society as on the continent. The noble families of England had so recently risen from the lower strata of society, and were still interested in the peaceful occupations of commerce and farming to such an extent, that they had not developed that exaggerated sense of honor which characterized their continental neighbors. Moreover, the prominence of Cavendish and Warwick, and the connection of the affair with the Virginia disputes added to its dramatic possibilities. Nor was it totally void of humor. Their lordships' ladies had long been close friends, and they did not now forget "their old familiarity" but met in prayer "daily to lament this misfortune." The two ladies also joined hands in a plea to the government to prevent the duel.[26]

The privy council had no idea of allowing these men to meet and had already taken steps to frustrate them in their purpose. The same day on which they left London, order was given for the closing of all ports to the two lords along with instructions that they should be returned to London if apprehended.[27] Cavendish, becoming ill, was stayed by a warrant in Sussex, and was there held in custody by the sheriff. Warwick, however, was able to evade the government's watch, and disguised as a fisherman got across the

---

[26] Chamberlain to Carleton, July 26, 1623, P.R.O., S.P. 14/149, 48; Chichester to Countess of Warwick, August 12, 1623, Manchester Papers, 160.
[27] P.R.O., S.P. 14/148, 126.

Channel in a small boat. Carleton, English ambassador at The Hague, had been instructed to do all within his power to prevent their meeting, but it was Trumball, "legion for his Majesty at Brussels," who found Warwick early in August and "stayed" him at Ghent. The king sent word requiring him to return to England. And thus was the attempted duel prevented.[28]

Chamberlain probably expressed the general opinion of those outsiders who for months had watched the ever increasing feeling in the companies which culminated in this attempted duel, when in writing to Carleton of the trouble between Warwick and Cavendish he declared:

The factions in those two companies are grown so violent as Guelfs and Gibelines were not more animated one against the other, and they seldom meet upon the exchange or in the streets but they brabble and quarrel. So that if that society be not dissolved the sooner, or cast in a new mould, worse effects may follow than the whole business is worth.[29]

The privy councillors, who had experienced many difficulties in conducting the investigation due to the injection of factional bitterness into their hearings, were also of the same opinion, and plans were already on foot for a reorganization of the business.

Attorney-General Thomas Coventry was instructed by the privy council on July 28 to examine the company's charters and the report of the Jones Commission with a view to the procedure necessary for recalling the patent and issuing another.[30] In accordance with these instructions, Coventry and Solicitor-General Robert Heath submitted on the 31st a joint opinion that the letters patent of the corporation might be annulled on the grounds of "the apparent abuses and miscarriage in the Plantation

[28] Chichester to Carleton, July 21, 1623, P.R.O., S.P. 14/149, 17; *ibid.* to Conway, July 25, 1623, P.R.O., S.P. 14/149, 42; Cromwell to Carleton, July 25, 1623, P.R.O., S.P. 14/149, 43.

[29] Chamberlain to Carleton, July 26, 1623, P.R.O., S.P. 14/149, 48.

[30] P.R.O., S.P. 14/149, 76.

and Government" as well as certain defects in the patent itself. As for the procedure to be followed, they suggested that, since the annulment of the company's privileges by legal action would take considerable time and since the distressing condition of the colonists demanded a more expeditious settlement of their affairs, the king might attempt to secure from the adventurers a voluntary surrender of their patent. If, however, they should not " upon consideration of their own weakness voluntarily yield up their privilege," it would, of course, be necessary to resort to regular legal action. In either case, it was advised that no steps be taken against the company until some decision had been made regarding the form of government to be substituted for the present. The king's position would be much stronger if, at the same time he demonstrated the need of some change, he might also offer the remedy.[31]

This counsel was accepted, but it was not until October that an attempt was made to secure the consent of the Virginia court to the annulment of its patent. While the delay may be accounted for, in part perhaps, by the fact that the months of August and September were an off season in London when many gentlemen retired from the city to their country estates, a more probable explanation is that in accord with Coventry's advice the time was used to complete plans for a reorganization of the company's affairs. This important task was assigned to a special committee of the privy council composed of Lords Chichester, Carew, and Grandison. They were instructed on July 22 to make a study of the problems and needs of the company, and to frame therefrom some more suitable plan for regulating the government of Virginia.[32]

The rejection by these lords of the joint-stock form of government and their decision in favor of a closer connec-

[31] Coventry and Heath to James I, July 31, 1623, Bancroft Transcripts, Virginia Papers, II, 165-171.
[32] *Cal. St. Pap., Col.*, 1574-1660, p. 50.

tion with the crown could hardly have caused much surprise in any quarter. The very choice of these three men
indicated the general intention of the government. All
of them had been closely connected with the colonization
and government of Ireland, especially Chichester, who had
been Lord Deputy of Ireland from 1604 to 1615, and
Grandison who had succeeded him in that office and had
retired from its duties only so recently as 1622. Their understanding of Irish problems was obviously expected to
give them special qualification for deciding upon the
future government of Virginia.

Moreover, of recent years the steadily mounting dissatisfaction over the lack of progress in Virginia had given
rise to an increasing disposition to regard the joint-stock
plan of management as ill suited to the needs of colonization and one of the paramount causes for the colony's
failure. It had been the burden of complaints by Warwick
and Smith that thereby small and inexperienced adventurers were enabled to secure control of the courts to the
injury of the plantations and of more substantial investors. Their demands required at least some modification
of the existing form of government. Captain Bargrave had
repeatedly objected that it enabled a few men to combine
their friends and dependents into a party of control to the
damage of lesser adventurers. He predicted the complete
ruin of the colony unless a closer dependence upon the
crown was established for the protection of all parties concerned. Captain John Smith's chief criticism of the company's government had been that there were too many
governors, most of whom had little knowledge or experience to qualify them for their important task. John Martin had in the preceding year proposed that Virginia be
made into a royal plantation, and the presence of Sir Julius
Caesar on the privy council assured a representation of
his views at that board in 1623.[33]

[33] Caesar Papers, Add. MSS. 12496, fos. 456-457.

It may be said, of course, that each of these men had an axe of his own to grind. It is significant, however, that the lords of the privy council, on whom had fallen the chief responsibility for charting the course of governmental policy in these early years of colonial experimentation, had given good evidence of their agreement with the opinions of Warwick, Smith, Bargrave, and Martin. In the attempt to revive organized settlement within the grant of the moribund North Virginia Company the organization of the London Company had not been followed. The establishment of the New England Council in 1620 is testimony of a reversion by the council and leaders of the colonial movement to earlier ideas that had been dominant at the granting of the first Virginia charter.

The substitute plan decided upon by Chichester and his associates was submitted to the adventurers on October 8, when Deputy Nicholas Ferrar and some few others of the company were called before the privy council. They were informed that his majesty " having taken into his Princely consideration the distressed estate of that Colony and Plantation occasioned as it seemeth by miscarriage of the Government in that Company," it appeared that remedy could be had only " by reducing the Government into the hands of a fewer number of Governors near to those that were in the first Patents of the Plantation." It was proposed that there should be issued a new charter under which the king would select a governor and twelve assistants to take over from the company all responsibilities of government. All future selections were to be made in the following manner: the assistants were to nominate three men from whom the king would choose one for governor, and vacancies in the ranks of the assistants were to be filled by the principle of coöptation with the king holding the power of veto. The governor and six assistants were to be changed in this fashion every two years.

The machinery of government in London was to be

duplicated in Virginia, where there were to be a resident governor and twelve assistants selected by the governor and assistants in England subject to the approval of the king. The authorities in the colony were to be directly responsible to their superiors at home, who in turn would be held responsible by the king. Thus might all important matters be " directed by his majesty at this Board." The proposal extended to nothing more than a reform of the government, and careful assurance was given for the protection of all private interests. The new charter was to provide ample guarantee for all franchises, land grants, and other propertied rights conveyed under the company's seal. Having received this outline of the provisions of the proposed charter, Ferrar was instructed to call within the week a full court for the Virginia Company and to submit the proposal to the adventurers with requirement of a speedy reply. And he was warned that, failing to get a voluntary surrender of the existing charter, the government would proceed against the company " in such sort as shall be just." [34]

A rather full meeting of 120 adventurers gathered together on the following Wednesday afternoon, October 15, to consider their reply to the privy council. Neither Warwick, Smith, Johnson, nor Rich were present, and the largest number of those attending were of the Sandys faction. With only eight dissenting votes the court requested that its answer might be delayed until the next quarter court, which was to meet on the 19th of November, since according to their charter a question of this weight could not be settled in an ordinary court.[35] Their lordships, however, were not at all satisfied with this response, considering it a mere pretense and evasion that could not be allowed when the important character of the business required all possible expedition. The adventurers were commanded, therefore, to return " a cleare direct and

[34] *Records*, II, 469.   [35] *Ibid.*, II, 471.

finall Aunswere" not later than the 20th of the month. It proved to be a flat refusal given by a court of about 70 adventurers on Monday morning, the 20th, at which nine of their number dissented from the majority vote.[36]

There was no other choice for the government now but to proceed by regular course of law against the company's charter. Accordingly, a writ of *quo warranto* was issued from King's Bench on November 4, and the suit was opened before that court on the 28th. There can be little doubt that the final decision of the court was dictated primarily by considerations of policy. Nevertheless, the suit carried some strength in that it was issued not against the company itself, nor against the whole body of adventurers, but rather against that part of them which followed the leadership of Sandys.

The case for the government was much stronger by virtue of the fact that a good number of the most substantial adventurers were willing to surrender the patent. Their numerical strength is somewhat uncertain. They were undoubtedly outnumbered by their opponents, but their strength was much greater than appears by the votes of the October and November courts. Most of them had by this time dropped attendance at courts, and the small dissenting votes of eight or nine recorded in the minutes represent no more than the voice of a few of their more garrulous partisans who delighted in disputation and debate, but were of comparative unimportance except that they added so many more to the numbers of Sandys' opponents. The real leaders of the opposition had long since given up hope of an effective voice in the courts and sought to advance their ends through direct dealing with the privy council. These men, as appears by the papers of Nathaniel Rich, had at first asked no more than the removal of Sandys' agents from the control of the company. According to certain propositions of Rich dated June 23, they wished

[36] *Ibid.*, II, 473-475.

the dismissal of the present managers "from all further meddling" with the colony and a reorganization of the company that would leave control in the hands of the older and more substantial adventurers.[37] But with the council's assurance that all private interests were to be fully protected and that the action against the company extended to nothing more than a revamping of the machinery of government, the Smith-Warwick coalition readily agreed to the surrender of the patent. They might well have expected that in the transfer of authority to a body similar to the old Virginia Council, or to the more recent New England Council, they would be given greater preference in the composition of its membership.

The suit, therefore, was in the nature of a charge against one faction or party of adventurers of having usurped authority for which they could show no warrant. Attorney-General Coventry declared that Sandys, Ferrar, Sackville, Cavendish, Southampton, and their partisans, who were listed by name, had for three years past and more used and claimed to have "without any warrant or regular grant" the liberties, privileges, and franchises of the company incorporated by the name of the "Treasurer and Society of Adventurers and Planters of the City of London for the first Colony in Virginia." And it was this charge that the government pressed throughout the proceedings before Chief Justice Ley. It was perhaps a doubtful point at law, considering the established practise of majority rule, and it is not at all certain that Coventry, as prosecutor for the king, expected to have to rely upon it too greatly.

It was occasion, however, for the last bitter dispute between the two factions and for further correspondence between the privy council and the company. In a court of November 12, Nicholas Ferrar reported the serving of the *quo warranto* on himself and other adventurers. The

[37] Manchester Papers, 379.

court proceeded then to vote that although the cause was prosecuted " by perticuler names," it was in fact a suit against the company itself since it called into question its patent. The defendants were, accordingly, instructed to secure counsel for their defense, and it was ordered that the costs of the suit should be borne by the common stock of the company. This action was confirmed in the quarter court of the 19th, at which time the Grand Committee, appointed the preceding spring to have charge of the company's defense before his majesty's commissioners, was also instructed to direct the defense before King's Bench.[38] Alderman Johnson shortly presented in protest a petition to the privy council signed by a number of adventurers and planters. Professing their willingness to surrender the patent as requested by the king " so farr as any way concerneth themselves for point of Government," they humbly prayed that an order might be given requiring that all costs occasioned by the pending suit be borne wholly by the defendants, "and no part thereof by the Companies publique Stocke nor by the goods of any the Adventurers and Planters that shew themselves conformable." On the same day, December 8, the councillors favored Johnson with the requested order, forbidding the adventurers to lay any charge for the suit upon the public stock, and requiring " that such as are willinge to surrender shalbe discharged from all contribution towards the expence of the saide sute both in their persons and their goods." [39]

Although Sandys' partisans were thus prevented, in so far as the costs were concerned, from making the cause that of the company, they proceeded to build their defense on that ground. Their attorney, Edward Offley, in answer to the Attorney-General at the opening of the suit on November 28, declared the defendants to be a body justified in assuming the privileges mentioned in the charge by virtue of the royal charters granted the company. Tak-

<hr>

[38] *Records*, II, 478-479, 494-495.   [39] *Ibid.*, II, 503-505.

ing each of the rights to which Coventry had objected, he sought to justify their exercise by the defendants in the provisions of the company's charters, and maintained that they possessed the full and lawful powers of the company under these grants. His prayer for dismissal of the suit, however, was denied, and on Coventry's motion the day of pleading was set for the Octave of Saint Hillary, January 20. On this day Coventry argued that the defense had failed to show sufficient cause and sued that the pretended company might be dissolved for the usurpation of the aforenamed powers, rights, and privileges. The court set April 11 for day of judgment, but a further postponement delayed the conclusion of the case until the Morrow of Holy Trinity. On that date, May 24, 1624, the chief justice handed down the decision that Nicholas Ferrar, Sir John Danvers, and the other defendants had failed to show sufficient proof of their right to the privileges claimed and were, therefore, convicted of usurpation of the said privileges which were now assumed by the king.[40]

With this decision of King's Bench all hope of a continued existence for the company was ended. A month earlier Sandys had entertained for a short time some hope of support from the house of commons. The strong feeling against Middlesex, on account of his opposition to the proposed war with Spain, seemed to offer an opportunity to enlist the commons in the company's cause by charging to the lord treasurer the chief responsibility for its reversals. On April 21, just six days after impeachment charges against Middlesex had been laid before the house of lords by Sandys and Sir Edward Coke, the council and

---

[40] The record of the suit is to be found in Coram Rege Roll, 21 James I, Mich., No. 1528, m. 39. Through the courtesy of Dr. Jameson the author was privileged to use a transcription of this document belonging to the Library of Congress, as also a translation made by Miss M. L. Moore under the direction of Mr. Hubert Hall which is scheduled for publication in the fourth volume of the company's records. A description of the document by Miss Kingsbury is found in *Records*, I, 103.

company for Virginia drew up a long petition to the commons. Prefaced by the usual summary of the possibilities of the colony, the paper declared that just when the company had overcome by time and diligence the natural difficulties incident to all new plantations, faction and discord proceeding from selfish ambitions threatened the complete ruin of the project. Many of the unjust oppressions from which they had suffered had originated with or were supported by the lord treasurer " out of his private and most unjust ends, not onely to allmost the utter overthrow of this noble worke butt allsoe to the Deceipt of his Majesty in his profitt and to the great prejudice of the wholl kingdome in matter of Trade, and dangerous consequence to the liberty of their persons." They desired the House to hear a full representation of their grievances and to favor the adventurers with some timely remedy for their ills.[41]

The petition was presented on the 26th, and upon motion of Coke it was referred to a committee of the whole house to meet in the afternoon of the 28th.[42] At the meeting of this committee Nicholas Ferrar, Sandys, Cavendish, and Danvers presented a long and prejudiced relation of their grievances on the points of tobacco, of the contract, of the acts of the Jones Commission, and of the proceedings against the company since the establishment of the commission.[43] They severely indicted Middlesex and Nathaniel Rich for their dealings in these matters, and frequently charged that they had suffered much by the malign influence of Count Gondomar and his successor who sought to destroy the company.[44]

[41] *Records*, II, 526-528.
[42] *Journals of the House of Commons*, I, 775. The Earle Diary for the Parliament of 1624 (Add. MSS. 18597, f. 163a.) is helpful in showing Coke's coöperation with Sandys in moving a committee for hearing the company's grievances. The author is indebted to Professor Wallace Notestein for access to a transcript of this diary in his possession.
[43] *Records*, II, 538.
[44] Sir Francis Nethersole gave a full account of the hearing before the committee in a letter of May 6 to Carleton: "In this strayteng of time as it was

The whole of it was so charged with prejudice, so largely
built upon supposition, and so calculated to take advantage of the current feeling against Middlesex and Spain,
that it merits little consideration except as the last desperate effort of Sandys to retrieve some measure of honor and
credit from the failure of the company. His hope of interference by parliament was quickly lost. For the king
promptly forbad the commoners to meddle further with
the question. In a letter written on the 28th and delivered
to the House on the following morning, James declared
that all questions pertaining to Virginia had been taken
under advisement by the privy council, which had already

---

apprehended there was notwithstanding a motion made for the hearing of
the late differences in the Virginia Company whereof your Lordship hath
heard too much, the contentions and factions occasioned by them being grown
so great that the members of that body could not possibly thrive till these
humors were corrected, nor the body do it of itself as was alleged, and thereupon though with much unwillingness the matter was entertained in our house,
and a Committee of the whole house appointed to hear the cause those which
are of the house and company being allowed free speech on the Committee,
but not deciding voices. At this Committee on Wednesday last, Mr. Ferrar,
Deputy of the Company, Sir Edwin Sandys, My Lord Cavendish, and Sir
John Danvers made a relation of the proceedings by order from the Company
in which they laid the great load upon my Lord Treasurer, charged the
Commissioners appointed by the King to hear and report the cause with
extreme partiality, and this burden upon Sir Nathaniel Rich that he since
his return out of Ireland hath been an active Instrument in them. They spared
not the Count of Gondomar and his successors, who they said had in charge
to use their uttermost endeavor for the destruction of the said Company and
their plantation, to which end they showed all the late proceedings to have
been directly intended, and among them all too long to repeat (for they spent
an afternoon in it) no one was more hard than that at the time in which the
Commission were to examine the behavior of Sir Edwin Sandys in his government, and of the former Governors in theirs, Sir Edwin was commanded
by my Lord Treasurer in the King's name to go out of this town where his presence was not then more necessary for the making of his own defence than for
accusing of his predecessors in that government of whose accounts he had
been an Auditor. And in this hard stage this was very remarkable that the King
being told of it by a great Lord disavowed my Lord Treasurer and gave
commandment for Sir Edwin's liberty to return. This and other circumstances besides the matter very foul as it appeared by the light they laid it in
made many which were unwilling to be no consent to have it ripped up. ..."
P.R.O., S.P. 14/164, 46.

gone to great pains in an effort to quiet the troubles of the company. His own special commissioners were making every effort to settle these questions justly and to the best advantage of the kingdom. And since interference by parliament would serve only to bring a renewal of factional feeling, all further discussion in the House was to be prohibited.[45]

Nor was there apparently any strong disposition among the members to take issue with the king. With the exception of those commoners who were personally involved in the Virginia disputes, the chief interest in the petition seems to have come from its connection with the general attack upon Middlesex. Upon receipt of the king's letter there was some apprehension that it might indicate a plan to stop the impeachment proceedings. According to Sir Francis Nethersole, the royal message was assented to by silence, although there were some murmurings that if the king could do this he might take any of the lord treasurer's business out of the hands of parliament.[46] With both Buckingham and Prince Charles supporting the impeachment of Cranfield, however, there was small likelihood of such an event, and the commoners' fears quickly subsided. Chamberlain in a letter written on the following day probably revealed the general sentiment of the House when he declared the king had "rid them of a thorny business touching Virginia and the Summer Islands which was like enough to have bred much faction and distraction among them, being followed on both sides with much eagerness and animosity; which to prevent the King hath resumed and reserved the whole cause to his own hearing, which is the best course could have been taken, and no doubt most pleasing to the major part." [47]

[45] King to Speaker of the House of Commons, April 28, 1624, P.R.O., S.P. 14/163, 71.
[46] Nethersole to Carleton, *op. cit.*
[47] Chamberlain to Carleton, April 30, 1624, in Lefroy, *Memorials of the Bermudas*, I, 337.

Having failed to arouse parliament to any effective steps in behalf of the company, the decree of dissolution by King's Bench on May 24 left the Sandys' party no choice but its acceptance. The last court was held on June 7, and with the record of that court the official minutes of the London Company are concluded.

Meanwhile, preparations had been made by the privy council for placing the affairs of the company and colony into what was virtually a receivership. The Jones Commission had, in fact, for a year exercised many of the functions of a receiver for the company. It had taken charge of all the company's records. All correspondence to and from the colony had passed through its hands. It had sat as a court of arbitration to hear numerous claimants against the company. And important measures for the colony's relief had been undertaken at the command of the commission and under its general supervision.[48] Justice Jones had been relieved of his duties the preceding October because of other pressing business,[49] but the remainder of the body continued active throughout the winter. They served not only to oversee the work of the company during the months preceding its dissolution, but as a fact finding body to compile much information that was of great value to the government in its attempt to devise some more satisfactory plan of management.

Another commission had been created to secure at first hand information concerning the conditions and needs of the colony. On October 24, 1623, John Harvey, later to become governor of the colony, John Pory, former secretary in Virginia, Abraham Piersey, for several years cape merchant, Samuel Mathews, planter and member of the Assembly of 1624, and John Jefferson, who, however, did not act, were constituted a special commission by the privy council

[48] Its work may be followed in the *Records*, II, 413, 424, 429-430, 431-432, 433, 441, 442, 444, 448-449, 458-460, 461, 463, 479, 486, 505, 507, 509, 510, 511, 517.
[49] *Cal. St. Pap., Col.*, 1574-1660, p. 52.

to conduct a personal investigation of the fortifications, provisions, boats, public works, and general conditions of the colony. The governor and council in Virginia were ordered to give them all possible assistance in their work.[50] It has been suggested that these men were sent from England to spy out any unfavorable conditions that would aid the king in his efforts to destroy the company. There is, however, no reason to believe that the privy council had any other purpose than to add to the general stock of information available for study in deciding upon the problem of government after the dissolution of the company, which by this date was merely a question of time.

Upon their arrival in America the following February, however, Harvey and his associates were given a rather unfriendly reception. The authorities in the colony, most of whom were agents of the Sandys faction, were not unnaturally sympathetic with the company in its quarrel with the government. A year before, their letters had been bitter and unqualified in condemning the company for its failure to provide for their needs. But now the threatened overthrow of the company made them apprehensive lest such an event might mean a return to martial law and the general conditions existing before 1618, and perhaps some move against the grants and privileges secured to them under the company's seals. It is not unlikely that they were encouraged in these fears by letters from the leaders of Sandys' party at home. At any rate, they had reverted to their older sympathies. When Harvey arrived the assembly, which convened on February 14, was engaged in " unmaskinge " Captain Butler's " Unmasked Face of our Colony," and in drawing up an answer to Johnson's " Declaration of the State of the Colonie in the 12 years of Sir Thomas Smith's Government." [51] Shortly afterward, they

[50] Bancroft Transcripts, Virginia Papers, II, 205-207; MS. Rec. Va. Co., III, Part i, 2.

[51] *Ibid.*, III, Part i, 4a, 9-11; Neill, *Virginia Company of London*, 406-407, 407-411.

forwarded a letter to the privy council defending the Sandys' administration in the point of its government and begging especially that they might retain their General Assembly.[52]

Harvey was early involved in a bitter dispute with the burgesses, who regarded his mission as that of an unfriendly attack upon their free institutions. On March 2 he endeavored to secure their endorsement of a paper to the privy council expressing their thankfulness to the king for the intended changes in government and the revocation of the old patents, which, as he explained, was proposed merely for the purpose of gaining royal favor for the colonists under the new dispensation. But the burgesses elected to run no risks of being led into signing away their liberties and, in rejecting his proposal, replied that in their opinion his majesty's intention to change the government proceeded from much misinformation.[53]

The dispute precipitated no little feeling between Harvey and the assembly. But he was able, nevertheless, to secure the grudging coöperation of the burgesses in gathering the information concerning the colony for which he had come. He sought their advice on four points: the most suitable site for the chief fortification of the colony, the existing and probable future relationship with the natives, the prospect for the future development of the plantations, and the best means for attaining the hope of a prosperous colony. Answer was given on March 9, declaring Point Comfort to be best situated for fortification. Their relationship with the Indians was pictured as " irreconcilable," and the greatest problem in securing a revenge on them was the shortage of man power. As for the colony's prospects, it was considered one of the " goodliest parts of the earth, full of rivers, good soil, fruits, and other gifts of nature." And there was, in their opinion, little doubt of the early development of Virginia into a prosperous state,

[52] MS. Rec. Va. Co., III, Part i, 5.   [53] *Ibid.*, III, Part i, 7a.

provided they were given adequate support from home against the natives and newly arriving colonists came well equipped with cattle, food, and clothing. Special care should be had "that ships come not over pestered, and with that plentie and goodness of diet, which is provided in England, but seldome performed." Immigrants should first provide themselves with good houses, and for the first year should attempt to plant only corn and a little tobacco to pay for their clothing. A supply of malt for the making of small beer would prevent physical disorders resulting from the unaccustomed drinking of water. When, by the guidance of these rules, the colony was well settled with people and provisions, they might proceed to the discovery of the land and the possible products of the country.[54] At least the planters had learned a few lessons in the art of colonization by the bitter experiences of recent years!

Generally speaking, the findings of the Harvey Commission offered great promise for the future of Virginia if its affairs were well directed from home. Much progress had been made toward recovery since the spring of 1623. The credit, however, belongs largely to the colonists. They had received some help from the company the preceding summer when the adventurers had been prodded to action by the privy council.[55] A magazine of food valued at £700 had been shipped in August, accompanied by the customary admonition to apply their labors at once to staple commodities which had been so long delayed that not only Virginia's enemies but her "well willers seem to stagger in an uncertainty of belief, either of the Countries fittnes for them, or of the sincerity of yours and our intentions for the accomplishing of them." [56] In addition to this, £1,800 had been subscribed by the adventurers for the relief of their own individual plantations.[57] But this aid was con-

[54] *Ibid.*, III, Part i, 6, 6a.
[55] *Records*, II, 458-463.
[56] MS. Rec. Va. Co., III, Part ii, 28-30.
[57] *Cal. St. Pap., Col.*, 1574-1660, p. 49.

siderably offset by the fact that most of the 300 and more
settlers sent during the summer and fall landed, as usual,
pitifully short of provisions. The council in Virginia entered a complaint in January, 1624, that might well have
been written four years earlier. The company's ships had
come "pestered Contrary to your agreements, Victualed
with mustie bred, the reliques of former Voyages, and
stinckinge beere, heretofore so ernestly Complained of,
in great parte the cause of that mortalitie, which is imputed alone to the Countrey." The year had been one of
great scarcity, but so far as was known none had died of
want.[58] By diligent effort, by raids on native food stores,
and by sending an occasional ship into the Bay, the authorities had been able to feed their people. And in the
spring of 1624 they were able to report that the colonists
were in good health and well supplied except for powder
and ammunition.[59]

At the same time John Harvey, in a communication to
Nathaniel Rich, reported the completion of his investigations. He had found the people to be more in number and
provision of victuals to be more plentiful than had been
expected after the death of so many men and cattle. There
was a shortage of ammunition and several plantations were
too thinly settled to provide adequate protection against
their "subtil and nimble" enemies. On the whole, however, he believed that, a decisive defeat having been administered to the Indians, "the Plantation with good government would undoubtedly flourish.[60]

The findings of Harvey and his associates were placed
in the hands of a third commission established by the privy
council for the final arrangement and settlement of the
company's affairs. On June 24, 1624, an order in council
constituted Lord President Mandeville, Lords Paget and
Chichester, Secretaries Calvert and Conway, Attorney-

---

[58] MS. Rec. Va. Co., III, Part i, 7-8.
[59] Ibid., III, Part i, 8a; Part ii, 40, 41a.
[60] Harvey to Rich, April 24, 1624, Manchester Papers, 400.

General Coventry, Solicitor-General Heath, Sir Richard Weston, Chancellor of the Exchequer, Sir Humphrey May, Chancellor of the Duchy of Lancaster, Sir Thomas Edmonds, Treasurer of the Household, Sir John Suckling, Comptroller of the Household, Sir Robert Killegrew, Sir Thomas Smith, Sir Francis Gofton, Sir John Wolstenholme, and Alderman Johnson a special commission to settle the problems of Virginia. Prefaced by a statement of his majesty's intention to issue a new charter to the adventurers conveying all former privileges to them with amendment only of such imperfections as concerned the government of the plantations, the order authorized all or any six of the commissioners, whereof two were to be of the privy council, to meet and decide upon all questions necessary to an expeditious settlement of the colony's affairs and its government. They were to keep in close touch with the privy council, and to report all their actions to that body.[61]

A formal commission was issued to them on July 15, wherein the king reviewed the history of his grants to the company and declared his discontent that the colony had not been more prosperous. Upon petition he had appointed a commission which reported that most of the people were dead and that those who remained alive were living in great want. Yet the commissioners had considered the country to be a land of great promise. The blame for its misfortunes they laid upon the company here, in which much trouble had resulted from placing the government in the hands of too many men. Upon the advice of the privy council, therefore, he had resolved to reform this " popular course " of government. The company had been dissolved, and it was now necessary to decide upon the new charter and to frame a government for the colony. These important tasks were committed to them. But since they were matters requiring great care and much time, they

[61] Privy Council Register, James I, Vol. VI, p. 342.

were to assume full control of the colony's affairs in the meantime. All business formerly belonging to the company was now within their jurisdiction, and they were to take charge of all public property held in the name of the defunct company until such time as it could be turned over to the reorganized corporation.[62]

This commission of important state officials and prominent leaders of the colonial movement proceeded at once to its duties. By order of the privy council on June 26, all records, books of accounts, and invoices of the late corporation were delivered to the council for the commissioners' use. Another order of the same date required that all stock, averages, dues upon accounts, merchandise, and profits upon lands " or other emoluments whatsoever belonging to the Publike of the late corporation of Virginia " should be reserved and accounted for to the commissioners to be held for the use of the new company which his majesty intended to erect for Virginia.[63] Their first important task was the settlement of the local government for the colony. At a meeting of July 16 this was held to be the most urgent problem of the moment, since news of the company's dissolution might lead to confusion and disorder in the colony if some immediate decision on government was not made. Accordingly, a formal commission was issued on August 26 to Sir Francis Wyatt appointing him governor of the colony and delegating Francis West, George Yeardley, George Sandys, Roger Smyth, Ralph Hamor, John Martin, John Harvey, Samuel Mathews, Abraham Piersey, Isaac Madison, and William Claiborne to act with him as a council. They were to enjoy powers

[62] Rymer, *Foedera*, XVII, 609-613. By the addition of Ferdinando Gorges, Sir Thomas Wroth, Sir Nathaniel Rich, Sir Samuel Argall, Captain Nathaniel Butler, Samuel Wrote, John Pory, Maurice Abbott, Anthony Abdey, and a large number of others, including several prominent merchants, the total number comprising the commission was increased to fifty-six.

[63] Privy Council Register, James I, Vol. VI, pp. 344, 345.

equal to those of any governor and council in the colony during the preceding five years, but were to be subject to such instructions as were given by the king or by his commissioners.[64]

The decision on the questions of the company's charter and of the machinery of government in England came more slowly. In the end, events did not proceed exactly according to plan. The new charter for the company was never issued. And while it continued on in the loose form of a trading company until after 1630, its importance ceases with 1624. Its stock of more than £100,000 had been irreparably lost, and, completely bankrupted, the company in time disappeared.

At least one serious effort was made by Sandys' followers to secure a renewal of the old patent. No permanent settlement of the company's affairs had been made at the death of James in March, 1625, and the recent coöperation of Charles with Sandys and other parliamentary leaders in support of a war with Spain appeared to offer some promise of securing from him a reincorporation of the old company. In fact, their advice on the government of the colony was sought by the king, and in reply the famous " Discourse of the Old Company " was submitted to the privy council. A long and prejudiced account of the company's history, laying much blame upon Middlesex and Nathaniel Rich, preceded a request for the reëstablishment of the company with its former privileges and rights. The question of government, in their opinion, should be determined according to the parties providing for the charges of the colony. In case this cost fell upon the planters and adventurers, it was only just that the government should remain with the company. But if the king himself intended to bear the cost, or a considerable part of it, the powers of government might be placed in a special coun-

[64] *Cal. St. Pap., Col.*, 1574-1660, p. 64 *et. seq.*; Rymer, *Foedera*, XVIII, 618.

cil, on which, however, the adventurers should not be altogether excluded from some voice.[65]

Though giving this advice a friendly acceptance, the king in his decision demonstrated that the opinions of the privy council at this time outweighed those of any special group in the formation of colonial policy. By a proclamation of May 13 Charles declared that the territories of Virginia, the Somers Islands, and New England did of right form a part of "Our Royal Empire," and that the government of Virginia should depend "immediately" upon the king and "not be comyted to anie Companie or Corporation, to whom it maie be proper to trust Matters of Trade and Commerce, but cannot bee fitt or safe to communicate the ordering of State Affairs be they of never soe Meane Consequence" — a significant indication of the effect of the company's failure on the development of imperial policy. Two councils, one in England and another in Virginia, were to be established for the government of the colony.[66]

The council in the colony, as we have seen, was already active. But the plan to establish another council in England was never put into effect. Instead, the functions of this proposed body gradually devolved upon the privy council. The Mandeville Commission became with time less and less active, and since many of its members were councillors, it was an easy transition to the assumption by the privy council of the chief responsibility for administering the colony's affairs. Thus Virginia became in every respect a royal colony.

The position of the Virginia Assembly remained for a time somewhat uncertain. In the plan of government proposed by Chichester in October, 1623, it had not been mentioned, nor again was there any reference to it in the com-

---

[65] Printed in *Virginia Magazine of History and Biography*, I (1893-1894), 155-167, 287-309.
[66] Rymer, *Foedera*, XVIII, 72.

mission to Wyatt and his council in August, 1624. Yet there seems to be little basis in fact for the strong fear of the colonists that the king intended some move against their free institutions. There is no evidence of an intention to reëstablish martial law. And there are to be found no direct objections to the assembly. The whole of the evidence supports the belief that the government's quarrel was almost entirely with the company and its administration. In so far as there was a quarrel with conditions in the colony, it seems to have been almost wholly confined to such conditions as could be charged back to the maladministration of the adventurers. The appointment of Wyatt as the first royal governor, the selection of Yeardley to succeed him upon his return to England in the fall of 1624, and the retention of most of the old councillors on the new council in Virginia may be taken as proof of confidence in these men and in their work. As already pointed out, objections to the " government of Virginia " refer primarily to the machinery of government in London, which in its democratic and popular form was considered a point of great weakness. There can be no doubt that substitute plans of government looked first of all to the rectification of this weakness, and any decision that may have been made on the machinery to be established in the colony itself must have been dictated primarily by the desire to provide whatever form of local government would work most smoothly and effectively with that at home.

Under such circumstances, it is not impossible that the assembly received little thought or, if it did, that it was considered advisable to leave its position in the new scheme to be determined upon more deliberation. This much is certain, the problem in 1624 was to remedy the demonstrated shortcomings of the government in England, and if the assembly was deliberately left out of all plans, the decision was dictated not primarily by objections to the assembly itself, but by problems nearer home. In the desire to substitute a more closely knit and more responsible form of government in London, the assembly may have been rejected on the ground that it might confuse and lessen the efficiency of a well ordered government. But in the records extant it is difficult to find support for the thesis that Chichester, Coventry, and Mandeville were engaged in a crusade against free and representative institutions in America. Although the assembly received no formal recognition for a time, there is recorded no attempt to prevent its continuance, and by 1627 it received full approval by the crown.

The Bermuda Company came through the investigations of 1623 with much more success than did its sister corporation. That colony had not suffered so severely as had Virginia, and the Jones Commission reported more favorably upon its condition and the prospect for its future under the company's direction.[67] Moreover, Warwick and Smith with their followers, who were more deeply interested in Bermuda than in Virginia, assumed control and took effective steps for a reorganization of the company's affairs. Its debts amounted in all to £1,400, and provision was made, backed by an order of the privy council on December 8, 1623, for the removal of these obligations. Of this burden £400 was to be borne by an imposition collected on all tobacco coming from the plantation that year. The remainder was to be paid by a levy imposed on the adventurers according to the number of shares held in the joint-stock.[68] Endowed thus with fresh life the company continued to direct the fortunes of the Bermuda colony until 1684 when its charter was surrendered to the king.

Did time and space allow, we might with profit follow Nicholas Ferrar into an early retirement with his mother

[67] Manchester Papers, 384.

[68] Cal. St. Pap., Col., 1574-1660, p. 55. For the assumption of control by Smith, which probably had the king's support, see Records, II, 501-503.

at Little Gidding in Huntingdonshire, there to lay up treasures "where neither moth nor rust doth corrupt, and where thieves do not break through nor steal." We might follow the more exciting adventures of the earl of Warwick's ships as they scoured the seven seas in search of the treasures of this earth, or move with him — that man hated and loved by so many people, that stalwart opponent of royal prerogative, that unyielding enemy of Spain, and that never failing friend of Puritans — through the most momentous years of English history to his death in 1658. We might pause for a moment at the grave of Sir Thomas Smith, as in 1625 he concluded a long and honorable career as one of England's most renowned merchant princes. We might mark the passing in 1629 of Sir Edwin Sandys, who had writ his name so large in the annals of parliamentary government, or of Nathaniel Rich, both his ally and his foe, in 1636. All of them famous in the history of two continents!

But we are concerned only with that portion of their lives in which they touched upon, or helped to shape, the fortunes of the Virginia Company. The story, as we have found it, is essentially one of commercial disappointment. Frequent mistakes in policy and in execution through years of unsuccessful pioneering in the field of colonial adventure had contributed to a heavy indebtedness under which the company languished without much prospect of relief. The difficulties of the situation and the conflicting interests of the adventurers had bred faction and distrust among them and left little disposition to coöperate for the removal of this burden. The failure in Virginia, the bankruptcy of the joint-stock, and the bitter strife within the courts seemed sufficient proof to the king and his councillors of the incapacity of the company's leadership under existing conditions and organization to achieve the high purposes for which the business was designed. For a corporation thus bankrupted in purse and in morale, it was

both natural and desirable to establish a receivership as
the first step toward some reorganization whereby the
affairs of the colony might be placed upon a more secure
footing.

If it has been a story worth telling, it is because the aims,
the endeavors, the disappointments, and the quarrels of
the adventurers in the London Company throw a pene-
trating light upon the many sided history of the origins
of our nation and of the beginnings of the British Empire.
Here can be made the closest study of the original purposes
with which the English set out to colonize America. The
records for the six year period covered by this work provide the most complete source at hand for an analysis of
these purposes in the actual attempt to achieve them. Here
may be found many of the factors which explain their
failure. The emergence, too, of less exaggerated hopes for
reward in their later activities may at least be traced in
embryo. Optimistic expectations of quick and ready wealth
in America were only slowly surrendered, it is true, but
the experience of the London adventurers may be considered as having brought ideas about colonization a little
closer to the realm of reality. Virginia, at any rate, was allowed thereafter to follow what was perhaps her most
natural development as a commonwealth of tobacco plantations. Such a course was for a time hardly considered
the most desirable, but bitter experience in attempts to
forestall this development argued against further efforts.
A greater appreciation of the stupendous tasks involved
in colonization may be considered another of the fruits
growing out of the company's collapse. It was many years
before Englishmen rid themselves completely of the idea
that colonizing required anything more than the transportation of their people to this new land of plenty. But
surely some of those who followed the trackless path across
the Atlantic after 1624 must have owed their survival and

later happiness to those first Virginians who laid down
their lives to demonstrate the importance of good food and
water, of adequate equipment in tools, arms, clothing, and
housing, and of proper care in the selection of sites for
settlement that were healthy and easily defended.

There were other important lessons which the men who
guided English colonial experiments thereafter sought to
draw from the company's history. The apparent disadvantages of the joint-stock plan of management were of real
weight in the attempt to find some machinery better
adapted to the proper direction of colonial affairs. In re-
verting to earlier ideas in the establishment of the New
England Council and in numerous experiments with the
plan of proprietary settlements, the experience of the Virginia Company was not without great influence. The government, too, had acquired a greater appreciation of both
its interests and its duties in this new type of national enterprise. In the tobacco negotiations there may be traced
the delineations of later imperial policies. The desire to
utilize colonial trade for the upbuilding of English commerce and the expectation of some financial reward for
the national treasury are both indicated, as well as the
counterbalancing policy of granting preference to colonial
products in the home market. Through these negotiations,
through the prolonged investigation of the company's
affairs, and in the establishment of a receivership there is
clear indication of the important rôle to be played by the
privy council in the machinery of colonial administration.
And in the events which made of Virginia the first royal
colony, there may be found many of the considerations
which later dictated an attempt to bring all colonial settlements into a more closely knit and better administered
unit under the direct supervision of the Crown and its
agencies.

It may be, too, that the study has been of value for reasons totally aside from these points of historical significance. Few of us in America ever pause to count the cost in pounds, shillings, and pence, and in terms of human suffering, at which the English people laid the foundations for this country. That in itself is a story worth recalling.

BIBLIOGRAPHY

IN view of Miss Kingsbury's exhaustive description and list of the various documents of historical record relating to the Virginia Company it is unnecessary to attempt here a complete bibliography for the company's history. The appended bibliography, therefore, is confined to the sources cited in the text with an attempt to indicate those collections that have been of most value in a study of the company's affairs after 1618. For a fuller treatment of the source material for the history of the company and colony the reader is referred to Susan Myra Kingsbury, ed., *Records of the Virginia Company of London*, 2 vols., Washington, 1906, I, 17–205.

Miss Kingsbury's volumes have furnished the most important single collection of sources used in the preparation of this work. Of her projected four volumes, only two, comprising a carefully edited copy of the official court book of the company from April 28, 1619, to June 7, 1624, have been published. Though these official court minutes must be used with care, representing, as they do, a partisan and biased account of the courts' proceedings and including only such information concerning the colony's affairs as Sandys chose to give to the public, they must, nevertheless, form the foundation for any study of the last years of the company's existence. The remaining two volumes, incorporating official and private correspondence between the company and its leaders and officials and prominent planters in America, official orders, commissions, and instructions of the courts and council, and a vast amount of valuable material in the public archives and private papers of adventurers and state officials, are in an advanced state of preparation. Through courtesy of Dr. Jameson of the Division of Manuscripts in the Library of Congress the author has been privileged to use these volumes, the third in galley proof and the fourth in manuscript. Most of the material included therein had been previously examined in the original, but the opportunity to work through Miss Kingsbury's volumes was of immeasurable value in checking and filling in certain gaps in the author's notes as well as in avoiding important errors of omission or oversight.

Other collections of sources are listed below.

I. MANUSCRIPTS, TRANSCRIPTS, AND FACSIMILES.

Much valuable material is to be found in the state papers preserved in the Public Record Office in London. It is especially useful in studying the relationship between the company and the government in handling such problems as tobacco and customs duties, and in following the course of government policy through the investigation and final dissolution of the company. The British Museum also afforded valuable assistance. Special mention should be made of the Caesar Papers and of the Official Papers of the Pitt Family found in the Additional Manuscripts. Sir Julius Caesar was a member of the privy council and brother-in-law to Captain John Martin. Some of his papers (Add. MSS. 12496) are valuable for a study of the possible connection between Martin's grievances against the company and the attitude of the government. Sir William Pitt was a member of the royal commission established in 1623 for an investigation of the company and colony, and it is in his papers that we find the copy of the official commission authorizing the investigation. (Add. MSS. 29975, f. 63.)

Of great importance for the study of Sandys' plans and methods of colonization, of the conditions which brought about their failure, and of the effect upon the morale and finances of the company is a collection known as the Manuscript Records of the Virginia Company, Volume III. (For full description see Kingsbury, *Records*, I, 44–48.) Of first importance for our purposes have been letters from the company to the colony between 1621 and 1623, letters from the colony to the company or to the king and his councillors between 1621 and 1625, and a miscellaneous collection of letters, instructions, commissions, and warrants relating to the colony and its affairs in 1623 and 1624 and to the activities of the privy council and the various commissioners through these critical years. These valuable documents form a part of the manuscript volumes acquired for the Library of Congress from Thomas Jefferson. The manuscripts are either original records or authenticated contemporary copies. They will appear in Miss Kingsbury's later volumes. This source has been cited in the text as MS. Rec. Va. Co.

Mention should be made of another volume of Jefferson manuscripts belonging to the Library of Congress, *Miscellaneous Papers,* 1606–1683, containing seventeenth century transcripts of letters, instructions, commissions, proclamations, etc., some of which fall within the dates of this study. (See Kingsbury, *Records,* I, 41–43.)

Three manuscript collections of private papers throw considerable light upon the company's affairs and significant developments in the colony. The first of these are the Ferrar Papers in possession of Magdelene College, Cambridge. Of the seventy-eight items relating to Virginia twenty letters from Sandys to John Ferrar are of unusual value in showing the chief importance of these two men in directing the company's business. Equally significant are over thirty letters from planters and adventurers in Virginia to Sandys which, with the official letters from the governor and council in the colony (mentioned above), furnish the most accurate key to an understanding of the true state of affairs in the colony under the management of Sandys and Ferrar. They are especially interesting for their repeated complaints of Sandys' overhasty methods of colonization, the sending of too many colonists, their inadequate provisions, and their great suffering by sickness and death. They are in sharp contradiction to the impression of progress and happiness gained from the court minutes, and furnish important substantiation for the serious charges presented against Sandys by his enemies in 1623. In the preparation of this volume use has been made of complete transcripts and photographs of letters and documents in the Ferrar Papers relating to Virginia which have been made under the supervision of Miss Kingsbury for the Library of Congress. Their publication in the forthcoming volumes of the company's records will be of great value to future students.

The Manchester Papers, at present in the care of the Public Record Office, have been consulted in the original. They supply the most accurate index to the interests and motives which inspired Sandys' opponents, especially the Warwick group. Henry Montague, Viscount Mandeville and later earl of Manchester, was lord president of the privy council at the time of the company's dissolution and head of the Mandeville Commission established in 1624 for the solution of problems remaining after the recall of the Virginia patent. The inclusion of papers relating to Virginia may have been due in part to Mandeville's official connection with the company's affairs. But the most important documents bear the mark of Nathaniel Rich's private papers, which could have come into this collection through any one of several close social and business connections between the two families. Rich was the chief spokesman for the Warwick group, the most active in pressing the charges before the royal commission of 1623, and his papers present a complete record of the grounds of objection to Sandys and the charges whereon he was indicted before the government. There are also some important letters to Rich and Warwick from America, most of them from Bermuda, which throw light upon the important interests of the Warwick group in that colony. Rich's papers are also helpful in studying the famous tobacco fight of 1622 and 1623. The Manchester Papers, while known and frequently referred to, have been generally neglected in studying the company's history through a disposition to discredit them because of their obvious bias. They are undoubtedly prejudiced, but no more so than the public statements of Sandys' partisans, and a study of them in conjunction with the private correspondence of Sandys and Ferrar shows that the written history of the company has suffered much from the neglect of this important source. A rather unsatisfactory catalogue of these papers may be found in the eighth report of the Historical Manuscripts Commission. Those papers concerning Virginia will be published by Miss Kingsbury.

A third collection, the Smyth of Nibley Papers belonging to the New York Public Library, consists of over sixty papers relating to Virginia between 1613 and 1634. The main body of them forms a valuable record of the settlement of Berkeley Hundred in 1619, and presents the most complete source for a study of the character and development of the private plantations which were one of the most significant movements in the company during its last years.

The Virginia Papers of the Bancroft Transcripts in the New York Public Library have also been of valuable aid for reference. They consist largely of accurate transcriptions of state papers now to be found in the Public Record Office.

The Original Correspondence of the India Company and several volumes of the company's Court Books preserved in the India Office at London have been of some aid in tracing the relationship between Sir Thomas Smith and the earl of Warwick.

II. OFFICIAL PRINTED SOURCES.

Acts of the Privy Council, Colonial Series. Vol. I, 1613–1680. Edited by W. L. Grant and J. Munro. London, 1908.

Calendar of State Papers, Colonial Series. Vol. I, 1574–1660. Edited by W. N. Sainsbury. London, 1860.

Calendar of State Papers, Domestic, 1619–1623. Edited by Mary Anne Everett Green. London, 1858.

Calendar of State Papers and Manuscripts, Relating to English Affairs Existing in the Archives and Collections of Venice, and in other Libraries of Northern Italy. Vols. XIV, XV. Edited by A. B. Hinds. London, 1908–1909.

Reports of the Royal Commission on Historical Manuscripts. *Report on the MSS of his Grace the Duke of Manchester.* VIIIth Report, Appendix II. London, 1881.

Journals of the House of Commons, Vol. I.

Journals of the House of Lords, Vol. III.

III. PRINTED COLLECTIONS.

Transactions and Collections of the American Antiquarian Society. Vol. IV. Worcester, 1860.

Force, Peter, ed. *Tracts Relating to the Origin, Settlement and Progress of the Colonies in North America.* 4 vols. Washington, 1836–1846.

Hazard, Ebenezer, ed. *Historical Collections.* 2 vols. Philadelphia, 1792–1794.

Lefroy, J. H., ed. *Memorials of the Discovery and Early Settlement of the Bermudas,* 1511–1687. 2 vols. London, 1877–1879.

Neill, Edward Duffield. *History of the Virginia Company of London.* Albany, 1869.

Rymer, Thomas. *Foedera,* etc. XVII, XVIII. Second ed. London, 1727.

" Lord Sackville's Papers respecting Virginia, 1613–1631." *American Historical Review.* Vol. XXVII (1922). Pp. 493–538, 738–765.

Tyler, Lyon Gardiner. *Narratives of Early Virginia*. New York, 1907.

IV. CONTEMPORARY ACCOUNTS AND DOCUMENTS OF SPECIAL SIGNIFICANCE.

Arber, Edward, ed. *Travels and Works of Captain John Smith*. 2 vols. Edinburgh, 1910. (A new edition with a biographical and critical introduction by A. G. Bradley.)

A Declaration of the State of the Colonie and Affaires in Virginia. Edward Waterhouse, London, 1622.

" The Discourse of the Old Company." *Virginia Magazine of History and Biography*. Vol. I (1893–1894) . Pp. 155–167, 287–309. Also to be found in Tyler, *Narratives of Early Virginia*, pp. 431–460.

Lefroy, J. H., ed. *Historye of the Bermudaes*. Hakluyt Society. London, 1882.

Rolfe, John. " Relation of the State of Virginia." *Virginia Historical Register and Literary Advertiser*. Vol. I (1848) . Pp. 101–113.

Wodenoth, Arthur. *A Short Collection of the Most Remarkable Passages from the originall to the dissolution of the Virginia Company*. Printed by Richard Cotes for Edward Husband. London, 1651. (New York Public Library.)

Orders and Constitutions, Partly collected out of his Maiesties Letters Patents, and partly ordained upon mature deliberation, by the Treasurer, Counseil and Companie of Virginia, for the better governing of the Actions and affaires of the said Companie here in England residing. Peter Force. *Tracts*. Vol. III, No. 6.

" Instructions to Governor Yeardley, 1618." (The so-called " greate charter " of Virginia.) A copy is in possession of the Library of Congress, and it has been published in the *Virginia Magazine of History and Biography*. Vol. II (1894) . Pp. 154–165.

" An Ordinance and Constitution for a Council and Assembly in Virginia." Manuscript Records of the Virginia Company, III. Another copy in Miscellaneous Papers, 1606–1683. Pp. 21–23. It will shortly be published in the third volume of the company's records.

The record of the *quo warranto* suit before Kings Bench by

BIBLIOGRAPHY 343

which the company was dissolved is found in Coram Rege
Roll, 21 James I, Mich., No. 1528, m. 39. By permission of
Dr. Jameson the author has used a transcription of this
document in the Library of Congress and a translation
made by Miss M. L. Moore under the supervision of Mr.
Hubert Hall. Miss Kingsbury is responsible for the discovery of this important document. For her description of
it see *Records*, I, 103.

V. SECONDARY WORKS.

Adams, Henry. Leading article on Captain John Smith as an
historian. *North American Review*. Vol. CIV (1867). Pp.
1–30.

Bancroft, George. *History of the United States of America*.
Revised ed. Vol. I. New York, 1884.

Beer, George Louis. *Origins of the British Colonial System,
1578–1660*. New York, 1922.

Beverly, Robert. *History and Present State of Virginia*. London, 1705.

Brown, Alexander. *Genesis of the United States*. 2 vols. Boston and New York, 1890.

Brown, Alexander. *First Republic in America*. Boston and
New York, 1898.

Brown, Alexander. *English Politics in Early Virginia History*.
Boston and New York, 1901.

Brown, Alexander. " A note on Mr. W. W. Henry's views of
'The First Republic in America.' " *Virginia Magazine of
History and Biography*. Vol. VI (1899). Pp. 324–334.

Bruce, Philip Alexander. *Economic History of Virginia in the
Seventeenth Century*. 2 vols. New York, 1896.

Burk, John Daly. *History of Virginia from Its First Settlement
to the Present Day*. 3 vols. Petersburg, 1804–1805.

Campbell, Charles. *History of the Colony and Ancient Dominion of Virginia*. Philadelphia, 1860.

Channing, Edward, *History of the United States*. Vol. I. New
York, 1905.

Craven, W. Frank. " The Earl of Warwick — A Speculator in
Piracy." *Hispanic American Historical Review*. Vol. X
(1930). Pp. 457–479.

Fiske, John. *Old Virginia and Her Neighbours.* 2 vols. Boston and New York, 1899.

Goodman, Godfrey. *Court of King James the First.* 2 vols. London, 1839.

Newton, Arthur Percival. *Colonizing Activities of the English Puritans.* New Haven, 1915.

Peckard, Peter. *Memoirs of the Life of Mr. Nicholas Ferrar.* Cambridge, 1790.

Robertson, Wyndham. " The Marriage of Pocahontas." *The Historical Magazine.* Vol. IV (1860). Pp. 289–296.

Scisco, L. D. " Plantation Type of Colony." *American Historical Review.* Vol. VIII (1903). Pp. 260–270.

Scott, William Robert. *Constitution and Finance of English, Scottish and Irish Joint-Stock Companies to 1720.* 3 vols. Cambridge, 1910.

Stith, William. *History of the First Discovery and Settlement of Virginia.* New York, 1865.

Young, Alexander. *Chronicle of the Pilgrim Fathers of the Colony of Plymouth.* Second ed. Boston, 1844.

INDEX

Abbott, Maurice, 43, 107, 143, 328n.
Abdey, Anthony, 43, 107, 328n.
Accounts, difficulties over auditing of, 43-44, 106-112.
Adams, Henry, 13.
Arber, Edward, 13.
Argall, Captain Samuel, 44, 50, 58, 59, 65, 76, 77, 197, 328n.; governor of Virginia, 36; discontent with his administration, 36-39; recall of, 46; and the earl of Warwick, 121-122, 128-130, 133-134; failure of attempts to try him, 122-123.
Argall's Town, 76, 174.
Arondelle, Peter, 193-194, 215.
Assembly, the Virginia, provision for, 67-68, 73-74; reasons for establishment of, 71-79; unimportance of in dissolution of company, 330-332; position after 1624, 332.
Auditors, for company's accounts, 43, 90-91, 106.

Baldwin, John, 220.
Ballot, use of in Virginia Company, 86-87, 91-92.
Bancroft, George, 11, 13.
Barbor, Gabriel, agent for Virginia lotteries, 149, 184.
Bargrave, Captain John, 42, 312; suit against Smith, 279, 280, 282; warns of Sandys' political sympathies, 276-278; criticisms of company's government, 279-283.
Barwick, Captain Thomas, 213.
Beer, George Louis, 22.
Berkeley, Richard, 59.
Berkeley Hundred, 59-60.
Berkley, Captain, 216.
Berkley, John, 187.
Bermuda, 84; representative assembly in, 68; and piracy, 136-139.
Bermuda Company, 68, 84; close connections with Virginia Company, 84-85, 91, 141; and tobacco, 225, 227n., 232, 234n., 238-245, 247-249; and the royal investigation of 1623, 258-260, 267-268; after 1623, 332.

Beverly, Robert, 4.
Blount, Charles, eighth Lord Mountjoy, 84n.
Bluett, Captain, 100.
Boroughs, the Virginia, 54-55.
Bourchier, Sir Henry, 267.
Briggs, Henry, 106.
Brown, Alexander, his treatment of the company's history, 12-21.
Buckingham, George Villiers, duke of, 143, 321.
Burk, John Daly, 11.
Butler, Captain Nathaniel, 85, 120, 140, 144, 299, 305, 323, 328n.; governor of Bermuda, 87; attacked for encouraging piracy, 137-140; and the earl of Warwick, 85, 134-135, 137, 306; his "Unmasked Face of Our Colony in Virginia etc.," 254-258, 299.

Caesar, Sir Julius, 119-120, 292.
Calvert, Sir George, 294, 326.
Campbell, Charles, 11.
Capps, William, 219.
Carew, George, Lord, 311.
Carleton, Sir Dudley, 310.
Cavendish, William, Lord, 119, 238, 244, 246, 248, 259, 260, 319; defense of the Sandys party, 262-263; 285-286, 290-291; replies to criticisms of "democratic government," 284-285; attack on Warwick, 306-308; attempted duel with Warwick, 308-310.
Chamberlain, John, comments on Virginia quarrels, 87-88, 310.
Chambers, George, 106.
Channing, Edward, 21-22.
Charles I, 329; proclamation settling problem of Virginia, 329.
Charles City, 54, 196.
Charter, the Great (the so-called Magna Carta of Virginia), 117, 186; identification of, 52-53; its character and provisions, 53-67; and private plantations, 60-67; and the colony's government, 53-54, 70.
Chichester, Arthur, Lord, 326; drafts

HATS

*A History of
Fashion in Headwear*

Easter Island hat

HATS

*A History of
Fashion in Headwear*

16020 1

HILDA AMPHLETT

DOVER PUBLICATIONS, INC.
Mineola, New York

Bibliographical Note

This Dover edition, first published in 2003, is an unabridged republication of the work first published by Richard Sadler Ltd., Mill Lane, Chalfont St. Giles, Buckinghamshire, Great Britain, in 1974.

Library of Congress Cataloging-in-Publication Data

Amphlett, Hilda.
    Hats : a history of fashion in headwear / Hilda Amphlett.
       p. cm.
    Originally published: Chalfont St. Giles, Buckinghamshire : Richard Sadler, 1974.
    ISBN 0-486-42746-3 (pbk.)
     1. Hats–History. 2. Headgear–History. I. Title.

GT2110.A55 2003
391.4'3–dc21
                                     2003043450

Manufactured in the United States of America
Dover Publications, Inc., 31 East 2nd Street, Mineola, N.Y. 11501

This book is dedicated
with deep affection
to the Hon. Mrs T. B. Hart,
to show my appreciation of her encouragement
and help during its production

FOREWORD

by

Mrs Greta Raikes

Lecturer on, and collector of, English costume

TRACING THE EVOLUTION of the Hat over two thousand years is an absorbing and monumental task.

Since we have now arrived at the second hatless age, the hat has become something of a curiosity, so people go to lectures about hats, dress up for 'old time' evenings in hats, and, when looking through the pages of this history, will realize how flattering *e* a hat to a woman, how dashing and important for a man. They may even feel deprived, and evince a twinge of envy, realizing that we are, at present depressingly unimaginative about our headwear.

In the history of clothing the Hat surely came first, and we may be sure that EVE found that leaves looked better in her hair than where she is reported to have worn them. And ADAM certainly must have used his to make a crown, and so, from the very start, the woman fascinated and the man dominated, and all with the aid of a hat.

Lectures on the subject of head-adornment are eagerly attended which is surely a sign that deep down in us all is a longing to be crowned with a glorious hat again; to sally forth in an elegant glossy hideous topper, or in a feathered, floppy, flowered cartwheel. Meanwhile, in our hatless era the men have turned, most successfully and romantically to the adornment of long hair, and some of the women to wigs, that can be changed in colour and shape to suit a mood.

To be able to peruse this book of pictures, representing so many eras and nationalities of headwear makes the realization possible that the wearers were forced to suffer untold headaches in their efforts to impress their contemporaries, and thus cause most of us to decide that perhaps we are better off without a hat, even if going bare-headed has taken away dignity and self-esteem from the men and gracious elegance from the women.

The ensuing pages will help you to decide whether to wear—or not to wear—a HAT.

Contents

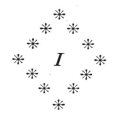

The First Millenium A.D.

FOR SELF-EVIDENT REASONS we have little or no information on the head-coverings of cloth, leather or other perishable materials worn in Western Europe before the Romans recorded some details. Crowns and helmets, however, being usually of metal, have survived in many cases, so that information is more abundant in the case of royal and military headwear.

There is some evidence that the Phrygian cap *(Fig. 1)* was introduced into Europe from the Middle East by the trading Phoenicians, who sailed along the Mediterranean coasts and the Atlantic shores as far as Cornwall, where they traded their famous cloths, dyed Tyrian purple, for tin and possibly other commodities such as oysters. The Neolithic, Bronze, and Iron-age peoples of Europe kept sheep and cattle and dressed and sewed leather. They also spun and wove wool and probably flax, so that it can be inferred that they made themselves protective caps and hoods and may have decorated them with beads or thongs.

Of the everyday head covering worn by Europeans before the Roman occupation and beyond the boundaries of the Empire, one fascinating example may be a clue to more widespread habits, at least in the northern parts of the Continent. At Tollund Bog near Viborg, Denmark, in 1944, the body of a man, thought by archeologists to have been a chieftain sacrificed for the sake of his people, was discovered in almost perfect condition, preserved by the bog-water for 2000 years. He was wearing a cap sewn from eight or nine pieces of leather with fur side inmost and conical rather than dome-shaped, crown with a band along the lower edge and a chin strap. *(Fig. 2)*. The head and shoulders of this man, who still wears his cap, can be seen in the National Museum at Copenhagen.

Pomponius Mela wrote that the natives of Britain dyed their bodies blue with woad, after they had been tattoed, as did the Scythians of the same period, and they probably tattooed their faces as well to make themselves look fiercer in battle. The term Picti applied by the Romans to this tattooing, eventually became the name for the peoples themselves.

Julius Caesar certainly found that the Iron Age

FIG. 1 Byzantine (South Italian) 6th cent. A.D.

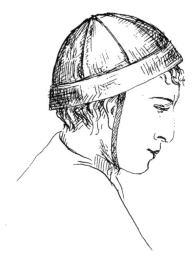

FIG. 2 Danish (*c.* 70 B.C.)

Britons of Kent and Sussex had by 54 B.C. reached a considerable degree of civilisation, and he records that they had long flowing hair and shaved every part of the body except the head and upper lip. Razors had long been known and many examples are displayed in museums.

Caesar's description tallies with the appearance of a fine bust, now in Rome, reputed to be that of a British chieftain, Caractacus (Caradoc to his own people), who was taken to Italy to march in the Emperor's Triumph. He is certainly of a Northern European type and has thick flowing hair, parted in the centre, with short waves like a fringe over his forehead, the rest falling to his shoulders. On his upper lip he has a handsome moustache.

Two main styles of veil were worn by Anglo-Saxon women. One had a hole made to fit the face, a fillet or crown holding the material in position on the head. The other was rectangular, draped over the head and down the back, and held in place with a band of metal.

The head-rail (known to the Saxons as the heafodhraegl) was made of linen or woollen fabric and was about two yards in length by one yard wide, and the method of donning this head covering was as follows: one end was passed from the left shoulder, over the crown of the head, down and under the chin from the right, then round the back to the left shoulder where the end was left hanging.

It was always coloured and often embroidered. *English Work,* a term for this embroidery, was designed in conventionalized patterns of spots and lines, and became famous, even on the continent. This head-rail was later, by the Normans, to be called the couvrechef, or coverchief, and continued to be worn well into the next century.

During the Roman occupation, the Celts of Gaul and Britain, at least south of Hadrian's great wall, became romanized, adopting the toga and tunic, and the custom, in the case of men, of wearing little head-covering, apart from military helmets when these were required. A fillet or band for the brow was another Roman custom adopted to some extent by the peoples they conquered.

At Mayence a double monument was unearthed of a man and woman, both seated, and from this we get an excellent representation of Romano-Gaulish dress of the period between A.D. 20 and A.D. 80. The woman *(Fig. 3)* wears a turban-like head-dress of gathered cloth, possibly wound round a large quoit-shaped foundation. From it streams a veil of the same material. Her husband is bare-headed and the hood of his cloak is thrown back to lie round his shoulders.

The hooded cloak or *bardocucullus,* which covered the head and fell in folds to the feet, served for both young and old. A British example, of about A.D. 300, is seen in *Fig. 4.*

The Saxons, who had never been subjected to Roman rule, arrived in successive waves when the Legions withdrew in A.D. 450. They dispossessed or conquered a race more civilised than themselves, and for a century or more men on both sides were preoccupied with almost perpetual warfare. Their

Fig. 3   Romano-Gaulish

Fig. 4   British Bardocucullus (*c.* 300 A.D.)

attire, therefore, became predominantly military in style and many helmets of the time have been unearthed by archeologists. We know, too, that conical caps of leather, wool fabric or felt, covered with metal bands, were sometimes worn, but men ordinarily went bareheaded. Hair remained long, loose and curled.

The Welsh bard, Aneurin, described the Teutonic tribes as wearing a profusion of hair, wreathing it with beads, and having many golden torques (bracelets) about their arms and necks.

In contemporary manuscripts the beards and long hair of the men are often coloured blue which may indicate that they were dyed with woad or other blue pigment.

Women, also wore their hair long, but braided and coiled at the nape of the neck. It is seldom seen in illuminated manuscripts as it is generally covered with the folds of the cloak as in *Fig. 5*. Compare this with the Roman *palla* the outer edge of which is frequently embroidered, or hidden by the veil or head-rail.

Christianity, filtering in from Celtic Ireland and Wales, and cemented by the arrival of St. Augustine, had its influence on the attire of the converted. The Church taught that to expose any part of the body, other than the hands, face and feet, was a sin, and prescribed more clothes and less adornment for the faithful, though not necessarily what they themselves followed. The Danes brought with them new fashions and particularly that of wearing their hair much longer. King Canute is described as wearing his

hair in profusion over his shoulder, but unfortunately the only illumination we possess that is supposed to represent the Danish king shows him with short hair and curly beard and is undoubtedly the work of a Saxon chronicler who had never seen the king in person and painted the so-called likeness many years later than the incident it depicted—the Marriage of Canute and Aelgyfe. In The Death Song of Labroc (8th–9th centuries) the hero is referred to as 'the lover of the lady, beautious in his locks', and there is an anecdote of a young Danish warrior who had been taken prisoner and who begged his executioner not to allow his hair to be touched by a slave or defiled by his own blood, so much pride had he in his long tresses.

Saint Gregory Nazianzen said of his sister, in commendation, 'She has no gold to adorn herself, no yellow hair tied in knots and arranged in curls, no transparent garments, brilliant stones or jewels.' We cannot help feeling sorry for her, but her brother's list of vanities is enlightening as showing what the gayer and less pious were wearing.

MILITARY

During their occupation of Western Europe the Romans encouraged or compelled men of the native races to serve in their armies, and they then wore the standard helmets of their conquerors *(Fig. 6)*.

This was the helmet for captains or centurions; the gladitorial helmet is seen in *Fig. 7*.

Fig. 8 is taken from a silver piece found in Britain, and represents the head of the first Christian

FIG. 5   Saxon

FIG. 6   Roman (96 A.D.)

FIG. 7   Roman (96 A.D.)

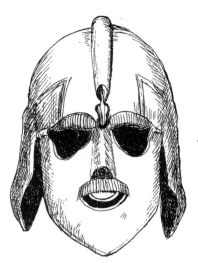

FIG. 10   Sutton Hoo Helmet

FIG. 8   Romano-British

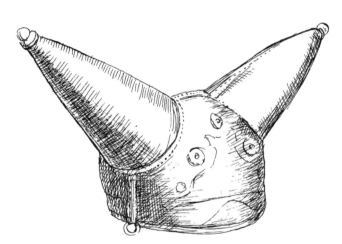

FIG. 11   Viking

FIG. 9   Celtic (800 A.D.)

FIG. 12   English or Irish (9th cent.)

FIG. 13   Burgundian (9th cent.)

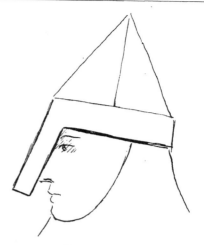

FIG. 14   Norman

Emperor, Constantine, on whose helmet the Christo-gram—Chi-ro can be seen.

Native Britains and the Celts, who resisted the Romans, also found it expedient to adopt a metal covering for the head as a protection during battle and *Fig. 9* shows a Celtic helmet which seems to have some—though not much—affinity with the Roman.

With the withdrawal of the Legions from the outlying regions of the Empire the way was left open for the raiding tribes of the Baltic and North Sea coastal areas to make incursions, and later to settle in the districts the Romans had vacated. The Angles, Jutes and Saxons, who colonized lowland England brought their own helmet styles with them. Among the treasures found at Sutton Hoo in the ship Cenotaph excavated in 1939 at Woodbridge, Suffolk, is the Anglo-Saxon moustachioed helmet of bronze, illustrated in *Fig. 10* and dating from approximately the middle years of the seventh century. It has movable ear-flaps, repoussé-work eyebrows, and shaped nose-piece, with a raised ridge over the crown to deflect the enemy's weapon.

Of a different style altogether, but doubtless at least as effective, was the true Viking-style helmet of *Fig. 11*, worn by raiders from the North in the eighth and ninth centuries. Historians have noted the resemblance of the prominent horns to the Sumerian and other Middle Eastern head-dresses

of prehistoric times, but this similarity is probably purely coincidental, and their purpose in this case was not of religious significance but to turn aside the enemy's spears or axes. They may also have been intended to inspire terror in their adversaries' ranks.

Western European helmets in the ninth century began to acquire the square shape illustrated in *Fig. 12* as worn by an English or Irish warrior. The protective ridge runs from front to back over the domed crown but the lower edge has now been forged into four points. Beneath the outward sweep of the metal cap the warrior can be seen to have short hair. Moustache and beard are carefully tended and the latter is bi-forked. In the illumination from which the sketch was made the helmet appears to be green, but this may have been artistic licence to add gaiety to the picture—that of several knights riding on horseback with spears in their hands, their leader carrying a pennant with a green fish device.

Another version of the square-brimmed helmet, this time with a feather attached, is shown in *Fig. 13* by a Burgundian soldier of the same period. Thus the original helmet of the Roman Legionaries had by this time been modified by widening the brim to a basic square shape. By the eleventh century it had taken a curved form and had acquired a *nazal* or metal piece projecting downwards to protect the nose, as in *Fig. 14*.

Eleventh Century

SAXONS AND NORMANS

THE MOST ILLUMINATING record of contemporary Saxon and Norman costume is the Bayeux Tapestry, which covers the period from Harold's visit to Normandy until William's arrival in England and Harold's death at the Battle of Hastings in 1066. The two national styles are always differentiated, and the contrast is seen most clearly in the hair-dressing. The Saxons by that time wore their hair cut short, and had long moustaches but no beards, whilst the Normans not only shaved their faces but also shaved the back of their heads from the nape to the crown, and that which, on a first glance, looks like faulty drawing is indeed a definite hair-style. In some of the scenes William's advisers are seen with the hirsute part of the head covered with a coif which passes from ear to ear and ties under the chin, but leaves the back of the head exposed the better to display this curious fashion. The front hair was combed forward and cut straight over the brows to form a fringe. This strange form of hair-dressing was brought over to England and persisted until about 1090 by which time the Normans had adopted the English style of letting their hair grow. The fashion

of shaving the back of the head is thought to have originated in Aquitaine and spread to Paris after the marriage of Constance, Princess of Poitiau, where the behaviour of the men was described by a contemporary writer as 'conceited' and their dress as 'fantastic'. Certainly the Norman style of hair-dressing led to an error of judgment on the part of Harold's spies, who reported to the king that William had 'more priests than soldiers.' *Fig. 15.*

As the popularity of long flowing locks spread beards and moustaches became general, especially among older men and by 1160 we read 'They shave their foreheads and have long curls at the back of their heads, a style adopted by Robert Courte-Heuse, Duke of Normandy.'

Field workers and artisans in this early period are known to have worn the so-called Phrygian cap of *Figs. 16* and *17*. It was a soft stocking cap with turned-back edge round the face, and had a peak or bulge at the top, jutting towards the front. Its origin is obscure but it is known to have been worn by the Phoenicians who traded along the Mediterranean coasts and the Atlantic shores at least as far as Cornwall. The God Mithras, particularly venerated

FIG. 15   Norman hair-style (1066) From the Bayeux Tapestry.

FIG. 16   English or French Phrygian cap (10–11th cent.)

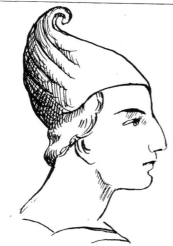

FIG. 17   Another style of Phrygian cap

FIG. 18   Saxon (Early English)

by the Roman Army, is always represented in such a cap, and it may be from representations of this God brought to England by the Romans that the style became popular.

A Saxon shepherd, however, might have a simple domed hat of wool or felt with an upturned brim, such as is shown in *Fig. 18*.

MILITARY

A Saxon helmet such as would have been worn by King Harold's soldiers at the Battle of Hastings appears in *Fig. 19*. It is conical in shape and reinforced round the lower rim with a studded band of a different metal, while a separate narrow band secures the side seams. This warrior has shortish hair, beard and whiskers and his neck is bare. Later a fringe of leather was added to protect the neck.

Among the Normans of the eleventh century and later a skull-cap shape of Roman derivation came into use again and this was finally ousted by the tubular form.

The Saxon chronicler describes William of Normandy when he became king of England, as wearing his helmet thrice every year. At Easter he wore it at Winchester, for Pentecost at Westminster, and in mid-winter at Gloucester. With it a tippet encircled his neck.

FIG. 19   Saxon Helmet

✳ *19* ✳

Twelfth Century

WOMEN

By the beginning of the twelfth century the head-rail worn by women in Saxon times had changed. It was now relegated to the back of the head and kept there with a bandeau or, if the wearer's social status warranted it, with a coronet. Between 1090 and 1130 the head-rail was so long that it had to be tied in knots at the back to raise it from the ground.

From about 1130 until roughly 1154 noblewomen adopted a new fashion; they divested the hair of all its voluminous draperies and grew it to its maximum length. Parted in the middle, it was allowed to fall forward over the shoulders in two plaits or coils *(Fig. 21)* which often reached to the wearer's knees. Matilda, in her effigy in Rochester Cathedral, has plaits which terminate in curls.

Each coil or braid was bound elaborately with ribbon bands or encased in silk—a useful device to disguise the fact that false hair or even tow was frequently added to increase the apparent length. Ultimately the plaits were encased in sheaths of silk, gold or silver, called *furians,* which were not unlike a modern umbrella case. If such a sheath was worn then all the hair was enclosed in it and it hung down the back *(Fig. 20)*. Otherwise the custom of plaiting the hair in two braids was varied and four might be worn, two hanging over the shoulders in front and two at the back. A coffin, discovered in Romsey Abbey in 1836, contained the body of a woman who had been buried during the reign of King Stephen (1135–1154). Everything had disintegrated except the hair which was intact, in plaits eighteen inches long. For a time these were preserved in a glass case in the Abbey.

With these plaits or coils women wore a loose veil draped over the head and a garland (or fillet) set on *(Fig. 21)* which often reached to the wearer's knees.

The weaving of cotton was established in France under Louis VII but linen was usually mixed with it. There were also available silks and siglatons and satin samite, but these came from the East. Sendals and taffetas came from Asia Minor. Silks went out of use temporarily about 1180 owing to the cessation of trade with the Moslems during the Crusades. Cloth then came into its own for most purposes.

FIG. 20   Early English

FIG. 21   French (1100–1200)

MILITARY

Fig. 22 shows a metal casque with link or plaques sewn to leather forming the *gorget,* which completely covers the mouth.

By 1146 French knights were wearing a Phrygian-style cap made of metal as seen in *Fig. 23* which is from the incised and enamelled tomb of Geoffrey Plantaganet, Earl of Maine and Anjou. The pointed metal cap or helmet is ornamented with golden leopards on a blue ground. The hair is shoulder length and conventionally represented in three waves or loops, whilst the beard and moustache are neatly clipped. As a funerary slab it is unique.

FIG. 22   Norman

FIG. 23   French (1146)

Thirteenth Century

WOMEN

SOME TWELFTH CENTURY styles persisted well into the thirteenth. A typical example of barbette, fillet and coverchief of the early years of this period may be seen in Freiburg cathedral *(Fig. 24)*. The hood and gorget, as worn by men in the previous century, was adopted by women of all ranks in this. It formed a protective covering for travelling and outdoor wear and was sometimes accompanied by a wide-collared cape, as in *Fig. 25*, which shows the German Queen Uta. Her cape holds the gorget snugly to her chin, while, probably to show her royal rank, her crown rests conventionally on the hood. The statue is so lovable and lifelike that 'one might speak to her and stand in hope of an answer'.

Climate, as always, had a marked effect on design and fashion and it soon became evident that on the whole Germany favoured the heavier and more cumbersome styles, with less hair visible, while Italy's styles were freer and gayer. England followed modified French versions.

Several innovations marked the early years of the thirteenth century. The *barbette* or chin strap (from the word meaning a little beard, and sometimes

FIG. 25   German

referred to as the *tresson* or *dorelet*) was introduced by Queen Eleanor de Guienne, queen to Henry II, and an example is shown in *Fig. 26*, taken from her effigy. All her hair is hidden under the coverchief on which is set her crown. The *barbe*, a development of the barbette, was adopted during the later years of the century and continued well into the second half of the sixteenth. It consisted of a piece of pleated fabric suspended just under the mouth and covering the lower part of the chin. An example is seen in *Fig. 27*.

The *wimple,* from a word meaning 'to flow in wavelets', came into fashion in the thirties. It consisted of a length of silk, linen or other soft cloth wrapped round the throat and passing under the chin from one side of the head to the other, and was pinned to the hair under the coverchief. *Fig. 28* shows a noble lady wearing both wimple and coverchief. Her coronet appears to secure the latter. When the wimple was worn without the coverchief it is possible to see exactly how it was fixed to the hair, which, like the chin itself, was completely concealed as in *Fig. 29*. The wimple has survived among religious orders down to the present day. Nowadays we regard it as unflattering to the wearer and prob-

FIG. 24   German

✳ 22 ✳

FIG. 26   Eleanor de Guienne. French (1204)

FIG. 29   English

FIG. 27   English (1403)

ably it was always restricting and uncomfortable, but it must originally have helped to keep the women warm in large medieval castles and convents. *Fig. 30* depicts a thirteenth century Italian nun wearing a wimple.

The *goffered fillet,* a new development of the plain linen headband, is worn with the barbette in *Fig. 31* It will be noted that the lady's waist-length hair is allowed to hang down loosely in heavy waves. In the original picture, from Germany, she has come out of her house to speak to a pedlar who has hung his wares—belts, purses, etc.—over a railing, and she carries a toy dog, of a breed popular in Germany at that time and possibly a type of dachshund.

FIG. 28   English or French

FIG. 30   Nun. Italian

FIG. 31   German

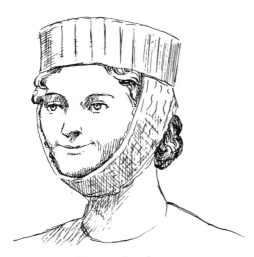

FIG. 32   French

A small *pill-box hat* was sometimes worn with the barbette as in *Fig. 32*, taken from the portrait of a donor in the cathedral of Bourges, France. Age has blurred the finer details but markings on the hat and barbette suggest they were made of woven straw and that a goffered linen barbe was worn under the chin-strap. This was evidently a form of outdoor attire and kept the hair tidy and the ears warm.

The fillet is pinked into pointed turrets in *Fig. 33* and the barbette passes right over the head which is covered by a small white skull cap.

Changing hair fashions resulted, as generally happens, in new styles of head covering. The long dangling plaits of the early years must have proved very irksome at a time when even the chatelaine of the castle or manor spun and wove or superintended her maids at such work, and also cared for her children and cut out and made clothes. So a more practical if somewhat bulky hair style was adopted towards the middle of the century. Many women first coiled their hair with ribbons, then wound the whole round their head, as in *Fig. 34*. Others particularly those of lesser degree, wore *bends* (from the Norman word *bendae* meaning ribbons or bands for the hair) in place of the coronet or garland which adorned the heads of noble ladies. Such bends were prohibited for religious orders.

During the whole of the thirteenth century young girls wore their hair uncovered except for such a bend to keep it in place (*Fig. 35*).

FIG. 33   English

FIG. 34   English (1250)

FIG. 35   English (1200)

FIG. 36   English (1225)

Personal preference naturally guided some women in their choice of head covering, as for instance Berengaria of Navarre, queen to Richard I. In *Fig. 36* she wears a light veil over her loose uncurled hair, and over the veil a crown.

The more generally adopted and rather clumsy vogue for winding ribbon-twined plaits round the head gave way to a simpler style of hairdressing. The whole mass of hair was caught into a net or bag and thus suspended at the nape of the neck. Such a device was known as the *crespine,* and a typical example is shown in *Fig. 37.* The crespine might be of plain linen, jewelled gold thread or wire, or, for working women, a rough cloth. In a further example *(Fig. 38)* the netted crespine is shown clearly. It does not reach the top of the head and a white cap covers the hair. With it are worn the bend, or fillet, and barbette. A few strands of hair may have been allowed to show in the previous figure but here all hair is banished from sight. Occasionally the crespine is modified into a single bundle at the back of the neck where it has the effect of a large snood.

Designing and making hair nets of silk and ear-bosses of gold tissue were recognised trades, and there was a flourishing market for artificial flower chaplets, made by *chapeliers des fleurs* in France. This was in line with the great interest in and development of materials and styles for clothes in general, for both

FIG. 37   French

FIG. 38   French

men and women. Sequins, already known far back in Ancient Egypt, were adopted as an English fashion in this century and used, not only for adorning the dress of both sexes but to trim hats as well.

Towards the end of the century the bycocket (or *chapeau à bec*) came into fashion for both men and women, as is explained in the section on men's hats. It was a hat with a crown and upturned brim brought to a sharp projecting peak in front. Crown and brim were frequently elaborately ornamented. *Fig. 39* shows a noble Italian lady in her bycocket, the crown of which is embroidered with a symmetrical pattern, and decorated with a single jewel in the front of the hat-band. In the original she is seen riding with her hawk on her wrist. Her side braids are turned up under the hat, as is her unplaited back hair.

Another noblewoman *(Fig. 40)* wears her bycocket style hat over a simple veil, the hair being allowed to flow freely beneath it. This drawing is made from an ivory, carved in low relief, in the British Museum.

FIG. 39   Italian (1310)

MEN

Men's headwear styles did not, apparently, change much during most of this century. By the end, however, the bardocucullus had been shortened to shoulder-length, thus producing the hood and cape *(gorget)* which continued in favour and was worn by all classes out-of-doors during the best part of the next hundred years. The illustration *(Fig. 41)* shows a shepherd wearing a hood and generously cut gorget, which falls in folds over his shoulders. The pointed hood is pushed well back on his curly head, and he is clean-shaven. A variant on this style may be seen in *Fig. 42* from an ivory plaque. Here we see St. Gallus reproving the bear. The hood now resembles a huge sock pulled over the head, with an opening for the face. The upper end hangs down over his shoulder and could, if necessary, be wound round the neck for extra warmth.

FIG. 40   English

What seems to be a metallic equivalent of the hood and gorget is worn by Robert Ros of Hamlake, one of the Knights of the Round Temple, in *Fig. 43*. His *coif-de-maille* is thrown back off his head, exposing his hair, an unusual representation of the period. He has a centre parting, with a short fringe, while the side hair is waved, first outward then back to the chin, where it again turns outward in curls. This was a style of masculine hairdressing that continued in vogue for over a century and was adopted by all

FIG. 41   English (1200)

classes, from king to labourer. *Fig. 44* is from the effigy of King Henry III and *Fig. 45* from an illuminated manuscript showing a labourer working in a field. Both men have identical hair styles, the king being differentiated only by his crown.

The Phrygian cap was worn during the first decades of the period but went out of fashion as men's styles began to change about mid-way through the century. Labourers wore a felt or straw hat with a brim for protecting the head and shading the eyes in outdoor work. The man sharpening his scythe in *Fig. 46* has a felt hat with turned down brim and another labourer in *Fig. 47* wears a straw, this time with brim upturned.

In a romance of the period the hero wears a linen hat to protect his hair from the dust of the underground passage he is required to traverse to meet his loved one when he goes to take the baths.

About the year 1270 professional men, like the surgeon in *Fig. 48*, often wore a round skull cap with a short stalk at the top. (His robe, like that of a monk, has a hood which could be drawn over both head and cap when visiting his patients.) Little caps of this kind were usually decorated with appliqué felt cut into scallops, or with a band of embroidery, such as we see worn by the elderly man in *Fig. 49*.

The hood and gorget were worn by men, as well as by women, but from about 1280 all classes and ages adopted a *coif* or close-fitting cap made of white linen and fastened under the chin with a strap. The coif seems to have been essentially a summer head covering and was particularly popular among travellers, huntsmen, soldiers and outdoor workers, as it prevented the hair from blowing across the face. The labourer in *Fig. 50*, with his wavy hair and fringe, has a coif with the linen gathered into the face at the side to ensure a close fit. The pikeman, also wearing this useful form of head covering, in *Fig. 51*, is one of a group in the illustration to a manuscript depicting Henry II and his men saying farewell to Thomas à Becket on his departure for France. A Spanish manuscript gives us *Fig. 52* in which the coif is worn by a musician who is playing a curved platterspiel or rudimentary bagpipe. His coif, though slightly smaller, is identical with the type worn in England. The manuscript from which *Fig. 50* is taken also includes a picture of a man wearing his coif in his bath, a tub with a tent-like curtain.

FIG. 42   Irish

FIG. 43   English (1250)

FIG. 44   English

Fig. 45   English

Fig. 48   French (1270)

Fig. 46   English (1250)

Fig. 49   French (1270)

Fig. 47   English

Fig. 50   English (1280)

But the coif was by no means confined to such groups as these. Any kind of hat or head-dress might be worn over the close-fitting coif, as is shown by *Fig. 53*, where a King has his surmounted by his crown, and by *Fig. 54*, in which the great Emperor Frederick wears a turned-up hat over the coif. The second of these two drawings is made from an illustration to *De Arte Vernandi cum Avibus*,[1] a treatise on hawking and on wild birds in general which the Emperor himself wrote before 1250. The shape of the hat here given is accurate but the decoration is only approximate because of a discoloration of the parchment. Other illustrations in the same book show attendants wearing either the coif alone or the coif surmounted by a form of bycocket hat (sometimes called the *chapeau à bec* because of the beak-shaped point at the front).

MILITARY

In the thirteenth and early fourteenth centuries the helmet was ingeniously constructed to close completely over the face. Narrow slits allowed the wearer to see while his eyes remained protected and the front was perforated with holes for breathing. We see such a closed helmet in *Fig. 55*. At this period helmets were often surmounted by heraldic emblems in the form of imposing crests.

For the Crusades, lighter, cooler armour was a necessity and the characteristic *chapeau de fer*, a light skull-cap with brim and chin-strap was the rule. *Fig. 56*.

FIG. 52   Spanish (1254)

FIG. 53   French

FIG. 51   French or English (1287)

FIG. 54   Italian

FIG. 55   English (1390-1410)

FIG. 56   Italian (1350)

5

Fourteenth Century

WOMEN

BY THE END of the thirteenth and beginning of the fourteenth century the crespine had developed into an extremely formal hair style *(Fig. 57)*. The plaits were now brought up on either side of the face to form two vertical, pillar-like structures which were supported by a frame hanging from a metal fillet above the brows. The fillet and frame were often concealed by a scalloped coverchief with a wimple hiding the neck and pinned on each side to the plaits, as in *Fig. 58*. This arrangement was stylized yet further towards the end of the century by placing a coronet over the coverchief and concealing the plaits entirely in a square network or reticulated caul of gold filigree work. (Hence the name given to it at the time: the *reticulated head-dress*). The example in *Fig. 59* includes an M-motif on the fillet and at the top of the square cylinders, which stood for the initial letter of the Virgin's name.

Such ornamental head-dresses were costly as well as beautiful and Chaucer is referring to one when he says, in his Legend of Fair Women, 'A fret of gold she hadde next her hair'. Women of less exalted rank wore a *volupere*, a cap tied with tapes, and the Carpenter's Wife, in Chaucer's *Canterbury Tales*, is described as wearing one, with a silk fillet.

Meanwhile in the thirteen-twenties some head-wear styles were worn by both men and women. Such was the cloth scarf, folded double, over a flat-topped hat, that we see in the English example in *Fig. 60*, which is a portrait of Queen Margaut. It

FIG. 58   English (1347)

FIG. 57   English (1340)

FIG. 59   English

can be compared with the German version, worn by a man in Fig. 81.

Decorative head ornaments were in fashion until well into the seventies. The inventory of Jeanne d'Evreux, dated 1372, includes two chaplets, and precious and imitation jewels. Many were sewn on gold net foundations and were gorgeously rich.[1]

The wimple was still an important item in women's attire and sometimes took eccentric forms. The style in *Fig. 61*,[1] for instance, is pinned to the hair, leaving a space between the fabric and the neck. The hair itself is parted in the middle and ripples down to the ears. Only the ends are plaited and turned up to the top of the head.

From about 1356 a new form of head-dress, apparently deriving from the goffered fillet, was introduced. The coverchief, of linen or fine lawn, was cut in a half circle, the straight edge was then goffered and, when laid over the top of the head, formed a wide frill. The goffering might reach only from eartip to eartip, as in *Fig. 62*, but was sometimes carried down as far as the chin, the curved edge also being bordered by frills *(Fig. 63)*. The same goffered frame to the face is shown in *Fig. 64* but here a fillet accompanies it and the ends of the coverchief contain the curled ends of the hair (or other weights to keep it down).

This arrangement was known as the Nebula head-

Fig. 61   English

Fig. 62   English

Fig. 60   English

Fig. 63   English

FIG. 64 English

FIG. 65 French

FIG. 66 Italian (1330)

dress. Two excellent examples of it exist in the church at Bray in Berkshire, where the two wives of Sir John de Foxley are commemorated with their hair dressed in the mode of the time when the effigy was completed; 1378.

The elaborate head wrappings which have been illustrated appear to have been popular only in England and Germany. In countries with a more temperate climate, particularly in the southern parts of France and in Italy the custom was not adopted. In *Fig. 65* a queen of France has very fair hair coiled into thick ringlets on either side of her face, the rest being left short and curly and uncovered. She has no veil, her only ornament being her crown. Simpler still is the style worn by the Italian woman (earlier in the century but still current) in *Fig. 66* who has wound her plaited hair round her head to form a natural chaplet.

Taffeta and samite, silk and wool were the materials most generally used for hats and hoods. The *chaperon* which, came into fashion for both men and women in the sixties, was made from all four fabrics. The first two, being stiffer, were used for styles with firmer, more sculptured lines, and the softer silk or wool for the draped styles with dagging that drooped from the rondel. *Fig. 67* shows the drooping arrangement, worn by a woman on horseback.

MEN

The coif, unless worn under a hat, as already described, was a summer or fine weather head

FIG. 67 French (1400)

covering; for the hood and gorget were worn concurrently with it. These latter developed in an unexpected manner during the early part of the fourteenth century. Chaucer believed that the changes taking place in clothes' styles were due to the arrival of the Hainaulters who came over with Queen Isabella. With Mortimer, Earl of March, she helped to dethrone Edward II and put Edward III on the English throne. The poet, listing what he considered extremes of fashion, mentions 'hoods over long and large and much hanging'.

The hood had, indeed, now developed from the crown of the head a lengthy tube which hung far down the back and was called a *liripipe. Fig. 68* shows a labourer wearing a hood, gorget and liripipe which is represented in the original as of fawn-pink fabric with the lining, where it shows in the turn-back round the face, in blue. Thus a field worker appeared warmly clad about the head and shoulders at the time the Luttrell Psalter was painted in 1340. A conical hood with its turned-back brim and long liripipe (now a lengthy ribbon) is worn by an aged German in *Fig. 69*.

It was customary at this time for both men and women to buy an ensemble consisting of three, four, or even five, pieces, all made from matching fabric, and even a century later we hear of Caxton buying himself material from a huxter woman at the Exchange to make a suit of four pieces. (A hood would make the fifth.) In 1305 the Count of Flanders had a scarlet outfit of four pieces, including a hood.

For more than a hundred years hoods such as those described assumed the most extraordinary and fantastic shapes, and from a mere point the liripipe varied to a two-foot tube and, later, to a ribbon two yards in length.

A further development of this head covering was to take the hood and gorget off the head and place what was formerly the face-opening on top of the head, with the gorget bunched to one side and the liripipe arranged on the other. The wearer could decide the actual arrangement for himself. In *Fig. 70*, for instance, a short liripipe points forward and the gorget is rolled up and wound round the forehead, the ends jutting out at the back. The labourer in *Fig. 71* has wound his liripipe round his neck and over the top of his head, the end just showing beneath his felt hat with its upturned and split brim. The ploughman in *Fig. 72* wears his hood and gorget in the same manner, but surmounts it with a bycocket hat put on with the point at the back (the reverse of the more normal practice).

Fig. 73 shows yet another way of wearing the liripipe, the little tippet ends being passed through slots at the neck. Again, in *Fig. 74* the wearer has padded his liripipe into a thick roll and has wound it round his conical hat. The flat end passes once round the roll and the tapered point projects at the side. *Fig. 75* is an arrangement somewhat resembling Fig. 70 but reversed, This man is a glass-blower and he and his companions in the trade favour a variety of hats. *Fig 76* shows one fit for Aladdin to wear.

Fig. 68   English (1330)

Fig 69.   German

FIG. 70   English (1335)

FIG. 73   English (1350)

FIG. 71   French

FIG. 74   English

FIG. 72   English

FIG. 75   English

Fig. 76   English or French

Fig. 79   Italian

Fig. 77   Italian (1320)

Fig. 80   French (1378)

Fig. 78   Italian

Fig. 81   German

By the end of the century the dandies of the time will have contrived something really gay from the hood and gorget, as will be seen in due course.

In Italy the coif continued to be worn by students such as the one depicted in *Fig. 77*. Over this he has donned a black velvet or cloth tammy-shaped hat, square at the corners and perhaps prefiguring, by some centuries, the mortarboard. Also Italian is the next drawing *(Fig. 78)* of a young man who wears a hat incorporating the coif. The cap has a rolled brim and padded top and the coif-section to cover the ears is made from matching material. For a last look at the fourteenth century coif, another Italian style has been chosen *(Fig. 79)*, where it is worn in front of the ears and is covered by a fur-edged cap, with a loose black or dark-coloured velvet crown softly falling over the rim. The coif continued in fashion until the end of the century. *Fig. 80* is a French example, worn by King Charles VI. It is worth noting that side whiskers were often worn with the coif with good effect.

By 1325 men had begun to let their hair grow longer. A handsome hat style from Germany *(Fig. 81)* is worn over fair curly hair. It is edged and decorated with navy blue and the maroon cloth scarf thrown over it is folded double, the peak being drawn over the hat brim. Both men and women favoured this style.

Two further developments from Italy, both dating from 1330, are shown in the figures which follow. In *Fig. 82* a strolling musician wears a vestigial coif with the strap dangling under an ornamental version of the hood, gorget and liripipe. The hat has a band of cloth in a dark colour which matches half of his parti-coloured robe, with a tartan or check top corresponding to the other half. His companion in *Fig. 83* has bobbed hair and a parti-coloured high crown to his close-brimmed hat, which is similar in shape to that in *Fig. 84*. These folk were mostly of the lower strata of society, probably the descendants of the much-despised yet much sought-after *jongleurs* who strolled from place to place playing music and reciting love-poems, putting up at inns and regaling the visitors with an evening's entertainment in return for food and a shake-down in a barn.

Older men, it seems, preferred comfort to the fashionable fads indulged in by their juniors, and in *Fig. 85* an old gentleman has put on a snugly fitting beret-type hat.

FIG. 82   Italian (1330)

FIG. 83   Italian (1330)

FIG. 84   Italian

. Two strange styles are almost certainly of this era though they are apparently unparalleled, at least in pictures or effigies. One is a man's hat with a metal knob *(Fig. 86)* and the other in *Fig. 87* a hood worn by an ecclesiastic. These may owe much to the artist's imagination.

By the 1360's men had contorted the gorget and hood and liripipe into many strange shapes and by 1369 had decided it would be better if it were made in three pieces, together known as the *chaperon*. One threefold form consisted of the *rondlet* or padded roll, of *Fig. 88* (from a French tapestry), fitting round the head and stuffed with silk or linen; the gorget, now cut into scallops called dagging which, when bunched together, gushed out from the top of the rondlet and fell over the left shoulder; and the liripipe, which had become a flat ribbon or length of cloth and was suspended from the rondlet over the right shoulder to give a balanced effect.

Another form of chaperon is given in *Fig. 89,* which is also French. The same style was taken up in England and was especially favoured by the aesthetes of the Court of Richard II.

Richard was only eleven years of age when he came to the throne and as he grew to manhood he was surrounded by young courtiers who garbed themselves and their wives with rich and beautiful fabric and jewels from other countries and were equally fond of stylish embroidery in silks and gold. The splendour of their apparel must have afforded

FIG. 85   German

FIG. 87   13th cent.

FIG. 86   13th cent.

FIG. 88   French

the citizenry a wonderful pageant when they rode abroad.

Masculine hair styles were fairly short for the greater part of the fourteenth century. The hair was usually parted in the centre and waved to just below the ears, where it was finished with a long curl or curls. *Fig. 90* shows this free style as worn by William of Hatfield, the second son of Edward III and Queen Phillipa, who died young and is buried in York Minster.

Apart from a trend towards looser, more natural waves and curls, this was the fashion until the time of Richard II (1377-1399). During his reign much care and thought was given to dressing the hair as also to clothes in general. Beards and moustaches,

which had been optional earlier, now became general, the former being small, pointed and sometimes forked.

The two styles which follow illustrate a popular type of hat of the thirteen-eighties. As both are worn with a hooded cloak it seems likely that they were made deliberately small and rounded in order that the hood could be pulled over them in inclement weather. *Fig. 91* is from a brass to Hughes Libergier, master mason, in Rheims Cathedral, and his hat has a short "stalk" at the top. A similar hat of the same period is seen in *Fig. 92*.

The bycocket hat, with crown and upturned brim brought to a point in front, was often decorated and was adopted by both men and women in the four-

FIG. 89   French

FIG. 91   French (1380)

FIG. 90   English

FIG. 92   French

teenth century. *Fig. 93* is a good example as worn by a gentleman while hawking. The crown is decorated with either real or embroidered peacock's feathers, and the upturned brim has a facing of *menu-vair* (miniver, the hair of the squirrel's belly).[1]

Note the knotted leather streamers which would tie under the chin on windy days. *Fig. 94* is an Italian example of the bycocket, with a split brim, and is reproduced from a design on a medal. Froissart says that beaver fur and ostrich feathers were used for the larger forms.

[1]Fairholt's *History of English Costume.*

FIG. 93   French (1325)

FIG. 94   Italian (14th-cent.)

6

Fifteenth Century

WOMEN

IN THE FIRST quarter of the century women still wore warm and comfortable hoods for travelling abroad, as in *Fig. 95*. But indoors fashions were very different.

By the beginning of the century the crespine and reticulated head-dress had become more exaggerated and now formed large box-like bosses over the ears. These projecting masses were given the name *templettes* and varied greatly in size and construction. Lady Joyce Thorpe in *Fig. 96*. lies in effigy on her tomb wearing a handsome example of this head-dress. The large templettes are covered with a reticulated design of gold fret studded with jewels, which continues above the fillet across the forehead. A coverchief with daintily scalloped or dagged edge is draped over the templettes and falls gracefully to the shoulders and above all this is a coronet of triangular shape moulded in metal and studded with jewels. It seems obvious that this unwieldy but exciting head-dress could have been lifted off entire by a handmaiden, when Lady Joyce's hair, which had been confined in the side boxes, would have fallen freely—doubtless to her great relief.

Another English style, but somewhat smaller and simpler, is worn by Catherine, wife of Michael de la Pole, whose effigy lies in the church at Wingfield, Suffolk *(Fig. 97)*. The Earl died at Agincourt and his wife herself erected this monument during her lifetime, as was the custom among many of the nobility to ensure a suitable and lifelike memorial. Thus the style of dress may belong to a date considerably earlier than their recorded deaths. The same discrepancy might arise when pious and grateful descendants erected memorials to their predecessors after a lengthy interval.

Catherine de la Pole's hair is confined by an open-ended fret of gold, surmounted with a plain band. A coverchief is draped over the back of the head and the open ends of the templettes fall in graduated flutes to the shoulder.

Fortunately plenty of examples of the templettes are available in pictures and carvings, and this interesting style, which lent itself to so many decorative effects, must have been extremely popular among the nobility. It was a time when the wealthy indulged in display. Many of their garments were covered with embroidered fruit, flowers, birds and heraldic designs, and contemporary fashions afforded

FIG. 95   French (1410)

FIG. 96   English

the opportunity to lavish rich materials on head attire as well. *Fig. 98* is a young French queen whose templettes and the crown are entirely studded with precious stones. Another French version, in *Fig. 99* shows how becoming the bosses could be on a young and beautiful girl. Her hair is parted in the centre and the locks at the side are coiled under the reticulated templettes. The rest of her hair is allowed to escape and cascade down to her waist. Here is a real fairy princess with her pearl necklace and ermine-trimmed cote-hardie.

Fig. 100 is from a corbel in Southwold Church, Suffolk, and although it is claimed to represent Mary Tudor, sister of Henry VIII the style is earlier, probably dating to before 1420. It somewhat resembles the head-dress worn by the Countess of Arundel in 1416. Here, in *Fig. 101,* is a fantastic version of the contemporary mode. She has the cylindrical templettes over her ears, and draped over these a dagged kerchief which, instead of lying over the closed ends, is extended on wires to form two horns. The total width is 22 ins, and to fit this structure her coronet has had to be enlarged proportionately.

Jan Van Eyck painted his wife, Margaret, wearing the new horn head-dress *(Fig. 102)*.

Another head-dress which, like its forerunners, could be lifted off in one piece and is a further development of the style we are considering appears in *Fig. 103*. Here the templettes enclose the ears and

FIG. 97   English (1415)

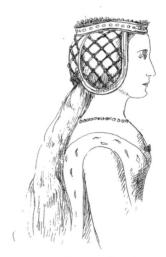

FIG. 99   French

FIG. 98   French

FIG. 100   English

are extended above the coronet, which follows its contours, into two crescent-shaped horns. The coverchief flows from beneath the coronet to the shoulders at the back.

This upward trend of the *templettes* merged into another style the *horned head-dress* which will be considered later.

Eyebrow plucking and face-painting was fashionable at this period and in a representation of the Virgin by Jean Fouquet she appears with her hair plucked from the forehead and neck so completely that she would seem to be perfectly bald.

Thus far it is obvious that one style of head-dress developed out of its predecessor, and so represented a continuous mode of thought.

We saw in the illustration where the templettes were small and the coverchief discarded that the back of the neck and the forehead had been shaved. This strange fashion of shaving the back of the neck and forehead, was done presumably to make the latter look higher and nobler *(Fig. 104)*. The vogue aroused much abuse from moralists, but was not therefore abandoned, and we can still read the advice, written by the Knight of La Tour Landry:—'Fair daughters see that you pluck not away hair from your eyebrows nor from your temples nor from your foreheads to make them appear higher than nature ordained.'

This desire to appear bald-faced may have originated in Italy as we see an example of it in

FIG. 101   English (1416)

FIG. 103   English

FIG. 102   Flemish (1430)

FIG. 104   French

Fig. 105. where the lady's hair is drawn tightly in a cone and bound with ribbon, while her neck and forehead appear to be shaven. (This style of hair-dressing was used for Lady Capulet in the accurately garbed film of *Romeo and Juliet* made in Italy in 1950.) From Italy, too, comes the similar style of *Fig. 106* but here accentuated by a bandeau. *Fig. 107* is also Italian and dates from 1395 but is in line with fifteenth century fashion. It is remarkable for the little plume of hair which is allowed to project over the pearl-studded head-dress of original shape.

Combined with the shaven forehead in *Fig. 108* is a fifteenth century 'pony-tail', displayed by the lovely Isotta Digliati, wife of Sigismondo Malatesta, in 1420. A hoop of gold, set with a single jewel, is placed over the crown of the head and the thick hair is drawn through it to cascade over the rim. A frame or support of some kind appears to have been necessary to keep it in this extended position. Such a method of holding the hair away from the head would have made for coolness in hot weather.

Italian women at this period were very proud of their hair and devised many ways of displaying it. In *Fig. 109* the hair drawn away from the shaven forehead is intricately coiled with an involved arrangement of plaits and ribbons. It has been aptly described as 'a snake's nest'. Lucrezia Borgia, a few decades later, was so proud of her golden hair that she washed it every week (unusual at that time), even pausing on her way to meet her prospective bride-groom in order to wash her luxuriant locks and dry them in the sun. A straw, halo-shaped frame was fixed round her head and her hair spread over it so that it was exposed to and bleached by the bright sunlight.[1]

An Italian woman in *Fig. 110* wears a small black velvet cap over the back of her head, her hair being firmly bound round it, to finish in a single heavy plait down her back. One more illustration from Italy *(Fig. 111)* shows an individual style developed from the chaperon worn by men. A twisted rondlet of two kinds of material over a padding is set round a 'brim' of hair pushed out by a 'foundation'. The side hair is wound into a coil, not plaited in this case, and held in position with several large hairpins. The lady wears the high-collared houppeland and has a shaven forehead and neck.

The Countess of Arundel in Fig. 101 wore her wide dagged coverchief erected on a wire frame. A different version of this mode is shown in *Fig. 112*. It is known as a Burgundian-French style, referred to at the time as *attour de gibet* that is, 'veils propped up gallows-fashion on long silver pins'.

The old templettes have developed into upturned horns and beyond them the coverchief is held out on wires. In some measure this erection seems to pre-figure the butterfly head-dress which will be described later, but in fact predates it by seventy years and is different in construction. The flowers on the cover-chief are real as they represent a festive decoration worn by the dainty lady on horseback who rides

---

[1]This device was called a *caluna* and an engraving in the Victoria and Albert Museum in London shows how it was used.

FIG. 105   Italian (1405)

FIG. 106   Italian (Late 14th cent.)

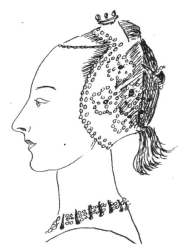

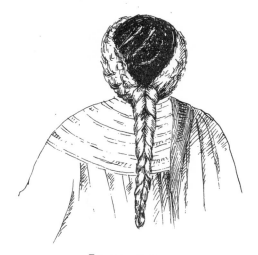

FIG. 107   Italian (1395)

FIG. 110   Italian

FIG. 108   Italian

FIG. 111   Italian

FIG. 109   Italian (1450)

FIG. 112   Netherlandish or French (1410)

FIG. 113   French (1412)

FIG. 114   Flemish or French (1438–40)

FIG. 115   English (1410)

FIG. 116   Italian (1400)

abroad on the First of May. *Fig. 113* is a similar head-dress in which no horns are visible and the forehead is shaven. It is known that this delicate and fairylike head attire was worn out of doors, but it is difficult to imagine how it could be sufficiently secured to enable it to stand up against gusts of wind.

Young women of the upper classes sometimes favoured short cut hair and no head-dress as in *Fig. 114,* and Englishwomen who travelled abroad must have conformed with local customs, as we see in *Fig. 115* which shows Margaret Holland, wife of John of Beanford, wearing a high-standing collar and natural curly fair hair confined only by a simple circlet of gold.

Although the templettes, coverchief and other striking forms of head-dress were so characteristic a feature of fifteenth century fashions, the hat was by no means completely discarded. While the templettes were being worn in Northern Europe, Italian women took to very large, cushion-shaped hats. The example in *Fig. 116* is possibly covered with small feathers or may be of soft ruched fabric, and is built over a frame set above simply arranged hair. This fashion, in varying forms, persisted for many years after its inception somewhere near the beginning of the century.

Giving the effect of a cushion hat, though not actually such, is the head-dress of an Italian serving woman in *Fig. 117*. Here the veil and wimple are kept in place with a swathe of fabric wound round the crown of the head.

Carrying the swathing to absurd lengths is the

style depicted in *Fig. 118,* and here again it may be presumed that the whole massive structure could be removed with the buckram lining intact when the knot under the chin was untied.

The large turban-effect cushion head-dress from Italy in *Fig. 119* or the Flemish version in *Fig. 120* must have been built over a wicker foundation, and therefore, although apparently heavier and more bulky than the templettes, could in fact have been lighter and easier to remove.

A last glimpse of these cushioned shapes *(Fig. 121)* gives us a back view of one that is only a padded satin rondlet and is open at the top. It originated either from Germany or the Netherlands, its colour is moss green and it has a crimson lining. The hair is parted at the centre and worn in long plaits down the back, one plait being caught up in the girdle at each side.

The templettes with the swept-up shape were known as the *bourrelet* after 1430, and are well shown in the portrait, painted by a Flemish artist, of Margaret, daughter of James I of Scotland and wife of Louis XI of France *(Fig. 122).* The hair is still shaven or plucked from the forehead and neck, and the templettes rise at an angle from the ears, being held in place on the forehead by a jewelled band which passes round the head. A very gorgeous crown, also curved upwards to accommodate the horns, is set on top. The sides are of fret, studded with pearls and hung with pendant pearl drops, while little feathery shapes in gold rise from the rim of the crown. A large jewel is set in the centre of the fore-

FIG. 118   Italian

FIG. 119   Italian

FIG. 117   Italian

FIG. 120   Flemish

head and the whole is richly resplendent. Here too, for the first time, appears the little black V in the centre of the forehead which persisted in all these off-the-forehead styles for fifty years or more. Its use must have been to lift the whole structure off the head where it had to fit tightly in order to stay in place. Balance would have been maintained by fixing the head-dress to the hair, though no fastening is visible.

Fig. 123 is a simple English version of this fashion.

Meanwhile the horns showed no signs of diminishing popularity. Jehan de Meung, the fifteenth century writer and author of the *Roman de la Rose,* describes them thus: 'I know not whether they call gibbets or corbels that which sustains these horns, which they consider so fine, but I dare venture to say that St. Elizabeth is not in Paradise for the having of such horns. Moreover, they make a great encumbrance; for between the gorget and the wimple may pass a rat or the largest weasel on this side of Arras.'

Fig. 124 is another illustration of the vogue, the lady here wearing a U-shaped roll over the horns. The veil has been conventionalized into twin lappets hanging down from the back of the head-dress, while—striking an odd note—the masculine liripipe is suspended from the roll. The little V-tag can again be seen on the forehead.

The horns in *Fig. 125* (German) are of gold fret, and the U-roll is balanced on them, with a straight-cut, ear-level veil.

FIG. 121   German or Netherlandish

FIG. 123   English

FIG. 122   French

FIG. 124

In France another development of the roll appears (*Fig. 126*). Here it is of patterned damask with two plain bands encircling it, and the U is wider and shallower. The padded roll is seen once more in *Fig. 127* (from France). In this case coin-shaped disks, or sequins probably of silver or gold, are sewn on it in three lines which follow the horned shape. This device was very popular, and may be seen in pictures where ladies are attending tournaments or masques or are spectators at the dramatisation of some biblical scene.

The Dutch women of the fifteenth century liked their headgear to be simpler and more solid. The 'horns' appearing in *Fig. 128* are rather like two cocoons jutting out horizontally from a fillet-edged cap, while the veil is dark, possibly black, in strong contrast to the little transparent tabs suspended from the French head-dress we saw in Fig. 124. *Fig. 129* is a further style from the Netherlands of about the same period, and illustrates Jehan de Meùng's description of a wimple round the neck and pinned under the horns. This is another sober style with no elaborate ornament, although the coverchief is heavy and rather clumsy-looking.

The banded horns, the U-roll, the dagged gorget and the becca are all incorporated in one headdress in *Fig. 130*. A German equivalent, portrayed in *Fig. 131*, is drawn from a carved poppy-head finial on a pew-end, and gives, in excellent detail, the immense fretted horns banded with a double row of

FIG. 125   German

FIG. 127   French

FIG. 126   French

FIG. 128   Dutch (1434)

FIG. 129   Netherlandish

FIG. 132   French

FIG. 130   French

FIG. 133

FIG. 131   German

FIG. 134

pearls across the forehead, the damask U-roll, thicker and heavier than those we have seen before, and the veil. The last-named commences at the forehead in a series of pleats held by a large carbuncle brooch, passes over the top of the head and after falling down the back is caught by the corners to the horns above the ears. A small ruched veil is also worn under the head-dress and crossing the forehead, the side hair being allowed to flow freely beside the cheeks.

The horns spread to their utmost width in *Fig. 132* which shows a French princess. *Two* horns on each side are needed to support the massive roll, now nearly flattened out horizontally and decorated with artificial flowers. Height, rather than width, is exaggerated in *Fig. 133,* and bulk seems to be the aim in *Fig. 134,* from a Flemish tapestry.

Lydgate, the celebrated monkish poet, in his 'Ditty of Women's Horns', satirised them thus:

> Clerkes record, by great authority,
> Horns were given to beasts for Defence;
> A thing contrary to feminity,
> To be made sturdy of resistance,
> But arch-wives, eager in their violence,
> Fierce as tigers for to make affray
> They have despite, and act against conscience,
> List not to pride, then horns cast away.

The horned headgear seen in *Fig. 135,* for example, is indeed, far from flattering, and in it a woman could scarcely be said to 'show beauty'.

As might be expected, the Italians wore their horns with a difference, and introduced a more fantastic touch. The horns in *Fig. 136* are of leather, laced along one side and tilted backward. The long hair, with centre parting, is pushed through the horns to fall in cascades down the back. Loose ribbons keep them in place, and a jewel, attached to a pearl and jewelled chain, decorates the shaven forehead. The front hair is waved and arranged in backward-sweeping ripples.

Another Italian style *(Fig. 137)* echoes the horned head-dress but is less cumbersome. Thick strands of hair are bound round with ribbons and then wound up like Catherine-wheels to form round ear-coverts, held in place by a broad ribbon band of the same colour passing over the top of the head and bearing a jewel inset with stones or pearls and laid flat in the centre. The custom of attaching a jewel or rosette on

FIG. 135   German (*c.* 1470)

FIG. 136   Italian

FIG. 137   Italian (1450)

the head in this way is referred to in a letter written by Laura Bentivoglio to the Marchese Gonzaga:[1] 'Today she (Lucrezia Borgia) wore a camora of black satin and gold foliage with a hem that looked like a flame of pure gold and such flowing sleeves as your excellency wears, and gold flowers and a necklace of finest pearls. Her head was dressed in the usual fashion with a very bright emerald on her forehead and a green velvet cap wrought with beaten gold . . . She enquired what were the latest Mantuan fashions and praised my head-dress. I promised to make her some caps in our style and send them to her. Certain rosettes that I wore on my forehead also pleased her and she begged me to show them to the jeweller and have them copied for her.'

Reference has already been made in this book to Lucrezia Borgia's pride in her long fair hair. (She was, of Spanish birth, although always associated with Italy.) In the next two drawings we see how this long hair could be dressed by high-born Italian ladies of her generation. *Fig. 138* shows a caul which she wore on her head with a sheath enclosing her long hair at the back—a style resembling closely that adopted by Saxon ladies four hundred years earlier. *Fig. 139* is somewhat similar, only here the caul is of fine net continued down the long strand of hair and tied tightly at intervals. It reached right down to the hem of its owner's dress. Motifs, either of appliqué fabric or metal, are sewn on the round hat with a

---

[1]Quoted by Julia Cartwright in her biography of Isabella d'Este, who married Francesco Gonzaga.

rolled embroidered brim, which is worn by a girl in a north Italian city, (see *Fig. 140*).

In 1470 the reticulated head-dress was still being worn and that of the Italian noblewoman, Bianca Sforza, in *Fig. 141* conceals all of her hair except a few wisps at her temples. Her short veil, after covering the head, dangles only as far as the nape of her neck, but the V-shaped loop can be seen at the forehead.

Four styles from the Netherlands follow. In *Fig. 142* there is a suggestion of horns in the upraised ends of the metal and jewelled fillet which is held in place by a fine chain attached to the points and passing over the back of the head, to be fastened to the rim of the circlet. A very fine gauze veil softens the rather hard lines of this style and the natural hair is wound round the head and under the coronet.

An incipient version of the *henin,* which soon became widely adopted, is drawn in *Fig. 143*. It is a cap, formed over a short cylinder of buckram, covered with a band of embroidery set with jewels. Once more a fine gauze veil is attached, flowing from the back of the head and falling over the forehead. No hair is visible and forehead and neck are shaven. The next two examples *(Figs. 144* and *145)* are also built over buckram shapes, in dark-coloured velvets, with a jewel at the centre front in each case. In *Fig. 145* a little fluffy hair is allowed to escape from the tall bell-shaped hat.

Fig. 146 is German and was contemporary with the horns. Again it is of velvet, this time emerald green, over a stiff shape, and is studded with jewels.

FIG. 138 Italian

FIG. 139 Italian (1495)

FIG. 140   Italian (1420–40)

FIG. 143   Flemish

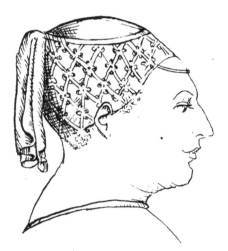

FIG. 141   Italian (1470)

FIG. 144   Flemish (1460)

FIG. 142   Flemish

FIG. 145   Flemish (1460)

Drop pearls and gold disks depend from the rim. In another German shape *(Fig. 147)* the contrasting velvet brim is turned back, wide in front and tapering at the back. The pointed crown is made of triangular sections and terminates in a button from below which sweeps a liripipe ribbon that increases in width as it descends. Over the forehead is a small veil. Note the pleated frill on the dress. This soon became a feature of hats.

In the Netherlands towards the close of the fifteenth century the pony-tail style of hairdressing, which we noted earlier in Italy, made its appearance and *Figs. 148* and *149* depict two examples. In the former the turban or bandeau, made from a long strip of fabric, is wound round and round the head like a thick bandage with the inner end free to fall at the back in a long loop to the waist. Over the forehead is the fine gauze veil we have seen elsewhere in Europe. The hair is taken up, through the bandeau, and fastened tightly at the top of the head, then plaited and left to fall down the back, where it is caught up in the loop from the bandeau. Undoubtedly this halo-style was a solid circlet and could be lifted off like a hat. Such turban effects had their greatest vogue after the fall of Constantinople in 1453 when Eastern influence was apparent in fashion as in many other aspects of life. *Fig. 149* has small reticulated ear-bosses and a padded roll swathed in criss-cross bands, which are embroidered and hold the bosses in place. The hair, with its

FIG. 146   German

FIG. 148   Flemish

FIG. 147   German

FIG. 149   Flemish

centre parting, is drawn away from the face and through an octagonal frame from which it then flows freely. The time and thought these head-dresses took to devise, make, don and discuss make today's simple head wear seem comparatively insignificant. Indeed, during the whole of the fifteenth century women's head-dresses were constructed with almost incredible intricacy and ingenuity. Some of these styles were favoured in certain periods, whilst others continued in favour for the whole century. Width was the keynote between 1430 and 1440 as we have seen. Later in the century height was the dominant factor. It was achieved in several ways, but at its most characteristic it produced the *henin*, sometimes called the *cornet* or *steeple*, which rose from the head like a tall thin cone. The henin was essentially a Continental style and originated in Burgundy. It is unlikely that it was ever worn in England. The name is claimed to derive from the Old French word *genhenner* (cf. Modern French *gêner*) meaning to incommode or inconvenience, but this seems a doubtful etymological conjecture. When the henin appeared in France Monstrelat reported in 1449 that a Carmelite preacher made children run after women who wore it and cry 'a henin! a henin!'

A veil, known as a *cointoise* and generally of gauze was either attached to the apex of the cone or swathed round it. Sometimes the ends of the veil hung loosely to shoulder level, at others they fell to the hemline of the wearer's robe. *Fig. 150* depicts a henin and cointoise from Burgundy and is dated 1440.[1]

The V-shaped loop which can be observed attached to the front of the horned head-dress is also visible in this illustration. It was a small tab, called a *frontlet,* attached to a frame of rigid wire netting covered with black fabric which passed over the front of the head. Frontlets of gold are mentioned in wardrobe accounts of Tudor princesses and no-one with an income of less than £10 a year was permitted to wear velvet frontlets.

A Frenchwoman in *Fig. 151* wears henin, contoise and frontlet. The style appears in illustrations to Froissart's Chronicles, but these were drawn con-

[1]The cointoise had been originally a military accessory, fixed to the crown of the tilting-helmet, under the crest (cf. also Fig. 219) and was designed to prevent the back of the head from getting overheated, a necessary precaution when the wearer was fighting in the East. See *The Chronicles of the Crusades* by Villehardouin and de Joinville.

FIG. 150   Burgundian (1440)

FIG. 151   French

FIG. 152   French

FIG. 153   Flemish

FIG. 154   French

FIG. 155   Flemish (1475–80)

siderably later than the scenes they represent. A pointed henin and a truncated version appear together in the same picture depicting a Court scene. The second of these resembling a chimney-pot *(Fig. 152)* would seem to be very solid and heavy, with two motifs, probably of jet beads, embroidered on the front, while the old liripipe or becca, starting from the top on the one side, passes under the chin and up to the top again, where it is fastened for extra security. Once more the V-shaped frontlet, with which to adjust the head-dress, is clearly visible. *Fig. 153* shows a shorter type of truncated cone.

Although *Fig. 154* came from an illuminated manuscript purporting to represent the marriage of Isabella of France to King Edward II of England a hundred years before, the artist has in fact depicted the bride wearing the costume of his own period. The supposed Isabella is pictured with a head-scarf under a bulbous, cushion-like head-dress, from the crown of which springs a tall thin henin, bearing at its apex a cointoise which is wound round the cone like a barber's pole, and flows from the top as a streamer. The jewelled fretwork with which the cushion part is covered is reminiscent of the reticulated work of fifty years earlier. It is difficult to imagine anything more absurd, and yet, to us, in our dingy business world, how romantic, in its association with the days of chivalry.

It is likely that for Froissart himself it had the same significance.

Pierre de Gros in *Le Jardin des Nobles* complained that 'the younger and more beautiful the ladies were, the higher were the chimneys that they carried.' The henin, equally with the horned head-dress, was the object of much abuse from clerics and moralists, though why they should select any particular modes rather than others for condemnation is difficult for us to understand. *Fig. 155* is a case in point. When an artist wished to portray the Temptation of St. Anthony he chose the henin head-dress as being, to his mind, evil (yet at the same time alluring) so he dressed the temptress in a gown and steeple hat with the addition of black velvet lappets and long suspended veil falling nearly to the ground. It is only when our eyes reach her feet that we realise these are actually talons and so we know that this charmer is really the devil in disguise.

The lappets mentioned above, continuing as a band across the front of the henin, anticipate the gable head-dress of Tudor times. A German version of the henin, again with lappets, buttoned back on themselves, and front band, is shown in *Fig. 156*. The head-dress appears solid and heavy and the wearer has her hair drawn back from the centre parting and nearly concealed beneath the border. The fabric swathing the crown (or steeple) falls from its underside seam.

Lappets, this time lengthy and of black velvet, appear once more in *Fig. 157*, which is Flemish and dates from 1498. The crown itself is also of black velvet (or possibly satin) and the veil does not start until half way up the crown. Smoothly laid over the steeple, it is seamed at the underside, and from there falls lightly behind the shoulder.

A twin-steepled crown from France is shown in *Fig. 158*, the two cones rising side by side. This departure from the normal henin shape indicates that its popularity was declining. Steeples were henceforward lower, and the head-dress was developing into another style altogether.

Meanwhile we must glance at a freak style that combines a number of ideas *(Fig. 159)*: the shaven forehead, the reticulated ear-bosses (or possibly a caul over the forehead), and the hat brimmed like that of the pilgrim in *Fig. 184*. The brim, split in four places and curled outwards, is of velvet, with a braid edge and contrasting lining. The crown rises like a miniature henin and the frontlet is still in evidence. Not unlike it in conception is *Fig. 160*

Fig. 156   German (1490)

Fig. 158   French

Fig. 157   Flemish (1498)

Fig. 159

FIG. 160   Netherlandish (1460)

FIG. 161

FIG. 162   Flemish

where the brim is twice split and the crown a little higher. Also worn during this period was the strange head-dress pictured in *Fig. 161* which comes from a group in an illuminated manuscript showing young men and women watching a tournament—a smart occasion paralleled in our own day by Ascot race meetings where spectators vie with one another in the fantasy of their hats. The last-mentioned style is, in fact, a sugar-bag shape split up in front to reveal the face, and with turned back wings which are stiffened or wired.

The Flemish woman in *Fig. 162* wears a hat which was possibly more serviceable than the foregoing but, in our view at any rate, not very becoming. Over a white linen coverchief she has placed a leather hat, the slashed brim of which is turned back against the crown in the manner of the much later cocked hat.

The Wars of the Roses between Yorkists and Lancastrians dragged on but the English aristocracy still flaunted their brave apparel, even though it was denounced by the Church as indecent. Eventually women gave up their horns and henins, not to please the moralists, however, but because an exciting new style of hat had developed. This was the so-called *butterfly* head-dress, particularly characteristic of the reign of Richard III (1483–1485). It spread its gauzy wings on either side of the wearer's head, and, although varying in detail, undoubtedly grew out of the steeple style, as a truncated cone still fitted the head. From this rose the veil erected on wires made as wide and high as ingenuity could contrive. An

FIG. 163   English

English effigy *(Fig. 163)* achieves in stone a very clever representation of such a butterfly head-dress. The winged veil descends in two thicknesses on each side from the top of the shortened henin set vertically on the head. As usual in the fifteenth century the hair is hidden. Another butterfly, in *Fig. 164,* was worn in the Netherlands. The rising cone, with a backward tilt, had a fretted border and is held in place with a stiffened ribbon that actually hooks over the ears. The transparent veil worn with it covers the forehead to just below the eyebrows and, starting in a V-loop at the centre of the shaved brow, spreads in flutes on both sides. *Fig. 165* is also from Flanders. It is an elaborate structure made up of a cone of cloth of gold, tilted almost horizontally back from the forehead, with a wide U-band for adjusting it and stiff metal clips in front of the ears to hold it securely. The veil is extremely diaphanous, rising from the centre of the forehead and simulating the earlier horns, finally falling to the shoulders.

A truly immense butterfly style in *Fig. 166* is French. It consists of a two-layered veil erected high over a gold cone and composed of fine gauze. Folding these intricate structures and keeping them in place must have presented many difficulties but they were worn, not only by the high-born and frivolous, but by many industrious and hard-working matrons, as will be seen in *Fig. 167* where the foundress and governess of a Flemish hospital has adopted it and, indeed, the 'fly-away veils' of some religious orders of our own time derive from the attire of these fifteenth century ladies. It is familiar to us as part of

FIG. 165 Flemish

FIG. 166 French (1480)

FIG. 164 Netherlandish

FIG. 167 French

the habit of the Sisters of Mercy *(Fig. 168)*. The butterfly is also worn today in Normandy from the locality of Caux and is known as the *cauchoise*.

The veil in *Fig. 169* must surely be one of the largest ever to have been worn. It is interesting to note that folding in the material is indicated by crossed lines, making it appear that these veils were laundered and folded for storage in a cupboard, from which they could be taken when required to be laid over the cone-shaped hat. Probably they were held in position with gold-headed pins such as may still be seen on fisher-girls in Holland. The disposal of the veil in this illustration is different from those so far illustrated. It hangs in a sweep from the forehead and is lifted into two horns by wire supports at the sides. Another device giving a similar effect is seen in *Fig. 170* where two pear-shaped boards covered in diaper-patterned fabric are arranged over the ears and attached to a band of the same material passing across the forehead. The band probably continued right round the head, securing the head-dress firmly. There are two veils, a fairly thick one which rises in twin horns from the headband, and a gauzy light one that covers the ear pieces and falls over the forehead to the eyebrows.

Striped fabrics, particularly silk, were much worn during this period, the most renowned coming from Ghent where a special Guild was formed early in the century exclusively for their manufacture. Stripes were seen on head-dresses as well as on clothes. It is difficult to decide, from a study of the stone effigy of Lady Margaret Neville, daughter of Reginald

Cobham Kt., *(Fig. 171)* of what fabric her head-dress is made but it is certainly striped, and the truncated cone, with turned-back lappets, anticipates the later Tudor styles.

Fig. 172 shows a young girl of about 1480 wearing a hat covered in striped silk. The illustration is taken from a brass of Sir J. Tirswick's family at Dagenham. The wife is wearing a wimple and veil, suited to an elderly woman still clinging to the subdued and decorous head-dresses of her youth, but her two daughters, in the heyday of their early married life, wear immense butterfly head-dresses. The two unmarried girls on the other hand have the chimney-pot hats seen earlier in *Fig. 172*, with hair hanging loosely to their hips.

An advanced style of butterfly veil, as worn by married women in England in 1484, is given in *Fig. 173*. The cone or caul is now meshed and jewelled and projects horizontally backwards from the head. (Cf. the earlier version in *Fig. 171*, where it was perched vertically.) The veil here is in two layers and is held out at the back over a wire support. The arrangement of such frames is well shown in several brasses where the thickness of the veil is indicated by graving only the supports, as though they show through the gauzy fabric. This is the butterfly veil at its daintiest.

The butterfly, like the henin, was not worn in Italy. Neither was the hair so severely concealed. A coil—real or false—was braided on the top of the head, leaving the rest to flow on to the shoulders. *Fig. 174,* with an attractive fringe over the forehead,

FIG. 168   Ghana (1902—but dating back to 15th cent.)

FIG. 169

FIG. 170 Netherlandish (1456)

FIG. 173 English (1484)

FIG. 171 English (1484)

FIG. 174 Italian

FIG. 172 English

FIG. 175 Italian

is a Venetian lady's choice of hair styles. It is varied in *Fig. 175* where the hair is drawn back smoothly from the centre parting and the sides are twisted or curled.

It would be erroneous to imagine that all English women—or for that matter all French women—covered their hair with exciting and elaborate head-dresses, or that only young unmarried girls wore their tresses loose. Lady Joan Cromwell of Tatter-shall, Lincolnshire, whose likeness in *Fig. 176* is adapted from her memorial brass, was married five times, yet has freely flowing hair confined only by a handsome decorated coronet or garland. With such examples available it is surprising that the claim is so often repeated that only unmarried girls wore their hair free and unconfined.

FIG. 176   English

MEN

The chaperon, worn with such dash and ingenuity by the giddy young courtiers of the time of Richard II, persisted well into the fifteenth century and reached extremes of absurdity before being discarded. Frenchmen were still finding new and fantastic arrangements, as in *Fig. 177*, where the rondlet is small, the liripipe absent and the bag-top flopping to the front. The back of the hat touches the scalloped or dagged edge of the houppeland at the rear. Indeed the houppeland often rose so high *(Fig. 178)* as to cover the wearer's chin and ears and reach up over the head and under the hat, so that it might almost be considered part of the actual headgear. In this example the edge of the collar, which now frames the face, is edged with fur. The hat itself is formed of a band (or rondlet) of curly fur, which may be astrakhan or lamb, with a crown of mottled silk. A clipped peacock's feather appears to form the trimming.

FIG. 177   French (1417)

The exaggerated shape from the Netherlands in *Fig. 179* features the rondlet, certainly, but from it springs a tall shape, in velvet over buckram, terminating in a soft bag and decorated with a jewelled brooch. The last example in this group, *Fig. 180* shows the chaperon with rondlet twisted into a soft crown and pleated gorget edged with embroidery falling over the left shoulder. The liripipe, by now (1410) a broad streamer, balances it on the right.

A style completely different from the chaperon seems to have been worn for riding, at any rate between 1400 and 1415 and is represented in *Fig.*

FIG. 178   French or Flemish (1420)

181. This hat, which is from either France or the Netherlands, consists of a buckram or straw shape, over which a length of velvet is drawn, and a small split brim that turns up at the front, with a feather sprouting from the wedge-shaped nick thus formed. (This may, however, have been an amateur's effort at hat-making, as the flutes caused by dragging the velvet over the crown can be clearly seen.)

By now the coif was losing its strings and becoming a close-fitting cap covering the hair. The unconventional Louis XI always wore one of these caps under a hat of plush or velour, perhaps 'brushed' as its surface is rough, and with a turned-up brim. *(Fig. 182).* A very unbecoming headress.

By the end of the century the coif as such had ceased to be worn in the daytime but a form of it persisted as a nightcap for men and women called *cuffie (coiffe)* or *cappeline* or sometimes *benducci* or *bendoni* (Italian), but they were all more or less alike, close-fitting, with a strap under the chin, and made of linen. Francesco Datini, Merchant of Prato, ordered three good cappeline, 'to wear at night, lined with black lining, the best and finest that can be found.' So four large white double caps and four double nightcaps were sent to him from London.

During the fifteenth century the hood and gorget underwent a good deal of modification. The hood proper still retained its popular appeal long after the coif had disappeared and the hood and gorget combination was valued for the warmth and comfort

FIG. 179   Flemish

FIG. 181   French (1410)

FIG. 180   French or English (1410)

FIG. 182   French

it afforded while travelling. In an illumination representing pilgrims setting out for the Holy Land, most wear this form of head-covering with, in every case, a different style of hat set above it. The first example chosen here *(Fig. 183)* shows one pilgrim in a heavy cloak, combined with which is a hood, without a liripipe but fashionably dagged around the face and over that a hat with upturned brim and a moulded truncated cone-shaped crown. He looks most suitably and comfortably clad for venturing on the high seas. One of his companions *(Fig. 184)* wears a deeply dagged gorget, the dags forming pointed lappets round the shoulders, and over the hood an unusual hat with upturned and outward curved brim, slashed in four places. The crown is bell-

shaped with a metal ring at the top. An older man in *Fig. 185* is ready to brave the elements with gorget muffled round his chin and three-tiered felt hat drawn well down over his eyes. The helmsman of the vessel wears a similar hat but with four tiers. Possibly these pilgrims are people of substance making a Grand Tour while at the same time wishing to acquire a reputation for sanctity.

Francesco Datini, whose nightcaps have been mentioned earlier, also had nine hoods, apart from those attached to his cloaks. The separate hood, unlike the hat, was not taken off in greeting but raised to the height of two fingers while bending the head before a bishop, magistrate or other superior. This was called *riverenze di cappuccio*.

FIG. 183   French

FIG. 185   French

FIG. 184   French

FIG. 186   Court Jester, from a French M.S. of Le Chevalier Delibre, dated 1480

Hoods were varied in shape and Villari complained that after the arrival of Walter de Brienne in Florence young men wore them in such long points that they nearly reached the ground and could be wound round the head like a scarf. And a doctor of Prato, Gabbedeo, thought himself elegant with his hood in a short point at one side so wide it could hold half a bushel of wheat.[1] Francesco Datini also owned five round berette, two (vermilion) to be worn over the cowl and three smaller for 'under the hood'.

At this period young men wore bells on their hats and at the waist so that they jingled as they moved (like the Lady from Banbury Cross).

The fool's cap and bells *(Fig. 186)* were derived from the hood, gorget and liripipe. After a style has passed it appears to be ludicrous, as do all fashions, until they are sufficiently ancient to be judged on an aesthetic basis only. The bells were also a feature of this passing period, and so became the figure of fun on the jester's garb. .

Individual taste seems to have governed the construction and arrangement of the chaperon throughout the decades during which it was worn. Sometimes the dagged gorget stands erect like a cock's comb; in other cases it lies like limp leaves over the rondlet which, as in *Fig. 187,* is completely hidden. At times the dagged fabric might be allowed to fall forward over the wearer's forehead; or it might trail out at the back. If the liripipe was suppressed altogether, then the dagging drooped over the edge of the rondlet to fall like a curtain at sides and back. No doubt the method of constructing the chaperon was largely prompted by the materials used: taffeta or samite would stand up stiffly and silk or wool would fall downwards. Fabric, dyed in France, or of woven stripes, from Ghent, was used for the chaperon and both hats and hoods were lavishly trimmed with fur.

The chaperon with its flat liripipe, now called a *becca,* remained popular until well into the middle years of the century, and it was customary (and probably more comfortable) to let the long streamer fall over the right shoulder and then tuck it into the belt as in *Fig. 188.* This shows a young man wearing it in what was doubtless considered the correct manner, rondlet set well on the head, folded gorget

FIG. 187   French (1410)

FIG. 188   Italian

FIG. 189   Flemish or French

[1]See *The Merchant of Prato* by Iris Origo.

✳ *65* ✳

falling over one shoulder, with the becca crossing the chest and then thrown casually over the left shoulder. When saluting a lady, a gentleman raised the rondlet from his head with his right hand, while supporting the streamer with his left, as can be seen in *Fig. 189*. We have come a long way in 150 years from the beginnings of the liripipe as a small extension of a workman's hood!

When the hat was not required on the head it could be conveniently slung over the shoulder by this same streamer *(Fig. 190)*. Here the top of the crown lies against the man's shoulder and the lining, made of stiff canvas, faces outwards. This is the origin of the badge of the Order of the Garter; a member of which order still wears it in this way with

his Garter robes while a feathered 'tammy' covers the head (Fig. 585).

The rondlet, whether worn by men or women, was sometimes given a bias twist. This is very noticeable in *Fig. 191* where the gorget is laid on the head and parts of it appear down each side of the face. The wearer is John Arnolfini, one of those wealthy Flemish merchants who at this time lived like princes. Van Eyck painted his portrait in 1430, in a chaperon of bright red, then a favourite colour. The cloth from which it was made was, in fact, known by its colour and called, simply, 'scarlet'.

Gorgets were often very elaborately dagged in these earlier years and men also shaved the backs of their heads. When not wearing the chaperon they

FIG. 190   Flemish or French

FIG. 192   Burgundian (1410)

FIG. 191   Flemish (1425)

FIG. 193   Burgundian

adopted a variety of hat styles. *Fig. 192,* from Burgundy, is a tall asymmetrical stove-pipe shape with a turned-up brim, and in *Fig. 193* another Burgundian noble wears the rondlet and large bag crown. Wide-brimmed beavers, sometimes with a point in the centre of the crown and of various colours, including white, were popular. Van Eyck painted another portrait of John Arnolfini, from which *Fig. 194* is taken, and here the sitter wears a large dark maroon-coloured beaver, in keeping with the merchant's fur-trimmed wide-flowing cloth surtout, to give an over-all appearance of sumptuous prosperity and comfort.

The chaperon had reached its heyday by 1430 and then its popularity began to wane. *Fig. 195* is an uncouth clumsy version and in *Fig. 196,* where it is worn by a clerk, it is so simplified as to be little more than a cylinder of fabric pulled on the head like a brewer's cap and left to fall loosely over the shoulder. These last two illustrations come from Italy.

For a short period Italians broke away from the trends of fashion in other parts of Western Europe and—at least in the Siena district—wore the curly-brimmed wide hat of *Fig. 197,* with its dandified, somewhat raffish look. The wide brim (probably felt) edged with gold braid is turned up on each side against a stiff bowler-shaped crown which may have been made of a closely shaven fur—perhaps dyed lamb. The wearer's hair is shorter than was customary in Italy at the time. There are few examples of such

Fig. 194   Flemish

Fig. 196   Italian (1430)

Fig. 195   Italian

Fig. 197   Italian

hats in contemporary art and it seems likely that they never became generally popular.

The cushion hat, which was then so much in vogue among Italian ladies, was also adopted by their menfolk, and in *Fig. 198* we see a man in the ubiquitous padded rondlet, attached to a long cushion-shaped variant of the bag top. Even one of the Three Wise Kings in a *Nativity* was represented as wearing the cushion-topped hat *(Fig. 199)*. It is decorated with gold ornaments in the form of daisies, with a crown perched above it to symbolise his kingly status, and with a halo behind to show that he is also a saint. The picture is by Gentile de Fabriano who died in 1428.

The cushion hat was not confined to Italy and was enlarged still further by piling one or even two more cushions on top of the first, as in *Fig. 200* from Flanders.

While the more sober-minded were still wearing the simple form of chaperon, with becca over the shoulder, Florentine dandies dressed in much richer and more fanciful attire, with every accessory to make them gorgeous and picturesque (while their girl-friends trailed yards of dagged silk in the dust and wore cushioned hats on their yellow hair).

The young men in the next three illustrations stand and gossip at a street corner, in the shadow of the Duomo. The year is 1450. One youth, in *Fig. 201*, has a soft velvet crowned hat with upturned brim faced with ermine. His hair is cut and curled, but

FIG. 198   Italian (15th cent.)

FIG. 200   Flemish (15th cent.)

FIG. 199   Italian (1428)

FIG. 201   Florentine Dandy (1450)

we cannot see whether it is parted in the centre as was the usual custom. His companion, in *Fig. 202,* has his hair brushed out in a bushy style general at the time and probably achieved by back combing or even plaiting at night to give a crimped effect by day. This youth has a hat also with an upturned brim and a large bag-top pulled towards the front. The hat of the third young man, *Fig. 203,* is evidently made from a fur such as curled lamb or astrakhan and is conical at the top with a deep brim flattened against it. All three youths have fair hair so we may presume that it was fashionable for men as well as women to dye their locks.

In contrast a French youth of about the same age and social standing wears a simple felt cap *(Fig. 204)* with his heavily gored doublet.

By the end of the first half of the fifteenth century the coif as a head-covering, had disappeared, except on old men as in *Fig. 205,* where it is fastened under the chin with an extension of the material of which it is made and not with a ribbon or strap as formerly. The wide embroidered strip passing from the front of the crown and down the back of the coif is probably there to hide a seam.

But for another 50 years the coif remained a static style for wearing under hats and caps of state. Thus we see it under the Doge's cap in *Fig. 206* where the strings are left loose. The cap itself resembles in style the ancient Phrygian head covering and may indeed have been retained as a form of traditional and ceremonial attire as is the judge's wig of today. It consists of a deep band and a shaped top rising

FIG. 203   Florentine (1450)

FIG. 204   French (1460–65)

FIG. 202   Florentine (1450)

FIG. 205   Italian (1438)

✳ *69* ✳

FIG. 206   Venetian

FIG. 209   Venetian (1499)

FIG. 207   French

FIG. 210   Venetian (1485)

FIG. 208   Netherlandish

FIG. 211   Italian (1470)

to a blunt point at the back. It was stiffened and quite hard to the touch.[1] Called a *dogone* it was worn with the traditional coif with hanging tapes.

In the British Museum there is an M.S. which shows the newly elected doge kneeling before an altar, wearing on his head only the coif, whilst behind him stands a page bearing a cushion on which reposes the dogone cap in red with a gold band. With the donning of this and the taking of the oath the new doge is installed as head of the Venetian State. This parchment is *The Promessio Covenant* of Antonio Grimoiu on his election as Doge on July 21st 1521. It sets forth the laws and customs of the Venetian State which he promises to observe.

In another *Promessio* in Latin, of Cristoforo Moro's election, he is shown kneeling before the Virgin wearing the coif but no cap; evidently a sort of short vigil before the final setting of the state cap on his head.

The coif is worn by a French king in *Fig. 207*. Here the soft upturned brim bears a decorative jewel and the crown is contained within the brim. This is not exceptional as several instances can be cited of a crown being worn with a hat, usually over a bycocket.

As the fifteenth century was a period of prosperity for the merchants of the Low Countries, their clothes including their hats, became increasingly sumptuous. *Fig. 208* shows a variant of the bycocket worn by such a merchant (probably the master of his guild as he is

wearing a gold chain). The brim is of contrasting colour and the cap worn below it is of velvet. The wearer's hair is well tended and long, conforming with the general European trend of the second half of the century.

Pictures by Botticelli and Carpaccio give other examples of these hair styles and the Venetian dandy of *Fig. 209* has well combed locks flowing on to his shoulders. His skull-cap with single feather is small, allowing the maximum amount of hair to show.

Feathers as a decoration for men's hats came into fashion during the third quarter of the century, at first as small plumes, as in *Fig. 210*, where one is worn at the back of a hat with narrow graduated brim. Such plumes might be curled or straight and sometimes they were sequined along the midrib or studded with gems. Later they gave way to larger feathers, from swans or peacocks, and these in their turn surrendered to the ubiquitous ostrich plumes which, in one form or another, remained an important feature of masculine hat decoration until the late eighteenth century.

Older men in Italy were much given to wearing the hard felt biretta type hat, usually in bright scarlet. Such a hat is seen in *Fig. 211* where the wearer's hair is rolled into a stiff curl over a bandeau which reaches from ear to ear.

A Spanish fashion that became *de rigueur* in 1467 or thereabouts and was copied in other countries was the tall six- or seven-sided velvet cap illustrated in *Fig. 212*. The same tall shape is worn by a Frenchman in *Fig. 213*. Made of velvet over buckram, it has the

---

[1] See an excellent example in the Ashmolean Museum, Oxford.

Fig. 212 Spanish (1467)

Fig. 213 French

FIG. 214   French

FIG. 217   French

FIG. 215   French or English

FIG. 218

FIG. 216   Portuguese

FIG. 219   Italian (c. 1490)

padded head-band or rondlet, with a small jewel as
its only decoration. The painting from which this
sketch was made shows another tall hat, varying only
slightly from the foregoing, and this is shown in *Fig.
214*. It has affinities with the tall henin women were
then wearing and has no brim or rondlet. Also tall,
but widening at the top instead of diminishing is the
white ermine hat of *Fig. 215* which may, however,
have been part of the attire of a young ecclesiastic.

In 1480 Oliver de la Marche writes of hats 'in
the Portuguese fashion', that is, round with a deep
thick fringe, as in *Fig. 216*, still another proof of the
originality and variety in the hat designs of this
period. Different again are the two which follow.
Fig. 217, from France, is a blue beaver, with gold
braid decorations in chevron form, and *Fig. 218* is a
type worn by some elderly men.

By the 1490's men in Italy were allowing their
hair to grow even longer and more luxuriant and
were brushing it over the brims of their caps, thus
showing it off to advantage. *Fig. 219* is such a Romeo
style, with small upturned contrasting brim. In *Fig.
220* the only head-covering is a minute soft cap over
shoulder-length curls and heavy turned-under bang
which entirely conceals the eyebrows. The same hair
arrangement but without the bang is seen in *Fig. 221*,
of a young Florentine gallant who was obviously
painted from life, though he appears in a picture of
the *Nativity* by Botticelli. His hat has an upturned
brim with a point at the front. The under surface is
of contrasting colour and two circles of braid decorate
the round domed crown of medium height. One tall
thin feather is inserted between the side of the brim
and the crown.

Although by this time the liripipe (or becca) had
lost its *raison d'être*, it was still retained as a trimming
even on such a sophisticated hat as in *Fig. 222*. The
artist who painted the original depicted Tobias, in
contemporary costume, setting out, with his fish
dangling on a string, to visit his uncle. His beaver
hat has an embroidered band with a jewelled buckle,
and his locks fall in a graduated line to his shoulders,
as in the two previous examples.

In Flanders the same hair style prevailed, at least
for younger men, and hats were appropriately simple,
with either high square or little round crowns, and
small brims touching the crown, as we see in *Figs.
223* and *224*.

Long hair held sway for a few more years—until

FIG. 220   Italian (1490)

FIG. 221   Italian (1490)

FIG. 222   Italian

✳ *73* ✳

FIG. 223 Flemish

FIG. 224 Flemish (1485)

the beginning of the sixteenth century—but at the end of the 1490's some larger hats appeared and were worn with it. Carpaccio shows such hats, gaily flaunting feathers, and a Flemish example is depicted in *Fig. 225*. Here the straight hair is uncurled but well brushed and tended, and cut in a straight line just below shoulder level. A soft green cap fits closely to the head and over it is a hat so large that it has to be held on with a ribbon passing over the brim and under the chin. The whole hat is covered with swan's feathers, while a complete wing of the same bird provides the immense plume. The effect is romantic and picturesque, but as the picture from which it was taken represents young people dancing in a garden and one of them has wings on his back, we may gather that a masque is in progress and that therefore the participants wear somewhat fantastic attire. The 'spectator' who is shown in the picture is much more soberly clad. Even so, it should be noted that the Prince, in Carpaccio's picture of the return of the Ambassadors, carried a befeathered hat large enough to need ribbons, which can be seen hanging from the inner side of the crown where they are sewn on to the felt.

Little 'pork-pie' hats, like that in *Fig. 226*, were to be seen on the heads of middle class Italian boys during the whole of the fifteenth and well into the sixteenth century.

MILITARY

When the helmet was worn during the fifteenth century, as indeed throughout the Middle Ages, the

FIG. 225 Flemish

FIG. 226 Italian (1470)

hair was usually cut short and now the head was shaved up the back and above the ears. It will be recalled that one of the accusations made against Joan of Arc at her trial before she was martyred in 1431 was that she had cut her hair short like a man. This was deemed irreverent and indecent. On the modern stage, in a play such as Shaw's *St. Joan*, she is invariably represented with a modern style 'bob', and when the accusation is brought against her the audience laughs, for nothing, to our eyes could look more feminine. But if the hair of the Maid was originally cut and shaven above the ears to accommodate her helmet she would have appeared to her contemporaries as indecently masculine. The normal way of cutting the hair with the effect of a small cap is shown in *Fig. 227*.

Fra Angelico represents a soldier of 1440 in a helmet and carrying a shield *(Fig. 228)*. The crown is still dome-shaped, as in the previous century, but the lappets are now incorporated as extensions of the helm, to cover the ears, and the link-mail gorget is worn. The face, it will be noted, is exposed. In the next illustration, *Fig. 229*, a closed helmet has a movable visor. This formed part of the *cap-à-pie* armour of the period, which, in all, weighed, 117 pounds. Another English helmet, the *basinet*, as worn by Sir Giles Capel in *Fig. 230*, shows how the armour of the time completely covered a man's head.

The Italian *barbuti*, of *Fig. 231*, dating from 1441, has no visor however, though it offered effective protection for the neck and most of the face.

FIG. 228   Italian (1440)

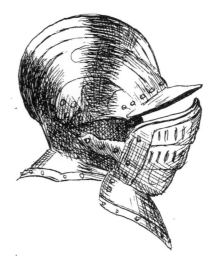

FIG. 229   English

FIG. 227   English

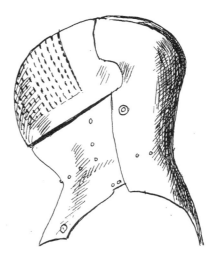

FIG. 230   English

* 75 *

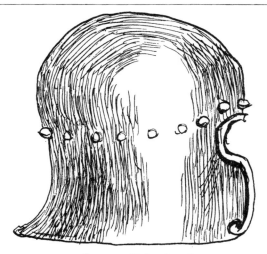

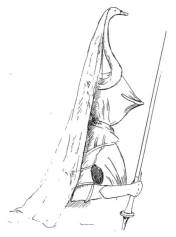

Fig. 231   Italian (1440)

Fig. 232

Fig. 233   Italian

Crests in the form of a swan, eagle, lion or other similar heraldic emblem surmounting the helmet had been introduced in the thirteenth century and remained an important accoutrement for the tourney until the fifteenth. In *Fig. 232* a knight flaunts a tall swan crest above his tilting-helmet, and from the apex a light *cointoise*, or gauzy veil, is suspended. Such a veil was introduced to shield the armour at the back and keep it from over-heating in the sun. Conspicuous and easily identifiable crests, like heraldic devices on the shield, were very necessary in tournaments or battle when the face was hidden by the visor and it would otherwise have been impossible to distinguish friend from foe.

A white coif was at first worn under the helmet to protect the head, but this was no longer needed when it became customary to sew a plush, felt or velvet lining inside the helmet itself. Francesco Donati, the merchant of Prato, Italy, embarked on his successful career by supplying arms and armour to the Papal soldiers stationed at Avignon during the Schism, when there were two Popes. He saw that there was trade to be had while one Pope resided in France and his court provided a rich market for artistic and warlike merchandise. In one of the many letters Donati wrote to his aunt he says 'Tieri lets his wife go with other women to make merry in the pleasure gardens and at every little feast, but mine was sewing helmets.'[1]

He means that she was sewing the linings into the helmets which he was to sell and so augment his trade.

The cushion hat, so fashionable in Italy in the middle years of the fifteenth century for both men and women, was also worn by soldiers on active service, impracticable and unsuitable as it may seem to us. A huge example can be seen in a painting by Paolo Uccello of the Battle of San Romano *(Fig. 233)* where it covers the head of a captain· who is flourishing his sword. *Fig. 234* represents a general who was called the Saviour of his Country, but apparently he found nothing incongruous in wearing, with his armour, a three-tiered velvet hat of immense proportions. This seems to be composed of the rondlet, or padded roll, and two tiers above, the higher being bag-shaped.

In the 1460's Spain appears to have taken the lead

[1] See *The Merchant of Prato*, by Iris Origo.

in popularising tall hats, for both civilian and military wear, and in *Fig. 235* a helmet of 1467 conforms with the current vogue. This Spaniard also wears shoulder-length hair with a moustache and bi-forked beard.

At the end of the century Italian soldiers (and the retainers of great noblemen) wore large hats with swans, or eagles' feathers—stiff, not curled like ostrich plumes.

FIG. 234   Italian (*c.* 1425)

FIG. 235   Spanish (1467)

7

Sixteenth Century

WOMEN

THE NEW CENTURY opened with the striking of flags in the matter of women's veils; gone were the flowing gauzes, and in their place came the heavy Tudor styles which lasted until they made way for the little close-fitting caps, invented by, or named after Mary Queen of Scots.

By the beginning of this century our previous sources of information; sculptured effigies, brasses, illuminated manuscripts and tapestries; are supplemented by oil paintings. Great artists mostly Flemish and German, were often commissioned to make portraits of royalty and wealthy patrons in countries other than their own. Holbein's portraits of King Henry VIII are a case in point.

During the period of transition (1485–1510) Holbein gives us one style that shows the passing of the butterfly gauzes. In *Fig. 236* the sitter still wears the veil attached to the little hinder peak of her closely fitting cap and it blows out on the wind, but it is no longer wired. The front of the cap, too, has already adopted the gable shape and the mass of hair at the back is now confined in the cap's double crown.

A further reduction of the veil is shown in *Fig. 237.* where the sitter has donned the cylindrical cap on which the butterfly gauzes were moulded but her veil is now very short, and is heavy being edged with a bobble fringe across her forehead, and it is now underneath and not over the cap. The general effect is of weight and solidity. Such a head-dress can no longer be described as a 'fly-away'; its wings have been clipped.

Although the well-known gable hood is regarded as so characteristic of the sixteenth century it was essentially an English style, and before describing it some continental fashions merit attention.

Bulbous, bag-shaped headwear was much worn in Germany and the Netherlands. The lady from the Low Countries in *Fig. 238* (who is companioned in a dance by the young man in the large hat with swan's feathers described in *Fig. 225)* wears a soft bag-shaped head-dress that is effectively brightened by stripes of gold thread embroidery. The bag is gathered into a gold band (probably soft and flexible) and is caught up into metal knob at the top. A little hair shows at the forehead, which is not shaven, and a large tress escapes from under the band and falls to her waist at the back.

Italy developed a turban shape which has some affinity with these circular styles but which almost certainly arose independently. Andrea Solario painted the exaggerated balloon head-dress of *Fig. 239* in the year 1516. Lines radiate from a central embroidered boss like the meridians on a globe and these cross other lines to give a lattice effect. The whole massive erection is worn over a red head-scarf of the kind Benvenuto Cellini called 'summer cloths'. A diaphanous gauze veil hangs in a long loop below a more restrained halo head-dress in *Fig. 240.* Here the rondlet is worn over the back of the head unlike the original horizontal arrangement.

Fine pleating, used as a frill, had become a feature of German costume by this time and in *Fig. 241* it forms the upturned brim of a hat, covering the eyebrows and terminating on a level with the top of

FIG. 236   German or English

FIG. 237 Flemish

FIG. 240 Italian

FIG. 238 Netherlandish

FIG. 241 German

FIG. 239 Italian

FIG. 242 Flemish

the bag of velvet or other cloth which forms the crown. No other example of this mode is known to the author.

A Flemish woman in *Fig. 242* wears a close-fitting cap swathed with a heavy linen cloth to give a turbaned effect. The cloth follows the liripipe tradition and falls on the right shoulder before crossing the breast and being thrown over the left shoulder.

What might be conveniently called the jelly-bag head-dress was by now very much enlarged, as we see in *Fig. 243* and no amount of decoration could make it becoming. A variant of the same style is worn in *Fig. 244* which is also German. An embroidered band encircles the forehead and short strands of hair emerge at the sides. (It has been observed

that German women unlike most others of Western Europe, often allowed their coiled or ringleted hair to show at the sides of their horned or other close-fitting head-dresses or caps.) In this illustration the balloon that rises from the band is embroidered with a semblance of the old reticulated pattern and a small scarf encircles it while a minute gauzy veil falls from the band to cover the eyebrows.

Another bulbous form of head attire from Germany in *Fig. 245* retains a suggestion of the gorget over the left shoulder and liripipe over the right. The linen of which it is made is stitched in multiple rows to stiffen the band and the top is padded with tow or horsehair. This was an exceedingly popular style dating from the end of the prev-

FIG. 243   German

FIG. 245   German

FIG. 244   German (1510)

FIG. 246   German

ious century, and the style *Fig. 246,* a turban gathered into a band and crossed with long streamers of the same material, was also much worn. This lady, be it observed shows a considerable amount of hair at the temples.

Fig. 247 is French—the famous Lady of the Unicorns—depicted on a tapestry. Her unusual head-dress may have been a creation of the artist's fancy since it is of soft fabric gathered closely and encircled at intervals with jewelled bands running from a wider band round her head. Her hair style is also unusual, being unconfined and uncurled; although her jewels show her to be a lady of quality dressed in her most handsome attire.

There were other indications that women were no longer willing to confine their hair in all-concealing swathings. The attractive style from the Netherlands in *Fig. 248* shows little rippling waves and curls descending on either side of the face from a central parting. The rest of the hair is twisted loosely, only the ends being turned under a small green cap which finishes with a hanging tassel on the left. Over this is set the crown or coronet. At this period, particularly in Germany, much pride was taken by both sexes in the hair as an adornment and many women wore it loosely waved to the shoulders.

The Portuguese lady of about 1510 in *Fig. 249* has dark silky hair which is arranged naturally with a simple knot at the nape of her neck. The head-dress consists of a padded roll, embroidered in the long

FIG. 247   French

FIG. 249   Portuguese (1516)

FIG. 248   Flemish (1508)

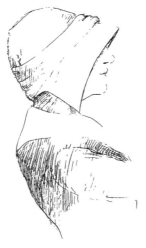

FIG 250   French (1505)

established reticulated design and fastened with a large jewel. The cord across the forehead is there only for decoration—a vestigial reminder of the old frontlet.

Fig. 250 is the linen coif or bonnet worn by the average French housewife in the early years of the century, the long becca being wound round the crown. Its simplicity is enhanced by the severe white collar.

The *gable,* a uniquely English style of hood was so revolutionary in shape and so generally worn in this country that it deserves a section on its own.

The henin, as we have seen, had vanished completely by the eighties of the previous century, to be replaced by the hood which, at first, had no inside framework to hold its shape. Made from velvet and usually black in colour, it had a front edge folded three or four inches back to form lappets on the shoulders, as we saw in earlier figures (326 and 327). By turning back the edge the contrasting silk lining was exposed and the edges were often embroidered with gold or coloured silk thread. The hood was usually slit part way up behind the lappets and the rest left to hang at the back in folds to just below shoulder-level. A cap or coif was worn under the hood and the black velvet frontlet was still sometimes seen. Of the few transitional shapes we can examine, the Englishwoman's head-dress in *Fig. 251* is noteworthy. She is a member of the Hobart family and wears the lappets—the final stage of the henin—covering the crown of the truncated cone. The whole construction is already heavy and solid, seemingly embroidered in semblance of the old reticulated design but possibly made from a large piece of brocade, with a woven pattern, folded back. A piece of wire under the front of the lappets gives it a square line on either side of the face and a point at the centre anticipates the true gable. The little V of the black frontlet is still in evidence. This is the last time we shall see it in this book.

The heavy pleats at the back of the cape head-dress in *Fig. 252* provide a further variation from this period of transition. The shape has something in common with the man's hood and gorget worn by a German in *Fig. 253* and in fact the English sometimes adapted and Anglicised German styles during the next fifty years. But the gable itself is exclusively English.

The change to the gable was almost abrupt but in line with the general trend towards sober, heavier clothes' styles. Gowns were of heavy velvet or cloth closely pleated and often with stiff waist-skirts under them. Women's attire was to become even more stately and cumbersome in the course of the century.

The *gable* proper, scathingly referred to also as the *kennel* or, according to variations in the shape of the framework, as the *diamond* or *pyramid,* now invariably incorporated a metal support which formed a base for the fabric of the hood. In cold weather and in draughty castles and mansions heavy head-dresses must have been comforting but Elizabeth Woodville, wife of Edward IV, lived in the same palaces and looked fairy-like in her fly-away butterfly gauzes.

The gable's popularity was such that it was general among all classes in England until nearly the end of the reign of Henry VIII, that is for about fifty years. At first it was worn with the hair centrally parted, the front strands neatly drawn to each side of the temples and showing below the point of the gable as in *Fig. 254.* This point is, indeed, most pronounced, leaving a tent-like gap between hair and head-dress. The front of the structure is edged with a band of jewelled embroidery, mitred at the three points to fit the shape and falling on either side of the face to the square neckline of the gown. This band is in reality part of the undercoif. The lappets proper increase in width as they descend from the centre of the gable to lie in front of the shoulders and they are sewn with precious jewels. The veil section of this head-dress is attached to the underlappets and falls down to the back in heavy folds.

Later, as in *Fig. 255,* the space between head and gable peak was filled in with plaits of hair bound with ribbon and laid crosswise in the aperture. This fashion was superseded in its turn by striped satin ribbons sewn into the head-dress as one of its permanent features and so concealing all the hair. Here the gable shape is accentuated by the inward curve of the narrower band, itself attached to a white coif, and the hood lappets are turned up at the ends and pinned on the crown. No doubt free hanging ends had proved inconvenient and fastening them up in this way was a simple solution.

Since napped cloths and velvet are apt to cling to other fabrics and materials, the one piece shape must have proved somewhat restrictive, and so the cape-piece, at first all in one like the hood, was later divided into three sections. The V-cuts which we saw in

FIG. 251   English

FIG. 254   English (1520–40)

FIG. 252   English

FIG. 255   English

FIG. 253   German

FIG. 256   English

Fig. 252 were extended to the top so that one part fell at each side of the face and the third hung down the back, giving greater freedom for the articulation of the neck and shoulderblades.

Fig. 256 is from another Holbein drawing showing a further advance. Here the inner ribbon is brought much farther forward and the lappet is flatter. Again the ends are taken up and fastened to the cap.

Holbein's drawings also show little gable-shaped caps of white fur, and the same kind were sometimes made from linen. Whatever the material, whether linen or fur, they were known as *lettice caps* and the hood with the flap turned back was styled a *bongrace*.

Meanwhile on the mainland of Europe the gable never became popular, and in the Netherlands a sixteenth century adaptation of the wimple and coverchief seems to have taken its place *(Fig. 257)*. Here the voluminous linen veil is draped about the head with a suggestion, in the backward-turned edges, of rudimentary lappets. Little hair is visible but the whole effect is not unpleasing. A second Continental example, *Fig. 258,* is also from the Low Countries and consists of a shaped linen cap with a bulbous crown and embroidered band passing over the forehead. The veil is also manipulated in line with the traditional Dutch cap and flutes forward over the brows, to curve outwards above the ears and become one with the cap. Meanwhile the tippet (old liripipe or becca) emerged from the right side, to pass over the head, where it is pinned to the

FIG. 257   Netherlandish

FIG. 259   German

FIG. 258   Netherlandish

FIG. 260   Flemish

bulbous head-dress and thence falls loosely to the right shoulder.

A German style which may owe something to the gable is seen in *Fig. 259* where a linen coif completely hides the hair and black velvet lappets are shortened to chin level. This severely sober style would seem more in keeping with the habit of a religious order.

Towards the middle of the century women's hair fashions were beginning to change and as more was allowed to show it became customary to wave or crimp it. *Fig. 260,* from Flanders, shows this incipient development. The crimped hair is drawn under a cap, the curved outline of which prefigures the style said to have been sponsored by Mary Queen of Scots and often referred to as the 'Marie Stuart'. In this case a brocade or velvet bag at the back holds the ends of the heavy tresses.

The caul, like the coif, was used as a basis for other head coverings, especially in Germany, where it was worn by both sexes. Those worn by women were of necessity larger, as they had to contain the heavy back hair, and a band was then added to allow some pretty curls to escape over the forehead and ears. Finally the caul was topped with a bigger hat whose brim was embroidered at the back and slashed at the front. The whole structure was then loaded with as many feathers as the brim would hold. *Fig. 261* is from a drawing of such a confection by Holbein in Germany in 1523 and is surely the culmination of all slashed beret styles to date. So unwieldy had they become that such an example had to be held on with a strap beneath the chin. The whole effect is fantastic but exceedingly decorative and it makes a handsome accompaniment for the wide sleeves and much cut and smocked bodice.

Cranach gives us another version as worn by Sybilla of Cleves in 1530 *(Fig. 262)*. A caul with a reticulated band tightly fitted to the head becomes, at the back, a bulbous excrescence divided into cross-sections by ribbons tied into little bows. The hat brim is higher now and the feathers drape over it in profusion.

Ear-pieces were not yet altogether discarded and they may be observed in *Fig. 263,* where a decorated caul encases ears and hair and is topped with a flat beret-type hat made either of brocade or embroidered silk.

The gable, so universally adopted by the English of all classes, changed little in basic design until the

FIG. 261   German (1523)

FIG. 262   German (1530)

FIG. 263   German

FIG. 264   French (1536)

FIG. 265   English

FIG. 266   French

closing years of Henry VIII's reign. In the forties it came under the influence of a French style of hood, the construction of which was similar to that of the gable but it had now lost its angles, swelling out at the sides into crescent-shaped curves. This change is said to have been introduced into England by Anne Boleyn and Catherine Howard. And, at last English women had begun to show their hair again, as in *Fig. 264*, where the velvet cap lined with white silk permits tight little curls to appear at the temples. The heavy veil had become smaller and by this time was relegated to the rear only. It is an altogether prettier and younger style.

A further departure from the rigid lines of the gable is depicted in *Fig. 265*. Here a simple band, encircling the head and widening towards the back, is recurved at ear level, leaving room at the temples for similar clusters of curls. The embroidery on the head-dress is handsome without being heavy and again the dark veil flows down the back.

In *Fig. 266* the same shaped cap is worn by Mary Queen of Scots with whose name it has become associated. This drawing also shows the traditional pleated barbe, for long denoting a widowed state. Mary's husband, Francis II of France, had recently died and she was not yet Queen of Scotland.

German women were also addicted to little caps in these middle years of the century and *Fig. 267* gives an example somewhat resembling the flat style worn by men in the Tudor period. The caul or snood has been retained and is highly decorated but the costume worn with it shows that the century was passing into its second—and in regard to fashion at least—more exciting half.

The reigns of Edward VI and Mary Tudor were comparatively uneventful in the history of costume, but with the accession of Elizabeth swift changes set in. Little caps and flowing veils disappeared. Hair was at last regarded by English women as a natural asset worthy of careful dressing and display, and as the century drew on coiffures became more and more elaborate. At first, however, they were still simple enough to enable a hat to be worn as well. *Fig. 268* is typical of the early Elizabethan period and the wearer's hair is puffed out at the sides, supporting a high-crowned 'topper', perched well forward with peaked brim coming down over the forehead. It is, to all intents and purposes, a man's hat, worn with a difference. The gold and jewelled hatband and ostrich feather themes are to recur for many years to come. Another Englishwoman *(Fig. 269)* has arranged her hair in puffs which conceal her ears and has also donned a very masculine style of hat—stiff with a narrow flat brim and hard, nearly flat top. A band of twisted fabric (probably the cyprus referred to on page 83) takes the place of the hat-band without making it appreciably more feminine.

From about 1570 hair began to be dressed much higher off the forehead and eventually was arranged over a pad or wire framework with a mass of curls on top. Later still in the century it rose to even greater heights, with the addition of false hair or a wig if necessary. Wigs were, indeed, very popular during the last decade or so of Elizabeth's reign. They were often golden or red as a compliment to the queen and sometimes women had their own hair dyed in the 'royal' colour.

When these new hair fashions were adopted all but the tiniest hats had to be abandoned. In *Fig. 270* the sitter wears on her hair, which is brushed back from her forehead, a little lace-edged cap, and perched on top of this a miniature version of a man's velvet hat with a curly brim. By the end of the century heads were decked only with little bows, jewels, gold ornaments or feathers.

Somewhat similar hair styles were worn on the Continent and in *Fig. 271* which is Flemish and *Fig. 272* (from Italy or Spain) show the heights to which they were ascending. The second and more fantastic

Fig. 267   German (1560)

Fig. 269   English

Fig. 268   English

Fig. 270   English

FIG. 271   Flemish

FIG. 274   German

FIG. 272   Italian or Spanish (1570)

FIG. 275   German

FIG. 273   English

FIG. 276   English or Flemish

of these two examples may indeed be a wig and it is adorned with a glittering jewelled set-piece and black bows at the ears.

Fig. 273 indicates how an Elizabethan lady when in bed convalescing, received her guests. She wore a lace cap over her hair (represented in this drawing by the small lower edging over her forehead), her ruff, and a thin gauze wired head-dress which makes another cap at the back and projects well over the face, pinned with a brooch below the ruff. The gauze is spread out over the pillow and through it can be discerned her ermine cape or wrap.

The wearing of ruffs by women raised a great outcry amongst the moralists; they were denounced as evil in the same manner as the henin and horns were met with opprobrium in earlier generations. It is difficult for us nowadays to understand why this piece of starched linen and lace round the neck should have been the object of vituperative abuse; it was a new inovation and therefore suspect. Crispin de Passe even went to the length of drawing a scene showing how the ruffs were laundered and stiffened with that which the moralist Stubbs called 'the Devil Starch' and the satire is forced home by the fact that all the participants of the scene, including the ladies and gentlemen who have brought their ruffs to be laundered are represented as dressed-up monkeys!

In Rowley's play *Match at Midnight* the stage directions are 'Enter maid with band-box' This term is used here in its original meaning—a box in which to keep bands or ruffs for the neck, and consequently a round box. When the maid is asked 'Where ha' you ben?' she answers, 'For my mistress's ruff at the seamstress's, sir.'[1]

The long cloak and hood worn by Dutch women at this period was called a 'huke'. The Duchess of Suffolk, when fleeing from Catholic persecution during the reign of Mary Tudor, donned one of these hukes as soon as she landed in Holland the better to disguise herself.[2]

MEN

In Germany at the very end of the fifteenth century men were still indulging in a last medieval fling of exotic and fantastic clothes and wore hats not seen elsewhere in Europe, although they followed the prevailing fashion of wearing the hair long and flowing. The young exquisite in *Fig. 274* has a sugar-bag shaped hat made of leather, with an upturned brim varying in width from front to sides. From the seam at the top of the crown fall numbers of cut leather strips. Dürer portrayed himself in an equally fantastic style *(Fig. 275)* and may have been the prime mover in such vagaries.

In medieval times the silhouette for a man had been a tall slender one, starting at the point of the elongated shoes, up the slim legs to an almost non-existent doublet with a tight waist, passing the head with its flowing locks and little cap to the point of the tall feather. Now comes a complete change (Henry VII and Henry VIII): square toes as wide as possible with bunchy material pulled through the slashes to exaggerate their short stumpiness; wide pleated skirts to their doublets, wider shoulders with masses of material in the sleeves, short clubbed hair, like the short stubbed toes, and upon it all a flat beret, pancaked on the head at right-angles.

But bedizenry remained. Everything was slashed and guarded and puffed and studded with jewels. Square silhouetted men and women looked soberer in outline than their slim antecedents, but they had more surface of material to ornament.

Costume was aesthetically dull and many artists began to clothe their sitters in fancy dress or fantastic versions of earlier ages. Discrimination has therefore to be exercised in selecting examples to illustrate this section in order not to include the products of the painter's imagination.[1]

In England King Henry VII (1485-1509), always rather underestimated and maligned because of his parsimoniousness, made a solid background for himself and his Court and amassed a fortune which his son, Henry VIII, was to squander foolishly if gloriously on the Field of the Cloth of Gold. In the older Henry's day the beret had a domed crown of velvet with upturned brim which was deeper at the sides and back than at the front. In *Fig. 276* it is worn with long wavy hair.

In France the first berets had a six- or eight-sided

---

[1] Quoted in Fairholt's *History of English Costume*.
[2] From the Steward's accounts of Richard Bertie, Duke of Suffolk, and his wife.

[1] This phenomenon recurred in the eighteenth century, when Gainsborough and his followers clothed powdered and bewigged gentlemen in Vandyck style costumes, and again in the nineteenth when some artists avoided the introduction of contemporary costume in their pictures.

brim turned up against the soft flat top *(Fig. 277)*. Such upturned brims were often slashed, the sections being laced together with gold, silver or coloured cords. French and Flemish tapestries of the period depict hunting and other scenes in which the participants invariably wear a beret-type hat. The brim is sometimes held in place by a cord passing over the crown of the head and under the chin. For decoration pheasant feathers are often used, as in this last figure. The main rib of such feathers might be jewelled as in the previous century, and were often fastened to the hat with an open-centred brooch. Hair is tightly curled and always shoulder length.

A German version of the beret is worn by Maximilian I in *Fig. 278*. His is of the contemporary shape but sober and made of plain velvet. In Italy Alberto Pio, Prince of Carpi *(Fig. 279)* wears a beret with a four-cornered brim. This Renaissance humanist has a hair-line moustache and the suggestion of a beard, at a time when most European men, except the elderly, were still clean-shaven. Alberto Pio's facial adornment is dark in colour, in strong contrast to his long golden hair, which adds weight to the supposition that Italian men dyed or bleached their locks.

Sometimes the splits in the brim of the beret made it possible for the hinder part to be let down as a protection against sun or rain (See *Fig. 280*) while the front was turned up against the crown and could be laced there by thongs or ribbons.

FIG. 277   French or Flemish

FIG. 279   Italian (1512) Alberto Pio—Prince of Carpi.

FIG. 278   German

FIG. 280   Flemish (1525)

Leaden or enamelled badges began to appear on hats in this period and continued to be worn for many decades, very often as a sign that the owner had been on a pilgrimage to a shrine (of. Shakespeare's reference to the 'cockle hat' in Hamlet. He alluded to the cockle shell emblem of St. James of Compostello.) But these devices by no means always bore a religious significance. Benvenuto Cellini (1500–1571), writing of the period of about 1525,[1] says: 'In those days it was the fashion to wear a little gold badge in one's hat, and noblemen or gentlemen liked to have them engraved with some emblem or device. I made quite a few of these badges, though it was very difficult work. Caradosso used to make them; his designs included more than one figure and as a result he never asked for less than one hundred gold crowns each. Because of this, not so much because of what he charged as because he was a slow workman, certain noblemen preferred to come to me.'

FIG. 281

A round beret with a contrasting peak is worn by a merchant in *Fig. 281*. (He is watching the weighing of his merchandise ready for shipment.) Such a style might be imagined as being the forerunner of the modern yachting cap. There is a single small brooch at the side and the wearer has shoulder-length hair, which is well combed and arranged and not too long for a business man of the time.

The beret lent itself to clever manipulation so that, suitably adjusted it could be worn with dash and style. A German youth in *Fig. 282* has set his cap at a jaunty angle on his short ringleted hair. It has the usual turned-up brim and small jewel and is worn with an effeminate ensemble including a necklace, such as is hardly to be found elsewhere.[2]

FIG. 282   German (1515)

Francis I of France in *Fig. 283* wears his hair short and clubbed and has donned a beret with a wider brim and no slashes, but bugles and a badge are sewn on the under side while the upper supports a single ostrich feather.

In Germany men took to wearing rather larger berets tipped very much to one side, the brim being slotted to allow ribbon to be inserted as a decoration *(Fig. 284)*.

The Italians never adopted the extreme styles of

---

[1] *Autobiography of Benvenuto Cellini.*
[2] This period, lasting about twenty-five years, is the only time in the history of European costume when men wore low-necked garments.

FIG. 283   French—Francis 1st

FIG. 284   German or Netherlandish (1520)

FIG. 285   Italian (1515)

FIG. 286   German

their contemporaries in other countries but they experimented with original styles of hairdressing, as in *Fig. 285*. Here the beret is not much more than a skull cap since it has no brim but the hair is brushed into large thick bunches on both sides of the face and reaches the shoulders. This form of coiffure, along with less eccentric styles, remained in vogue amongst the younger set for about a quarter of a century.

In 1507 Francesco Gonzaga, being in Rome, wrote home to his wife Isabella in Mantua for a new hat and she replied: 'As soon as the felt hat, which is being made after Bernardus del Armaria's directions, is finished, I will have it covered in velvet and embroidered with such taste that it shall be the finest and most gallant thing in the world!'

A strange mode adopted by some men in Germany in these early years of the sixteenth century was the embroidered caul. Into it all the hair was thrust, except for a few wispy strands at the temples. Maybe the hair was cut short to accommodate the tilting or field helmet, as there is an excellent example by Lucas Cranach of a knight in full armour with such a caul. The short crop may have seemed so unsightly when the helmet was removed that the caul was used to conceal it. In *Fig. 286* the close bag shape is elaborately designed in sections to ensure a good fit and has a band of contrasting braided fabric placed over it at an angle. A jewel is set in the front. As a head covering it was well devised but, even so, not particularly becoming. Another caul is worn in *Fig. 287*, which dates from 1518. This is worn by a German and is decorated somewhat differently from the foregoing. Round it, at an angle is set a wreath of artificial flowers as though thrown casually into position. Note, too, the fringe of whiskers under the chin of this elegant young man.

The caul, like the coif, was often worn indoors, while for travelling a large hat could be conveniently worn over it. In *Fig. 288* for example another scion of the German nobility has set over his netted caul a broad-brimmed beret, sewn with jewels and supporting in the brim a number of small ostrich feathers. High embroidered collars to smocked shirts, like the one in this illustration and previously seen in Fig. 361 were a handsome feature of male attire at this date and in this portrait we may notice a narrow and apparently insignificant edging to the collar. As the years pass, however, this will increase in width and importance until it becomes the massive ruff of

Elizabethan days and this in its turn will have a decisive influence on hairdressing styles.

So far only Continental examples of snood (or caul) for men have been discussed and indeed it seems never to have become popular in England. Only two examples are known to the author, both drawn by the German artist Holbein. The first is a miniature of Henry VIII's illegitimate son, the Duke of Richmond, who was buried at Framlingham, Suffolk, and here the attribution may be erroneous and what appears to be a caul might in fact be a night-cap since the young man is attired only in a white shirt. The second painting is of Sir Nicholas Poinz *(Fig. 289)* and, curiously enough, the original drawing from which the painting was made shows

only vaguely defined hair and no caul. But, to keep the hat at the angle at which it was worn required an embroidered strap passing over the crown of the head and round the nape of the neck.

Fig. 290 is our last example of a German hat of this period and it eschews fantasy completely. Influenced, very probably, by the barbaric splendour of his Russian neighbours, the Duke of Brandenburg has enhanced his simply styled tall beaver hat only with an edging of black fur—probably kolinsky. An enamelled plaque is placed at the centre front, with the jewels attached above and below it. His moustache is carefully trimmed and his beard cut short at the chin, but two pointed tufts have been allowed to grow out at each side. This was an instance of the

Fig. 287   German (1518)

Fig. 289   English

Fig. 288   German

Fig. 290   German (1530)

barber's craft made famous by the Elector of Saxony. In this drawing can be seen a further example of the white frill at the neck—a significant forerunner of the ruff to come.

Meanwhile in England the small feathered beret was just coming into vogue and the young man in *Fig. 291* wears such a hat. Gabriel Harvey referred to this fashion in his satire *Speculum Tuscanisimi* where he said 'A little apish hat couched flat to the pate like an oyster'. Edward VI was also depicted wearing an almost identical hat style.

The Steward's Accounts of Richard Bertie and his wife Catherine, Duchess of Suffolk, give an idea of the prices of hats then obtaining in England in the middle years of the century. One item entered is 'A hat of thrummed silk, garnished, and a band of gold, for my master at his coming to Grimsthorpe. 18s.' This was a very expensive hat in terms of money values at the time.

By the 1560's the beret with flat brim was passing out of fashion and has never, since then, returned to favour for men. Stowe in his *Memoranda* bitterly regrets the change and records his dissatisfaction thus: 'Sir Thomas Lodge was L. Maior in 1563, that same year, to ye great slaunder of ye whole city in ye end of his maioralitie professed to be bangerowpte... The same ware a beard and was ye fyrst that beinge Maior of London ever ware any, ye which was thought to many people very strange, to leve ye comly aunsyent custom of shaving their beards: nevertheless, he ware ye comely ancient bonete with iij coners as all his predysesours had done ... But ye next year after, Sir J. Whit, being maior, ware both a long beard and also a round cap that wayed not iiij ounces wh. seemed to all very uncomely.' Evidently the combination of long beard and round cap was quite shocking to the citizens, even more so than his 'predysesours' going 'bangerowpte'. The square beret, however, survived, and an example is seen in *Fig. 292* where the wearer is shown with a beard.

In Henry VIII's day it had been customary for Englishmen to be clean-shaven, despite the royal example, as we have seen, but under Elizabeth England became 'valenced' and nearly all men grew beards. The colour and shape of these was so varied that they became a butt for all the playwrights of the time, including Shakespeare.

Thus, in *Much Ado About Nothing*, Benedick, falling in love, has shaved off his beard, which causes mirth to his friends:

Claudio. If he be not in love with some woman, there is no believing old signs; 'a brushes his hat' o mornings; what should that bode?

Don Pedro. Hath any man seen him at the barber's?

Claudio. No, but the barber's man hath been seen with him, and the old ornament of his cheek hath already stuffed tennis balls.' The joke here being that tennis balls in Elizabeth's time were stuffed with goat's hair.

Again, *In a Midsummer Night's Dream,* Quince says to Bottom: 'You must need play Pyramus.

Bottom. Well, I will undertake it. What beard were I best to play it in?

Quince. Why, what you will.

Bottom. I will discharge it in either your straw colour beard, your orange-tawny beard, your purple-in-grain beard; or your French crown beard —your perfect yellow.'

After Elizabeth came to the throne (1558) hats once again came into fashion and their high crowns contrasted dramatically with the shallow berets of the earlier reigns. Lord Burleigh, one of the founder Governors of Trinity College, Cambridge, thought it incumbent upon him to issue an edict against graduates exchanging their scholarly flat caps for the new-fangled headgear, on penalty of a fine. Nevertheless, the young bloods of the day persisted in sporting the recently introduced gathered velvet hats with an ostrich or peacock plume, or a lace-trimmed brim, or a soft crowned piece of nonsense made of satin resplendent with a jewelled buckle.

Another edict, made by the Sumptuary Court, that all above the age of six, except nobles and persons of degree, must wear the flat, beret-shaped hat on Sundays, and must be able to show that they owned one, was intended to foster the wool trade and yet it had to be repealed in 1597. In spite of these official decrees during the last decade of the sixteenth century, hats became almost as varied as in the early fifteenth. The 'cumly' four-cornered beret was displaced by the chimney-pot style, broad brimmed velour, or soft gathered velvet bag with stiff brim, referred to as the *bonet*. Some of these hats are illustrated here. *Fig. 293* is a style that was favoured by Sir Edward Hoby of Bisham Abbey, who has not yet acquired the beard which was usually grown with advancing years. His hat is a tall, but not firmly

FIG. 291   English

FIG. 292   English (1569)

stiffened, beaver or velvet with a narrow brim and pointed lace edging (later known as Vandyck lace) round the crown in place of the usual hat-band. A triangular pearl jewel and ostrich feather complete the trimming. Such a hat was called a *copotain*, and in *The Taming of the Shrew* (V.1.70) Petruchio is made to say 'A velvet hose, a scarlet cloak and a copotain hat.' These shapes were also seen without the feather and with nap (thrummed felt). In the latter case they looked very much like beaver.

Sometimes, instead of lace, the copotain was decorated with braid or ribbon. Feathers were much affected and Stubbs, the sour moralizer, says 'Men are content with no kind of hat without a great bunch of feathers of divers and sundry colours. Many get a good living dyeing them and selling them and not a few prove themselves fools by wearing them.'

Worsted braid, called *galon* (or galloon), was commonly used as a hat band by 'the man in the street' of the day, as it was cheap and very durable. A black gauzy fabric called *cyprus* was very generally swathed round the crown just above the brim. This was not unlike the Victorians' beloved crepe, but did not necessarily indicate that the wearer was in mourning, though it might do so, having a suitably lugubrious appearance.

Shakespeare mentions this fabric in *A Winter's Tale* as being one of the commodities carried by Autolycus in his pedlar's pack.

'Lawn as white as driven snow,
    Cyprus black as any crow.'

Another copotain hat is worn in *Fig. 294* by a

FIG. 293   English (1572)

FIG. 294   English (1585)

FIG. 295   English

FIG. 296   French (1577)

FIG. 297   French (1578)

member of the Cartwright family in 1585. It is trimmed with a jewel of considerable size and intricate workmanship supporting an aigrette.

The mariners engaged in the expeditions made by Drake, Hawkins and Gilbert were bringing back new feathers from far countries and gold was flowing into England, having been deflected in the Spanish Main from its intended destination. Silver from Peru was arriving by the same means at this time, when trade flourished and piracy was considered legitimate business. The Queen herself and her favourites decked themselves out with much of this treasure.

One of the master mariners, the great Raleigh, is presented in *Fig. 295* wearing a discreetly handsome velour hat with a new and strange kind of feather not found on this side of the Atlantic. It is held in place with a brooch consisting of one pearl drop. Men now favoured pearl earrings, sometimes suspended from both lobes but more often from one only. Raleigh's ruff, though not very massive, shows that the width was increasing and it now takes its characteristic shape, tucked up close under the ears. Hair and beard are carefully trimmed and in proportion.

An incipient ruff, with a different style of hat, is worn by the ill-fated Charles IX of France, a son of Henry and Catherine, in *Fig. 296*. He looks out on the world sadly from under his soft silk or satin hat, with its dark ribbon band punctuated with jewels, and his little bunch of feathers gives it 'style'.

Another French variant, of about 1578, is the velvet hat with a buckram foundation in *Fig. 297*. The brim, which dips a little over the brows, is edged with cord and the crown bound with a satin ribbon which is twisted into a rosette at the front. A jewelled brooch is fastened into the centre of the rosette.

So quickly did styles change in the closing years of the century that Ben Johnson's foolish knight in *The Poetaster* just cannot keep up with the fashions. By the time he has bought a new hat, suit or sword it has already become démodé so that he never becomes the fashionable man-about-town he wishes to be.

CHILDREN

At the beginning of the century little boys for the most part, wore skull caps with hair brushed out all round, but more elaborate caps and hats were made for the sons of the nobility. In *Fig. 298* the small son of Charles VIII of France has a cap of white satin

FIG. 298 German (1500)

FIG. 299 German (1528)

damask, the material also used for his gown which is worn under a white apron. The cap is seamed down each side and a lap is turned back over the forehead, exposing the edge of a white coif, which covers the head like a bonnet and ties under the chin with a bow under the right ear. The son of Sybilla of Cleves, a rather older boy, seen in *Fig. 299,* is dressed in a style prevailing for adults in 1528. With his heavily bobbed hair he wears the slashed red beret then coming into vogue, with a bias twist of contrasting material slung over one side and a jewel with three stones set in the centre of the band.

The son of Isabella Gonzaga of Mantua, whose letter to her husband is quoted on page 80, went to Rome with his tutor when he was ten years old and we are told that he rode through the streets clad in white and gold brocade with a cap of purple velvet on his fair curls. (He gave a gold-embroidered cap to one of his servants, for which he was rebuked by his mother.) On another occasion he 'rode at the Pope's side, looking', wrote Stazio Gadeo, 'as beautiful as an angel in a suit of gold and peacock satin, with a white velvet cap and fine white feathers . . . fastened by a diamond clasp with the letters ACRV, which His Holiness thus interprets: *Amor cara ritorna vivo*—Dear love come home safe.'[1]

Fig. 300 shows a tiny English girl in a version of the Tudor cap and snood, with her little plaits showing at the temples, and *Fig. 301* portrays the small brother of Charles IX of France in a hat much like

[1]Quoted by Julia Cartwright in her *Life of Isabella d'Este.*

FIG. 300

FIG. 301 French (1576)

FIG. 302   Flemish

FIG. 303   English

FIG. 304

that of his senior which was illustrated in Fig. 296. It has the same baggy crown, narrow brim, side tilt and bunch of feathers.

RURAL ENGLAND

For the country straw hats were often worn and they are referred to in *The Tempest* (IV.1.136) 'Make holiday. Your rye-straw hats put on.' In John Lyly's *Euphues or the Golden Legacy,* of 1592 the author describes the countryman's head attire in these words 'His bonnet was green, whereon stood a copper brooch with a picture of St. Denis, and to want nothing he had a fair shirt of white lockram whipt' over with Coventry blue of no small cost.

The exquisites of Elizabeth's Court were now using make-up on their faces, as witness Benedick's behaviour when he believes Beatrice is in love with him.

Claudio: 'And when was he wont to wash his face?

Don Pedro: 'Yes, or to paint himself? for the which, as I hear, is what they say of him.'

Hall, in his Sixth Satire, mentions this effeminate habit.

. . . 'Wear curl'd periwigs, and chalk their face
    And still are poring on their pocket glass.
    Tir'd with pinn'd ruffs, and fans and partlet
        strips
    And busks, and verdingales about their hips.'

THE LOWER ORDERS

Outdoor workers, such as the shepherd in *Fig. 302*, needed warm, comfortable clothes in winter. His cap

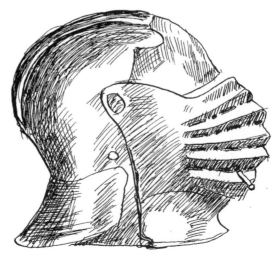

FIG. 305   North Italian (1500)

has a top of red cloth which might well have been the sort of style worn by his wife, wool probably being part payment for his services to the master. As a minder of sheep he could also get fur easily and the soft fur edge to his cap is more likely to have been *budge*—dressed lamb's skin with the fur outside—than coney (rabbit), in spite of the fawn colour.

Other workers, apprentices and so on, wore beret shapes of nondescript character, the most usual being the flat style of *Fig. 303.*

Straw hats were also worn in summer by field workers. In *Fig. 304,* from a picture of the Holy Family, Joseph has put spectacles on to read a book and wears the wide-brimmed straw hat of the time. It seems probable that this figure was a portrait either of the artist himself or of his old father, for he bears no resemblance to St. Joseph in other artists' portrayals, where he is traditionally shown with a beard, a staff and a chisel or plane.

MILITARY

In the early years of the sixteenth century the visored helmet, completely, or almost completely, enclosing the face, was the rule, and *Fig. 305* is a North Italian example dated 1500. *Fig. 306,* of 1510, is English and *Fig. 307* is a casque made in Nuremberg in 1556. The Italians and the Germans specialised in the making of armour and their products were often intricately decorated as in this instance. There existed, apart from an armourers' company, a separate guild of helm makers. For a long time Englishmen bought their armour from

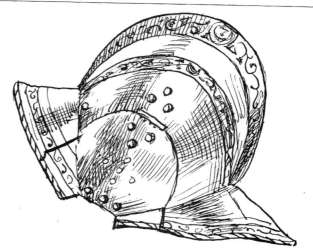

FIG. 307   German (1556)

FIG. 308   Italian (1525)

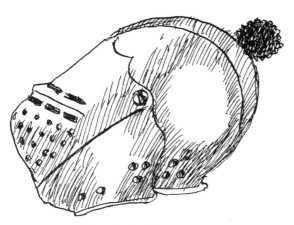

FIG. 306   English (1510)

FIG. 309   German Lansquenet

Milan in Italy or Augsburg in Germany, and even Henry VII's armoury—the first Royal Armoury in England—was staffed by Italians.

The incongruous habit of wearing civilian style hats with coats of mail was noted in the preceding century and it persisted into this. *Fig. 308* is an instance of what we are tempted to call 'military millinery', and shows Romanino's 'Armed Warrior' wearing a large felt hat with ostrich feathers.

In Germany the beret, worn at this period by civilians, and sometimes of great size, was also sometimes seen on military men. The hat-brim in the portrait of a Lansquenet in *Fig. 309* is slit and ribbon slotted through to make a pattern of contrasting splashes of colour. Three ostrich feathers sprout boldly from the top and the whole is worn over a close-fitting cap, with strings that could, presumably, be tied under the chin to keep this handsome piece of headwear in place.

Seventeenth Century

WOMEN

THE DEATH OF Queen Elizabeth I, and the accession of James I—rather than the opening of a new century —marked a change in English fashions, chiefly an accentuation of the bizarre. Anne of Denmark, James's queen till her death in 1620, loved display but used it without taste or discretion. The flamboyant and ungainly clothing of Elizabeth's reign was elaborated still further with ribbons, jewels, fancy leather work, artificial flowers, embroideries and lace. All found their way on to hats and headdresses.

Although Britain had been noted since medieval times for the quality of her embroideries, lace-making had originated in Spain and Italy and perfected in the Low Countries and France. It was a late arrival in England but immediately became immensely popular. Both men and women at this time wore doublets and bodices of embroidered linen with caps or bonnets of matching material trimmed with lace. Ladies' hats, often of black velvet trimmed with ostrich plumes, were as dashing as those of their husbands and sons. They were usually perched at an acute angle at the side or back of the head and worn over a cap. *Fig. 310* is a quaintly delightful picture of his wife by Rubens. Her hat, not unlike his own, with a kicked-up brim and embroidered hat-band, is perched on top of her starched lace cap and must have been pinned in position, for the narrow high crown could not have accommodated a human head. Such a hat was known as a *chapeau de poil*, later misnamed *chapeau de paille*.

Fig. 311 indicates these and other changes still to come. The little cut-work cap is surmounted by a large-brimmed beaver which flaunts a cavalier type feather. The clusters of side curls remind us that the days of Nell Gwynne are not far distant.

After the first quarter of the century and until well into the eighteenth men, as we shall see, dominated the fashion scene, and there is little difference between the hat styles of the two sexes.

The bizarre style of *Fig. 312*, which shows Queen Maria Theresa of Austria, wife of Louis XIV, about the year 1625, seems to have been peculiarly her own. It was not copied even by her own ladies.

On the death of Anne of Denmark in 1620 and until James's death five years later, there was no feminine influence at the English court. On the

FIG 310 Flemish (1610)

FIG. 311 English (1620)

accession of Charles I, however, his French wife, Henrietta Maria, initiated a period of elegance in clothes and hairdressing. Stiff and cumbersome garments were banished, soft silks and satins replaced quilting and padding, and the low corsage and Medici collar superseded the incommodious ruff. Hairdressing showed the same feminine influence. Women's hair was allowed to assert its own natural beauty, curled if necessary and combed into little tendril-like fringes, called *favourites,* over the forehead, the side tresses flowing free, with a softly wound coil at the back as in *Fig. 313*. Large heavy hats would have spoiled the effect and so for a time, until well into the seventies, they were discarded. Sometimes a little white cap, with a lace edge lying against the hair, was worn in the house, and out of doors the hood of the cloak was pulled over it. A craze for protecting the complexion set in in the 1630's and in winter the hoods were often drawn in so that they completely circled the face. A mask covered forehead and nose and a band concealed the chin. In fact the entire face was hidden except for the mouth.

The 1640's were turbulent years in England. The Civil War and the advent of the Commonwealth brought about divergent trends in hats and hair styles. For a time sober, even severe fashions were adopted by Cromwell's adherents and their wives, whose Puritan caps and plain white collars are familiar to us from many pictures. The Royalists, on

FIG. 312   French Maria Thresa, Queen of France. Prado

FIG. 314   English

FIG. 313   English (1638)

FIG. 315   Danish

the other hand, wishing to dissociate themselves from the Roundheads (so called from their close-cropped hair), went in for gay, dashing clothes and are noted for their handsome hats, worn by men and women alike.

With the Restoration, Commonwealth austerities disappeared, and gaiety bubbled up again everywhere.[1] *Fig. 314* gives an idea of a Restoration lady's hat, side-tilted and adorned with the ubiquitous plumes. Plumes are also worn on the Danish lady's hunting hat, illustrated in *Fig. 315,* which may have been chosen for more formal occasions.

Midway through the century, little black caps with a pointed peak were in fashion for a while. They were an admirable foil to the long, free-falling hair styles of the time.

A strange departure from most fashion trends is shown in *Fig. 316.* Although worn here by a young girl, women depicted in paintings of Dutch church interiors also wear this odd headpiece, which may, therefore, have had some ecclesiastical significance. It is difficult to decide what the shiny substance is—possibly it was a lightweight wood such as was used for clogs. From the back flows a long gauzy black veil which may be the cyprus mentioned on page 95.

Holland gives us also the next three styles, all practical and utilitarian and worn by ordinary folk far outside court circles. The Dutch housewife in *Fig. 317* has covered her carefully coiled hair with a little scarf that fastens under the chin with a brooch. Some of these head-scarves were sewn into shape to form caps. Other women favoured pieces of linen or other fabric, quickly and artistically adjusted. The working women in *Fig. 318* wears the very small cap, shaped in linen and fitting closely over sleek head and neatly coiled bun, which we so often see in Dutch paintings. For Sundays she might wear a cap of the same shape but embroidered in black thread. The third of this group, *Fig. 319,* illustrates a market woman who wears a black straw hat with downward-sloping brim over her indoor white cap. The little crown echoes the shape of the cap crown and probably fits snugly over it.

For country wear in summer straw hats were usual in England, France, Germany and Spain. In

---

[1]The disfigurement of so many effigies and monuments in English churches, under Cromwell's orders, has lost to England a great wealth of historical evidence of sartorial details.

FIG. 316   Dutch

FIG. 317   Dutch

FIG. 318   Dutch

1667, Samuel Pepys, recording the return from a visit to his father at Bampton, writes 'At Hatfield, being come back and weary in the walk, the women had pleasure in putting on some straw hats, which are so much worn in the country, and did become them mightily, but especially my wife.'

In the 1660's hair-styles departed from the simple elegance of natural-looking ringlets, and curls were held rigidly away from the head on wires, as in *Fig. 320*. In France the preference was for curls arranged close to the head, except for two long corkscrews, standing well away from the face on each side *(Fig. 321)*. On such curled heads might be placed a small black velvet hat with flowing ostrich feathers *(Fig. 322)*.

The little "quiff" over the forehead is not a remnant of the fifteenth century *frontage* but a flattened lock of hair called a *foretop* in imitation of Queen Catherine of Braganza who came from Portugal to wed Charles II wearing such a lock of hair in the old-fashioned manner. It was considered a little ridiculous by the London beauties but was adopted in moderation by those who wished to conciliate or flatter her. In his diary Pepys says of Catherine of Braganza, seen in *Fig. 323*, "Her foretop was long and turned aside strangely". And here is Samuel Pepys's description of the same beauties: "I followed them up Whitehall and into the Queen's preserve where all the ladies walked, talking and fiddling with their hats and changing and trying one another's

FIG. 319   Dutch

FIG. 321   French (1662–28)

FIG. 320   English (1664)

FIG. 322   English (1660)

by one another's heads and laughing. But above all, Mrs. Stewart, in this dress, with her hat cocked and a red plume . . . is now the greatest beauty I ever saw."

During the reign of William and Mary, or a little before, women began to sweep away their curls, as in *Fig. 324*, where the side hair is drawn on to the top of the head and at the back is allowed to fall in two loose ringlets. With the severely low, plain neckline without necklace or lace kerchief, the full effect of good features and complexion colour was no longer overshadowed.

Throughout history women have adopted men's styles from time to time, but, until the seventeenth century, only in inessentials. *Fig. 325* is not of a man, as one might suppose, but of Henrietta Cavendish,

Lady Huntingtower, wearing full masculine outfit, save for the breeches. This vogue was deplored by the critical Samuel Pepys. The sitter in the portrait wears her own curly hair, or at any rate a very naturalistic wig, a cocked hat with feather fringe and a single pearl ornament on the underside of the brim to relieve the austerity.

Indoors, in the 1670's, little lace caps were fashionable, always with a ribbon bow in front and above the massive curly fringe. Towards the end of the century this form of head-dress became more and more elaborate. The *fontange*, as it was called, after its inventor, Mlle. de Fontage, generally consisted of a white cap of linen, cambric or lawn, with a small round caul or bag which fitted over the bun at the

FIG. 323   Spanish

FIG. 325   English (1723)

FIG. 324   English

FIG. 326   French

FIG. 327   English (1610)

FIG. 328   Dutch (1600)

FIG. 329   English

back of the head. Attached to the front of the fontange was a series of stiffened, fan-shaped pleated lace frills, forming the *pinner*. These were graduated in height, the tallest being placed at the back. A wire frame called a *commode* held the erection in place. The pinner was usually arranged with forward tilt, and two long streamers attached at the back fell behind the shoulders. A whole set of technical terms were invented to identify variations in the arrangement of this head-dress. A double pinner, for instance, was called a *settee*, a bonnet and pinner together were known as the *frelange*. Sometimes it was simply known as the *tour* (or tower). The mode spread from France to most European countries between 1690 and 1710, and was at its height at the turn of the century. *Fig. 326*, although dating from 1710, is a typical example of this French style. Under the whole confection the hair was curled and sometimes arranged in two coils, one on each side of the forehead. Or false curls might be inserted under the front of the fontange. Small curls, placed near the ears were called *confidants*.

MEN

During most of this century men led the way in hat fashion which reflected the exuberance and extravagances governing taste in general. Very few innovations were introduced in women's hats, which, on the whole, were copies of styles worn by their menfolk.

In 1604 James I incorporated the felt-makers of London in a Mistery or Guild, granting them 'divers privileges and liberties'. This attempt to support home industries and cut out competition from the import of French and Spanish beavers and felts indicates the popularity of both materials.

Fig. 327 shows a transitional style of 1610 in beaver. The brim is broadening and the crown growing taller but as yet it shows none of the elaborate trimming soon to appear. *Fig. 328* gives an inkling of the developments to come. A Dutch style, its crown is higher and a string of beads is thrown negligently round it. The effect is gay and spontaneous. The Dutch could afford to be cheerful and lively at this time, having recently thrown out the villainous Spanish Duke of Alva and built up a solidly prosperous little kingdom for themselves.

By the time Charles I came to the English throne hats had reached a perfection of grace and elegance never since surpassed. *Fig. 329* is the earliest version, with a wide brim cocked up at the back, allowing an ostrich feather of considerable size to be tucked between it and the crown and to droop gracefully over the edge. The quill appears to be diamond-studded and such a hat would almost certainly have had an ornamental band round the crown. 'He looks for all the world, with those spangled feathers, like a nobleman's bedpost', wrote a contemporary.

For sheer romantic appeal, however, nothing has since surpassed the Cavalier's beaver hat and feather, and so it has figured in innumerable paintings, both contemporary and later, from Abraham Bosse down to Ernest Crofts.

FIG. 330   English

Men now allowed their hair to grow long and to fall freely. The lovelock over the shoulder which looked so daring in the case of the Elizabethan Earl of Southampton, became a commonplace. In *Fig. 330* we see that Charles I was no longer the short-haired lad, the 'bobbed youth' that he had been dubbed earlier.

Long flowing locks and large cavalier hats achieved a nice balance and the one was calculated to set off the other. How these impressive gentlemen looked without their hats can be seen from the next two illustrations. *Fig. 331* is the Spanish Duke of Pastrina, who allowed his black hair to hang over his shoulders to his elbows, uncurled and unwaved. *Fig. 332* shows the hair of a Caroline courtier at its natural best, before the vogue for the wig set in.

FIG. 331   Spanish

The 1660's saw a dramatic change in men's hair-dressing styles: they gave up their own hair to wear wigs, a habit that was to endure for 150 years. Many reasons can be advanced for the custom. Maybe some men found their own hair insufficiently long, thick and wavy to meet the dictates of fashion. Or perhaps it seemed simpler to put on one's hair like a hat, leave it on a dummy stand and pull on a comfortable nightcap in the privacy of one's own room. When necessary one could send one's hair to the hair-dresser to be washed and re-dressed instead of spending hours submitting to his ministrations in person. One could, moreover, indulge one's preference for colours other than one's own or flatter one's ego by concealing greying or thinning locks.

Samuel Pepys has many references in his *Diaries* to the new fashion, after its inception about 1664. He refers, for instance, to the trouble of keeping his own head clean and trimmed, is tempted to experiment with a border or periwig and finally falls in

FIG. 332   English

with the trend. When he hears that the King is about to wear a periwig he remarks 'I never until now observed that the King is mighty grey'.

By 1665 the wig had become indispensable for all except countrymen and artisans, and even these followed suit where possible, servants often wearing their masters' cast-off periwigs.

About 1638 the large flat-brimmed beaver or felt hat that was to develop into the simple style worn by the Puritans is seen for the first time. *Fig. 333* marks the beginning of the Puritan vogue: tall-crowned hat set well on the head, hair uncurled, and plain collar with only the narrowest of lace edging.

On the Continent the taste for romantic styles persisted. In Holland, indeed, the cavalier hat was exaggerated to absurdity, as we see in *Fig. 334*, dating between 1645 and 1654. Grotesquely large, its upturned brim completely hides the crown. A more moderate French version appears in *Fig. 335*. Set squarely on the long combed-out hair (with its lovelock tied in a bow) this hat is trimmed with a contrasting feather laid along the brim.

Fig. 336 shows a gentleman of the Netherlands wearing a periwig in its earliest form, assimilating natural hair as far as possible. The effect is that of a luxuriant crop of hair, wavy and long, and over it the hat necessarily has to have a larger crown. This huge model is of beaver, with several ostrich plumes (instead of one as previously) symmetrically placed inside the upturned brim and drooping over the

FIG. 333   English

FIG. 335   French (1650)

FIG. 334   Dutch (1645)

FIG. 336   Netherlandish (1660)

sides. The crown, it will be noted, is lower than in earlier years and between 1666 and 1670 fashionable hats had low flat crowns and wide stiff brims like those worn by Spanish dancers of the twentieth century. *Fig. 337* shows this new mode with bows of ribbon on the brim.

All these large hats, whether of felt or beaver, were expensive, and could cost £3 or more. At today's values this would be very costly.

In their own homes, with the wig set aside on its dummy stand, a gentleman swathed his close-cropped or shaven head in a velvet bag. *Fig. 338* indicates how the bag was adjusted when it was worn by Henry Fitzroy, Duke of Grafton, the natural son of Charles II.

By 1680 the wig had become very important indeed, as we see in *Fig. 339*. It now has a multitude of curls, is longer and more enveloping and apparently there is no attempt to give the false hair an appearance of naturalness.

Meanwhile a completely new hat style, known to us (but not to its wearers) as the tricorne, had made its appearance in Europe and was to remain a favourite until nearly the end of the eighteenth century. An early example of this three-cornered shape, adopted by Peter the Great of Russia in 1670, is shown in *Fig. 340*. It will be noted that, a little more unconventional than his contemporaries farther west, he still wears his own hair, of moderate length.

The tricorne was a further development of the

FIG. 337   English (1678)

FIG. 339   English

FIG. 338   English

FIG. 340   Russian (1676)

low-crowned hat of James II's time, the flat brim being turned up on three sides, with one of the points so formed centred over the forehead. Although the shape remained static and was adopted all over Europe for so long, individual wearers asserted their independence by slight differences of decoration. Along the upper edge of the brim feather fronds might be sewn, the under-edge being faced with gold braid, as in the one worn by Peter the Great above. The ribbon cockade later became a feature of military uniform hats.

Ribbons and plumes became rarer as the feather frond edging won favour, though nearly fifty years later, in 1717, John Gray could jauntily comment:

'While wretched is the wit, condemed forlorn,
Whose gummy hat no scarlet plumes adorn.'

Among the élite, however, metal braid or lace made from gold or silver thread was steadily gaining favour. *Fig. 341* is a typical example of a cocked hat with a feather fringe round the brim. It is worn by a French general with one of the heavily curled wigs now in fashion.

By the 1680's wigs, like men's clothes, had become weighty and cumbersome. Hyacinthe Rigaud, French painter of the court of Louis XIV, has given us some magnificent portraits showing that *homo sapiens* was now little more than a mere prop for a mountain of clothes surmounted by a colossal wig. *(Fig. 342)*.

In England small caps were worn by fox-hunting lords down from the shires and were affected by young gentlemen who possibly never rode to hounds or in a race in their lives. Such a cap *(Fig. 343)* dating 1681 was the prototype of the present day jockey cap.

CHILDREN AND YOUNG PEOPLE

During the earlier years of the century babies were still tightly wrapped in swaddling clouts (or cloths) and had linen hoods to cover the head, as in *Fig. 344*. Older children were generally dressed in modified versions of adult styles, and as men, as well as women, enthusiastically adopted lace as a trimming, it is not surprising that we find plenty of it on boys' clothes. *Fig. 345* shows a young Flemish boy of the period in a lace-edged cap or bonnet to match his collar.

Lace is also worn by the little girl in *Fig. 346* (from a painting by Lely). Her front hair is taken back over her lace cap and pinned in loose curls to the crown of her head, from which several ringlets are allowed to fall freely. It is evident that her pretty, richly auburn hair is being trained to look like her mother's.

By the sixteen-sixties ostrich plumes and large hats were very generally worn (among those, at least, who could afford them) and *Fig. 347* shows a little girl from Holland so attired. Over her silky fair hair the hat, of black velour, is tied on with red ribbons and has a matching ribbon band round the crown. From the back rises a cluster of red, black and white ostrich feathers.

While the Stuarts in England were beginning to dress their hair in more natural styles, Spanish ladies, some years behind the rest of Europe in matters of fashion, still dressed theirs and their little

FIG. 341   French

FIG. 342   French (1680–90)

Fig. 343   English (1689)

Fig. 346   English

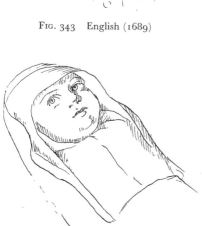

Fig. 344   English (1630)

Fig. 347   Dutch (c. 1666)

Fig. 345   Flemish

Fig. 348   Spanish

FIG. 349   English (1610)

FIG. 350   English (late 16th and 17th cents.)

daughters' stiffly and most formally. The Infanta in *Fig. 348* has her hair drawn rigidly back from the forehead and then plaited or twisted into numerous separate strands tied at the ends with vermilion ribbons. The whole must have been supported on a wire frame of some sort in order to stand away from the head in such a manner. A spray of ostrich feathers is attached to the front and droops towards the left shoulder.

The student in *Fig. 349* wears the seventeenth century version of the mortar-board with "iiij cumly corners" regarded as so admirable by the chronicler John Stowe.

MILITARY

The wig and cocked hat were as much a feature of seventeenth century military attire as of civilian and *Fig. 341* shows a French general in both. The brim of the hat is edged with a feather fringe.

When standing armies took the place of feudal or even city companies of soldiers—as in Holland—uniforms became standardised and were authorised or altered only by order of the king or government. Red coats were officially introduced in England in 1645 in this way and were worn with the plain felt hat, or breast-plate and *morion*. The latter, illustrated in *Fig. 350*, had been introduced at the very end of the previous century but can be regarded as a typical military style of the seventeenth. It was later replaced by the three-pointed cocked hat.

Eighteenth Century

WOMEN

WE HAVE SEEN in the previous chapter how, by the turn of the century, the head-dress known as the fontange or *tour* was the height of fashion. Its popularity lasted well into the eighteen-hundreds. *Fig. 351* exemplifies the style as worn by older women in England. The arrangement of fan-shaped pleats is low but supplemented with stiff ribbon bows and a deeper lace edge to the cap. The hair is rather more simply dressed than in portraits of younger women at the time but artfully arranged curls are trained becomingly over the temples. *Fig. 352* of a French woman wearing a fontange, shows an unusual instance where the double row of goffered folds continues all round the face to the shoulders. Height is added by fabric (or ribbon) peaks on the crown of the head.

Lace, it should be noted, was popular for outdoor as well as indoor wear. In *Fig. 353* it edges the kind of hood favoured by older women throughout the greater part of the century.

Indoors women invariably wore domed caps of lace or linen and also kept them on in the street in fine weather.

The high *tour* of the late seventeenth century and early eighteen-hundreds fell into disfavour as the years went on. Instead, the little flat lace cap called a *pinner* became all the rage. It took various forms, sometimes having lappets (or tabs of ribbon) that could be tied under the chin and *Fig. 354* gives an example of the pinner with side lappets left unfastened. The cap, fitting snugly over the head, is encircled with a ribbon and bow. This style was favoured by a princess, sister of Frederick, Prince of Wales.

As with women's head-dresses in Tudor times, the loose-hanging lappets were found to be inconvenient (too apt to dip in the soup, perhaps) and were removed to the top of the head to be out of the way. Soon they disappeared altogether. In *Fig. 355* the wearer has turned up the lappets and pinned them to her cap where, at least at one side, they are fastened in place with a starry brooch. A little frill of lace with Vandyck points is added across the forehead.

The pinner continued in favour till the middle years of the century and is seen at its prettiest in *Fig. 356* in which narrow pleating graduated to-

FIG. 351   English

FIG. 352   French (1725)

FIG. 353   English (17th cent.)

FIG. 356   English

FIG. 354   English

FIG. 357   English (1722)

FIG. 355   English (1735)

FIG. 358   German (1732)

wards the centre is carefully adjusted over simply arranged hair. Hats could be conveniently and comfortably set on the head without removing the cap, or pinner, if the wearer so wished. In *Fig. 357* a pretty English girl may be observed in a shady straw with plain ribbons round the crown, over a lace (or broderie anglaise) pinner. In Germany the same custom obtained, as we see in the drawing of the country girl in *Fig. 358*. Her rustic straw bonnet almost conceals the pinner but it is there—just visible as a small lace cap behind the front ringlets and covering her bun at the back.

A little later in the century a youthful style made its appearance. Fine muslin or gauze was then used for the little caps and a bright-coloured lining added to show through the nearly transparent white fabric.

For a few years in mid-century women experimented with other forms of head adornment. A contemporary writer observed 'They wear no caps, only substitute a variety of trumpery ribbons'. But the change took time to establish itself, as is indeed evident from the next illustration, dated 1760, and coming from France, *(Fig. 359)*. Here a dainty little cap with ribbon bow over the forehead is covered by a neat dark bonnet with a velvet border. The picture from which this is taken shows a mother dressing her little daughter to go out. She is pinning the bonnet to the cap while the child eyes her reflection in a mirror.

For excursions into the open air older women adopted a cap with spreading wings on either side of the face, called a *pulteney*, *(Fig. 360)*.

In France during the reign of Louis XV women's hair was simply and elegantly dressed (See *Fig. 361*), waved and powdered and set with little bunches of artificial flowers. A band of ribbon with a bow often encircled the neck and completed the effect when the decolletage was very low, as here. Mme. de Pompadour, who was noted for her exquisite taste, probably started the practice, or, recognising its grace and attractiveness, adopted it and so made it fashionable.

In *Fig. 362* the Venetian lady of our illustration has had her white-powdered hair dressed in this way. Her mantilla is of fine black lace and a black tricorne is placed over all. The hat flaunts a white ostrich feather, kept in place with a large jewelled brooch. With such an ensemble a *mask* was often worn, sometimes of black velvet, sometimes shaped to the face in

FIG. 359   French (1760)

FIG. 360   English

FIG. 361   French

papier maché. Loo masks were half-masks, covering the face to the nose only and worn in fine weather: on windy days a whole mask took its place.

> 'Loo masks, and whole, as wind do blow
> And mis abroad's disposed to go.'

This illustration and the succeeding one indicate clearly how faithfully women copied men's hat styles at this period. *Fig. 363* is an extravagant version of the cocked hat from Germany. The lady from Strasbourg who wears it has donned what is possibly the largest example ever seen on a female head. A very small jewel fastens the upturned brim to the crown at the front and the severity of the effect is offset by a soft lace fichu and laced bodice.

In France, about the year 1757, a new and pretty hat shape was introduced and became a great favourite with artists, who saw its picturesque value. Worn as in *Fig. 364* over the simple Pompadour hair style, it consisted of a circle of straw or goffered linen rising steeply at the back of the head to provide a platform for a profusion of artificial flowers, ribbons and feathers. It had no crown worth mentioning but more flowers and ribbons were tucked behind and beneath the tilt at the back, so helping to balance it on the head. For an English version see *Fig. 365* and note the cap visible at the back.

During the latter half of the century sophisticated court circles in several European countries, notably France and England, affected artless-seeming rustic styles which were supposed to represent the dress of shepherds and shepherdesses. (They are familiar nowadays in many examples of Dresden, Sèvres and other porcelain figures.) *Fig. 366* is a pretty dyed straw hat from France, showing the craze for idealised shepherdess attire.

In the seventeen-sixties women began to pile their hair higher and higher, eventually reaching such outrageous dimensions as to call forth sarcasm, abuse and endless caricature. In *Fig. 367*, dating between 1775 and 1780, the hair has been raised over a high foundation, with formal curls on either side and a tight little roll at the back. Obviously such a style could not easily support a large heavy hat and in this English example (called a half-moon toupée) it is lightly tied with a dark scarf and ornamented on the raised crown. *Fig. 368* is a further English instance of the high-piled hair style, with each tuft arranged separately and layered to form a three-tiered structure, surmounted by another small scarf. The wearer, from whose portrait this sketch was adapted, was a pretty, gentle type of mother with her young child, and by no means an eccentric exhibitionist, so we can judge from this that the mode was generally prevalent. From *Fig. 369*, which gives the back view of one of these creations, this time from France, the height can be gauged by comparing it with the width of the wearer's shoulders. A thick plait of hair is turned up and fastened with a ribbon, while the front is mounted on a frame and the whole topped by three ostrich feathers and three aigrettes. *Fig. 370* shows an English example, simpler but no less bulky.

For outdoors in fine weather a second scarf or kerchief, usually made of gauze was thrown over the head-dress.

FIG. 362   Venetian (1714)

FIG. 363   German

FIG. 364   French (1777)

FIG. 367   English (1775–1780)

FIG. 365   English (1760)

FIG. 368   English (1778)

FIG. 366   French

FIG. 369   French

FIG. 370   English (1780)

FIG. 371   English (1780–1800)

FIG. 372   English

To accommodate these voluminous hair styles a large collapsible hood called a *calash*, constructed in sections like the hood of a carriage, was invented.[1] It pulled up over the head by a string attached to the whalebone hoops which supported the contraption. Even the less bulky and more moderate versions of this fashionable form of hair-styling needed hats with very large crowns such as can be seen in *Fig. 371,* Here the crown and brim are made of cloth or velvet and the whole is trimmed with bows of the same fabric. The wearer has her hair done on the style called the *banging chignon.*

One very real danger run by the wearers of these elaborate head-dresses was fire. While candles were still the main source of illumination accidents were not uncommon. Samuel Pepys mentions one such incident. 'Here I also, standing by a candle that was brought in for sealing a letter, do set my perriwig afire, which made such an odd noise, nobody could tell what it was till they saw the flame my back being towards the candle.'

The Duc de St. Simon a contemporary of Pepys at the Court of Louis XIV, records in his *Memoires:* 'On Friday night Mme de Charlus was supping here with a large company. She was ill-dressed as usual but for once, most fashionably wearing one of those head-dresses called *commodes*, that were not fastened in any way to the ladies' heads. They were vastly high contraptions and were removed or put on just as men put on or take off their wigs and nightcaps. Mme de Charlus was sitting next to Le Tellier, the Archbishop of Rheims. As she was removing the top of a boiled egg, she leaned forward to take salt, and accidentally stuck her head into the flame of a neighbouring candle. The Archbishop, seeing her on fire, hurled himself at the head-dress and flung it to the ground, whereupon Mme de Charlus in amazement and fury at finding herself de-wigged for no apparent reason threw the egg into the Archbishop's face and it ran down all over him. He did nothing but laugh, and the entire company was in fits at seeing the ancient grey dirty head of Mme de Charlus and the omlet she had made on the Archbishop. Especially comic was her rage and abuse, for she imagined she had been insulted and would hear no excuse and then suddenly perceived that she had been left bald before the world. By this time Mme la

[1]See drawing in *History of English Costume.*

Princesse de Conti had sent for another but before it could be placed on her head there was plenty of time to contemplate her charms and for her to continue with her furious protests.

The *commode* mentioned above was 'a frame of wire two or three stories high fitted on the head, and covered with tiffany or other thin silks; being now compleated into the whole head-dress'.[1]

Women went to extraordinary lengths to achieve these elaborate high-piled coiffures. They used *cushions* (pads made of horse or cow hair, tow or wool) to support their own hair or additional false locks. *Rolls* were smaller devices for the same purpose. 'I had my head-dress roll on', writes Anna Green Winslow in her diary in 1771. 'It makes my head ache and burn and itch like anything. This famous roll is not made wholly of red cow-tail but is a mixture of that and horsehair—very coarse, and a little human hair of yellow hue.'

The hair was manoeuvred into a variety of shapes: buckles, shells, spindles, locks, parcels, dragons and serpents etc. plastered with pomade and often powdered as well.

For the country the straw hat maintained its popularity and usefulness. (Straw, as a decoration for women's jackets and men's coats, also, had become quite 'the rage'.) Girls and women might wear light, wide-brimmed leghorn straw hats over their *mob-caps* as in *Fig. 372*. Here the folds of the cap are encircled by a dark-coloured ribbon. A second ribbon forms the hat band and is tied in a knot in front. The frill at the neck is dainty and feminine but the coat with its revers has a masculine look somewhat out of keeping with the rest.

Mob caps varied slightly in form but all were drawn up with a tape where the brim and crown met and so could be laid flat for laundering and ironing. All were starched. *Fig. 373* is a French style, worn without a hat, and *Fig. 374* is the even less pretentious cap of a young working woman. In both these cases the hair is unpowdered. *Fig. 375* shows the mob cap at its best, and *Fig. 376* illustrated the immense hat now necessary to accommodate both high-piled hair and mob-cap in addition.

During the last twenty years of the century women's hair styles increased still further in dimensions but now it was width rather than height which

[1] Ladies' Dictionary. 1694.

FIG. 373   French

FIG. 374   English

FIG. 375   English (1780)

was every woman's aim. Hats, of course, had to conform to the new hair fashions and at the same time they became more ornate, as we see from *Fig. 377*. In this picture the sitter has a fuzzy wig probably of the type called *herisson* (or hedgehog). Her tall-crowned hat is edged and banded with bias-striped ribbon and is surmounted with the ever-popular ostrich feathers. From the left side and over the brim to the shoulder falls a cascade of more ribbons. Nowadays we might regard such over-exuberance of trimming as ridiculous but in this case the effect is not unattractive.

Long locks falling down the back and over the shoulders were now favoured and it became easier to support the enormous 'picture' style we call the

Gainsborough hat, which can be seen in *Fig. 378*. It was made famous by this artist's portrait of the lovely Duchess of Devonshire who wore it for her sittings. Made of felt or beaver, and with ostrich plumes sweeping up and over the crown, which was bound round with ribbon, it was steeply tilted to show to advantage the grey powdered wig. The hair has an artfully tousled appearance at the top and side with loose ringlets down the back.

A wig, which is plainly a herisson, or hedgehog, of shapeless fuzziness, appears in *Fig. 379*, as worn by the Spanish Marquise de San Andres. It is loaded with ostrich feathers, bunches of ribbon, lace, strings of beads, and jewelled brooches. Accounts of such monstrous wigs credit them with being the resting

FIG. 376   English

FIG. 378   English

FIG. 377   English (1780–1800)

FIG. 379   Spanish

place for model sailing ships, flower gardens and other set pieces, but the author of this book has failed to find any contemporary portrait featuring them. It may well be that in attempting to throw scorn on the current absurdities writers have resorted to artistic exaggeration. It is true, however, that incongruous ornaments such as a coach-and-six, a farm-yard with piglets, plates of fruit, and so on, were made in blown glass and, being very light, they could be pinned to false hair as a form of decoration. The Spanish portrait of Queen Louise *(Fig. 380)* approaches the level of caricature and vulgarity. Here is piled-up hair bearing a load of lace, ribbons and feathers, without taste, orderliness or discretion.

By way of contrast note the restraint of the style adopted by the French artist, Madame Labelle-Giuard, in *Fig. 381*. Daintily curled hair is balanced by a wide straw hat with judiciously few ribbons at one side and one ostrich feather and a little aigrette at the other.

In *Fig. 382,* from Sweden, we again have high-piled hair but this time draped with a *fascinator* of net and ribbon, decorated with shell-like twists of what may be ribbon or fabric. Voluminous hair-styles could display such fascinators and lace scarves to advantage. A black lace mantilla typical of Spain is so worn in *Fig. 383*. It is held in place by a comb, itself decorated with rosettes of ribbon and lace.

In the last decade of the century the feminine addiction to men's hat styles we saw earlier is still

FIG. 380 Spanish

FIG. 382 Swedish (1785)

FIG. 381 French (1790) Mme Labelle-Gurard. Self-portrait

FIG. 383 Spanish (1780–90)

FIG. 384   English or Irish (1794)

FIG. 385   French

FIG. 386   English (1730)

very evident, as may be readily seen in *Fig. 384.* Here the Countess of Tyrcomil favours a tall masculine type hat enhanced by a rosette in front and displaying the usual ostrich feathers drooping gracefully over the top of the crown. Her wig is tied with ribbon bows, in the manner of her husband's, and her coat, masculine in cut, sets off the mannish hat. That such an outfit was planned for travelling is stressed by the large woolly muffler swathed round the throat. She is thus ready to face the gales in the strait or the highwayman on the heath.

MEN

Wigs became ever more popular and were worn throughout the eighteenth century. Like every other fashion, they were subject to change and development. The *toupée* was introduced about 1730 and was one such modification. It was a method of brushing the wearer's natural front hair back over the wig, thus eliminating the ridge between wig and scalp that would otherwise have been obvious. After being stuck in position with pomatum, natural hair and wig were heavily powdered, thus concealing any difference in colour. Hair powder was introduced at the beginning of the century but was not generally used until the eighteen-forties. The powder used, had by law, to contain starch, and those coiffeurs who sold starchless powder were fined or imprisoned. From then on, for about fifty years, it was adopted throughout Europe, especially for evening and social occasions.

Eventually wigs became so formalized that no attempt was made to give them a natural appearance. In fact men sometimes had their own hair dressed to simulate a wig and some wigs were even made of feathers. Apparently feather wigs became particularly popular among clergymen, usually in the form of a *toupée*. 'For some swore it was an owl in a feather-top wig.'

Fig. 385 shows a full wig with centre parting and symmetrical peaks at each side, as worn in France.

In 1745 Horace Walpole wrote: 'I could have no hope of getting to his ear for he has put on such a first-rate tie-wig that nothing without the lungs of a boatswain can ever penetrate the thickness of his curls.'

Fig. 386 gives us a good example of a sedate, well-fed higher-class Englishman with his centre-parted, heavily curled wig, and our next illustration, *Fig. 387* provides an excellent idea of a clerical wig, as formal as that of a modern judge. It would undoubtedly have had a small queue at the back since the full-bottomed wig without a queue, such as Dr. Johnson favoured, was discontinued by young men after 1730 and by their elders some years later. By mid-century long queues had become an essential part of the wig, whatever style the latter assumed, as we can see from *Fig. 388*. Here the lengthy pigtail is bound with ribbons and tied with a bow at each end. That part of the wig which covers the head is still small enough to accommodate the large tricorne hat with its brim typically ornamented with what may be feather fronds or a narrow lace frill.

Because wigs, like hats, could be donned or doffed

at will and wig styles were so exaggerated, hats became untenable with them, and, instead, a small collapsible hat called a *chapeau bras* was carried under the arm. By the end of the century the chapeau bras was made to fold flat so that the sides of the brim met and concealed the soft crown.

The feather fronds of the seventeenth century gave way to gold and silver galloons (from Fr. *galon*) and a wide band of braid decorated the brim of the cocked hat until well into the eighteen-hundreds.

Beaver fur was the most popular material for making hats, and such hats were called *castors* (from the French word for the animal). When part beaver and part coney (i.e. rabbit) they were known as demi-castors. Nicolas Rowe in *The Biter* says 'I do not

FIG. 387   English

FIG. 389   English

FIG. 388   English

FIG. 390   Italian

FIG. 391   English

FIG. 392   English

FIG. 393   English

think a demi-castor with fashionable edging a very gentlemanlike kind of ornament'. Although he wrote this in 1705, he might have expressed the same personal opinion at any time during the rest of the century.

After 1760 the bag-wig depicted in *Fig. 389* was generally adopted, possibly because it was tidier and more practical wear for professional men with work to do. As in this picture, the queue was confined in a silk bag which closed with a drawstring, itself concealed by a large black ribbon bow. Sometimes, as in *Fig. 390,* from Italy, the bow had long ends which were brought round to the front and tied in a second bow over the cravat. This style originated earlier at the court of Louis XV and was called a *solitaire.*

'Now quite a Frenchman in his garb and air,
His neck yoked down with bag and solitaire.'[1]

The English wig in *Fig. 391* is the simplest version of these fantastic fashions.

In 1763 the vogue for wigs seemed for a time to be losing ground and consequently the wig-makers petitioned the king to encourage the trade by 'not wearing his own hair'. Their appeal was ridiculed by the timber merchants, who suggested that wooden legs should be worn to encourage their trade in wood.

The cocked hat took various new forms at this time, some of them exaggerated versions of earlier fashions. The points were frequently elongated as in *Fig. 392* a style which in England was known as the 'Egham, Staines and Windsor', from the triangular position of these three towns in relation to one another.

Where the brim touched the crown it was often held in place with a ribbon cockade, and many flaunted jewelled brooches. Mrs. Delauney writes in 1709 'The King's hat was buttoned up with prodigious fine diamonds'.

Cockades, as worn by the military, were seen on civilian hats and the front of the hat was then given a smart pinch as in *Fig. 393* where, it will be noted, the front peak has become less prominent and sharply pointed—a foretaste of the two-cornered hat to come. A contemporary writer (1753) observes 'The fore part of my hat was considerably elevated so that it now no longer resembles a spout but the corner of a mince-pie'.

Most hats still had a gold galloon round the brim,

---

[1] *The Modern Fine Gentleman,* 1746.

as we have seen in Figs. 392 and 393. The *Keven-huller* hat was a 'heavy dragoon type' with wide gold braid, and the *Denmark Cock* high at the back, low in front and tilted forward.

In Scotland, farther from the fashion centres, some local styles were independently adopted. The small round toque for instance in the wearer's tartan *(Fig. 394)* sits well on a small white wig and its feathers give it dash. The style looks handsome and dignified.

In *Fig. 395* a splendid tricorne, with the usual feather sandwiched between brim and crown, is worn by a young Spanish grandee the Conde Fernan Nuñez. His hair is unpowdered, showing that towards the end of the century the custom was going out of fashion. His side-whiskers too—quite exceptional in the eighteenth century and seldom seen in conjunction with a cocked hat—are in advance of his times, as they did not become popular until worn with the 'topper' twenty-five years or so later. The young Conde has fine eyebrows, if they are his own, but it was quite a feature of the period to wear eyebrows of mouse fur.

During the last years of the century Spaniards, at least, confined the long queues of their wigs (or their own hair) in a snood of net or patterned fabric, with front edge midway across the crown of the head, passing behind the ears, and tied at the top with a ribbon bow. The man in *Fig. 396* also wears side whiskers in the manner of the Conde Fernan Nuñez (and the Barber of Seville!).

In England the tricorne was, at least in some

FIG. 395   Spanish (end of 18th cent.)

FIG. 396   Spanish

FIG. 394   Scottish (18th cent.)

FIG. 397   English (1778)

FIG. 398   English

FIG. 399   French

quarters, losing favour, and most of the younger men in George Morland's pictures are painted with a round beaver hat having a brim of medium width, firm flat crown, and buckled bands placed one above the other, as shown in *Fig. 397*. The next illustration *(Fig. 398)* is another version of the same kind of hat, worn with a similar style of wig. Maybe the young country gentlemen Morland liked to depict were the first to adopt this more practical and comfortable headgear, which was also very handsome.

A hat called the *Nivernois* became fashionable about the year 1775. In the memoirs of William Hickey we read of a Mr. John Rider who 'returned from his French excursion . . . with a little skimming dish of a hat—the brim not four inches deep, two of which was covered with silver lace and immensely wide in front . . . The hat he purchased in Calais. It had been introduced by the Duc de Nivernois and was therefore known as the *chapeau Nivernois*. I obtained a Nivernois even more outr é than Rider's.'

Ballooning was taken up with enthusiasm at the end of the century, and, like most new sports, made new demands on hat designers. Here, in *Fig. 399,* is a French pioneer in this branch of aeronautics. He wears a cap of leopard skin over his powdered wig, which is tied loosely with a black bow. There also exists a delightful engraving of a Major Money, who is being rescued after his balloon has come down in the sea. He looks in the circumstances unexpectedly immaculate, his white wig still securely hugging his head, not a hair of it awry.

Both men and women in England and France

FIG. 400   English or French

FIG. 401   French (1793)

wore the type of soft cloth hat with turned-up fur brim that we see in *Fig. 400* for riding and it was known as the *montero* (Spanish *montera*).

Fig. 401 shows a style and shape made famous later by the Duke of Wellington. Here it is worn by a Frenchman, member of the National Assembly in the eighteen-nineties. The steeply turned-up brim bears a bunch of ostrich feathers and is sewn with gold galloon on the under side which, now, becomes the outer one.

It will be seen that the wearer of the hat in the preceding illustration has no wig. In this last decade wigs went out of fashion with comparative suddenness. France was always a fashion pace-setter, even in her most troublous times, and during the French

reasonably small and is of beaver, coney or felt, with an uprolled brim. He flaunts his political allegiance with a tri-colour sash tied round the brim but the incongruity of the ostrich feather militates against the effectiveness of its symbolism. The apparently unkempt hair and unfashionable moustache of this *citoyen* also seem to strike a discordant note but were no doubt adopted to underline his allegiance to the people's cause.

A third member of the Assembly, M. Barbaroux, sports the light-coloured beaver hat now entering the scene *(Fig. 403)*. It has a simple band and buckle but no feather. There will be no return to powder and wig: monsieur's hair is his own and carefully tended. Sad to say, this young man, fearing that the

FIG. 402   French

FIG. 403   French (1793)

Revolution and after, so great was the fear of being thought an aristocrat and sent to the guillotine that people completely abandoned the wig. Powder, too, was part flour, and the *sans coulottes* were starving, so powder, too, was discontinued, for obvious reasons. Pitt's belated attempt to raise funds by a tax on powder finally killed the practice in England: and powder was henceforward given up here, except by the very elderly who could brook being called guinea-pigs, and felt under-dressed without it. Influenced by France, English men and women also abandoned their wigs.

Another member of the French National Assembly, Le Conventionel J. B. Milhaud, strikes a strange new note in *Fig. 402* with his round hat which is

noise of gunfire he heard was made by soldiers coming to arrest him, lost his nerve and shot himself!

Throughout the eighteenth century comfortable caps were worn by men when the wig was removed, as we have noted, and even when wigs were no longer the mode caps of white cotton or embroidered linen were worn in bed. Harriette Wilson, in her *Memoirs*, remarks 'But something I determined on; so miserably tired was I of Craven, and his cocoa trees and his sailing boats, and his ugly cotton night-cap. Surely, I would say, all men do not wear these shocking night-caps, else all women's illusions had been destroyed on the first night of marriage.' Harriette Wilson was wrong. Men were very fond of their cotton night-caps and clung to them firmly until nearly the end of the following century. We have only to think of Cruikshank's illustrations to the novels of Dickens to recall many examples.

CHILDREN

In this century it was still customary to dress children in miniature versions of the styles worn by adults and in *Fig. 404* we have a small *pinner* worn by a little girl. Such a cap often had white streamers at the back.

A tiny boy is shown in *Fig. 405,* wearing a French bonnet edged with lace and held in place with a thick belt-like band. His little sisters would wear pinners like their mother's of the same construction as in Fig. 409 (See page 129).

An Austrian prince whose portrait, *Fig. 406,* dates from 1760 has his head completely covered in a pleated lace bonnet adorned with a feather.

Fig. 407 provides us with an idea of mid-century hair styles and hats such as would be worn by a lad of between ten and twelve. His tricorne resembles his father's but his own curled brown hair is not powdered (although parents and governesses are known to have powdered children's hair for special occasions). A ribbon bow ties this young boy's queue and holds it neatly away from neck and shoulders. Chardin, who painted the original portrait, also produced an exquisite picture called *The Reprimand* in which a boy, dressed like the one in our illustration, is ready for school, his books tucked under his arm, while his mother, with his hat in one hand and a brush in the other, scolds him for its dirty condition.

Boys in those days were evidently as fond of snatching each other's hats and throwing them into a pond or a puddle as they are today.

We have seen how straw hats were much worn by girls and women in the country. *Fig. 408* proves that little boys wore them as well. This young man has a hat with a blue moiré ribbon band and rosette.

Ribbon was even more popular for little girls and in *Fig. 409* we can admire the large blue ribbon bows that trim the wearer's cap of broderie anglaise. Such a cap was similar in construction to the mob-caps described on page 119.

In Denmark in the seventeen-eighties boys were wearing the type of cap seen in *Fig. 410*. It has a stiff and shiny peak shading his eyes and, instead of a conventional crown, a tapering bag ending in a tassel and resembling a brewer's cap. We may possibly suppose that such a cap was the forerunner of the twentieth century students' caps with their stiffened peaks and soft tops, as seen in Germany, the Scandinavian countries and other parts of Europe.

Eighteenth century students wore the tie-wig when it became fashionable, the hair being drawn away from the face and the curls bunched together to form a queue, which was then tied with a black ribbon.

During the last half of the century the heads of small babies were covered with a cap, embroidered or edged with lace. From a list of the clothes worn by infants admitted to the Coram Foundling Hospital we may read 'A male child, about a fortnight old, very neatly dressed, a fine holland cap with cambric

FIG. 404   English

FIG. 405   French

FIG. 406   Austrian (1760)

FIG. 409   English (1790)

FIG. 407   French (1750)

FIG. 410   Danish (1785)

FIG. 408   English (1788)

FIG. 411   English (1808)

border, white dimity sleeves etc.' Mention is also made of 'a male child a week old, wearing holland cap with plain border, edged forehead . . .'

MILITARY

Military headwear in the eighteenth century seems to have been uniformly tall-crowned, as the following examples make it clear. The first, in *Fig. 411,* is the fur hat of the 10th Hussars, a regiment raised in Hertfordshire in 1715. Its plume is red and white. The second, in *Fig. 412,* is an English Grenadier's sugar-loaf cap of 1770 and the third, *Fig. 413,* an officer's hat worn at the Battle of Seringapatan in 1799. The crown and brim of the last of these three are of felt and the hat has a feather crest and plume. It accompanies a white wig with ribbon queue.

In 1799 soldiers of all ranks were ordered to wear their hair in a queue or pigtail up to ten inches in length, tied with a black ribbon, level with the upper part of the collar.

The first *busby (Fig. 414)* was introduced in 1760. It is a tall hat of bearskin, black sable or black Persian lamb.

The English soldier in *Fig. 415* has a powdered tie-wig such as he would wear in civilian life, with the queue upturned and fastened with a ribbon. Over it his *fantail* cocked hat, edged with braid, is squarely set. Such fantail hats were introduced in 1780 and this example was worn two years later.

Fig. 412   English (1770)

Fig. 414   English (1760)

Fig. 413   English (1799)

Fig. 415   English

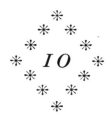

10

Nineteenth Century

WOMEN

FASHIONS FOR WOMEN changed dramatically early in the 19th century; gone were the fichus, the hooped skirts, the towering wigs and the powder and pomatum. Everything had to be simple and flowing *à la grecque*. Was this not the Age of Reason? Paris, after its revolution, led the way.

The Countess of Brownlow, though writing much later, speaks of the styles she saw in her younger days:—'The Peace of 1802 brought, I suppose, many French to England, but I remember only one, the celebrated Mme. Récamier who created a sensation . . . by her dress which was vastly unlike the unsophisticated styles and poke bonnets of the English women. She appeared in Kensington Gardens, à la antique, a muslin dress clinging to her form like the folds of drapery on a statue, her hair in a plait at the back and falling in small ringlets round her face and greasy with huile antique. A large veil thrown over her head completed her attire and not unnaturally caused her to be followed and stared at.'[1]

[1]*Slight Reminiscences of a Septuagenarian.* 1867 by the Countess Brownlow.

Ancient Greece was not the only distant country to influence fashion designers. The travels of Lady Wortley Montague in the Far East were undoubtedly responsible for the popularity of the turban which many women adopted early in the 19th century. It could be worn with dress or undress. (See *Figs. 416* and *417*).

Both of these last two examples illustrate the new short hair styles which became popular with the younger set at this time. Harriette Wilson[1] is said to have worn her hair shortly curled all over her head like an untidy school-boy and certainly her beaus liked ruffling her curls; whilst Ida de St. Elme, in France, author of the *Memoirs of a Contemporary*, recounts that at a dinner at Prince Talleyrands' being asked if she curled her hair with papelots and how, on her admitting it, he went to a drawer and took out a bundle of bank notes and with these put her hair in curl-papers, so that she went home a richer woman.

But even in this era of simple hairdressing a good deal of false hair must have been worn. Readers of

[1]See the Memoires of Harriette Wilson.

FIG. 416

FIG. 417 French (1812-20)

FIG. 418   French (1802)

FIG. 419   Swedish (1810)

FIG. 420   French (1810)

Les Misérables will remember how poor Fantine sold hers to support her child, and newspapers of the time carry such advertisements as the following, from the *Morning Post* in 1800: 'Correct imitations of nature for Ladies of Rank and Fashion . . . Full-Dress Head-dresses, made of long hair, judicially treated to correspond with Nature price 4 to 20 guineas. Real natural curl head-dresses are made of hair, originally straight but curled by baking, boiled, etc., 3 guineas. In order to account for the apparent high prices it is necessary to observe that there are as many qualities of Hair as of silk, fur or wool . . . all collected at fairs from French peasants which (from the very convulsed state) is now very dear, no part of it men's hair'.

The poke bonnets mentioned in Lady Brownlow's memoirs were indeed all the rage in England. They took various forms, from the tallest, resembling upturned waste-paper baskets, to low coal-scuttle shapes. The next three illustrations show a few of them. *Fig. 418* is a French model, of 1802, made of straw and embellished with loops of ribbon on the crown, the ends passing over the brim and tying under the chin.

The Swedish bonnet *(Fig. 419)* of 1810 is typical of many for everyday wear. Of light straw, with ribbon bows at the back of the crown ending in the usual streamers for tying, its trimming consists of a large bunch of artificial marguerites with black centres. A much more striking and elaborate style, also of 1810, is shown in *Fig. 420*. Such fantasies were termed *"Incroyables"* or *"Merveilleuses"*. The brims often projected so far forward as nearly to hide the whole face, and Gilray caricatures them, calling their wearers *"Les Invisibles"*.

Hats themselves had wider brims and in *Fig. 421* we have an ornate version, the crown decorated with tartan ribbon and the brim having bows above and beneath it, with a long matching ribbon loop.

Ribbons such as these and in many other colours and designs, which had been almost exclusively worn by men in the seventeenth century, became the prerogative of women and children henceforward. Millinery, especially bonnets with their tie-strings, demanded vast quantities of ribbon and bows appeared on evening dresses throughout the century.

The most exquisite figured silk, satin and velvet ribbons were made in France, St. Etienne being the centre of the industry. It is estimated that 100,000 people were employed in their production, and by 1855 47 million francs worth of velvet and embroidered ribbons alone were sold in the Department. The figure rose later to Fr. 111 millions. 350 manufacturers employed 30,000 workers at 15,000 ribbon looms.

By the end of the first quarter of the century fashions were again changing. Simple muslins over a coloured foundation of satin, however lovely, offered little scope for variety. Under the influence of Queen Adelaide, waists began to sink to normal levels, skirts got stiffer and hair styles more elaborate. Puffs and rolls and peaks—indeed excrescences of all kinds—marked this period. In the fairly sophisticated coiffure of *Fig. 422* the back hair is raised to a

close bun on the crown of the head, while side curls are trained to lie over the temples.

Although younger and less sophisticated women wore natural ringlets (see *Fig. 423*) hair-styles were becoming ever more artificial and elaborate among the leaders of fashion. Bouffant sausage-like rolls, such as those illustrated in German examples *(Figs. 424 and 425)* are arranged symmetrically at each side of the forehead and over the ears, and on top are placed ribbons, broderie-anglaise frills, feathers, and sometimes artificial flowers for good measure. A velvet bow with drooping ostrich feathers might complete the arrangement.

Fig. 426 is French. It shows similar formal curls, this time with a felt hat and ostrich feathers.

FIG. 421   French (1826)

FIG. 423   English

FIG. 422   French (1821)

FIG. 424   German (1835)

FIG. 425　German (1830)

FIG. 426　French

FIG. 427　English or French

For evening wear, hair arrangements varied from the very loose 'wind-blown' effect depicted in Sir Thomas Lawrence's portraits, to the excessively formal style of *Fig. 427*, which, since it is worn with no cap or other head-covering, shows clearly how the curls appeared from the side. The back hair is carried up to the crown of the head where it is tied and manipulated into two large rolls, to which aigrettes and other features add height. (Balancing this upswept style, drop ear-rings were in favour.)

The lace frill framing the face, with black felt or velvet hat and ostrich plume trim, recurs in *Fig. 428*. In *Fig. 429,* an English style, the lace does not completely frame the face, but is kept in place by a band across the top of the forehead. With the centre parting, the bonnet-shaped hat, and feathers, the Victorian era is nearly at hand.

One more example, with many ribbon bows, as well as the usual feathers, can be seen in *Fig. 430*.

Older women found the bonnet, with appropriate variations very becoming, and in *Fig. 431* (German, 1820) such a woman wears a style typical of her age group: her lace-edged cap of linen is tied under the chin and has back-fullness to accommodate her own bun of hair. The black velvet ribbon with bow over the forehead is a pleasant addition.

For outdoor wear in cold weather a good example may be seen in *Fig. 432* (also German, and of 1820). Here a shape, almost identical with the previous one, is made of dark cloth with a fur band set round the face.

By the 1850's, caps, even for older women, had become bigger, with baggier tops and lace frills. Such an enlarged version can be seen in *Fig. 433*.

Both bonnets and caps were much favoured by Queen Victoria and they were still in vogue at the end of the century, though varying in shape, trimming, size and the angle at which they were worn.

Fig. 434 shows the Queen herself, in early married life, wearing a very large bonnet that has a softly falling lace frill, like that of a lampshade attached to the brim. A ribbon bow ties at the throat and little roses frame the face. The cascade of ostrich feathers at the left side is balanced by a ribbon rosette on the right.

A style which probably most people, at least nowadays, would consider smarter and more stylish is the chic little Austrian straw of *Fig. 435,* set well back on the back of the head of the Empress Marianne.

FIG. 428 English

FIG. 431 Scottish or English

FIG. 429 English (1830–35)

FIG. 432 German (1820)

FIG. 430 English (1831)

FIG. 433 English (1856)

Fig. 434   English (1840)

Fig. 437   English

Fig. 435   Austrian (1840)

Fig. 438   English (1850)

Fig. 436   French (1860–70

Fig. 439   English (1852)

Her hair has a centre parting and is drawn straight back over the temples, while two side plaits are pinned into circular shapes like catherine wheels rather high over the ears. Lace and flowers are tastefully arranged to complete this attractive bonnet.

By 1875 a rather different style had been evolved, as in *Fig. 436*, where a small straw set well away from the forehead and having the usual ribbons, flowers (or feathers) has an embroidered scarf placed over the crown and ears and finished with a ribbon bow and streamers under the chin.

The elaborate curls of the 1830's had given place to sleeker styles in the forties *(Figs. 437 and 438)*. Carefully combed hair is worn under the feminine version of the contemporary man's muffin hat in *Fig. 439*. The brimless shallow crown is encircled with velvet ribbon and has a small feather plume on the left side.

The trend for loose-hanging, sleekly brushed locks did not last longer than a decade and by the 50's there was a return to curls and the large Leghorn hat for country wear.

Smaller, neater, forward-perching hats became fashionable as the years went on, as we see in the three styles that follow. *Fig. 440* is a small straw (or fur-felt) with rosette, short feathers and narrow ribbon ruching. Unlike bonnets, such hats were kept in place by a ribbon passed under the hair at the back. A similar trend is shown in *Fig. 441*—a black velvet toque with a matching velvet ribbon to keep it secure. This time large light-coloured ostrich feathers are used for decoration. *Fig. 442* is of a small French model hat of this period (the 70's). Set well forward, like the two previously described, it shows how heavy masses of hair could be arranged to fall in looped curls—not plaits—at the back, the side hair being drawn across from the temples. The custom of massing the hair heavily at the back in a banging chignon, oiled and curled and fixed in various ways, became very popular and, when nature did not provide enough, false hair was added. Over the large bun (or chignon) very small brimless bonnets of the kind shown in *Fig. 443* fitted snugly. For evening, during these closing years of the period, the hair could be worn as in *Fig. 444* waved and curled, then taken into a loose bun on the crown of the head, with two ringlets falling down the back of the décolleté dress.

The chignon is seen again in *Fig. 445* which shows

FIG. 440   English (1870)

FIG. 441   English (1870)

FIG. 442   French (1870)

FIG. 443   English (1872)

FIG. 446   English or French

FIG. 444   French

FIG. 447   English (1880)

FIG. 445   English (1872)

FIG. 448   French (1883)

a lady in riding habit and topper. Women had borrowed this style of hat from their menfolk in the 1870's and it became part of the formal attire for riding—possibly useful as a kind of crash helmet. It is still, sometimes, worn for hunting.

Forward-perching hats were high fashion as the century came to a close. *Fig. 446* is a good example. The narrow brim of this small, high-crowned black velvet model nearly touches the eyebrows. The heavy back hair is allowed to fall to the nape of the neck and is then fastened on the top of the head with a comb. Over the chignon the long ends of softly tied ribbon bows fall to the shoulders and contrast in texture with the wider band of moiré circling the crown.

Fig. 447 (English, 1880) is a lacquered straw with nearly conical crown swathed in dark coloured fabric and with contrasting feathers arranged over the top. At last ribbon-strings were going out of fashion, and this and later hats were held in place with long hat-pins—thrust through the crown and hair and out at the far side. The heads of these pins were often very decorative and the tips might be protected by small ornamental guards.

This chapter has already made it clear that women took great pride and pleasure in their millinery in the last 25 years of the nineteenth century and on the whole hats were by far the most tasteful items of their wardrobes. It was the period when the bustle was at its most prominent, and at least fourteen yards of fabric went into an ordinary, everyday dress. The modistes of France then, as for many decades past

and still to come, set the millinery styles for Western Europe. The next six illustrations are all from a French periodical, portraying costume and hat styles, called *Le Petit Echo de la Mode* of 1883. *Fig. 448,* gives the rear view of a straw model with the under side of the brim drawn up into flutes and then turned up to reveal the banging chignon. The tiny crown is decorated with flowers and the whole harks back to the bonnet in having strings that appear to tie beneath the chin. *Fig. 449* is another straw, this time white, the brim once again underlined with silk and tilted at the back and front, though rather less steeply. The trimming is a natural-looking bunch of wild flowers—poppies and daisies with ears of corn—over a moiré ribbon with a tiny jacquard design woven into it. The whole effect is very gay and summerlike. The hat in *Fig. 450* is of somewhat similar design but with brim tilting down at the back and front. The underlining is deep in tone, possibly red, and seems to match the broad ribbon round the crown. This time the flowers are garden varieties—roses, delphiniums and lilac. The French at that time, when flowers were fast gaining in popularity, made the most perfect reproductions of real flowers of any nation in the world— as they still do.

The elaborate design in *Fig. 451* more closely resembles a bonnet than a hat in shape and effect. The ruched silk of which it is constructed is manipulated into a sharp peak well above the parted fringe and the trimming consists of an ostrich feather and rosette of lace, on which are set three swallows in full flight, wings outspread and beaks meeting at the

FIG. 449   French (1883)

FIG. 450   French (1883)

FIG. 451   French (1883)

FIG. 452   French (1883)

FIG. 453   French (1883)

centre. A broad ribbon band secures the whole with a bow at the throat.

The hat in *Fig. 452* is probably intended for cooler weather wear as it is made of patterned fabric over buckram, with velvet swathed round the crown and fastened—or at any rate trimmed—with two buckles. Once more, at the end of the century as at the beginning, we have those ubiquitous ostrich feathers, of which the supply seems to have been inexhaustible.

The lace cap, too, is still in evidence, and *Fig. 453* is the type called a *fascinator*. A double fold hangs down to the shoulders at each side of the face and small dark bows or velvet cut into the shape of leaves surround the crown.

Women at this time adopted the man's straw boater *(Fig. 454)* especially for the river, the gentle ladylike sports of the period, and for country wear. Even young members of royal families wore this distinctly unflattering and uncomfortable form of headgear, while their elders mounted on their upturned frizzed hair little wisps of hats like that in *Fig. 455.*

Veils, to cover both hat and face and tie in a tiny knot under the chin or at the back of the brim came into fashion in the last years of the nineteenth century. In *Fig. 456* one is seen in spotted net and worn over a typical toque of the period.

MEN

Wigs and powder had virtually disappeared by the beginning of the century, and men soon began to have their own hair cut short. At a ball in April, 1802, Miss Berry[1] notes that Vestris the dancer and Jacques Lafitte were almost the only men there to be frizzed and powdered, and Bertie Greathead, in his diary of the following year, describing a visit to Paris, remarks that 'What Eyre called "The fashions of frizzling the hair and scattering powder on the heads of men" had gone out and there were now only "Black Crops" at Madame Récamier's ball'.

Caps, now no longer needed to disguise or protect the shaven or near-shaven heads of the wig-wearers in their more relaxed moments, were still worn, especially for smoking, and by many elderly men until the end of the century. Smoking caps were generally of pill-box shape and often embroidered;

[1]*Miss Berry's Journal*, Vol. II p.1740.

FIG. 454   English (1895)

FIG. 457   German

FIG. 455   English (1895)

FIG. 458   Spanish (1800)

FIG. 456   French (c. 1890)

FIG. 459   German

FIG. 460   French (1841)

FIG. 463   French

FIG. 461   English (c. 1812)

FIG. 464   English

FIG. 462   French

FIG. 465   French (1820)

sometimes beaded. *Fig. 457* shows a German gentleman of somewhat advanced years in a velvet cap trimmed with a tassel. The peaked cap worn by the Spanish artist Goya in *Fig. 458* (from a self-portrait) has an almost modern appearance compared with the headwear of the eighteenth century, and a snugly fitting cap trimmed with fur is shown in *Fig. 459*. A French cap of 1841, adapted for civilians from a military kepi, appears in *Fig. 460*. Such a cap might have a soft cloth crown and japanned leather peak or be made entirely of leather.

Meanwhile for street wear the beaver sometimes took exaggerated shapes in the early years of the century and in *Fig. 461* a dandy of about 1812 wears one with a large curved brim slanted deeply down at back and front. A simpler, handsomer example of approximately the same date is worn by a Frenchman in *Fig. 462*. The beaver retained its popularity for many more years—until, in fact, it was ousted by the 'topper'. High crowned beavers of the 1840's are seen in *Fig. 463, 464* (with its gracefully wide brim), and *Fig. 465*. Both the latter are white in colour.

A forerunner of the shape of hats to come had been the 1822 stovepipe style of *Fig. 466*, invented by John Heatherington, a London haberdasher, in the late eighteenth century but not generally adopted until the nineteenth. (Indeed, it was the cause of a riot, when Heatherington was charged with 'inciting a breach of the peace for having appeared on the public highway wearing upon his head a tall structure having a shining lustre and calculated to frighten timid people. Several women fainted at the

sight, children screamed, dogs barked and a small boy had his arm broken.') The public at length became inured to these alarming sights and by the middle years of the century this style of hat was generally worn. They now had narrower curled brims and flat-topped crowns, and *Fig. 467* gives a version of the stove-pipe that had been such a disturbing innovation fifty years before and which, in a slightly modified form, as the 'topper' or silk hat, was to be a leading fashion until the twentieth century opened, without serious competition, except from the bowler.

The custom of covering men's high hats with silk (hence the term 'silk hats') had been introduced as far back as 1830. At first the main structure was covered with silk plush but as this proved both heavy and expensive the 'head' (or crown) was later made of 'gossamer'—calico stiffened with shellac—and over this the silk plush, with shorter pile, was sewn with neat invisible stitching. A height of $5\frac{3}{4}''$ for the crown was usual but later the chimney-pot had a crown of $7\frac{1}{2}''$ and there are records of the 'kite-high dandy' hat with a crown of $7\frac{3}{4}''$.[1]

Fig. 468 depicts the topper as it was generally

[1]Most of this information regarding hat structure has been obtained from Christy's, the renowned London firm of hat manufacturers, who still make a greater range of hats than any other hatters: stiff and felt hats for men and women, fezzes for the Near East, mortar-boards for students and scholars, uniform hats for police and firemen, Tudor hats for Beefeaters at the Tower of London, embroidered cocked hats for Bank of England doorkeepers, and innumerable other special types.

FIG. 466   English (1822)

FIG. 467   English

FIG. 468   English (1870)

known by 1870. F. W. Fairholt, F.S.A., whose book on costume gives an invaluable contemporary picture of fashions of the period, held strong views in hats of this kind, then at the height of their popularity. 'Anything more inconvenient, ugly and disagreeable was never invented, yet so much are we accustomed to yield to the habit of fashion that no change is attempted in these 'march of intellect' days by way of improving what we allow to be bad and all feel to be uncomfortable' . . . I can think of no excuse for it save that it gave a certain supposititious height to a man, and that in turn tended to be dignified.

Caps made of tweed, with adjustable ear-flaps, such as we can observe in *Fig. 469* were introduced in the eighteen-sixties for deer-stalking in the Scottish Highlands (hence the popular name "deer-stalkers") and the harder cloth hat of *Fig. 470* was worn for other kinds of sport.

Sobriety was indeed the leading characteristic of men's clothes throughout the nineteenth century—since, in fact, the Industrial Revolution with its factories and smoke had made gay colours and choice fabrics undesirable and unpractical in the grimy surroundings of industry. True, prune red, dark green and royal blue had lingered on for men's suits until the depressing effects of Queen Victoria's retirement from public life after the Prince Consort's death, made themselves felt. Subsequently black became the rule for all males—a gloomy state of affairs from which only now, more than a hundred years later, we appear to be emerging.

To the topper for wearing with these dark clothes

FIG. 469   English (1860)

FIG. 470   English (1861)

FIG. 471   French (1865)

were added the bowler and the collapsible opera hat during the last quarter century. The latter was a tall hat of black silk and could be folded, concertina-fashion, for placing under the seat at the opera house or theatre. It was not intended for carrying under the arm like the *chapeau bras,* as is sometimes stated, and was alternatively called the *gibus,* after its French inventor, M. Gibus.

About this time men covered their heads with little round hats, reminiscent of the smoking cap, but intended for outdoor wear. Such an appropriately named muffin-hat is seen in *Fig. 471.* This example is made of stiffened black velvet and trimmed with a tassel at the back.

By the end of the century the bowler *(Fig. 472)* and the *boater (Fig. 473)* were the dominant styles for males, other than 'working men', i.e. manual workers, who wore the cloth cap.

We have records of prices paid for bowlers in 1884 (between 1/11d. and 5/11d. each) and for the straw boater (1/6d. to 2/6d.) but we must remember that subsequent changes in money values exaggerate their apparent cheapness.

The young Victorian man-about-town in *Fig. 474* is wearing a straw boater of the period. This was originally introduced for gentle sports on summer days but quickly became extremely popular with everyone. It is still part of the uniform of many boys' schools in England today, and till recently was, along with his striped apron, a mark of the butcher's trade.

Boaters were made in white or speckled straw,

FIG. 473   English (1885)

FIG. 474   English

FIG. 472   English (1884)

FIG. 475   Irish (1808)

with a ribbon band and possibly a hat-guard (to anchor it to the lapel) costing a shilling extra.

CHILDREN

Most little girls in the nineteenth century, like their mothers, wore a bonnet. Indeed it was even more suitable for an active child, with its ribbon-tie under the chin to keep it in place. Certainly in the simple forms children's bonnets took, they were very becoming. *Fig. 475* is a charming example, worn by a young Irish girl, thirteen or fourteen years of age. A band of blue ribbon (to match the blue eyes of this colleen?) is slotted through each side of the lacquered straw and the ends tie at the throat. Her fringe peeps below the brim while the rest of her hair falls in glossy waves to her shoulders. *Fig. 476* shows a French straw at the opening of the century.

Very small boys also wore bonnets, *Fig. 477* shows an English toddler in his. It is made of lace insertion with a small cluster of artificial flowers over his left temple. The older brother in *Fig. 478* has a tammy-like cap, with a shiny peak and tassel.

In the latter years of the century, children's hat styles developed much on the same lines as those of adults. *Fig. 479* is a little girl's hard felt hat. The hard-peaked cap continued to be worn by students on the Continent of Europe, and by English boys until the fifties. Later they gave way, in this country, to the soft-peaked versions which at one time marked the wearer as belonging to the 'working classes'. A crossing sweeper, for instance, might wear a cap like that in the photograph from which *Fig. 480* is drawn. Boys with wealthier fathers, who could afford to send them to Eton or other public schools wore a topper like a man's *(Fig. 481)*, with, of course, the famous down-turned Eton-collar, tie and short jacket. Such a topper cost 6/11d. in 1895.

In the 1890's hats modelled on those worn by coastguards at that date were favourites for young boys to wear with their sailor suits. Made of felt or straw with a ribbon band round the crown and streamers down the back, they were smaller than the so-called sailor-hat of white straw that came a little later. The example in *Fig. 482* is a rather large one.

At the very end of the century baby boys also wore round hats with upturned brims, though trimmed more appropriately to their age. *Fig. 483* is such a tiny boy's hat, of straw with white lace ruching on the lower side of the brim and surrounding the front

FIG. 476   French (1810)

FIG. 477   English (1811)

FIG. 478   English (1810)

FIG. 479　English (1872)

FIG. 482　English (1890)

FIG. 480　English (1889)

FIG. 483　English (1899)

FIG. 481　English (1895)

FIG. 484　French (1892)

FIG. 485   English or American (1898)

FIG. 488   English (1899–1900)

FIG. 486   English

FIG. 489   English (1803)

FIG. 487   French (1890–1900)

FIG. 490   English

edge of the hair. A feather is perched at the top for good measure, and it has bonnet-type strings.

A small girl of this period *(Fig. 484)* might wear a starched broderie-anglaise hat pulled in with tape, which could be untied for laundering, and over it was placed another hat—of soft silk, often in red. Her hair was encouraged to curl and hang in the fashionable ringlets, by twisting it in rags or curl-papers at night. In the picture, the hair is side-parted and tied with a bow which is allowed to show beneath the hat-brim.

All girls in the last decade or so wore their hair combed out loosely or in long curls, with a large bow on top to keep most of the front hair out of their eyes. *(Fig. 485)*. A large—one might say an enormous—bow trims the teen-age girl's hat in *Fig. 486*.

By the nineties a small velvet *capote (Fig. 487)* was a youthful and simple style for the older girl. The example chosen here is purple, adorned with green and mauve ribbons.

For most schools a tartan tam-o'-shanter was the general rule. It had little shape to recommend it, and often hung down behind like a jelly-bag finishing in a pom-pom.

Uniform hats for schoolgirls were not generally adopted until the close of the nineteenth century and then only for "private" schools (i.e. those not established and maintained by local authorities). They bore the school badge, on the hatband, as in *Fig. 488*.

MILITARY

In 1800 the cocked hat was replaced in England by a black cylindrical lacquered *shako* (from the Hungarian *csako)*, which had a leather peak and was ornamented with a plume or tuft in front, but officers continued for a time to wear the felt hat 'fore and aft' (instead of 'thwartship'), as well as other styles such as the towering construction of *Fig. 489*. This was adopted by the Honourable Artillery Company in 1803. The front is of black fur surmounted by a white plume and the felt brim is cut away and curved.

Five years later the queue was given up and the shako was ordered for all ranks. The cocked hat was no longer allowed because of the difficulty it presented when the wearer wanted to sling the rifle over the high, wide brim. *Fig. 490* is the first shako to be worn in the British army. At the time when war with Napoleon became inevitable English officers had a saxe-blue uniform and a high and handsome shako-like hat *(Fig. 491)*, with masses of feathers and a glossy peak.

In 1808 the fear of Napoleon was at its height and as an inducement to young men to join in the defence of their country ornate military styles were introduced for volunteers. *Fig. 492* is such a hat worn by a private in the Light Company of Westminster Volunteers. It has one plume of black fur and an extra one of feathers, red below and white above. The hat itself is of felt with gilded leather at the sides.

Napoleon's own staff wore most original and outstanding hats and in *Fig. 493* we have a square-topped style which has been copied from a contemporary lead soldier exquisitely modelled with great

FIG. 491   English

FIG. 492   English (1808)

accuracy, which was exhibited at the Guildhall, London. The hat was yellow, like the larger part of the plume, of which the rest was blue. Bands of saxe-blue encircled the whole hat which was saxe-blue and black. Silver braid runs across the top of the crown from the four corners, dividing it into triangles.

The Emperor's brother-in-law, seen in *Fig. 494,* was more elaborately turned out, with bedizenry that ill-befitted an officer and gentleman of the era. His 'fancy dress' uniform includes a hat with three ostrich feathers and three aigrettes as well as a ribbon crossing transversely from the lower edge to the top of the crown, where it terminates in two gold tassels. The band along the lower edge is decorated with gold braid.

The next illustration, *Fig. 495,* shows one of Napoleon's officers on parade in 1812. Note the bandage beneath the towering hat, and the tassel dangling before his eyes. Cocks' feathers cascade from the top of the fur and velvet crown. Not, one would suppose, a uniform hat intended for active service!

Also Napoleonic is the *Bonnet de Police* worn by a lieutenant in *Fig. 496.* Navy blue cloth makes the cap and the trimming is of gold braid. This shako is another from the collection of lead soldiers referred to above. *Fig. 497* is a 'Jingling Johnny', a musician of Napoleon's Imperial Guard. The term in fact applies to the staff he is carrying, which is decorated with bells. The crest here is of horsehair in alternate stripes of red and white, with a white plume in a

FIG. 494   Italian-French (1808)

FIG. 495   French (1812)

FIG. 493   French

FIG. 496   French (1812)

FIG. 497   French (1812)

FIG. 498   French (1812)

gilded sheath. The rest is navy blue felt to match his uniform with its white facings.

Another showy and, it would seem to us, very impractical form of uniform helmet was worn by dismounted French curassiers in 1812. *Fig. 498* shows one of them with its band of light fur round the domed and crested metal crown, its japanned leather peak and a long plume of horsehair descending far down the wearer's back.

About this time, in Belgium, Carabineer officers wore the silver coloured helmet of *Fig. 499* decorated with, at the front, a gilded lion's head, a black crest and a white plume.

In 1815, the year of Napoleon's defeat at Waterloo, the Royal Horse Artillery wore the hat shown in *Fig. 500* its black fur crest, white plume and royal blue band. (This illustration is made from a water-colour drawing by R. Wyman). In the same year the Life Guards wore a helmet *(Fig. 501)* which had a red and white plume in a gold mount and a black fur crest on a red band.

By 1816 a new type of shako was introduced for all British regiments. It was bell-shaped and made of beaver with a lacquer top. A two-inch band of gold or silver lace decorated the upper edge and half an inch at the bottom.

An Officer of the Light Horse Volunteers wore the white plumed shako with its sweeping plume of *Fig. 502* in 1825. By 1828 the design of the British shako was changed, the cockade being discarded and twelve-inch plumes added for officers. The whole was now given a black leather peak. Later the large

FIG. 499   Belgian (1812)

FIG. 500   English (1815)

FIG. 501   English (1815)

FIG. 502   English (1825)

FIG. 503   Russian (*c.* 1850)

shako was replaced by the 'Albert shako', introduced by the Prince Consort. Kilmarnock forage caps came in in 1837, doubtless owing to the Royal interest in things Scottish for which Queen Victoria was so well-known.

In the eighteen-forties one division of Russian Curassiers of the Guard adopted the Prussian-type helmet seen in *Fig. 503* and Ivan III introduced the double-headed eagle as a crest, giving it an even more Germanic appearance. It was retained until the First World War.[1]

By 1853 an officer of the 38th South Staffordshire Regiment was distinguished by his tall shako, seen in *Fig. 504.* Three years later, in 1856, both men and officers were permitted to wear moustaches and whiskers and eventually the shako was replaced by a blue cloth-covered helmet with a centre peak. This was a fashion borrowed from Germany.

For service in India, Artillerymen were authorised, in 1857, to wear a white helmet round which was swathed a dark blue roll of muslin. This was called a 'pagri'.

By 1860 a captain of the Rifle Division, Honourable Artillery Company, wore an all black uniform, including the hat with its shiny leather peak. The young officer of this Company, in *Fig. 505* has the copious side-whiskers and longer, brushed-out hair that was now permitted.

Fig. 506 shows a helmet introduced in infantry regiments for privates in 1882.

The tiny pill-box was another innovation and in *Fig. 507* it is worn, with a tilt to the side and a strap under the chin, by an English Recruiting Sergeant.

Meanwhile two interesting styles were introduced in the French army. *Figs. 508 and 509* are variations of the bicorne, the first with points fore and aft, the higher topped with feathers and the other trimmed with deep braid. The second style, contemporary with the foregoing, is a peaked cap with a small truncated cone crown shown in *Figs. 510 and 511.* The first of this pair is of japanned leather throughout and the other has a soft top.

SPECIAL GROUPS OR OCCUPATIONS

Although the wig went out of fashion at the close of the eighteenth century, it was retained for some

[1]For further information on military headgear see *European Military Uniforms* by Paul Martin, 1967.

FIG. 504   English (1853)

FIG. 505   English (1860)

FIG. 506   English (1882)

FIG. 507   English (1895)

FIG. 508   French

FIG. 509   French

FIG. 510   French

FIG. 513   English

FIG. 511   French

FIG. 514   English (1810)

FIG. 512   English (1887)

FIG. 515   English (1834)

ceremonial and official occasions, notably in the English Law Courts, where bewigged barristers and judges *(Fig. 512)* are still majestic and impressive figures.

In academic circles the mortar-board *(Fig. 513)* deriving from the square cloth cap of Tudor times, had remained almost static but acquired a flat square top with a tassel, and a braid finish to the head-piece.

Lower in the social scale it was usual for tradesmen and other groups of workers to be identified by their headwear, sometimes for protection in rough jobs but largely as a distinguishing mark when they sought custom or wished to advertise their availability.

As far back as 1810 dustmen *(Fig. 514)* wore a coal-scuttle shape hat of black leather with a large flap down the back to protect hair and shoulders. They announced their arrival with appropriate loud cries as they entered the street, since customers paid them direct. It was not yet a municipal responsibility. (Mr. Doolittle, the dustman in the stage and film versions of Shaw's "Pygmalion" wore such a hat.) Coalmen wore a similar shape and for the same reasons.

The fisherman of 1834, when not wearing a striped stocking cap like that of a brewer, sported the comfortable and quite handsome tam-o'-shanter *(Fig. 515)*. Note the ribbon passing round the cloth hat band and ending in two streamers at the side.

Another tammy shape, but with a flat top and a stiff band and flat ribbon bow, was worn by London firemen in the 1890's *(Fig. 516)*. Postmen, from the eighteen-nineties right through until the outbreak of the 1914-1918 war, wore the cap represented in *Fig. 517*, with peak of japanned leather and tapering, forward-tilting top of navy blue cloth and a narrow band of piping round the crown. Such a hat was known to the Victorians as a "cheese-cutter".

Carpenters wore square cotton caps with a flat top like an opened paper bag, as we can see in contemporary illustrations to "Alice in Wonderland".

Artists often wore the becoming and comfortable tammy type cap which is illustrated in *Fig. 518* and became the favourite headwear of Richard Wagner.

FIG. 516   English (1897)

FIG. 517   English (from 1890)

FIG. 518   German

Twentieth Century

WOMEN

IT IS TEMPTING to say that women rode into the new century on their bicycles. Taken up by Society, who, at the very end of the "nineties", cycled round and round Battersea Park, London, or the Bois de Boulogne, the bicycle soon meant emancipation for women as surely as did the enfranchisement bill. On their iron steeds, which needed no feeding or expensive stabling, they could explore the countryside on equal terms with men.

This adventure into sport necessitated different clothes. The celebrated Mrs. Bloomer had introduced her own special outfit to a shocked world conditioned by Victorian prudery. Divided skirts, offered as a compromise, were much worn during the early nineteen hundreds. We condemn them nowadays as heavy and clumsy, but they were one step forward towards our own practical sports clothes. To wear with her divided skirt and probably to sustain the masculine flavour of the outfit, a little trilby hat *(Fig. 519)* with upturned brim and small feather was chosen.

Very conveniently for our chronological purpose, motoring, too, began to transform the world as the century opened, and the specially designed motoring hat came in with it. *Fig. 520,* from an advertisement of 1905, is a flat, peaked-tammy shape of what is probably the same cloth as the coat. A plain white or beige net veil protects the lady motorist's complexion from the dust and keeps the hat from blowing away. Roads were then mostly of grit or gravel, cars open and the occupants exposed to the weather.

Of the same shape but without the veil is the hat in *Fig. 521*, in tartan cloth and described in the caption to the original picture as "Suitable for cycling or the Highlands". Hatpins would keep such a hat anchored to the wearer's bun and possibly also to the uprolled side puffs of her hair.

Fig. 522 is a French designer's conception that verges on the absurd. It includes a specially designed mask for the lady motorist! Goggles fixed over it protect the eyes and a peaked cap like that of a yachtsman is set on top.

The decade or so before the First World War— referred to loosely in Great Britain as the Edwardian period—was an age of very feminine hats in great variety, large as a rule and nearly always lavishly trimmed. In retrospect we may regard it as a time

FIG. 519 English

FIG. 520 English (1905)

when hat fashions had their last fling before war swept away all fripperies. *Fig. 523* is among the best of the modiste's creations of these years. It is suitably designed to balance the wearer's hairdressing style, with its centre parting, soft full waves on either side and loose plaits (or coils) taken up from the nape, where a few fluffy strands are left to twine naturally. Lightly set (but certainly firmly pinned) on top, the hat is of fine black straw, trimmed with four or five blue flowers and accompanying leaves, a swathe of black tulle, and some cock's feathers sweeping over the brim.

For summer wear of the period women bought coarse but floppy cream straws, decorated with wide (often red) satin ribbons, ostrich feathers and artifi-

cial cherries. *Fig. 524* is such a hat. With the boa of ruched ninon or gauze, the whole impression is very feminine, and one can imagine the young lady in the picture in a deck chair at Lords or reclining under a red parasol, in a punt at Henley.

The young lady of *Fig. 525*, with the nautical emblems embroidered on her sailor collar, wears for bathing a tammy shape made of cotton with braid along the rim. It was sold for 2/1 1¾d. by John Lewis's of London in 1908.

For smart occasions in London, Paris or any other great European capital city *Fig. 526* might have been designed in purple velvet, tilted well forward over the lightly dressed hair and with a bunch of pink roses under the turned-up brim. *Fig. 527* shows the

Fig. 521   English (1906)

Fig. 523   English (1906)

Fig. 522   French

Fig. 524   English (1902–28)

FIG. 525   English (1908)

FIG. 528   French (1912)

FIG. 526   English or French

FIG. 529   English (1910)

FIG. 527   English (1908)

FIG. 530   English

style of coiffure which supported hats of this type. The short front part of the hair is frizzed into a bunch of curls (probably with a hot iron) and the back smoothed into a coil like a conch shell. As the lady is wearing a tea-gown of *foulé* cloth and lace she might well be a hostess "at home" to her friends. If so she would be the only one present without a hat; her guests would retain theirs.

The frizzed fringe remained in fashion until 1914, as did the veil, and they are both seen *Fig. 528*. This veil-trimmed hat has a medium sized brim surmounted with flowers and ribbons, but hats were changing—getting larger and larger. Both brim and crown increased in size and the latter might reach the absurd proportions of *Fig. 529*. Such a style was worn by nearly everyone in the Enclosure at Ascot when public mourning was imposed for the death of King Edward VII. The occasion was known as the *Black Ascot*, and the hats worn, like this one, were nearly all of fine black straw, trimmed with an enormous ribbon rosette and a matching swathing caught to the crown with a brooch at the centre front. The veil, of spotted net, is also black.

Another indication of the extreme lengths to which millinery designers went at the time is the toque in *Fig. 530*. It has quite a narrow sloping brim, but the crown is banded with lace, roses cluster under the brim, veiling descends at the back, and—ultimate horror in modern eyes—the huge crown is surmounted with what looks like a dead pigeon straight from the poulterer's shop. (A large-brimmed hat of the same period, at one time on view at the London Museum, had on its crown a whole stuffed peacock.) The theatre could, of course, indulge in any fantasy with impunity. In *Fig. 531* we see the beautiful English actress Camille Clifford in an enormous hat of chiffon and feathers. The silk chiffon was folded into a flat ribbon-like band and then sewn round in ever widening circles with edges over-lapping until the required size was obtained. (We saw something of the kind, only more judiciously carried out in the section on the Middle Ages).

For the opera an aigrette *(Fig. 532)* was set in the front of the hair which was either back combed to form the full puffed roll, or combed over a foundation or *transformation*, a narrow padded U-shaped roll. The rest was arranged in loose coils and pinned to lie flat on top with width at the sides.

By 1910 the huge crowns had been reduced to

FIG. 531   English

FIG. 532   (1912)

FIG. 533   English (1913)

FIG. 534   English (1910)

FIG. 537   English (1917)

FIG. 535   English (1912)

FIG. 538   English (1924)

FIG. 536   (1890–1914)

FIG. 539   English (1925–27)

more reasonable proportions, but brims were still very wide. Velvet ribbon had long been a popular trimming, and is used on the straw hat for summer in *Fig. 533,* but now hat shapes themselves were often covered with piece velvet for cooler wear as in the two hats shown in *Figs. 534 and 535.* Feathers are prominent features of both.

Old ladies still sometimes wore a cap of lace and ribbons *(Fig. 536).* Many made their own and were very proud of them. The cap foundation or 'shape', as it was called, was bound with fabric cut on the bias and pleated back and front to produce a domed effect. On this, the lace, specially stiffened, was arranged very tastefully, a longer piece being pleated and allowed to fall down the back and hide the bun. Some caps had streamers to tie beneath the chin, but most were attached to the hair with special pins, much shorter than the ordinary hat pins of the time, and having little round coloured or pearl knobs. Bunches of ribbons (usually blue, pink or mauve) were set in the centre and occasionally a small spray of forgetmenots or lilac added.

The First World War brought fundamental changes to our whole way of life—not least in the clothes worn. Women, in particular, took on a completely new aspect. Skirts were cut off at the knee and hair at the shoulder. Hats of necessity were smaller.

Fig. 537 shows a matron's toque of about 1917. She still retains the veil, but that is soon to vanish— not to reappear for many years. Another toque, without the veil in *Fig. 538* is pulled down over the

"earphones", the plaited coils of hair fixed over the ears and deriving their name from the recently introduced "wireless".

But the great "hit" of the 1920s was the *cloche* which swept Europe in nineteen twenty six and seven *(Fig. 539).* It had a deep inverted-bowl-like crown, usually though not necessarily of felt, and descended well over the eyebrows. By this time hair was worn as a bob, that is, cut off level with the ear lobes, or a shingle (trimmed closely up the back of the head) so no bulk had to be allowed for in the crown. The *cloche* was worn with the knee-length low-waisted dresses and coats of the time, and is historically unique.

Other hats, besides the brimless cloche, were pulled far down over the eyebrows. For summer there were straws with downward curved brim, trimmed with flowers and ribbons, but fashion demanded that they, too, should almost conceal the top half of the face *(Fig. 540).*

Two years later, the cloche having finished its short but notorious life, women turned to more becoming styles such as the Leghorn *(Fig. 541).* Another Leghorn, this time an open work design being worked into the brim is seen in *Fig. 542.* With its curling brim and reasonable proportions it may be regarded as one of the most graceful hat fashions of the Twentieth Century.

Leghorn straw was plaited in and around the town of that name and was made from a special kind of wheat, cut green and bleached. Hats made from it were expensive, but a cheaper kind, of Tuscan straw, was also available.

FIG. 540   English (1926)

FIG. 541   English

FIG. 542   English (1920)

FIG. 543   American or English (1909)

MEN

Possibly the most striking innovation in men's headwear in the first few years of the new epoch was the panama, a straw hat light in weight and white or cream in colour, with a rather wide brim *(Fig. 543)*. Introduced from the other side of the Atlantic, it was intended as a summer hat mainly for vacations at the fashionable resorts. Panama hats were made exclusively in the northern part of Peru and Southern Ecuador, the best coming from Catacaos, a small village on the edge of the Sechura Desert. Their quality depended entirely on the selection and the preparation of the fibre grown near the coast, the straw was "woven" or "plaited" by the villagers into the desired shapes and designs and the edges not trimmed off or neatened before sale to enable merchants to judge the quality.

Although to a casual observer men's hats may not appear to have changed much in the years prior to 1914, a number of styles were in fact worn alongside the topper, the trilby[1] *(Fig. 544)* and the bowler: the *Homburg (Fig. 545)* that King Edward VII brought back from Germany; the *cheerer (Fig. 546)*, a hard felt like a bowler but with a flat top which was a favourite with farmers; a few *deer-stalkers*, familiar to us from illustrations to the Sherlock Holmes stories; and the *boater*. Very strict codes obtained about the wearing of this or that style for occasions etiquette prescribed as appropriate.

---

[1]Named after the heroine in George Du Maurier's novel of that name published in 1912.

FIG. 544   English

FIG. 545   German and English

Thus we can appreciate the two anecdotes connected with King Edward VII on this subject, the first being that when the Russian Ambassador asked "Bertie" whether he thought it proper for him to attend the races since he was in mourning, the Prince had promptly replied "To Newmarket, yes, because it means a bowler hat, but not the Derby because of the top hat". From the same source as the quotation cited above comes one as amusing. One day during the London season King George V saw Sir Derek Keppel, his Master of the Household, entering the Palace in a bowler hat. "You scoundrel," he chaffed him "What do you mean by coming here in that rat-catcher fashion? You never see me dressing like that in London". (From 'Family Album' by the Duke of Windsor).

Since the First World War, men's formal hat fashions have not changed greatly. The boater has almost disappeared (except among schoolboys) the panama is rapidly following it into obscurity—in England at least—but there have been one or two minor additions. Many men go hatless nowadays (1960s) but the following five styles are still in vogue. *Fig. 547* is the bowler, whose brim and crown have undergone subtle alteration from time to time and district to district, but which has remained basically static and is regarded on the Continent as the English city man's uniform. *Fig. 548* is the topper, still worn for race meetings and weddings, though nowadays usually grey or fawn in colour. *Fig. 549* is the homberg with a new look—a stiffer brim and crown with a less "pinched in indentation". *Fig. 550*

FIG. 547   English (1957)

FIG. 548   English (1957)

FIG. 546   English

FIG. 549   English (1958)

is the comfortable "pork-pie" hat that has crossed the Atlantic from the United States. In the late 1950s these were supplemented to some extent by the Robin Hood style *(Fig. 551)*, a tweed hat in Lovat green, particularly favoured by the men of Sandhurst and by young Guards Officers in mufti, who tipped it well forward over the brows.

From the U.S.S.R. has come the astrachan (or other fur) hat *(Fig. 552)* for winter, first popularised by the then Prime Minister, Mr. Harold MacMillan, after a visit to Moscow.

SPECIAL GROUPS AND OCCUPATIONS:
WOMEN

The sun-bonnet *(Fig. 553)* is always associated with women field-workers, farmers' wives and the country, as it was essentially a protection from the sun, and it was a common sight in the countryside until 1910 or thereabouts. Made of linen or calico, it was stitched round the brim and pulled on the crown with tapes that could be released for laundering and ironing. Another bonnet which lingered over into the twentieth century was the Quaker lass's poke style *(Fig. 554)*, a relic of early Victorian days.

The Salvation Army uniform bonnet is still with us and a very familiar and necessary part of the "Army's" equipment. It acts as a passport into districts where women social workers might be unwelcome if in mufti. The illustration in *Fig. 555* is drawn from life and is a portrait of Mrs. Doreen Harrison, an "Egham Songstress" as the title on her collar-tab describes her. The crown of the modern

FIG. 551   English (1960)

FIG. 552   English (1962)

FIG. 550   English or American

FIG. 553   English (1870–1910)

FIG. 554   English or American (1908)

FIG. 555   English (1966)

FIG. 556   English (1908)

bonnet is a little larger that it was in its early days of the "Army" when it had to fit over the small bun at the back of the head. The fine navy blue straw and matching silk ribbon are of good quality, as is the whole uniform. A maroon piping round the brim denotes that the wearer is an officer.

Girls who went "into service" in Edwardian England wore caps suited to their rank in the domestic hierarchy, from the scullery maid to the personal maid serving the lady of the house. But the parlour maid, who was so essential to the formal tea-party of the period and who was on show, had to have a particularly smart and spotlessly fresh appearance, hence the importance of her afternoon cap (which was more elaborate than her morning one). A typical example is worn by the little maid in *Fig. 556*. Her hair, like that of her mistress, is brushed up on the top of her head and arranged there in a series of curls or a flat bun, with a little curly fringe over the forehead. Around the bun the cap is neatly and becomingly pinned. Probably of white broderie anglaise (machine-made from the eighteen-sixties onward), it was tied in position with long streamers which hung far down the back. There were other styles, some without streamers, but all like the apron were heavily starched. Beige caps and aprons with velvet ribbons came in some years later.

Costers' wives and daughters living and working in the East End of London in the Edwardian period may have worn dilapidated chip straw boaters like the one in *Fig. 557* when going about their daily work, but on high days and holidays they donned a

FIG. 557 . English (1900)

flat-brimmed white straw with a deep velvet band round the rather high crown, plus several huge ostrich feathers dyed in brilliant colours—purple or scarlet, yellow or emerald, or a combination of any of these. If real feathers were not available, then they made them from coloured paper, and the whole was worn with great dash and style. *Fig. 558.*

With the development of air travel in the twentieth century air hostesses have become famous for their smart appearance, and national air lines vie with one another in fitting them out with spruce and becoming uniforms *(Fig. 559)*. Hats are always important items, and like their suits are generally designed by famous fashion houses. *Fig. 560* is a cap worn by a British European Airways stewardess in 1959. It is of

stitched cloth and has a cloth cockade with a badge at the side. *Fig. 561* is the style worn by a French Air Hostess in 1966.

Another badge of service to the community is the nurse's cap. Matrons of large hospitals, such as St. Thomas's in London, *Fig. 562*, usually wear a starched linen hat, the shape varying from hospital to hospital. Nurses' caps for the lower grades are now made sensibly of white paper (as were carpenters' square hats in the 19th century). The paper cap, which was introduced from America, has a turned-back brim round the face, rather like a Dutch bonnet, and the side flaps are taken round to the back and the three points pinned together, making an admirable shape. These caps remain clean and fresh

FIG. 558   English (1912)

FIG. 560   English (1959)

FIG. 559   English (1945)

FIG. 561   French (1966)

for about three weeks and are then discarded, thus saving the huge laundry bill of earlier times.

SPECIAL GROUPS AND OCCUPATIONS:
MEN

As so many distinctive hats and caps which denote a particular occupation have been worn within living memory or are well known from photographs, only a selection and some lesser known facts are discussed in this section.

A railway guard of 1910 *(Fig. 563)* wore a pillbox shape with a stiff peak, two rows of braid round the top, and a badge showing the company for whom he worked.

Station-masters of main-line stations continued to wear the civilian topper as a status mark but at other stations they wore, till recently, a flat, hard-topped cap with leather band, gold braid and badge of the line they served. *(Fig. 564)*. In recent years all British Railway uniforms, including hats, have been modified in the interests of comfort and in closer conformity with Continental customs, to the regret, perhaps, of the more nostolgic among us.

The London police constable's high navy-blue helmet *(Fig. 565)* has an honourable status and adds authority, as for instance while directing traffic, and, many consider, dignity to his appearance. One of its original functions was to act as a crash helmet in a fracas, hence its height and strength, leather strap, and metal tip to the crown.

FIG. 562   English (1950)

FIG. 564   (1938)

FIG. 563   English (1910)

FIG. 565   English (1945)

FIG. 566   English (1961)

FIG. 569   English (1958)

FIG. 567   English (1930)

FIG. 570   English (1966)

FIG. 568   English (1959)

FIG. 571   English (1959)

The fireman's helmet *(Fig. 566)* is now of a utilitarian dark grey colour, but it was formerly of shining brass and a fine comforting sight flashing in the light of the flames.

Until the Second World War municipal roadsweepers in the City of Westminster wore the blue felt hat of *Fig. 567* with one side of the wide brim fixed to the crown by a badge bearing the City coat of arms.

Peaked caps *(Fig. 568)* but usually with a soft instead of a stiffened top, are worn by other municipal employees, such as gas-inspectors or drivers, throughout Great Britain.

Two examples of modern peaked caps for official wear, both associated with the sea, are seen in *Figs. 569 and 570.* The former, with stiffened top, is part of the uniform of an English naval commander, and the latter is worn by a fellow-countryman for duty as a docks superintendent.

Another flap-topped cap, but without a peak, is shown in *Fig. 571.* It is that of a young Royal Naval Seaman and bears the name of the ship to which he is attached.

Lifeboatmen and fishermen clung to the sensible, waterproof sou'wester *(Fig. 572)* of what is now a traditional design, with adjustable brim. The amateur yachtsman has copied it in a brilliant yellow colour to assist rescuers in finding him should his boat capsize.

Fig. 573 is the unusual headgear worn till the present day by London's Billingsgate fish porters but now fast disappearing. It is chiefly of wood and costs approximately £10. The flat top is, for the balancing piled-up fish boxes.

The "bumaree" (or market porter) *(Fig. 574)* wears a hat of white or royal blue linen with the peak invariably turned to the side or back. It may be seen in London's Smithfield meat market on any weekday.

Fig. 575 is the better known chef's hat, no doubt originally intended to protect food from stray hairs but now an impressive and coveted symbol of the professional cook.

The modern coal-miner's hat, with hard top and lamp fixed to the front is illustrated in *Fig. 576* and somewhat similar hats are worn in other types of mining.

The topee for tropical wear *(Fig. 577)* goes back to the days when Africa and parts of Asia were being explored by Europeans. It has a facing of green

FIG. 572   English (1950)

FIG. 573   English (1958)

FIG. 574   English (1966)

fabric under the brim to soften harsh sunlight, but when worn today the crown is generally lower than it was in the nineteenth century.

Sir Robert, later Lord Baden-Powell, who established the Boy Scouts' Association in 1908, modelled on Boer War uniforms the khaki hats which boys (11–18) and Rover Scouts (over 18) wore for many years *(Fig. 578)*. Wolf cubs (8–11) were enrolled some time after the Association was set up and wore a coloured peaked cap with distinctive braid. *(Fig. 579)*.

Prior to the First World War the "British working man" was addicted to the comfortable cloth cap of characteristic shape with which he is always associated in pictures and in literature. He still wears it but so do young professional men and many others on informal occasions. Personal preferences have influenced shape and cut a little, as we can see from comparing the working lad's cap of *Fig. 580* with that of the older man in *Fig. 581*.

The London costermonger or street trader, well known through several centuries for his sturdy individuality, has invented a unique form of headwear *(Fig. 582)*. It was commonly seen at Hampstead Heath and other fairs until recently and is still worn proudly by the Pearly Kings and Queens of London's East End. An ordinary cloth cap is covered with pearl buttons, sewn close together in patterns, and matching the suit (or dress in the case of the Pearly Queens) which is similiarly decorated.

FIG. 575   English (1958)

FIG. 577   English

FIG. 576   English (1962)

FIG. 578   English (1925)

Fig. 579   English

Fig. 582   English

Fig. 580   English

Fig. 583   English (1961)

Fig. 581   English (1900-1959)

Fig. 584   English (1958)

FIG. 585   English

FIG. 586   English (1959)

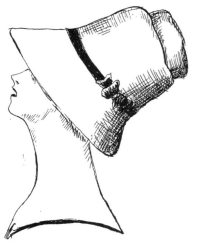

FIG. 587   English

In complete contrast but evidencing the same instinct for display among young males is the tough crash helmet worn by the motor-cyclist in *Fig. 583.* Most such helmets are brightly coloured or patterned in striking lines or segments.

A ceremonial hat of ancient lineage is that of the Queen's Bargemen in *Fig. 584,* and another enduring link with the past is the special velvet hat with plumes worn by members of the Order of the Garter with the Garter robes. *(Fig. 585)*. It still retains its ancient shape and royal blue colour.

The barrister's wig *(Fig. 586)*, with symmetrically arranged side curls and ribbon queue, dates back, with little modification, to the eighteenth century, and like the judge's wig we saw in Fig. 512 is still a picturesque feature of London life during Legal Sessions.

WOMEN: 1945 TO PRESENT DAY

Women's hat fashions change so quickly and so frequently nowadays that only a few outstanding examples have been chosen to represent the period following the Second World War.

In the late nineteen-fifties hats with deep crowns and face-shading brims, which critics have referred to as "the waste-paper basket shape," were in vogue for a season and many were seen at Princess Margaret's wedding in Westminster Abbey. *Fig. 587* is sketched from a fashion photograph of the time.

Most women would consider a much prettier fashion that which followed in the early nineteen-sixties when many hats were made from fur, in natural tones or dyed in light, bright colours. The softening effect of the fur at the hair-line or farther forward over the brows is recognisably flattering to the majority of women and so it is not surprising that the fur hat retained its popularity for a period of some years, though varying in shape and height and the angle at which it was set on the head. One of the earliest in this fashion, dating from 1964, is illustrated in *Fig. 588.* It is in white with a single pink flower as a trimming. Another becoming millinery style was very much worn in 1965 and 1966. This consisted of a simple brimless shape covered completely with fabric petals or leaves or made from swathings of nylon net or tulle (pure silk net), and an example is seen in *Fig. 589.*

The beige silk toque of *Fig. 590* was contemporary with the earlier fur hats but had a shorter fashion run, its hard lines making it much less easy to wear unless by women with exceptionally perfect features.

Many modern girls and women eschew hats altogether, concentrating rather on carefully planned hair styles, and, probably for this reason, the head square, once the prerogative of South and Central European peasants, is now generally popular, particularly as it may be conveniently folded and put away in handbag or pocket when not required on the head (See *Fig. 591*). The best of these squares—especially those made from pure silk—are printed in good colour combinations and often with exquisite designs bearing the name of the artist. Italy, the home of the European silk-spinning industry, is deservedly famous for her output of such squares, but

French and English weavers and fabric designers also supply the market with very fine examples.

Successful attempts have been made to give them a firmer shape to fit the head, by quilting or padding the inside of the fold at the centre front, and silk is by no means the only fabric of which they may be woven. Cotton, wool, nylon, rayon or other fibres lend themselves to the square shape and are often given a rain-resistant finish.

Cheap, mass-produced rain hoods which fold into a very small space have proved their value as a device for protecting the hair or a fragile hat during a shower and most women these days make a habit of carrying one. They have largely replaced the earlier mackintosh (rubberised fabric) hoods and

FIG. 588   English (1964)

FIG. 590   English (1964)

FIG. 589   English (1965)

FIG. 591   English (1953–66)

FIG. 592　English (1961)

FIG. 595　English (1905)

FIG. 593　Italian (1902)

FIG. 596　English (1914–1918 war)

FIG. 594　South African

FIG. 597　German (1914)

hats which, however, are still sometimes sold and worn with matching coats. A child's mackintosh hat of the year 1961 is drawn in *Fig. 592*.

MILITARY

The tradition that persisted through so many centuries that military headgear should be flamboyant and picturesque dies hard, and even as recently as 1902 the uniform hat of the Italian Basaglieri had long drooping cocks' feathers reaching to the shoulder *(Fig. 593)*. Practical considerations, however, prevailed during the South African campaigns and fighting men in the Boer War needed the large shady hat of soft felt with brim that could be lowered to shield eyes or nape which we see in *Fig. 594*. Even so, a touch of the picturesque is added by the feather trim. The soft khaki felt hat of the Boer War proved acceptable and comfortable and its shape was retained for the Civil Imperial Volunteers. *Fig. 595* shows how it was worn by them in 1905.

At the outbreak of the First World War the peaked cap proved a light and practical form of headwear for all ranks, but under shellfire the metal helmet (or 'tin hat') protected the head against shrapnel. It varied in shape among the warring nations and in some cases was worn over a head-hugging woollen cap (first designed for the Crimean War in 1851), known familiarly as the 'Balaclava helmet', or simply 'Balaclava'! *Fig. 596* shows an English soldier in both kinds of 'helmet' in the 1914–1918 War.

We have come a long way from the times when the headgear of the fighting man was conspicuous and impressive—designed in fact to strike awe and terror in the enemy's ranks. During the highly organised wars of this century when the element of surprise has been so important a tactical factor, military uniforms including head wear have been deliberately made as inconspicuous as possible—field grey or khaki as a rule—and often camouflaged as well. But the idea of inspiring terror in one's enemies endures. Kaiser Wilhelm in *Fig. 597* wears a hat which was part of the uniform of the Todthussaren in 1914 which bore in the front the device of skull and crossbones.

Other traditional headwear includes the helmet of the Life Guards *(Fig. 598)*, so conspicuous a part of English pageantry and official parades. The high sweeping plumes are of horsehair, some being red and some white. Another full dress uniform hat is

FIG. 598   English (1958)

FIG. 599   English

FIG. 600   Scottish (1958)

Fig. 601   Scottish

Fig. 604   Hungarian

Fig. 602   Scottish

Fig. 605   Greek

Fig. 603   Italian

Fig. 606   English (1939–45 war)

that of the officer of Her Majesty's Yeoman of the Guard in *Fig. 599*.

Scottish and Irish regiments have maintained their own striking uniforms and on occasion such as the Battle of Waterloo have marched into battle wearing bearskins or other distinctive head wear. (It will be remembered that Highland Regiments earned for themselves the nickname 'the Ladies from Hell' by virtue of their attire and their intrepidity in both World Wars.) A Scottish piper of the Black Watch in *Fig. 600* wears a uniform renowned throughout the world. The Royal Company of Archers, guard of honour in Edinburgh, still has its cap with one, two or three feathers denoting rank *(Fig. 601)*. The Company was founded in 1676 and became a royal bodyguard in 1822. A cap of the Glengarry type *(Fig 602)* worn by the Cameronians (Scottish Rifles) is both distinctive and easy to wear.

Other countries, also have till recently preserved their own fine outstanding uniform hats and helmets. *Fig. 603* is a helmet worn between the Great Wars by Italian Dragoons and *Fig. 604* a Hungarian officer's busby of the same period.

Fig. 605. A military hat worn today by the Greek Evzones.

We conclude with some examples of recent hats or caps for active service. The English R.A.F. forage cap in Air Force blue cloth with badge of wings and crown was made to fold flat for tucking conveniently under belt or shoulder straps *(Fig. 606)*, and the beret of the Commando Regiments in *Fig. 607* was just as simple and practical, with its close-fitting leather binding. Both were worn with distinction in the Second World War.

FIG. 607   English (1939–45 war)

Crowns

THROUGHOUT MOST OF the long period covered by this book it was a convention among sculptors, wood-carvers, painters and other artists to portray royal personages and saints in a crown or coronet as an easily recognisable sign of their high estate.[1] Such symbols, always ornamental in themselves, often add to the dignity of the wearer and the pictorial effect of the whole.

The earliest form of regal head-dress in the Western world was the plain gold fillet or band. Offa, king of the Mercians, who ruled from A.D. 757 to 796, is represented as wearing a double circlet of jewels (beads or pearls) and Behrtulf whose reign lasted from 839 to 852, wears a simple gold band, with, in the centre front, a decoration of a half-moon lying on its back. When the tomb of Edward the Confessor was opened in the reign of James I it was

[1]The Romans conferred the *corona* however, on their national heroes as well as their emperors. To wear a circlet of oak leaves (for rescuing a fellow-soldier in battle) or of herbs and grasses gathered on the field of victory (for the leader who rescued an army from defeat) was considered as much an honour as the gold band worn by the first man to scale the walls of a beseiged city.

established that this Saxon king had been buried with a circlet of gold, one inch wide.

Tassels or strings often hung from the crown or coronet, fillet or garland as we see in *Fig. 608*, taken from a crudely fashioned coin of the period representing King Harold. Such pendant strings were called *vellae* or *ansulae* and were originally tied under the chin. They may still be seen on the Pope's tiara. A story is told of how Ralph, Archbishop of Canterbury, in a rage, snatched the crown from the head of King Henry I so breaking the ansulae that had secured it.

Many examples of crowns and coronets have been shown in earlier pages because the hair-styles or head-coverings with which they were worn exemplified particular trends or fashions under consideration. A few other instances which are intrinsically interesting, merit special attention.

Some of the Early English crowns were square, if the delineatinions in miniatures of the ninth to twelfth centuries can be regarded as accurate and are not faulty drawing on the part of the original artists. King Edgar in *Fig. 609*, for example, seems to have been one such king to wear this inconvenient shape. Another peculiar style graced the head of

FIG. 608   King Harold (1065)

FIG. 609   English 9th to 12th-cents.

St. Edmund *(Fig. 610).* It is shown in his *Life* written about 1125. His was a pearl-set coronet, like that of King Harold shown earlier in Fig. 608 and this form was eventually replaced by the radiating diadem. The rays themselves later became foliated in various ways, usually acquiring a smaller pearl- or jewel-studded point between the higher, leaflike shapes.

These are exceptions, however, and it was usual to show the crown as a thing of beauty in itself, as would have been the jewelled circlet from a silver head on a reliquary box of the twelfth century in *Fig. 611.* This is very probably of Sicilian origin.

Fig. 612 comes from what is thought to be a portrait of Constance of Aragon, first wife of Frederick II, Emperor of the Holy Roman Empire, as a crown of similar shape was found buried with her. The pendant of pearl tassels hangs from the ears and is not part of the handsome crown she wears. They undoubtedly show Byzantine influence, which became general all over Europe during the Crusades until after the fall of Constantinople.

The reputed crown of the Emperor Charlemagne is worn in *Fig. 613* by Ferdinand II. It, too, derives much of its grandeur from the example of Byzantine craftsmanship but is lighter than those of the emperors and saints of Constantinople.

The more typically Western European foliated style is drawn in *Fig. 614* from the portrait of King Richard II in Westminster Abbey.

FIG. 610   English

FIG. 612   Italian (12th cent.)

FIG. 611   Possibly Sicilian (12th cent.)

FIG. 613   Frankish

From the fourteenth century onwards Western European crowns have in general conformed to this fundamental shape, with, varying forms of elaboration and enrichment.

The British State Crown of *Fig. 615* therefore, although designed for Queen Victoria in 1838 and here worn by her great-granddaughter, Queen Elizabeth II, has a long and honourable lineage. In contrast to the comparatively simple silhouette and decoration of that of King Richard, it contains 2,783 diamonds, 277 pearls, 17 sapphires, 11 emeralds and five rubies. Among the jewels are the Black Prince's ruby, Edward the Confessor's sapphire, and four large pearl ornaments once belonging to Elizabeth Tudor. The crosses on the Crown of England were introduced by King Richard III and the arches date from Henry VII's coronation in 1485.

For somewhat less formal occasions the present queen of England wears a lighter symbolic head-dress—the tiara of *Fig. 616*.

Another twentieth century crown but probably deriving from pre-historic times is the head-dress of Lucia, Queen of Norway *(Fig. 617)*. The girl chosen to be the Queen of Light wears lighted candles amidst a profusion of dark green leaves. This is undoubtedly a survival of an ancient witch-cult, now christianised. Only unmarried girls were allowed to take part in the Farandole, a Norwegian processional dance not unlike the Helston Furry Dance of Cornwall in that the dancers held hands

Fig. 614   English (*c.* 1380)

Fig. 616   English (20th cent.)

Fig. 615   British (20th cent.)

Fig. 617   Norwegian (20th cent.)

FIG. 618

and wound in and out of the village houses. As the Farandole was performed at night the girls either carried lanterns or wore 'a round of waxen tapers on head.' Jeanne Boisdeau described this custom in 1594 and reported that the participants danced back to back and were led by a great black goat always associated with witchcraft and black magic. The oldest person followed, holding its tail, and the rest came after, holding hands.[1]

Fig. 618 represents the specially designed coronet worn by Prince Charles at his Investiture Ceremony when he became Prince of Wales, July 1969.

[1] *The God of the Witches,* by Margaret Murray.

Ecclesiastical Head-dresses

Fig. 618. THE CARDINAL'S RED hat was introduced by Pope Innocent IV in the 13th century. Formerly worn on the head, it is now only carried on the cardinal's coffin or on state occasions. The illustration shows one worn in the 14th century.

Figs. 619 to 622. The next five figures represent the evolution of the Pope's tiara. Thus, in the period 1073–1085 Pope Gregory VII wore a conical hood with a jewel pinned into it above the forehead. His staff also is very simple, far from the floriated crook of later days *Fig. 619*. A further development is shown in *Fig. 620* where Pope Innocent III wears a conical hat, with ansulae, a darker band, scalloped, at the edge and the whole jewelled. It comes from

FIG. 618   Italian (14th cent.)

FIG. 620   Subiaco

FIG. 619   Italian

FIG. 621   Italian

'Subiaco. In *Fig. 621* is depicted the Papal crown of Pope Alexander VI showing a modification of the cone and even more jewelled.

Fig. 622 is the tiara of 1776, worn by Pope Pius VI. It has now a rounded top and is surmounted by a cross.

Fig. 623 shows the Pope's tiara of the present day, 1966.

The mitre as we know it came into being about the beginning of the 11th century: before that a phrygian cap was worn tied with a cord, the ends of which hung free behind. One of the earliest examples is that shown on Peter Lombard, Bishop of Paris 1159 with horns over each ear. Then the whole was shifted round until the horns were back and front and so it assumed its present form. They were embroidered with birds, hares, etc. and often made of brocade.

Fig. 624 represents a mitre of 1315 and is Italian.

Fig. 625. A cardinal's biretta 1959.

FIG. 622   Italian

FIG. 624   Italian (1315)

Fig. 623   Italian

FIG. 625   Italian (1955)

Traditional or National Styles

WITHIN LIVING MEMORY national and traditional costumes, including becoming head-dresses and hats, were a common sight in nearly all European countries but they now have to be sought out in the remoter regions, and if the present deplorable trend of Westernizing the whole globe continues at the rate it is doing at present these distinctive head-dresses will have vanished before the next century opens. If we had something beautiful for them to emulate it would not be so regrettable, but even then why must everyone sink their individuality in one style no matter whether suitable to the climate, colour of skin or occupation?

When mass-produced goods penetrated into the

FIG. 626   Welsh

FIG. 628   Scottish (1835)

FIG. 627   Welsh (19th cent.)

FIG. 629   Scottish

remotest areas, until then largely self-sufficient, several changes resulted. People no longer had the time or felt the compulsion to make and decorate elaborate clothes or replace them when they fell into disrepair. In some districts they were discarded altogether. In others they have been lovingly and carefully stored and are brought out and worn only on special occasions.

Fortunately for posterity artists and photographers have preserved a detailed record of many types of costume, in rich variety and often in colour. This evidence proves that many peasant peoples have a natural feeling for aesthetic values, and a collection of drawings made during the last century is particularly revealing in this respect.[1]

Here we are concerned with authentic styles, many of which still persist, and with the simpler but accurate versions which the traveller may even now expect to encounter in certain areas. A few ceremonial examples are also included as these are often of great historic interest.

England can boast of no true national costume, unless we may so regard the ribbons and bells of the morris dancers.

In Wales the tall black hat worn over a fluted cap seen in *Fig. 626* was frequently seen until the 1870's, especially on market days when countrywomen came down from the mountains. It is still worn at the

annual eisteddfods, but is recognised as archaic—a deliberate and laudable effort to sustain Welsh national identity. In his diary for 1871 the Reverend Francis Kilvert wrote: "At Llanyadock for the first time on our journey we saw a Welshwoman in a tall peaked hat . . . Mrs. Hannah Whitney said she wore the high Welsh hat in Clyro forty years ago. Then it wore out and she did not get another so they went out of fashion."

Another type of Welsh cap, from Glensevern is shown in *Fig. 627*, taken from a small sketch in a book on nineteenth century Welsh clothes. Such caps were made of black (or occasionally white) linen with a pale blue quilted satin turned-back brim, and were decorated with a small bow over the forehead and ribbons to tie under the chin.

Scotland, as so often, asserted its independence of English fashions.

The fine Scottish tammy of *Fig. 628* is dated 1835. Followed by the Glengarry, *Fig. 629*, a folding hat with streamers, and the Balmoral, *Fig. 630*, it has continued in favour with men when they wear the kilt, until the present time.

Ireland had its own version of the tammy or "bonnet" with two pompoms on top, and in *Fig. 631* we see Paddy happily digging peat.

In France many examples are still extant. Normandy and Brittany can boast distinctive styles of headwear that have been proudly worn for generations and may still be seen, though they appear to be gradually passing out of use. *Fig. 632* is a linen or cambric cap as worn by Breton girls in 1910. The

---

[1]Some of these styles here referred to representing the area that was Silesia and Bohemia appear in Figs. 681, 682, 688, 689 and 690.

FIG. 630   Scottish

FIG. 631   Irish (1925)

FIG. 632   Brittany (1910)

FIG. 633   Brittany

FIG. 634   Brittany (*c.* 1924)

young Breton dandy still likes to bring out his gala hat for special occasions and in *Fig. 633* he is on his way to his wedding, while his bride in *Fig. 634* has a traditional white peaked cap of the Roscoff district, with a point at the back and embroidered turned-back frill framing the face. Such a cap could be laid out flat for laundering. Still in Brittany, an old weaver of St. Barbe wore the soft felt hat with wide ribbon of *Fig. 635*.

Tourists to the South of France are familiar with the straw hats which have raffia trimming, little or no crown, and ribbon tie strings, for sale in many shops, but they may not realise that they are purchasing a form of true traditional headwear *(Fig. 636)*.

The two following illustrations are from the small state of Liechtenstein. The becoming straw hat of *Fig. 637* with moiré ribbon round the crown and streamers tying under the chin was photographed in 1925, as was the neat cap with forward flopping peak to the crown worn by the old gentleman in *Fig. 638*.

The typical Swiss straw hat of *Fig. 639,* with shallow crown and wide flat brim, is placed over a cap of frilled lace which is pinned to and encircles the bun or coil of hair at the back.

The Low Countries have always been especially noted for characteristic head-dresses and caps, though the so-called "Dutch bonnet" is only one of many regional variations. The more recent or contemporary types are illustrated here. Gold pins are still a decorative feature of many, and may be seen at the centre front in *Fig. 640,* where a girl from

FIG. 635   Brittany

FIG. 636   France (1960)

FIG. 639   Swiss

FIG. 637   Liechtenstein (1925)

FIG. 640   Zeeland

FIG. 638   Liechtenstein (1925)

FIG. 641   Dutch

FIG. 642   Volendam

FIG. 645   Dutch (1940)

FIG. 643   Dutch

FIG. 646   Dutch

FIG. 644   Netherlandish

FIG. 647   Belgian

Zeeland wears an elaborate lace-trimmed bonnet with wide stiffened lace forming a halo-frame round her face. From another district in Holland comes the lace cap worn by the girl in *Fig. 641*. This time the accompanying wide frill falls in sculptured folds at the back and the gold pins are replaced by gold-coloured clips at the temples.

The women of Volendam, until recently an island but now part of the large area reclaimed from the sea, is well known for styles peculiarly its own and more closely approximating to the winged bonnets regarded as typically Dutch. Such a lace cap is shown in *Fig. 642* and the girl who wears it has also donned a straw bonnet-shaped hat for wearing out of doors. A more elaborate cap of lace and cambric with prominent wings is shown in *Fig. 643*, and this also comes from Volendam. Sketched in *Fig. 644* is another Dutch cap, perhaps barely becoming to our eyes but warm and snug in a country where cold north and east winds often sweep in unimpeded over the flat meadows bordering the North Sea. It is worn by a young girl and ribbons passing through slots in the crown and brim keep it securely in place on her head.

A not unusual sight in Scheveningen, Noordwijk and Fishwick is the fisherwoman of *Fig. 645* in her white starched cap with its proudly worn and very decorative gold hair pin. Only one is shown here but sometimes two or more are added, giving a gay, jaunty effect. A contrasting style is that of the young girl from Marken whose cap *(Fig. 646)* is made from fawn holland, embroidered in reds and blues and tied with embroidered straps.

A Belgian milkmaid in *Fig. 647* is dressed in her "Sunday best", a gay little hat worn over a fine lace cap with wings at the side. No doubt this had its origin in the distant past when such caps were general.

Another district known for its own distinctive styles is Alsace and probably the most typical is the large bow head-dress of *Fig. 648*, whilst dating from the end of the nineteenth century, is a style which is attractively simple *(Fig. 649)*.

German country people are still faithful to their traditional styles, many of which were officially revived during the nineteenth century to encourage a national sense of unity. The best are nowadays

FIG. 648   Alsatian (first quarter of 1920)

FIG. 649   Alsace

FIG. 650   German

✳*189*✳

FIG. 651   German (Black Forest area)

FIG. 652   German

FIG. 653   Austrian (1957)

brought out for gala occasions, but in the Black Forest districts many women still work in the simpler of their local attire, their hair being bound with black velvet ribbons. The men usually wear a western-type suit with their own local hats. Women's hats with large decorative pompoms *(Figs. 650 and 651)* are still to be met with and the author understands that here in the Black Forest unmarried girls wear red pompoms and wives wear black ones. Another strange shape from this area is the flat-topped disk shape with hollow centre of *Fig. 652* which is trimmed with circles of coloured beads.

Nearly every Austrian village has, or had until recently, its own hats and head-dress styles. One of the most fanciful, in *Fig. 653* hails from Berganze. The brim is of lace stretched over a wire frame and is fitted half way down the crown of the embroidered cap section. It was worn for festive occasions at least until 1960. The Austrian province of Carinthia provides a gala head-dress *(Fig. 654)* which is typically eastern European with its wide embroidered velvet band encircling the head. Several layers of accordion-pleated frills, in white lawn or linen, rise steeply above it and long wide ribbons, woven with a floral pattern, are suspended from the back.

In the Carpathians shepherd boys have worn the attractive broad-brimmed hats swathed with velvet or ribbon round the crown seen in *Fig. 655* which dates from 1945. Such headwear is in complete harmony with the thick leather or cloth coats donned for protection on exposed mountain slopes.

Fig. 656 depicts the livery hat of a Hungarian coachman as it was worn in 1924 and it may perhaps be regarded as a national style. But indisputably the Sunday hat worn by the youth in *Fig. 657* is in the true folk tradition. This example was seen in 1920 but the same shape with its rather exotic trimmings can still be sometimes seen in country villages.

Italian peasants, like those in France and Holland, have for hundreds of years realised the potentialities of lace for making up into or trimming caps or other forms of headwear, and in *Fig. 658* a country girl wears a frilled lace cap dating from 1890. It is attached to the back of the hair with an ornamental long-headed pin.

The specially designed medieval costume of the Swiss Guards at the Vatican includes the cloth tammy-shaped hat seen in *Fig. 659* which carries on a long tradition, as does the curiously-shaped but

FIG. 654   Carinthian

FIG. 657   Hungarian (1920)

FIG. 655   Hungarian or Czechoslovakian (1945)

FIG. 658   Italian (1890)

FIG. 656   Hungarian (1924)

FIG. 659   Swiss Guard in Rome

Fig. 660   Italian (1927)

Fig. 663   San Marino (*c.* 1925)

Fig. 661   Sardinian (1956)

Fig. 664   Spanish

Fig. 662   Sardinian

Fig. 665   Spanish

imposing hat of the Italian Carabinieri of *Fig. 660*.

Sardinia, as is to be expected in the case of a mountainous island, has retained its own local styles of costume and headwear, though some, alas, are fast disappearing. *Fig. 661*, for instance, shows a head-dress worn by a Sardinian shepherd as recently as 1956. It is of soft knitted material, tubular in shape, like a stocking. One end fits round the head and the rest is flattened and folded, first forward to shade the eyes and then back again to shield the neck. Another stocking cap style is worn by the Sardinian mountaineer in *Fig. 662,* but here the loose bag-shaped section is allowed to fall beside the face at one side.

In the Republic of San Marino two representatives are elected bi-yearly and in *Fig. 663* we have the ceremonial hat (and accompanying scarf) which they wear at their installation. It is of ermine and has a flat velvet top.

In Spain the ceremonial attire prescribed for the bull ring includes several hats of distinctive shape and historic interest. The matador's in *Fig. 664* is of astrakhan, and the side projections and flat decorated top to the crown are almost certainly unique. The picador's hat in *Fig. 665* is quite different, being made of felt with a leather chin strap and a small horn as decoration. Many young Spaniards who are not picadors by profession have borrowed and adopted this hat shape, and it may be seen in many parts of Spain in daily wear.

Although the wearer in *Fig. 666* is a Sardinian, the hat sketched at the Festa della Madonna Remeda in 1945 is typically Spanish and is placed over a white shawl or scarf. In the Seman Santo Procession in Valladolid the *confradéas* (congregations) wear the strange peaked hoods of *Fig. 667* as they carry through the streets "Pasos" with representations of Christ's Passion. Head and shoulders are completely covered, leaving only slits for the eyes.

The stocking cap of the Portuguese fisherman in *Fig. 668* has some affinity with the caps worn by Sardinians in Figs. 661 and 662, and it is tempting to regard all these and others like them characteristic of Mediterranean countries as deriving from the Phrygian style described earlier in this book. If indeed they are, then the shape has persisted without a break for more than 2000 years. In the present instance the stocking shape has an astrakhan border with a tassel terminating the bag which

Fig. 666   Sardinian (in Spanish style hat, 1945)

Fig. 667   Spanish Valladolid (1959)

Fig. 668   Portuguese

FIG. 669   Portuguese

FIG. 670   Norway

FIG. 671   Norway

hangs over the wearer's left shoulder. Very different is the headwear seen in *Fig. 669*. Here a Portuguese peasant woman wears the equivalent of a man's trilby over her dark headcloth or scarf.

In the Scandinavian countries caps and head-dresses peculiar to particular localities are still fairly general. Three from Norway are illustrated here. The first, in *Fig. 670*, and known as a *Skaut*, is the goffered fly-away head-dress of a married woman from Hardanger. Next *(Fig. 671)* comes an interesting style seen at a christening. It is in embroidered linen with a stiffened point at each side and a small pointed brim. The third example, in *Fig. 672*, is worn by a little girl. It is seen from above, to show the cloth top with bands of braid wound round the crown, a narrow fluted frill for a brim, and two ear pieces which may, if desired, be buttoned under her chin.

Young girls of Garpenberg in Sweden were wearing in 1922 the kind of cap seen in *Fig. 673* which bears some resemblance to the Cap of Liberty made famous during the French Revolution.

Farther north the men of Lapland are faithful to the hat shown in *Fig. 674*. It has survived through many generations and is snug and well padded to keep out the icy cold of winter. The cloth is manipulated into two horn-shaped points that rise from the top and the Lapps often add braid or colourful embroidery similar to that decorating the tunics worn by both sexes.[1] Women also trim their caps

---

[1]*Reindeer are Wild Too* by Joan Newhouse.

FIG. 672   Norway

FIG. 673   Swedish

FIG. 676   Lapland (1963)

FIG. 674   Lapland

FIG. 677   Alaska or Iceland

FIG. 675   Lapland

FIG. 678   Eskimo

FIG. 679   Polish

FIG. 682   Slatina (1845)

FIG. 680   Polish (1925)

FIG. 683   Russian (1903)

FIG. 681   Slatina (1850)

FIG. 684   Russian

with bands of embroidery, as we see in the two following illustrations *(Fig. 675)* of a young woman, and *(Fig. 676)* of an older one.

In the Arctic Eskimo women have their traditional 'parka' of fur *(Fig. 677)* which, besides being supremely warm, also provides a becoming frame to the face. The Eskimo child in *Fig. 678* has a comfortable woollen turban style cap, possibly of knitted fabric.

Polish peasants have always been fond of elaborate and striking headwear and the bridal head-dress of *Fig. 679* is a good example. It is made of ruched ribbon woven with a floral design, surmounted by an imposing spray of artificial flowers at the front and accompanied by a dark veil. The following example *(Fig. 680)* shows a Polish woman in a hat formed from a velvet circlet placed at a becoming angle over a dark head-scarf.

Russian and Polish peasants in the middle years of the nineteenth century had long plaits at either side of their faces as we see from *Fig. 681,* and soldiers in both armies are known to have retained them even though one imagines they would have afforded a perfect hand-hold to the enemy in hand-to-hand fighting. In *Fig. 682* a gamekeeper from the same district (Slatina) and of the same period has a felt hat tilted rakishly at a becoming angle and two small ribbon streamers at the back.

In the vast land masses now contained within the U.S.S.R., with their contrasting climates and customs, it is not surprising to find a wide variety of headwear styles. This was particularly evident before the 1917 Revolution, and several of the illustrations which follow date from the early years of this century. *Fig. 683* is the handsome head-dress worn by the Princess Zenaide Yousoupoff in 1903. Its tall peak is studded with rubies and other precious stones and in the centre is the great diamond called the Polar Star.

At the same period some Russian peasants wore the tall, flat-topped hat of *Fig. 684,* with its narrow brim and double bands of twisted cord round the crown. The man's hair, it will be noted, has been allowed to grow fairly long, as was the custom in those days.

In Georgia astrakhan was, and still is, a favourite material for men's hats and the type seen in *Fig. 685,* in the shape of a simple cone, is called a *bourka*.

From Latvia we have a splendidly embroidered

FIG. 685   Georgian, now Russia

FIG. 686   Latvian

FIG. 687   Siberian

✳197✳

felt cap, worn by a peasant woman on special occasions *(Fig. 686)*.

In Siberia, especially in the north, fur or reindeer skin are, not unnaturally, widely used for making hats, as in the case of the country woman of *Fig. 687* who has also attached silver disks and dangling tassels to the ends of her plaited hair.

A German artist visiting Roumania and Slovakia in the early years of the nineteenth century came back with some exquisite drawings he had made of local attire. *Figs 688* and *689* are from two of his sketches made in 1816 and both show high head-dresses. That of the woman has three ribbons of contrasting colour passing down from the top and under the front edge, with a bunch of ribbons

suspended from the back. The man's hat looks strange to us and his long hair even more so—especially the tied loop at the end of the side lock and his exceptionally long moustache.

In 1835 a young man from Slovakia was sketched in the hat shown in *Fig. 690*. It is of brown felt with a double wreath of artificial flowers, one ostrich plume and two cock's feathers. Somewhat similar hats are still to be seen today in Central European villages.

Most Eastern European peasants are famous for their attractive holiday attire, accompanied by colourful and often highly decorative hats and caps. The countryman from Ruvenia, Czechoslovakia, in *Fig. 691* has a shallow-crowned hat with brim of

Fig. 688   Slovakia (1816)

Fig. 690   Slovakia (1835)

Fig. 689   Slovakia (1816)

Fig. 691   Rumania or Czechoslovakia

Fig. 692   Slovakia

Fig. 695   Armenia

Fig. 693   Silesia

Fig. 696   Montenegro (1910)

Fig. 694   Armenia

Fig. 697   Serbia (1925)

medium width and decoration of twisted ribbon. His hair has been allowed to grow long enough to cover his ears. The Slovakian farmer in *Fig. 692* wears his hair uncut and in four long plaits, two in front and two at the back, and on his head a small felt hat with shallow domed centre.

Silesian peasant women, like the one in *Fig. 693,* assumed a most elaborate head-dress of wired-out lace, forming a winged frame for the tight-fitting bonnet which is gathered into folds beneath the chin.

From Armenia comes the studded band and padded roll draped with a white cloth or veil, worn by the lady in *Fig. 694.* It is curiously reminiscent of the medieval rondlet and coverchief described in earlier sections of this book, and in the next illustration *(Fig. 695)* an Armenian patriarch has a peaked, cowl-like head-dress of watered silk and a most venerable beard.

In Montenegro before the First World War nearly all Montenegrins, from King Nicholas downwards,

wore a pillbox hat of the kind shown in *Fig. 696.* Material and decoration varied according to the owner's purse and preference, some being embroidered and some having badges, as seen in the sketch. This hat has a band attached to a soft top, but many of them had flat stiffened tops.

Serbian women in 1925 wore the kind of head-dress drawn in *Fig. 697.* It consisted of a deep band of embroidery supporting a goffered linen top and was encircled by velvet ribbons finished with small bows. At the same period women of Kupinovo wore the pastoral head-dress depicted in *Fig. 698.* It was richly embroidered and braided and had a padded square tab of the same material projecting vertically from the crown.

Malta provides us with a unique cloak-cum-hood style in black silk or cotton, called a *faldetta,* which is worn by many women throughout the island *(Fig. 699).*

Fig. 698   Kupinovo, Serbia (1925)

Fig. 699   Maltese

Non-European Hats and Head-dresses

IN VIEW OF the fact that all parts of the world are rapidly becoming Westernized, and that before many more decades have passed the head-dresses of non-European peoples will have disappeared it has been thought reasonable to include those hats and hair-styles still to be seen by travellers in remote regions.

All examples have been taken from 20th century photographs.

The peasants and others who made the hats we have been examining within this book have the advantage of living within reach of the various trades where articles for hat-making are always obtainable, whereas natives in the wild have to be content with the materials at hand, and so their various head-dresses, which are based on leaves, rushes, flowers, feathers and even mud, are much more ephemeral. They have to be made more often and cannot be put away in a non-existent cupboard for the next gala occasion—the wreaths and leis of the Tahaitian girls being the extreme example. These latter head adornments have to be made fresh

several times a day. Thus the natives' head attire depends entirely on their environment, but they may, nevertheless, show great artistry in what they choose to put on their heads.

Starting in the high altitudes of Tibet we have

FIG. 701 Tibet

FIG. 700 Tibet

FIG. 702 Tibet (1965)

eight examples of really interesting head styles. *Figs. 700* and *701* show two high-ranking ladies with horned head-dresses, and in *Fig. 702* a veil of real human hair, usually bought from China, descends behind the wearer's back.

Lama Yongden in his novel '*Mipam, the Lama of the Five Wisdoms*' gives one an insight into the wearing of such a creation:—'The *gyalmo,* in her own room with the help of her maids, took off her jewels, her outer dress and the upper part of her tall coiffure, which was arranged in the Tsang fashion, but the two wooden horns on which this contraption rested, which were firmly held in place by the coils of her hair, could be removed only once a month, when the princess had her hair washed and re-dressed by her maids. These two stick-like supports, about 14 ins in length, projecting on either side at a slight angle compelled the lady to sleep lying flat and motionless on her back. Accustomed from the years of her girlhood to wearing these horns, they did not seem to incommode her, and her husband trustfully accepted the proximity of his horned consort, who, by a sudden movement, might have blinded him.'

Religious motives differentiate the next two hat styles, *Figs. 703* and *704,* the former being the original of the red-hat sect, and the latter of the yellow-hat or reformed sect. *Fig. 705* represents the hairdressing of a Tibetan student and *Fig. 706* shows a back-view of the 'Memen Oroit' or fur-trimmed hat of Tibet

FIG. 703   Tibet (1956)

FIG. 705   Tibet

FIG. 704   Tibet (1959)

FIG. 706   Tibet (1960)

which has a quilted top in red silk with a flap over the neck in blue silk and red streamers. This style is in use at the present date, as is *Fig. 707* where a lama wears a ceremonial hat whilst chanting religious songs beside a mandala.

Unfortunately many Tibetans have a penchant for Western hats; thus, from Fosco Mariani's book we have a description of hair-styling by a lama.

'Lobsang, whilst giving his personal interpretation of the Buddhist Four Noble Truths puts down his prayer wheel and starts combing his long hair with the nicety of an official scrutinizing a document. 'I wash my hair once a week,' he announces with a certain pride. Having been in contact with the British for so long he has acquired unusual habits of

cleanliness. He now looks like an old maid dressing up for the fair. His face is invisible completely covered with his hair. When he considers he has combed it enough, that is to say, when every hair is perpendicular and parallel he divides it into two with his hands. He plaits the two sides. When three quarters of the work is done, Lobsang's deft and agile fingers insert into the hair a number of ribbons, coloured pink, cobalt, green and sky blue. The ribbons on each plait end in a long many-coloured tassel and this makes the final effect very effective.'

But he spoils it all by placing on the top a homberg hat!

Travelling southwards to Nepal we see as in *Fig. 708* the head-dress of a Nepalese Court lady in the

FIG. 707   Tibet

FIG. 709   Nepal (1957)

FIG. 708   Nepal (1910)

FIG. 710   The King of Bhutan (1925)

FIG. 711   Bhutan (1920)

FIG. 714   Apa Tani (1960)

FIG. 712   Bhutan

FIG. 715   Assam

FIG. 713   Apa Tani—Himalayas (1962)

FIG. 716   Assam (1958)

early years of the century. An embroidered 'pill-box' hat elaborately embroidered, is worn with plaits.

Fig. 709 gives a very inadequate picture of the gorgeousness of the Nepalese crown which is still worn on regal occasions. It is a diamond, pearl and emerald studded cap, surmounted by a plume of feathers from the tail of the Bird of Paradise.

A little further south, in Bhutan the king wears a head-dress in the style of *Fig. 710,* whilst the Dah Raga, acting head of the Buddhist church wears the hat with split, upturned and embroidered brims as in *Fig. 711.* For another Bhutanese style see *Fig. 712.*

In the foothills of the Himalayas is the almost unknown valley of Apa Tani. *Figs. 713* and *714* reveal the individuality of the little known inhabitants of this valley. The man's hat is made of cane with two small feathers fastened to the front, the hair being wound into a top-knot, which is kept in place on the forehead with a brass skewer. It is a disgrace to an Apa Tani if this knot be cut off by an enemy.[1]

The woman wears her black hair curled into a top-knot, wooden nose-plugs, and has elongated her ear-lobes and passed through them large gold rings. There is a facial decoration of a line down her forehead.

The Nagas, so far, have not adopted European fashions, and for ceremonial occasions the head-dresses in *Figs. 715* and *716* are donned; at other times a plucked flower is pushed into the hair for decoration.

Continuing south into India we find that the turban still holds its own in many places. *Fig. 717* shows that of a Kashmiri embroiderer. It is made of fine white muslin. *Fig. 718* is a looser style and comes from Baluchistan. *Fig. 719* is made of striped red satin and was worn by high-ranking Indians in the early years of the century. (It is of the 15th Ludbiana Sikhs of the 1st Brahmins.)

Many, so turbaned, came over for Queen Victoria's funeral in 1902. *Fig. 720* is a more elaborately arranged turban of a high-class as worn in 1957. A bizarre head-dress decorated with steel knives is that of the head-executioner of Revah in 1912. *(Fig. 721).*

Figs. 722 and *723* are hat-styles from Kandy. The first is that of a man of position and the second a fancy head-dress worn by a Kandian dancer.

[1] See *The Hidden Valley* by Ursula Bower.

FIG. 717   Kashmir

FIG. 718   Balchestan

FIG. 719   Indian

FIG. 720   Indian (1957)

FIG. 723   Kandy, Ceylon

FIG. 721   Indian (1912)

FIG. 724   Japanese (1958)

FIG. 722   Kandy, Ceylon

FIG. 725   Japanese

FIG. 726 Japanese

FIG. 729 Japanese (1945)

FIG. 727 Japanese

FIG. 730 Japanese

FIG. 728 Japanese Utamaro (1753–1806)

FIG. 731 Japanese Aince

FIG. 732   Korean merchant

FIG. 733   Korean

FIG. 734   Korean

Figs. 724 and *725* give the traditional head-dresses worn by the Prince and Princess of Japan in 1958. In *Fig. 726* a more conservative lady of Japan wears a hair-style derived from those of the last century which may be seen in Japanese idiom in *Figs. 727* and *728.*

A modern Japanese girl at a fête would decorate her head with the hoop and artificial roses depicted in *Fig. 729,* whilst a Shinto priest clings to his distinctive hat as in *Fig. 730.* A peasant of Ainu, north Japan, wears as head decoration only a wide ribbon band which supports his prayer box over his forehead. *(Fig. 731).*

A Korean merchant still wears the hard japanned hat with ribbons to tie under the chin, and dresses his moustache and beard as in *Fig. 732,* whilst a Korean gentleman is seen in *Fig. 733* wearing the Kasi hat, which name covers many similar shapes and is strictly regulated to the importance of the wearer. A further example of Korean head-wear and which is of metal is given in *Fig. 734.*

In Meos, Indo-China, a fashionable maiden would have been seen, in 1925, wearing the basket-like hat in *Fig. 735.*

In *Fig. 736,* we may see a typical silk cap of a Shanghai merchant and in *Fig. 737* a Chinese coolie wears a hat of straw, tilted sunways to shade his head and face.

A head-dress from Manchuria is portrayed in *Fig. 738.* This lady wears a curiously-shaped board covered with black silk, and on which she has arranged fresh or artificial flowers, which can be removed and re-arranged for the next occasion. This allows great scope for personal artistry.

Two Mongolian hats follow. *(Figs. 739* and *740).* The latter may have some European qualities but is tastefully arranged for an Oriental.

The Emperor of Annam, King Khai Dinh, a man who thought evidently that one could be a modern ruler and an oriental and still retain the character and charm of his country, without sinking everything into the Western mould, is seen in *Figs. 741* and *742* wearing, firstly, his Imperial diadem and secondly the hat he wore for military occasions as Commander of the Army, which is shaped on the coolie's straw but ornamented to suit his exalted position. These were photographed in 1921.

Two Formosan styles follow. *(Figs. 743* and *744).*

An old man of Herat wears a knitted hat of

FIG. 735   Incas, Indo-China (1925)

FIG. 738   Manchurian

FIG. 736   Shanghai

FIG. 739   Mongolian

FIG. 737   Manchurian

FIG. 740   Mongolian (1940)

FIG. 741   Annam

FIG. 744   Formosa

FIG. 742   Annam (King Khai Dinh 1920)

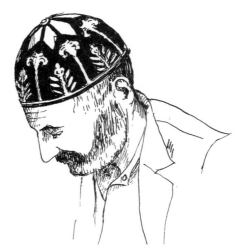

FIG. 745   Afghanistan, Herat (1960)

FIG. 743   Formosa

FIG. 746   Afghanistan (1960)

traditional design very similar to the crocheted caps made by the men of Menkes *(Fig. 745)*.

Figs. 746 and *747* illustrate the headgear worn to-day by the fine Afghan horsemen.

Fig. 748 shows a Karakul hat made from the pelts of sheep, and worn by the more modern and sophisticated men in Afghanistan.[1]

Next, in *Fig. 749* we have the usual hat of a Kashkai shepherd which he wears with a European suit. Also worn with European clothes is the padded-bandeau hat with a soft top favoured by the men of Hunza. The sitter for *Fig. 750* was a school teacher. With this headwear, a long cloak to the ground,

swinging wide from the shoulders, makes a handsome and dignified turn-out, and is to be seen on most of the males in the Hunza Valley.[1]

In *Fig. 751* a little girl of Baltit, Hunza, wears a pill-box embroidered cap, which the women make and wear with some distinction.

Here, in *Fig. 752*, may be seen the traditional head-dress of a Muslim of Iraq. Over his head, which is shaven to a stubble is worn a skull cap of bright coloured material. This, in our illustration, is hidden by the shawl-like drapery called a *kaffia*, on which a pattern like wire-netting is woven on a white background. This denotes that the wearer is of

---

[1]See *North from Kabul* by Andrew Wilson.

[1]See the *High Road to Hunza* by Barbara Mons.

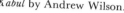

FIG. 747   Afghanistan (1961)

FIG. 749   Kashkai shepherd (1956)

FIG. 748   Kabul (1960)

FIG. 750. Hunza (1950)

FIG. 751   Hunza

FIG. 752   Iraq (1959)

FIG. 753   Yemen (1955)

a sect of muslims known as Sheas who believe that the cousin of Mahomet Ali and his descendants are in the direct line of the Prophet. To keep the kaffia in place two padded rings are worn, one larger than the other, to fit the head.

Fig. 753 portrays His Majesty Imam Ahmed, King of Yemen. The turban is of damask satin with woven motifs worn over a black cap and finished with a streamer bearing a fringe.

Fig. 754, is from a photograph of a Kurdish mountaineer who wears over his long ringleted hair a felt fez swathed in a striped scarf. And in *Fig. 755* a soldier of the Desert Patrol of the Arab Legion, in 1955, wears a head-scarf of red and white edged with small white pompoms, which, like the kaffia is held in place with a padded roll to which is fixed his military badge.

Headgear has always had a profound significance in the East. One glance at a man's head and you knew his religion and his social status. The fez is not really Turkish but of Greek origin. Two centuries ago the Turks wore turbans, and were devastated when ordered to abandon them and adopt the fez. This was ultimately tolerated, but when the order came for substituting a modern European hat they could find no compromise except the cap with its peak put on back to front, for no Moslem must wear a brimmed hat because it prevents him putting his forehead to the ground when praying in the mosque.

Fig. 756 shows the fez as worn by an Egyptian.

In *Fig. 757* a modern Turkish woman, dressed for her wedding wears traditional costume with the woman's version of the fez which has a heavy silk tassel.

An Anatolian woman *Fig. 758* (1940) wears the *yemeni* which confines her hair, and over that and her shoulders she has placed the *yazma*, or head-shawl. This may be of plain or printed cotton, but if plain it is invariably embroidered beautifully as the one pictured.

A Tartar of Azerbaijan on the Caspian Sea (now in Russia) wears a large hat *(Fig. 759),* probably of bearskin, with a collar of astrakhan. The tartars trade extensively in astrakhan fur which is the pelt of a young sheep, killed and skinned directly it is born.

Fig. 760 portrays the hat of a Dervish of Bokhara. It is of dark cloth with lambskin top and pompom. Another Dervish—this time of Mush—wears a

FIG. 754 Kurdish mountaineer

FIG. 757 Turkish (1750)

FIG. 755 Arabia

FIG. 758 Anatolia (1940)

FIG. 756 Egyptian

FIG. 759 Azerbaijan

FIG. 760   Bokhara (1935)

FIG. 763   Jerusalem

FIG. 761   A Dervish of Musk

FIG. 764   Egypt

FIG. 762   Palestine

FIG. 765   Cairo

large hat such as is figured in *Fig. 761*. It is made in four sections (like a European tea-cosy) embroidered and edged with fur.

Two orthodox Jews of Palestine are seen in *Figs. 762* and *763*. The former wears a felt fez over long hair, and the latter, being arrayed for prayers, wears the phylactery on his forehead.

Fig. 764. Here an Egyptian woman wears a face veil, *benco*, and a head veil, *tahah,* a yashmak of dark blue muslin. Note the metal nose-piece to keep the light material from being drawn into the nose and mouth.

Fig. 765. The turban or hat (for it is made on a foundation) here portrayed is worn by Baba Sirri, Sheik of Beltache, Chief of a monastery near Cairo.

A young girl of Biskra, admired for her dancing, wears a head-dress composed of metal plaques joined together with links and studded with semi-precious stones. With it she dons large earrings and a light scarf draped over her head. *(Fig. 766)*.

A head-dress seen here *(Fig. 767)* is part of the gala costume of the Druce ladies, but it is now almost, if not entirely disappeared. This was taken from a traveller's photograph of about 1925. It is not a left-over from the European henin, being a wooden pole on top of a hat, not a cone fitting the head.

Arab women of Zanzibar, when not veiled wear the *barkoa,* as shown in *Fig. 768;* and in Muscat, Oman, a slightly different yashmak prevails, *(Fig. 769)*.

Fig. 766   Biskra

Fig. 768

Fig. 767   Druce (1925)

Fig. 769   Muscat, Oman

FIG. 770 Tunisian

FIG. 773 Borneo (1956)

FIG. 771 Malay

FIG. 774 Balinese

FIG. 772 Burmese

FIG. 775 South Sea Island (1959)

The Sphi of Tunis wears a hat of straw three times as large as an American cowboy's. It is fringed at the edge and is worn over a frilled and pleated head scarf. *(Fig. 770).*

A Malaysian lady of rank here, *Fig. 771*, wears one of the prettiest of tiaras. It is of gold and enamel, and the design of daisies rises above the clustered leaves.

Very different is the queer head arrangement of a woman of a Burmese woman of the Padung tribe, who elongate their necks with an increasing number of brass rings. The assembled scarves over a dark base on her head can be removed, but the brass rings cannot or her neck would collapse. *(Fig. 772).*

Fig. 773 is a more sophisticated hat as worn by a young woman of Borneo. The hat is made of woven raffia, and little wisps of straw stand up in the manner of feathers. Note the long-drawn-out earlobes on to which rings are threaded.

Fig. 774. A more familiar (at least from photographs) head-dress is that of the Balinese dancer.

. A South Sea Island belle here in *Fig. 775,* wears a festive head-dress composed of beads, mirrors, feathers, and bleached human hair.

Tahitian girls invariably choose real flowers for their head adornment as in *Fig. 776*, and charmingly offer such garlands to their European or American guests.

Crossing to South America we find that the women of the Andes mostly wear a bowler-shaped hat, white if for a particular occasion as is given in *Fig. 777*. Tchifferley said, when passing over the Andes on his famous 'Ride' in 1924 that whenever these

FIG. 777   Andean

FIG. 778   South American (1956)

FIG. 776   Tahitian

FIG. 779   Cuzco

FIG. 780   Titicaca (1930)

FIG. 781   Peru

FIG. 782   Brazil

women passed him they took off their hats with both hands in greeting, and although he noticed that it was not the custom to reply in kind, he found it difficult when passing not to raise his hat in response. But *Fig. 778* gives us another Andean feminine hat. It is a large straw with upturned brim bearing on its edge an absurd little bow.

Three Peruvian caps follow *(Figs. 779 to 781)*. The first is from Cuszco, worn by an American-Indian, who is peddling water. It is to be noticed that he still bears the stamp of his Inca forbears. His cap is made of material, padded at the top to allow him to carry burdens on his head. Another Indian cap is seen in *Fig. 780*. The wearer comes from the Lake Titicaca district and he wears the traditional cap with ear-flaps, which is beaded in conventional patterns and is typical of his people. A third example is figured in *781*.

The Indians of the Amazonian basin mostly go bare-headed and unclothed, and some of the Jivero men still wear their hair long as in *Fig. 782*. It is ornamented with red and yellow toucan feathers.

Yet in *Fig. 783* we may see a charming hat worn by a Campa Indian of the Amazon valley whilst out shooting with his bow and arrows.

Fig. 784 is not, as it may appear, a rather extra-ordinary boy scout, but a Colorado Indian who has plastered his hair vermilion with the juice of achioto seeds.

Fig. 785 represents a Paraguayan hunter's hat or helmet made of jaguar skin.

A final interesting head-dress from South America is this given in *Fig. 786* of a woman of Tehuantepec, for it is formed from the frock of a small child. A girl was found in a wreck on the coast, and the villagers, believing that her dress brought them luck, have, ever since then, made their head-dresses in this shape. It is arranged with the frilly skirt over the head, the opening for the child's head at the back and the sleeves hanging down to the wearer's waist.

Here, in *Fig. 787* a Mexican caballero wears a large sombrero made of cross bands of woven straw.

A Labrador trapper *(Fig. 788)* wears a warm hood of thick cloth and fur-edged round the face.

The male Tauregs of Central Sahara still (1959) wear their veils *(Fig. 789)*. The custom probably originated as a protection against the sand-storms of the desert, but their women-folk are not veiled. The men do not remove their veils even when eating.

FIG. 783   Amazonian Indian

FIG. 786   Tehuantepec

FIG. 784   Colorado (1956)

FIG. 787   Mexico

FIG. 785   Paraguay

FIG. 788   Labrador (1959)

FIG. 789   A Tuareg of the Sahara (1959)

FIG. 792   Mr. Odinga, Chairman of the Kenya National Party (1960)

FIG. 790   Belgian Congo

FIG. 793   Northern Rhodesia (c.1926)

FIG. 791   Nigerian

FIG. 794   Algiers

Head-dressing in Africa varies from tribe to tribe when the wearer has not already adopted European clothes. *Fig. 790* is from a traveller's photograph of a member of the Manghbettus tribe. He has ivory hair-pins each with three disks, carven from the solid tips of the elephant's tusks which, to him symbolize the sun.

Fig. 791 is the quaint hair style of a Nigerian child.

Fig. 792 dates from 1960 and shows Mr. Odinga, Chairman of the Kenya National Party in traditional dress.

From Northern Rhodesia comes the large hat of *Fig. 793*. It was photographed in 1926, so in all probability is discarded by now.

Elaborate hair-dressing is done by Algerian natives and probably the most bizarre is that in *Fig. 794*.

Fig. 795 is the male Sudanese hair style. The hair is shaven to the crown of the head and the rest of the fuzzy hair is stuck and moulded into this extraordinary shape. Other members of the tribe wear small curls like cowrie shells all over the head. The bumps across the forehead are tattooed cicatrices.

The Turkana, a nomadic people of Lake Rudolph, Kenya, shave the tops of their heads and interweave hair from dead relatives into their own remaining hair, sticking it together with gum and decorating it with feathers *(Fig. 796)*.

The next three examples are from New Guinea. *Figs. 797, 798* and *799*. The first is a Papuan of New

FIG. 795   Sudanese

FIG. 797   New Guinea

FIG. 796   Tuskana, Lalu Rudolph, north of Kenya

FIG. 798   A New Guinea Islander

Guinea. He is wearing a bonnet of black fuzzy material, which is sewn on to a beaded band. (1925). The next figure is a New Guinea Islander who has on his head a circlet surmounted with feathers and to which are attached also cords with tassels. He has ivory nose-plugs and many metal ear-rings. The third represents a warrior, wearing the plumes of a Bird-of-Paradise. The bodies of the birds are veridian green and black and the tail feathers red to orange. The head-dress is made up of a curly fur, bound and dyed raffia, leather bands, a large shell and many cowrie shells. The chin decoration is white and the nose plug yellow. His face is stained black.

Michaela Dennis in her famous book, *Leopard in My Lap*, describes such a chieftain thus:—

'Mai-Mai's impressive appearance was enhanced by the brass medal bound round his forehead which was bestowed upon him by the Australian government showing that he was a *tul-tul* responsible for the maintenance of peace and order in New Guinea. He had with him about a hundred followers, their parrot feathers and cassowary plumes waving, shells on their chins, mother-of-pearl and gold lip shells— one represented a man's wages for fifty day's work. He wore on his head the fabulous Greater Bird-of-Paradise feathers which leapt and wavered like flames.' The King of Saxony Bird-of-Paradise tail feathers are also worn by these chieftains. They are bright blue with black divisional markings. They are also described as wearing, 'A coronet of irridescent green beetles, kapoul fur and Paradise plumes.' Their faces are often painted half red and half green.

Our final example, *Fig. 800*, is that of an Australian aborigine who besides painting his face and body in patterns wears on his head a wreath of magic leaves.

FIG. 799   New Guinea (1958)

FIG. 800   Australian Aborigine   with magic head-dress of leaves

A list of Sources

Abbreviations:— B.M. British Museum. N.G. National Gallery. N.P.G. National Portrait Gallery.
Ms. Manuscript. V and A. Victoria and Albert Museum.

1. Ravenna. Mosaic; The Three Kings.
2. Tollund Bog Burial. Copenhagen.
3. F. W. Fairholt's 'Costume in England.'
4. F. W. Fairholt's 'Costume in England.'
5. Ms. See King Edgar offering charter to Christ, or Cott: Ms Claudius B lv B.M.
6. Carved relief. Rome.
7. Museum, Naples, reproduced in a History of Pompean Art.
8. From a coin found in Britain. B.M.
9. F. W. Fairholt's 'Costume in England.'
10. Sutton Hoo Boat Burial. B.M.
11. Viking Helmet found in River Thames. B.M.
12. Ms. The Golden Psalter. Abbey Library. St. Gall, Ireland.
13. Ms. Burgundian.
14. F. W. Fairholt's 'Costume in England.'
15. Bayeux Tapestry. There is a good colour reproduction in book form.
16. From the Winchester Psalter. B.M.
17. From a 12th cent. Bestiary in the Bodleian Library.
18. Saxon Stone carving. V and A.
19. Ms. B.M.
20. Statue of early French queen. Corbeil.
21. Virgin and Child. Norman. B.M. Nero C lV.
22. F. W. Fairholt's 'Costume in England.'
23. Funerary slab to Geoffrey Plantaganet, Earl of Maine and Anjou.
24. Freiburg Cathedral.
25. Queen Uta in Naumburg Cathedral; near choir screen.
26. Queen Eleanor de Guienne, wife of Henry II.
27. Philippa, Duchess of York. Stothard's Monumental Effigies.
28. French Ms. B.M.
29. Ms. B.M.
30. Italian Fresco.
31. The Manesse Ms. (Minnesingers) Heidleberg University.
32. Bourges Cathedral.
33. Ms. B.M.
34. Stothard's Monumental Effigies.
35. Ms. Psalter of St. Louis. 'Jephtah and his Daughter' Bibliotheque. Paris.
36. Queen Eleanor, Consort of Henry II. Stothard's Monumental Effigies.
37. F. W. Fairholt's 'Costume in England'.
38. Ms. 13th or early 14th century. B.M.
39. Ambrogio Lorenzetti in the Palazzo Publico. Siena.
40. Ivory Mirror Back. B.M.
41. Gothic sculpture.
42. Ivory by Tutilio, a monk. Abbey Library. St. Gall, Ireland.
43. Stothard, from the effigy in the Temple Church. London.
44. Effigy in Westminster Abbey.
45. Ms. The Months. B.M.
46. Luttrell Psalter. B.M.
47. Bedford Book of Hours. B.M.
48. Ms. See the Lambeth Bible.
49. Statue in Rhiems Cathedral.
50. Ms. Franco-Flemish. B.M.
51. Ms. 1169. Becket says good-bye to King Henry 11 and King Louis of France.
52. From the Codex by Alfonso X, King of Leon and Castille.
53. French Ms. B.M.
54. *De Arte Vernandi cum Avibus* by Frederick II, in the Vatican.
55. A basinet from the Tower Armoury.
56. Chapeau de fer. Fra Angelico. Florence Academy.
57. Brass to Lady Harsick. South Acre. Norfolk.
58. Brass to Margaret de Walsham, 1349.

59. Brass.
60. Queen Margaret in Lincoln Cathedral.
61. Joan de Badlesmere of Leeds Castle.
62. Stothard's Monumental Effigies.
63. Stothard's Monumental Effigies.
64. Brass to Margaret, wife of Richard Torrington, Berkhampstead, Berks.
65. Ms. French. B.M.
66. Giotto. Padua, Arena Capella.
67. Hunting Scene. French. Ms.
68. Luttrell Psalter. B.M.
69. German. 'The Deposition' by Hieronymus Bosche.
70. Luttrell Psalter. B.M.
71. Luttrell Psalter. B.M.
72. Luttrell Psalter. B.M.
73. Luttrell Psalter. B.M.
74. Luttrell Psalter. B.M.
75. Sir John Mandeville's Travels. B.M.
76. Sir John Mandeville's Travels. B.M.
77. Duccio da Siena.
78. 'The Deposition' by Fra Angelico. Uffizi. Florence.
79. Dante by Andrea Castagno.
80. French Ms. B.M.
81. Manesse Ms. (Minnesingers) Heidelberg University.
82. Simone Martini. Church of St. Francis. Assisi.
83. Simone Martini. Church of St. Francis. Assisi.
84. Cited by Joan Evans in *Costume in Medieval France*.
85. German Painting of 'The Marriage of the Virgin'.
86. German Painting of 'The Marriage of the Virgin'.
87. German Painting of 'The Marriage of the Virgin'.
88. French Tapestry.
89. French Tapestry.
90. Effigy in York Minster.
91. Funerary Slab of Hughes Libergier in Rhiems Cathedral.
92. Weeper on French Tomb.
93. Cited by Joan Evans in *Costume in Medieval France*.
94. John VIII Palaiologue. From a Medal.
95. Weeper from a French Tomb.
96. Stothard's Monumental Effigies.
97. Stothard's Monumental Effigies.
98. French. A statue of a queen which was once coloured.
99. Ms. The Romance of the Rose. B.M.
100. From a Corbel in Southwold Church. Suffolk.
101. Stothard's Monumental Effigies.
102. Jan Van Eyck. Antwerp.
103. Stothard's Monumental Effigies.
104. Stothard's Monumental Effigies.
105. From a painting by Antonio Pisanello.
106. The Story of the Cross by Piero della Francesco. Church of St. Francis. Assisi.
107. Portrait of a Lady by Paolo Ucello.
108. Isotta Digliarti, wife of Sigismondo Malatesta, from a medal.
109. Simonetta Vespucci by Antonio Pollaiuolo. Musée Condé.
110. Fra Angelico. Uffizi. Florence.
111. Portrait of a Lady. Metropolitan Museum. N.Y.
112. Ms. Pol de Limbourg. Cluny Museum.
113. Ms. French. A Tournament Scene. B.M.
114. French Tapestry.
115. Ms. Margaret of Holland, Wife of John Beaufort. B.M.
116. 'The Presentation of the Virgin' by Giovanni de Paolo. Bearstead Collection.
117. 'Our Lord Appearing to his Mother' by Frei Carlos. Lisbon.
118. St. Veronica by Robert Campan. Drawing.
119. From the Monypenny Breviary. Augustus and the Sybil.
120. Jean Fouquet.
121. Jaques Daret. 'The Presentation in the Temple.'
122. Margaret of Denmark by Hubert van der Goes. Holyrood Palace.
123. Stothard's Monumental Effigies.
124. Flemish Tapestry. Metropolitan Museum. N.Y.
125. Tapestry. V and A.
126. Tapestry. V and A.
127. Ms. Lovers in a Garden. French. B.M.
128. Jacqueline of Bavaria. Dutch School.
129. Rogier van der Weyden. Berlin. Kaiser Friedrich Museum.
130. From Strutt. B.M. Ms. Roy 15. e. Vi.
131. Stall end. German wood carving.
132. The Queen of France. Ms. Christine de Pisan presenting her book.
133. Ms. Douce 213. Bodleian Library Oxford.
134. Tapestry. V and A.
135. German.

136. Portrait of a Lady by Lorentino d'Arezzo.
137. The Duchess of Urbino by Piero della Francesca.
138. Lucrezia Crivelli by Bernado Martini. (Mr. Newall.)
139. Italian.
140. Florentine stone head, painted.
141. Bianca Maria Sforza. by Bembo. Brera Gallery. Milan.
142. Hans Memlinc. Bourges Hospital, St. Jean.
143. Hans Memlinc. Buckingham Palace.
144. Hans Memlinc. Buckingham Palace.
145. Hans Memlinc. Buckingham Palace.
146. The Master of the Virgo inter Virgines. Walker Gallery. Liverpool.
147. A deposition. Hieronymus Bosch.
148. "Birth of the Virgin" by Roger van der Weyden. Munich.
149. Hans Memlinc.
150. Burgundian.
151. Froissart's Chronicles. B.M.
152. A lady in the Ms. 'The Marriage of Isabella and Edward II'.
153. Portrait of a Lady by Pietrus Christos.
154. Ms. The Marriage of Edward II to Isabella.
155. Ms. The temptation of St. Anthony. B.M.
156. German. A man and woman making music. Drawing.
157. Hans Memlinc. The wife of Jean Portinari. N.Y.
158. Fairholt's 'Costume in England.' From Eton College.
159. Ms. A chatelaine and her handmaiden weaving.
160. Ms. The Chronicle of England by Jean de Wavrin. B.M.
161. Ms. Froissart's Chronicle. At a Tournament. B.M.
162. Quentin Matsys. Louvre.
163. Stothard's Monumental Effigies.
164. Rogier van der Weyden. Portrait of a Lady. N.G.
165. Rogier van der Weyden. Portrait of a Lady.
166. French Tapestry. N.Y.
167. Rogier van der Weyden. Guingore de Salines, foundress of the Hotel-dieu. Beaune.
168. 'Charity,' by Mme. Uranie Colin-Libour.
169. Ms. Loyset Lieder, Brussels 9967 f.39.
170. St. Eligius (detail) by Petrus Christus. P. Lehmann Coll: New York.
171. Stothard's Monumental Effigies.

172. Brass in Dagenham Church, Essex. A daughter of Sir T. Urswick, 1479.
173. Margaret of York, wife of Charles the Bold. Brussels.
174. Portrait of a Lady by Vittore Carpaccio. Gallieria Borghese.
175. Portrait of a Lady by Domenico Ghirlandaio. Church of St. Maria Novello. Florence.
176. Brass of Lady Joan Tattershall, Lincolnshire.
177. French Tapestry. 'The offering of the Heart.' Louvre.
178. Ms. The Chronicles of Jean Creton. B.M.
179. Ms. French. The Riding Party. B.M.
180. The Chronicles of Jean Creton. B.M.
181. Ms. The Chronicles of Jean Creton. B.M.
182. Louis XI by Jean Fouquet. Privately owned. N.Y.
183. The Travels of John Mandeville. B.M.
184. The Travels of John Mandeville. B.M.
185. The Travels of John Mandeville. B.M.
186. French Ms. of Le Chevalier délibéré. 1480.
187. The Chronicles of Jean Creton. B.M.
188. Portrait of a man by Domenico Ghirlandaio.
189. Ms. The Romance of the Rose. B.M.
190. Ms. Froissart's Chronicles. B.M.
191. Jan van Eyck. Kaiser Friedrich Museum. Berlin.
192. Pol de Limbourg. Cluny Museum.
193. John the Fearless by Hubert van Eyck.
194. Jan van Eyck. N.G.
195. Pisanello. Vision of St. Eustace. N.G.
196. Fra Angelico. Deposition. Florence Academy.
197. Sienese School. N.G. of Scotland.
198. Fra Angelico. Deposition. Florence Academy.
199. The Adoration of the Magi by Gentile de Fabriano.
200. Tapestry. V and A.
201. Florentines outside the Cathedral. ⎫ From a
202. Florentines outside the Cathedral. ⎬ painting
203. Florentines outside the Cathedral. ⎭ on a coffer
204. Ms. French.
205. Statue.
206. Ms. B.M. Also good representation in Bellini's Picture in N.G.
207. King Louis XII and his wife Margaret. Flemish or French School. Ince Collection.
208. Panels of an Altarpiece. German School. Lubeck.
209. Carpaccio. Venice.

210. Botticelli.
211. Francesco Sforza by Bembo. Brera Gallery. Milan.
212. Nuno Goncalves. Janelas Verdes Museum.
213. Ms. Froissart's Chronicles. B.M.
214. Ms. Froissart's Chronicles. B.M.
215. Ms. Froissart's Chronicles. B.M.
216. Cited in Joan Evans *Costume in Medieval France.*
217. Charles VII of France by Jean Fouquet.
218. Ms. Chronicles of England by Jean de Wavrin. B.M.
219. 'The Flagellation' by Luca Signorelli. Brera. Milan.
220. 'Moses and his Sons.' by Bernardino Pinturriccio.
221. 'The Nativity,' by Botticelli.
222. Antonio Pollaiuolo. Turin.
223. Hans Memlinc. The Grand Bastard. Musée Condé.
224. Hans Memlinc. Portrait of a Man. Privately owned. N.Y.
225. Ms. The Romance of the Rose. B.M.
226. The Emperor Constantius's Dream by Piero della Francesca. Church of St. Francis. Arezzo.
227. Portrait of Henry V. Artist Unknown. N.P.G.
228. Martyrdom of S.S. Cosmo and Damien by Fra Angelico. Louvre.
229. Tower Armouries.
230. Basinet worn by Sir Giles Capel. Tower Armouries.
231. The Tower Armouries.
232. Ms. 'A Tournament' Froissart's Chronicles. B.M.
233. Paolo Uccello. The Battle of San Romano. N.G.
234. Fortunata degli Uberti by Andrea del Castagno St. Appollonia. Florence.
235. Nuno Goncalves. Janelas Verdes Museum.
236. Hans Holbein. Ashmolean Museum.
237. Conrad Van Creutznach. Portrait of a Lady.
238. Ms. The Romance of the Rose. B.M.
239. Italian.
240. Laura Battiferri by Bronzino.
241. Portrait of a Lady by Johann Kemmer. Leipzig.
242. The Raising of Lazarus by Gerard David.
243. Sibylla von Freyberd by Bernard Strigel. Munich.
244. Anne de' Ysembourg by Grünewald. Musée de Gotha.
245. Portrait of a Lady by Michael Wolgmut.
246. German engraving signed L.M.
247. Tapestry. The Lady of the Unicorns.
248. Portrait of a Lady by Jean Hay Clouet.
249. Simon Bennick. Genealogical tree showing the Alliances between Spain and Portugal.
250. French.
251. A lady of the Hobart Family.
252. F. W. Fairholt's 'Costume in England.' Ms. Royal. 16. F 2.
253. Quentin Matsys. Prado. Madrid.
254. Barbara Yelverton by School of Holbein.
255. Katherine of Aragon by J. Courvus. N.P.G.
256. Holbein.
257. Portrait of a Lady by A. Benson. Antwerp.
258. Portrait of a Lady by Bartel Bruyn.
259. The Countess of Egmont by Jean Hay Clouet. Col M. Friedsam. N.Y.
260. Mabuse. Portrait of Jacqueline de Burgoyne.
261. Holbein. Dress Design.
261. Cranach. One of Three Sisters. Vienna History Museum.
263. Anne of Cleves by Hans Wertinger of Landshut.
264. François Clouet.
265. François Clouet. (School of). Mme de Rendan.
266. François Clouet. Wallace Collection.
267. Portrait of a Young Woman, by Cranach the Younger. Vienna. Kunsthistoriches Museum.
268. Portrait of a Lady by George Gower.
269. Isobel Humble from tomb in Southwark Cathedral.
270. Miniature of an unknown young lady wearing a hat by Isaac Oliver.
271. Lady Jane Dormer, Countess of Feria by Antonio Moro. Prado.
272. The Duchess Maddalena in her wedding dress by Peter de Witte called 'Candido', Munich.
273. Mary, Queen of Scots by Nicholas Hilliard. (The Duke of Portland).
274. The Knight and the Lady by Israhael van Mackenem.
275. Self-portrait by Albert Dürer. Prado. Madrid.
276. The Marriage at Cana by a Spanish-Flemish artist. N.G. of N.Y.
277. Tapestry. Hunting the unicorn, from the Château de Chaumont. Now in N.Y.
278. Maximilien I. by Bernard Strigel. Bearstead Collection.

279. Albert Pio, Prince of Carpi by Baldesarre Peruggi of Siena. N.G.
280. The Nativity by Mabuse. N.G.
281. Ms. A Merchant weighing his Freight. Artist Unknown. Clarendon Press.
282. Portrait of a Young Man by Hans Baldung Grien.
283. Francis I. Probably by Clouet. (Col. Michael Freedsam.)
284. The Card-players by Lucas Van Leyden. (The Hon. Mrs. R. Plunkett).
285. Portrait of a Man by Giovanni Busi de Cariani.
286. The Card-players by Lucas van Leyden.
287. Casimir von Brandenberg by Hans von Kulmbach. Alte Pinakothek. Munich.
288. Count von Gelre of Zutphen by Jan Swart of Gronigen.
289. Sir Nicholas Pointz by Holbein. (The Earl of Harrowby.)
290. The Duke of Brandenberg by Lucas Cranach.
291. Ludovico Martinengo by Bartolommeo Veneto. N.G.
292. A good example is to be seen on John King, Bishop of London. Christchurch.
293. Sir Edward Hoby. Artist Unknown.
294. Sir Richard Cartwright by Paul van Somer. Aynhoe Park.
295. Sir Walter Raleigh by Marcus Gheerhardts. N.G.
296. King Charles IX of France by Francois Clouet. Louvre.
297. Portrait of a Man by Corneille de Lyon.
298. The son of Charles VIII. Louvre.
299. The son of Sybilla of Cleves by Lucas Cranach. Warwick Castle.
300. Portrait by J. Seisenegger. N.G.
301. The Duc d'Alençon by Francis Clouet.
302. The Shepherd by Pieter Brueghel. Vienna.
303. Holbein.
304. The Holy Family by the Master of the Birth of Mary.
305. Tower Armouries.
306. Tower Armouries.
307. Tower Armouries.
308. Portrait of a Man in Armour by Girolamo Romanino. N.G. U.S.A.
309. German. Possibly by Dürer
310. Portrait of his wife by Peter Paul Rubens. Munich.
311. One of the daughters of Lord Teynham from his Monument at Lynsted. Kent.
312. Maria Theresa of Austria, wife of Louis XI by Pierere Mignard. Prado.
313. Henrietta Maria by Vandyck.
314. Sir Peter Lely.
315. Karel van Mander. Leonora Christina daughter of Christian IV.
316. Esmerenta van Beresteyn by Pieter Claesz Soutman. Waddesden.
317. 'The Duet' by Gabriel Metsu.
318. 'An Old Woman Asleep' by Pieter de Hoche. Wallace.
319. Conversation Piece by Q.C. van Brekelenkam. Ryksmuseum.
320. Barbara Villiers, Duchess of Cleveland by Samuel Cooper.
321. Hortense Mancini. Miniature.
322. Portrait of a Lady by Peter Lely.
323. Catherine of Braganza by Dirk Stoop. N.P.G.
324. Portrait of a Lady by Isaac Whood.
325. Henrietta Cavendish, Lady Huntingtower by Geofrey Kneller. Ham House.
326. From a French Engraving.
327. Supposed portrait of Sir Philip Sidney. H.M. the Queen.
328. 'Gallant Company' by Willem Beutywyck.
329. Sir Nicholas Bacon. Self-portrait. (Col. G. H. Bacon).
330. King Charles I by Vandyck. Louvre.
331. The Duke of Pastrina by Juan Carreno. Prado. Madrid.
332. The Duke of Richmond and Lennox by Vandyck. Metropolitan N.Y. Copy at Ham House.
333. David de Ganges. 'The Saltonstall Family.' Sir Kenneth Clark.
334. 'Players at tric-trac.' by Willem C. Duyster. Prado.
335. 'The Gamesters' by Matthew le Nain. (Lord Mount Temple).
336. Portrait of a Man. Artist Unknown.
337. Fairholt's 'Costume in England'.
338. Charles Fitzroy, Duke of Grafton, by Godfrey Kneller.
339. James Butler, 2nd Duke of Ormonde by David Loggan.
340. Peter the Great of Russia.
341. William Hogarth.

342. Philippe de Courçillon, Marquis de Dangereau by Hyacinth Rigaud. Musée de Versailles.
343. Fairholt's 'Costume in England.'
344. David de Ganges. 'The Saltonstall Family' Sir Kenneth Clark.
345. Child with a Hawk by Philippe de Champagne. Louvre.
346. Lady Percy by Sir Peter Lely. Syon House.
347. 'Child with a hen.' by Johannes van Noordt (M.W.T. Leatham, Esq.).
348. Princess Mariana by Velasquez.
349. Thought to be a portrait of Sir Richard Lovelace.
350. The Tower Armouries. The Mansion.
351. Catherine Wilkenson by Thomas Hill.
352. From a drawing by Bernard Picart in the Ashmolean Museum.
353. Mrs. Hurt of Castern. Artist Unknown.
354. A sister of Prince Frederick in 'The Music Party,' by Philip Mercier. N.P.G.
355. Henrietta Wolters by Jan Mauritz Quinkhardt.
356. Portrait of a Lady. Artist Unknown.
357. Peg Woffington by Joseph Highmore. (Mrs. Fothergill).
358. Elizabeth Oberbuchler by Antoine Pesne. Ducal Museum, Braunschweig.
359. 'The Morning Toilet' by J. B. Chardin.
360. Mary Wingfield, wife of St. Aubyn by J. S. Schaak.
361. Portrait of a Woman by Jean Marc Nattier.
362. See paintings by Guardi and Longhi.
363. The Lovely Strasbourg Woman by Nicholas de Largillière.
364. See Engraving of Bagrigge Wells. The Long Room. 1772. *The Pleasure Haunts of London* by E. B. Chancellor.
365. Eleanor Frances Dixie by Liotard. Nottingham Art Gallery.
366. Melle Doré by Francois Drouet. V and A.
367. Mrs. Gwyn (The Jessamy Bride) by Daniel Gardner. Wallace Collection.
368. Lady Eardley by Gainsborough.
369. Engraving by J. Moreau.
370. Mrs. Carnac by Gainsborough.
371. Portrait of a Lady by Daniel Gardner.
372. 'The Charming Muser' by William Ward.
373. Portrait of a girl. Greuze. Musée Condé. Chantilly.
374. At the Alehouse Door' by Henry Singleton.
375. Portrait of a Lady by Nathaniel Dance. V and A.
376. 'In St. James's Park' by George Morland.
377. Miss Taylor by Sir Joshua Reynolds. (Coll; M. Maurice Kann).
378. The Duchess of Devonshire by Gainsborough.
379. The Marquese de San Andres by Francisco Goya.
380. Queen Marie Luise of Spain by Francisco Goya.
381. Self-portrait by Mme. Labille-Guiard.
382. Queen Caroline Mathilde by Sturz. Fredericksbourg Castle.
383. Donna Barrona de Goicoechea by Francisco Goya. (Don Felipe Modet.)
384. Lady Tyrconnel by John Downman.
385. Self-portrait by Nicholas Largillière.
386. Henry Fox, Lord Holland by J. G. Eccart after J. B. van Loo.
387. The Rev: Cotton Mather by Peter Pelham.
388. Conversation Piece. Artist Unknown.
389. See Engraving of Bagrigge Wells. 1772. (*The Pleasure Haunts of London* by E. B. Chancellor, or Joseph Highmore, The Green Room, Drury Lane).
390. Portrait of a gentleman by Fra Galgario.
391. John Mortlock of Cambridge by John Downman. (Mrs. J. J. Lias).
392. Self-portrait by Gainsborough.
393. Horatio Nelson by J. F. Rigaud. (Earl Nelson. Trafalgar House).
394. The 11th Earl of Eglington by Sir Joshua Reynolds. Buckingham Palace).
395. Conde Fernan-Nunez by Francisco Goya.
396. Men Flying Kites. by Francisco Goya.
397. 'At the Tavern Door' by George Morland. (Sir E. Marshall-Hall).
398. 'Jack in the Bilbows' by George Morland. Parker Gallery.
399. Dr. John Jeffries by John Russell. (Coll: G. H. Gibbs, Esq.)
400. Lady Henrietta Harley by John Wotton.
401. M. Augereau. Artist Unknown. Engraved by Portman.
402. J. B. Milhaud by Louis David. Louvre.
403. M. Barbaroux. Artist Unknown.
404. Princess Louisa Ann, by J. E. Liotard. Windsor Castle.

405. La Benedicite by J. B. Chardin. Louvre.
406. The Archduke Francis of Austria by Anton Raphael Mengs. Prado.
407. 'The Card-castle' by J. B. Chardin. N.G.
408. The Marquess of Hertford by John Downman. Wallace Collection.
409. Miss Brummel by Thomas Gainsborough.
410. August Hennings by Cornelius Hoyer.
411. From a water colour drawing exhibited in the Guildhall Museum.
412. 'The March to Finchley' by William Hogarth. The Coram Foundling Hospital.
413. From a painting exhibited at the Guildhall Museum.
414. From a painting exhibited at the Guildhall Museum.
415. 'In St. James's Park' by George Morland.
416. Princess Pauline Borghese by B. Anguissola.
417. Mme. de Stael by Marie Eleanore Godefroid.
418. Mme. Ingres by J. D. Ingres.
419. Portrait of a Lady by a Swedish artist.
420. *Incroyables et Merveilleuses.* Chapeau de Paille d'Italie, 1815. (Engraved by H. Vernet. V and A.).
421. From a French fashion plate.
422. Mlle. Pegler by Alfred Stevens.
423. Portrait of a Lady. Artist Unknown.
424. Portrait of a Lady by Emanuel Peters.
425. Grafin Sidonie Potoka de Ligne by Emanuel Peters.
426. Portrait of a Lady by J. Mansion.
427. Dress design of 1830.
428. A daughter of John Orbell of Bury St. Edmunds. Artist Unknown.
429. Lady Blessington by A. E. Chalon.
430. Fashion plate of 1839
431. Mrs. Painter of Boskenna, Cornwall by John Opie.
432. Anna Maria Ellenreider. Portrait of a Woman. B.M.
433. Portrait of a Lady. English School.
434. Queen Victoria by George Dawe. Buckingham Palace.
435. The Empress Marianne of Austria by M. M. Daffinger.
436. Mme. Threse Morbille-Degas by Edgar Degas.
437. Lady Dorothy Neville by G. Watts.
438. 'Art class on the Beach' by George Leach.
439. From a Dress Plate.

440. From a photograph.
441. From a photograph.
442. From a Dress Plate.
443. 'Sunday Morning' by G. G. Kilburn. (Mr. W. S. Wilding.)
444. Dress Design.
445. Dress Design.
446. 'The Fair Toxopholites' by W. P. Frith.
447. From a photograph.
448.
449.
450. From *Le Petit Echo de la Mode*. 1883.
451. In the author's possession.
452.
453.
454. From a photograph.
455. From a photograph. A royal group.
456. 'Woman in a Veil'. August Renoir.
457. One of the brothers Grimm. Artist Unknown.
458. Self-portrait by Francisco Goya.
459. Portrait of an old man. By Anna Marie Ellenreider. B.M.
460. Portrait of his father by Gustave Courbet.
461. Col. Mellish with his jockey Buckle. Artist Unknown.
462. M. Seriziat. by Louis David. Louvre.
463. Self-portrait by Jean Antoine Gros. Musée de Toulouse.
464. John Taylor. Sir J, Watson Gordon. (Hon.Coy. of Golfers. Edinburgh.)
465. 'At the Bonapartist Club' by Boilly-Cazenove. Cluny.
466. Portrait of a man in a Stove-pipe Hat. R. Bonnington.
467. From a fashion plate.
468. From a photograph.
469. Queen Victoria greeting Prince Albert on return from a hunt. by Sir Edward Landseer.
470. From a fashion plate.
471. The Picnic. Manet. Louvre.
472. From a fashion plate.
473. From a fashion plate.
474. From a dress or fashion plate.
475. Portrait of a Irish girl by Adam Buck.
476. The Lady Montagu. J. A. D. Ingres.
477. Miniature portrait of a Boy by S. J. Stump.
478. Master Beecher on his Pony by F. C. Turner.
479. 'Sunday Morning' by G. G. Kilburn. (Mr. W. S. Wilding).

480. From a photograph of a London crossing-sweeper.
481. From an advertisement.
482. From an advertisement
482. From a photograph.
483. From a photograph.
484. Portrait of Rose W. by Boutet de Monville.
485. From a photograph.
486. From a photograph. A royal group.
487. From a coloured fashion plate.
488. From a photograph.
489. From a water-colour painting exhibited at the Guildhall.
490. From a water-colour painting exhibited at the Guildhall.
491. Colonel Tarleton by John Hoppner.
492. From a water-colour painting exhibited at the Guildhall.
493. From a contemporary lead-soldier.
494. Murat by Jean Anton Gros. (Coll: Prince Murat.)
495. Revue de la Garde Consulaire. by Jean Antoine Gros. Malmaison.
496. From a contemporary lead soldier.
497. From a contemporary lead soldier.
498. Drawing by Christoph Suhr (1771-1842).
499. From a contemporary lead soldier.
500. Painting in water-colour exhibited at the Guildhall.
501. Contemporary water-colour painting.
502. Contemporary water-colour painting.
503. From a lithograph by A. Ladurner.
504. Water-colour by H. Martens. Parker Gallery.
505. From a water-colour painting exhibited at the Guildhall.
506. From a photograph.
507. From a photograph.
508. Napoleon III as a young man.
509. One of the sons of Louis Philippe by Horace Vernet.
510. Ditto.
511. Ditto.
512. From a photograph.
513. From a photograph.
514. Drawing of the 'Cries of London'. Artist Unknown.
515. From a water-colour painting by William Derby of 1843. V and A.
516. From a photograph.

517. From a photograph.
518. From a medal by Rudolf Meyer.
519. From a photograph.
520. From an advertisement.
521. From an advertisement.
522. From a French advertisement.
523. Miniature portrait of a Lady by Lionel Heath.
524. Miniature portrait of a Lady by Lionel Heath.
525. From an advertisement for John Lewis.
526. From a photograph.
527. From an advertisement. Marshall and Snellgrove.
528. 'Winter' by Melle Louise Abbema.
529. From a photograph of the Ascot races.
530. From an advertisement.
531. From a photograph.
532. From an advertisement. Peter Robinson.
533. From a photograph.
534. From a photograph.
535. From a photograph.
536. Miniature portrait of an elderly woman by Rosalie Emslie.
537. From a photograph.
538. From a photograph.
539. From a photograph.
540. From a photograph.
541. Elaine de Chair by Frederick Whiting.
542. From a photograph of the author's sister.
543. Joseph Popsel by Bohumel Kubista.
544. From a photograph.
545. From a photograph of King Edward VII.
546. From a photograph.
547. From an advertisement.
548. From a photograph at Ascot.
549. From a photograph.
550. From a photograph.
551. From an advertisement.
552. From a photograph of Rt. Hon. Harold Macmillan.
553. 'Drying clothes' by Mrs. Allingham.
554. From a photograph.
555. Drawn from life. Mrs. Doreen Harrison of Egham.
556. 'The Convalescent' by Claude Calthrop.
557. From a photograph.
558. Mrs. Stafford of Paradise Row by Sir William Nicholson. (Viscount Cowdray.)
559. From a photograph.
560. From a photograph.

561. From a photograph.
562. From a photograph.
563.
564. } From photographs lent by Railway men.
565. From a photograph.
566. From a photograph.
Examples 567 to 584 are all from photographs.
585. Portrait of the Marquis of Lansdowne in garter robes by Philip de Laszlo.
586. From a photograph.
587. From a fashion photograph.
588 to 592 all from photographs.
593. Self-portrait by Fortunino Matania.
594. From a hat of the Boer War in the possession of Rt. Hon. Harold Macmillan.
595. From a photograph.
596. Self-portrait by William Orpen.
597. From a photograph.
598. From a photograph.
599. From a photograph.
600. From a photograph.
Figs 601 to 607 are from photographs.
608. From a contemporary coin.
609. Ms. Psalter. 'David and Musicians'. *c.*150 B.M.
610. St. Edmund feeding the hungry. 1125. Pierpont Morgan Library. N.Y.

611. Silver-gilt head of a reliquary from Basle Cathedral. B.M.
612. Constance, wife of Frederick II. Stone.
613. Charlemagne's Crown worn by the Archduke Ferdinand.
614. Portrait of King Richard II from Westminster Abbey.
615. The Royal State Crown. From a photograph.
616. From a photograph.
617. From a photograph.
618. Simone Martini. An Altarpiece. N.G.
619.
620. 5 Phases of the Pope's Tiara.
621. } Bust by Pasquali de Caravaggio.
622. From a photograph.
623.
624. Simone Martini. An Altarpiece.
625. A Cardinal's beretta from a photograph.
All National hats and native head-dresses are taken from traveller's photographs or from photographs reproduced in a 12 volume book entitled *The People of all Nations.*
Exceptions are:—*Fig. 632* which is from a painting by Henri Royer, and *Fig. 649* from a painting by August Riedel.

Glossary

ALAMODE. A plain kind of silk, like lutestring, thick and loosely woven. Time of Mary I.

ARMAZINE. A kind of strong corded silk used for ladies' gowns and for gentlemen's waistcoats, from the time of Elizabeth I to George III.

ARMET. A helmet which could be worn with or without a beaver. Called a *great* armet *with,* and a *little* armet *without.*

ARMILAUSA. A surcoat to which was attached a hood, in use amongst both Saxons and Normans, often made wholly of silk (as mentioned in a deed of King Ethelbert) and worn over armour.

ATTOUR DE GIBBET. A scathing name for the henin.

AYRSHIRE WORK. Embroidery for caps, bibs and babies' long dresses, executed on very fine muslin or cambric in delicate patterns, using openwork to emphasise the designs. Early 18th cent.

BACKCOMBING. To comb the underneath hair backwards so that, when the top is turned over it, it produces a large soft roll, or gives a fluffed-out appearance.

BADGES. Worn on hats, originally as decoration, but later in trades to denote the firm or company for which the wearer works. They were made of lead, silver, gold or cloisonné work. Benvenuto Cellini mentions making these hat badges and describes the figures, animals or other devices he modelled for them.

BAG-WIG. A wig, the queue of which was tied back and enclosed in a black silk bag, which had a draw-string to close it. Mid 18th cent.

BALMORAL. A Scottish tammy-hat of cloth with back streamers of ribbon, and a feather in front.

BAND. A collar of linen or cambric, usually stiffened with starch or, if allowed to fall limply on the shoulders, was called a falling-band. Hence band-box in which to keep collars.

BANG. A roll of hair or a fringe over the forehead.

BANGING CHIGNON. A woman's hair bundled into a net or kept in place with hair-pins, placed at the back of the neck. 19th cent.

BARBE. (literally a beard). A piece of pleated linen or other white material worn under the chin, or just below the mouth, and descending on to the breast. Possibly denoting that the wearer was a widow. Middle English.

BARBETTE. (little beard). A flat chin-strap attached to each side of the fillet. 14th cent.

BARDOCUCULLUS. A hooded cape worn by both sexes in Roman and Saxon times.

BASINET. Helmet of the time of Edward II and III, and Richard II.

BAUDEKYN. A beautiful material, usually shot with gold, like a brocade, supposedly first made in Babylon. Henry III wore baudekyn.

BEAVER. A visor of a helmet.

BEAVER. Fur of the animal of that name extensively used in the making of hats. See Caster. Middle English.

BECCA. A long flat streamer worn attached to the right side of a hat. 15th cent.

BILLYCOCK. From 'William Coke' who ordered the first hard felt hat of the 'bowler' shape.

BIRETTA. A soft flat-topped cap, often with four corners. Late 15th and early 16th centuries. Name of a Cardinal's soft hat.

BOATER. A straw hat with a hard brim and crown, with a ribbon round the crown, especially worn in summer for river boating.

BONGRACE. A frontlet attached to a hood. Tudor period.

BONNET. A small soft hat for men (Hamlet. "Put your bonnet to his right use; 'tis for the head." Shakespeare. 16th cent.) Later for women and worn to the back of the head and secured in place with ribbon bows. Now almost confined to babies' caps. There was a sun-bonnet for little girls, late 19th cent. made of printed calico which had a frill at the back to keep the sun from the neck.

BOWLER. A hard felt hat, usually black, but sometimes grey or brown, named after the inventor.

BROCADE. A material used in 17th and 18th centuries for ladies' dresses and men's coats, originally called *brocat*, silk interwoven with threads of gold or silver—not unlike a baudekyn. 1563.

BRODERIE ANGLAISE. Embroidery on linen or cambric or muslin, with the material cut away to enhance the design. Hand-made until late 19th cent., later by machine.

BUCKRAM. Middle English, from the Italian *boucheraine*, a kind of fine linen or cotton fabric, stiffened with gum or paste. Used as an expression of false strength by Shakespeare's, 'Buckram knights'. 'Four rogues in buckram let drive at me.'

BUDGE. Lamb's skin with the wool dressed outside.

BUSBY. A tall cap of bearskin, black sable fur or black Persian lambskin, having a bag hanging out of the top on the right. Worn by hussars, artillery men and engineers. 1760.

BUTTERFLY HEAD-DRESS. A head-dress worn by women in the 15th cent. composed of a truncated cone cap on which light veiling was erected by means of wires. These are seen on brasses of the period.

BYCOCKET. A hat for men, sometimes adopted by women, which had a high pointed crown and an upturned brim with a point to the fore, and sometimes, as the name implies both back and front. Middle English.

CADDES. Worsted, used to ornament the clothes of the lower classes in the 16th century, and also used for garters.

CAFFA. A rich silk material of the time of Henry VIII.

CALASH. A large bonnet for the head used at the time when powdered wigs made hats for women impracticable. See the drawn examples F. W. Fairholt's Costume in England.

CALICO. A cotton stuff named from Calicut in India. Early 17th cent. Sometimes used for linings of hats.

CAMET. A material of wool and silk, suitable for hoods and gowns, made from the hair of the camel. Middle English.

CAP. Any close-fitting head-gear.

CAPPER. A man who made caps, often referred to in old account books. Thus in an account book of 1579, headed 'Payments made on the behalf of the Earl of Oxford' is the following entry, 'To

William Tavy, capper, for one velvet hat, and one taffeta hat, two velvet caps, a scarf, two pairs of garters with silver at the ends, a plume of feathers for a hat, and another hat band. £4. 6. o.'

CAPPELINE. A small skull-cap worn by archers in the middle ages.

CASQUE. A helmet.

CASTOR. The reddish-brown unctuous substance having a strong smell and nauseous taste obtained from two sacs in the inguinal region of the beaver, used in perfumery, hence 'castor' used for a beaver hat. A demi-castor was half beaver and half coney. Castor is the French word for the beaver.

CAUL. A close-fitting cap, usually of net-work, enclosing the hair worn, as a rule, by women, but occasionally by men as in Germany in the 17th cent.

CHAPEAU BRAS. A hat of beaver or felt made to fold in half so that it could be carried under the arm, and so avoid ruffling the wig. Last half of 18th cent.

CHAPERON. The final phase of the gorget, hood and liripipe, worn hatwise. 14th and 15th cents.

CHEERER. The top hat with a rather low crown and curled brim, usually brown, which was favoured by gentlemen farmers in the late 19th, early 20th centuries.

CHIGNON. A large roll of natural or false hair, worn by women at the back of the neck. 1783 onwards.

CHINTZ. Cotton cloth or calico, printed with flowers or other devices in different colours. India.

CHOUX. A bun of hair resembling a cabbage. End of 18th cent.

CIRCLET. A band for the hair, often of gold.

CLOCHE. A bell-shaped hat worn covering the eyebrows, 1926–7.

CLOCKS. A term applied to the wide ruffs of the 16th cent.

CLUMP WIG. A powdered wig, bushed at the sides and clumped off short at the ears. Mid 18th cent.

COASTGUARD. A small boys' hat in straw or felt, with turned-up brim and ribbon streamers, in imitation of those worn by coastguard men. 19th–20th cent.

COIF OR QUOIF. A close-fitting hood or bonnet for the head, usually made of linen and tied under the chin with tapes or strap and buckle, and worn by all classes of men during the 13th and 14th centuries.

COIF DE FER. A hood of mail worn by soldiers. 12th cent.

COINTOISE. A pendant scarf from hat or helmet. Originally the cloth worn by Crusaders to keep their helmets cool in the heat of Palestine; later as a decoration when jousting; the same term being applied later to the veil worn by women which floated from the top of their henins. It is the original of the heraldic 'mantle' or wavy scrolls around a coat of arms.

COMMODE. The term applied to the tall lace head-dress worn by women in the 18th cent.

COPOTAIN. A tall crowned hat made of felt or velvet worn by men, and adopted by women to some extent in the 16th cent.

CONFIDENTS. Small side curls, bunched at the temples favoured by women at the end of the 16th cent.

CORNET. Another derisive name for the henin.

CORONET. The head ornament of the nobility. In the early 12th century usually a plain circlet of gold worn round the forehead and hair, later becoming decorated with jewels until these decorations denoted the wearer's rank—duke, earl, marquis, baron and viscount.

COSMETICS. A preparation for the beautifying hair or complexion, used by both sexes from the earliest times.

COTTON. Woven originally in the East, but also in this country at an early period.

COVENTRY BLUE. 16th cent. A special colour, worn particularly by pages and servitors, and therefore eschewed by the nobility for which reason there are so few English portraits in which the sitters are wearing blue.

COVERCHIEF. A covering veil for the head worn by women; a development of the Saxon head-rail or *couvrechef*.

CRESPINE. A golden net caul worn by ladies in the 14th and 15th centuries—sometimes called a dorelet.

CUSHION. A padded roll made into a head gear, with sometimes another or even two rolls on top, worn by both sexes, particularly in Italy. 16th cent.

CYPRUS. A fine black material, often bound round crowns of hats.

DAGGING. The cut edges to hats and gowns or round the gorget edge worn by both men and women in the 15th centuries. The dags were usually simple scallops, but at times serrated like the edge of a leaf.

DEMI-CASTOR. A hat made of half beaver, half coney, 18th–19th centuries.

DIADEM. A crown or other head gear as a badge of royalty. (Poetical) 'Diocletian ventured to assume the diadem. It was no more than a broad white fillet set with pearls which encircled the Emperor's head.' Gibbon.

DIMITY. Stout cotton cloth, ribbed and figured, used undyed.

DOLLY VARDEN. A straw hat, tilted forward over the forehead named after a Dickens character in *Barnaby Rudge*.

DOGONA. The Doge's hat of state.

EAR-RINGS. Ornaments worn at different periods by both sexes to decorate the lobes of the ears. Men wore them in Elizabethan and Caroline times and natives still elongate the lobes of their ears to thread ornaments through them. The hole is made by a sharp instrument, then a small stick pushed through to keep the hole open and the size of the stick gradually increased until the skin is merely a thin thread.

ENGLISH WORK. Embroidery for which the English became noted early in the 12th century and which consisted of geometrical designs.

FALDETTA. A combined hood and cloak worn by the women in Malta.

FASCINATOR. A soft frilly scarf of silk or wool worn over the head for evening wear, in place of the hat. 18th–19th cent.

FAVOURITES. The small curls arranged on the forehead at the time of Charles I and Charles II.

FEATHERS. A favourite form of hat decoration and head-dresses of all nations; in Europe from the 14th century until the end of the 19th, with a revival in the small feather tucked into the band of the Robin Hood hat of 1960. Particularly favoured by all natives, special varieties being reserved for chiefs such as the Quetzal feathers of the Aztecs, the Duke of Saxony Paradise plumes by the New Guinea Islanders, and the eagle plumes of the red Indians. Knights wore plumes of immense size in the tops of their helmets, and in 16th century Germany, every lansquenet's hat was profusely adorned with ostrich feathers. Many birds are now protected, particularly the Birds of Paradise. Aigrettes were banned from women's hats early in this century. In the London Museum is an Ascot hat bearing a whole peacock!

FELT. Old English. A kind of cloth made of wool and fur, or hair rolled, beaten and treated by suction until it adheres into a compact substance with the aid of less or size. Fine felt is matted not woven. Hairs and furs are chiefly used for hats.

FEZ. (From Fez in Morocco). Of Turkish origin. A close-fitting felt hat without a brim, crimson with a black tassel in centre top.

FILLET. A band round the forehead, sometimes goffered.

FLOWERS. Worn by Greeks and Romans as garlands for the head and freshly plucked for banquets or special occasions. Artificial flowers were made as early as the 13th century and made into chaplets.

FORETOP. A loop of hair turned aside on the forehead. 17th cent.

FRET. The caul of gold or silver wire worn to conceal or confine the hair.

FRIEZE. A coarse woollen cloth, 16th cent.

FRONTLET. A band for the forehead, worn partially concealed by the head-dress in the 14th and 15th centuries.

FUR. Extensively used in the making of hats, either the whole hat, such as the bearskin, busby, or parka of the Eskimos, used with the fur either inside or outside, and also for decoration on felt or other hats. Miniver was the choice for hats in the middle ages, but beaver, coney, astrakhan and budge were also used, the latter by countryfolk.

FURIANS. Long cases of silk, plain or striped, into which Saxon ladies put their long plaits or coils of hair.

GABLE. Tudor head-dress for women, named from its shape. Sometimes called the kennel.

GALLOON OR GALON. Worsted lace or braid, later made of gold or silver.

GAUZE. A transparent stuff of silk or cotton used for veils, probably named from Gaza where it was manufactured in the 13th century.

GIBUS. A collapsible black silk opera hat, named after the inventor. (French).

GLENGARRY. Scottish folding cap of cloth, with black ribbon streamers at the back, and often with a badge in front.

GOFFERING. Material waved or pleated with hot irons.

GORGET. A covering for neck and shoulders.

GUARDED. Edged with lace or braid.

HEADRAIL. (Heafodhraegl). The head-covering worn by Saxon women.

HELMET. Metal or leather head protection worn by soldiers of nearly all periods.

HENIN. A tall cone-shaped head-dress worn by women in 15th cent.

HERISSON. (A hedgehog). A name gives to a fluffy wig for women in the 18th cent. It was usually powdered.

HOLLAND. A coarse linen, used for caps, unbleached.

HOMBURG. A hard felt hat worn by men in early 20th century. Introduced by Edward VII, from Homburg in Germany.

HOOD. Any soft head covering closing round the neck and shoulders.

HORNS. The two excrescences on the top of women's head-dresses in medieval times which brought upon them so much abuse from reformers.

HOUVE. A hood over a hat.

IRON HAT. The flat-topped helmet worn by Crusaders. (See figures on the Doge's Palace, Venice).

JABOT. Originally the frill down the front of a man's shirt, edging the opening. Later, a falling frill over a woman's bodice.

JAPANNED. Leather treated with lacquer, and made hard stiff and shiny by a Japanese process.

KAFFIA. The shawl-like drapery worn over the head and kept in position by two padded rings, worn by the muslims of Iraq. 1961.

KASI. A Korean hat.

KETTLE HAT. The iron hat of a knight in the middle ages.

KEVENHULLER. A type of tricorne hat, very large and heavy. 18th cent.

KOKOSHNIK. Russian woman's head-dress—heavily jewelled.

KOLINSKY. The Siberian mink. An expensive fur worn by Russians until the 1917 Revolution.

LAPPET. The lace pendants of a lady's head-dress.

LAMBEQUIN. A covering for the helmet to protect it from wet and heat.

LAWN. A delicate linen fabric, brought to England during the reign of Elizabeth I, and used for ruffs and ruffles.

LEGHORN. 1735. A kind of straw plaiting for hats and bonnets made from a particular kind of wheat, cut green and bleached, imported from Leghorn, Italy.

LINEN. Cloth made of flax.

LIRIPIPE. The extension of the top of the hood into a long pipe, worn, in the 14th and 15th centuries by men.

MASKS. Coverings for the face to disguise the identity of the wearer (often religious, such as those worn by witch doctors, initiates, etc.) but much favoured by the Venetians in the 18th century, to facilitate intrigues.

MACARONIS. A name given to the exquisites of the 18th century, and especially to their small tricorne hats perched on immense wigs. 'Stick a feather in his hat and call him Macaroni.'

MEMEM ORIOT. Mongolian fur-trimmed hat.

MINIVER. *(Menu-vair)*. A valuable fur made from the squirrel's belly, and much used on hats in the 14th and 15th cents.

MITRE. The head-dress of a bishop, usually made of brocade over buckram, and sometimes jewelled.

MORION. Helmet. 16th cent.

MORTARBOARD. A graduate's cap with square top, named from the likeness to a builder's board for mixing mortar.

MUTCH. A woman's cap. In the treasurer's accounts for James VI of Scotland (later James I of England) is the entry 'Ten elnes and a half of Tours taffeta for a gown; four elnes and a half of black velvet to be her skirt and lay out the hem of her gown, and one quarter of black velvet to one *mutch*.' These for the nurse, Isabel Colt.

NEBULA. The 14th century head-dress with goffered frills round the face.

NIVERNOIS. A very small tricorne hat, named after the original wearer, the Duc de Nivernois.

PARKA. The fur head-dress of the Eskimos.

PATCHES. Black spots of velvet stuck on the face to enhance the whiteness of the skin, mentioned by Shakespeare, and later by Pepys. At the height of the fashion (18th cent.) the spots were cut into various shapes such as a moon or stars and even a coach and horses. Glapthorne, in his *Lady's Privilege* says, 'Look, you, signor, if't be a lover's part you are to act, take a black spot or two. I can furnish you; twill make your face more amorous, and appear more gracious in your mistress's eyes.' 1640.

PEPLUM. A coverchief worn over the head and round the neck.

PERIWIGS. (See text). Wigs made of human hair, horsehair, feathers or tow, worn over a shaven head.

PHRYGIAN CAP. A hat shaped like the French Cap of Liberty.

PINNER. A ladies' lace and cambric head-dress of the early 18th century.

PLAITS. Hair divided into three and woven under and over; a method of hair-dressing in all times and countries, even the Polish and Russian soldiers adopting it in the early 19th century.

POKING STICKS. Instruments for shaping the flutes of Elizabethan ruffs originally made of wood or bone, later of steel.

QUOIF or COIF (See latter spelling).

RETICULATED HEAD-DRESS. A net of silver or gold wire forming side pillars to the face, in which the hair was concealed.

ROBIN HOOD HAT. A soft felt or stitched cloth hat with a small brim and feather, which came into fashion in 1959.

ROLL. The hair turned up above the forehead, or an artificial pad to turn the hair over.

RUFF. A circular collar, usually made of goffered pleats, in favour with both sexes in the 16th and early 17th centuries.

SALADE. A light helmet for soldiers. 14th cent.

SAMITE. A rich silk interwoven with gold, or embroidery. 'In the myddes of the lake Arthur was ware of an arme clothed in whyte samite.' Malory.

SARCENET. Now spelt sarsenet. A fine silk. (Saracenic.)

SATIN. A close woven silk with a high gloss on the right side 13th century onwards.

SAY. A sort of thin woollen cloth, suitable for hoods; one of the earliest cloths made in England.